Re-Viewing Resistance in Namibian History

Edited by
Jeremy Silvester

University of Namibia Press
www.unam.na
Private Bag 13301
Windhoek
Namibia

© 'Introduction: Re-Viewing Resistance, Liberating History', Jeremy Silvester, 2015
© Individual chapters, stated authors, 2015

All rights reserved. No part of this publication may be reproduced, stored in any retrieval system or transmitted in any form, or by any means, e.g. electronic, mechanical, photocopying, recording or otherwise without prior permission of the author.

Earlier versions of the chapters in this book were presented at a conference organised by the AACRLS project, 7-9 December 2009.

AACRLS
Archives of the Anti-Colonial Resistance and the Liberation Struggle

First Published:	2015
Cover photograph:	© John Liebenberg 1985
Design and layout:	John Meinert Printers, Windhoek
Printed by:	John Meinert Printers, Windhoek

ISBN: 978-99916-42-27-7

Distribution:
In Namibia by Demasius Publications: www.demasius-publications.com
In South Africa by Blue Weaver: www.blueweaver.co.za
Internationally by the African Books Collective: www.africanbookscollective.com

Contents

List of Contributors v

List of Abbreviations viii

Map of Namibia ix

Introduction: Re-Viewing Resistance, Liberating History 1

1 Transforming the Traumatic Life Experiences of Women in Post-Apartheid Namibian Historical Narratives 22
   Ellen Ndeshi Namhila

2 Hendrik Witbooi and Samuel Maharero: The Ambiguity of Heroes 38
   Werner Hillebrecht

3 The Vagciriku-Lishora Massacre of 1894 Revisited 55
   Shampapi Shiremo

4 Revolutionary Songs as a Response to Colonialism in Namibia 71
   Petrus Angula Mbenzi

5 Of Storying and Storing: 'Reading' Lichtenecker's Voice Recordings 89
   Anette Hoffmann

6 Colonialism and the Development of the Contract Labour System in Kavango 105
   Kletus Muhena Likuwa

7 Liberals and Non-Racism in Namibia's Settler Society? Advocate Israel Goldblatt's Engagement with Namibian Nationalists in the 1960s 127
   Dag Henrichsen

8 The Caprivi African National Union (CANU) 1962–1964: Forms of Resistance 148
   Bennett Kangumu Kangumu

9 Brendan Kangongolo Simbwaye: A Journey of 'Internal' Exile 160
   Bennett Kangumu Kangumu

10 The Kavango Legislative Council 170
    Aaron Nambadi

11	The 1978 Election in Namibia 178
	Timoteus Mashuna
12	Waking the Dead: Civilian Casualties in the Namibian Liberation Struggle 192
	Jeremy Silvester and Martha Akawa
13	Okongo: Case Study of the Impact of the Liberation Struggle in the Ohangwena Region 207
	Lovisa Tegelela Nampala
14	The Liberation Struggle Inside Namibia 1966-1989: A Regional Perspective from the Kavango Regions 221
	Herbert Kandjimi Karapo
15	The Gendered Politics of the SWAPO Camps during the Namibian Liberation Struggle 240
	Martha Akawa
16	Solidarity with Liberation in Namibia: An Analytical Eyewitness Account from a West German Perspective 252
	Reinhart Kössler
17	Finnish Solidarity with the Liberation Struggle of Namibia: A Documentation Project 266
	Pekka Peltola
18	Colonial Monuments in a Post-Colonial Era: A Case Study of the Equestrian Monument 276
	Helvi Inotila Elago
	Comment: Colonial Monuments – Heritage or Heresy? 292
	André du Pisani
19	Heritage Education in the School Curriculum: A Critical Reflection 298
	Gilbert Likando
Index 307	
About the cover photograph 317	

List of Contributors

Martha Akawa (PhD in History, University of Basel; MA History, University of Western Cape) is a History Lecturer and Head of Department for Geography, History and Environmental Studies at the University of Namibia. A revised version of her PhD thesis, entitled *The Gender Politics of the Namibian Liberation Struggle*, was published in 2014 by Basler Afrika Bibliographien. Her areas of interest include heritage issues and Namibian history, particularly the liberation struggle. Email: makawa@unam.na

André du Pisani (PhD in Philosophy, University of Cape Town) retired at the end of 2013 as Professor of Politics at the University of Namibia. He has published widely on the politics of Namibia and Southern Africa. He is also a photographic artist, collector of visual art, and a published poet.

Helvi Inotila Elago is currently studying for an MA in Heritage Management at the Athens University of Economics and Business and University of Kent. She was previously a Programme Assistant in Namibia for fesmedia Africa, the media project of the Fredriech-Ebert-Stiftung; worked at the UNESCO Windhoek Cluster office as a Culture Programme Assistant; and was a researcher and co-author of the report entitled *Heritage into Education: Education into Heritage*, for the Namibian National Institute for Educational Development (NIED). She has also worked on the exhibition plan for the proposed City of Windhoek Museum. Email: inotila@gmail.com

Dag Henrichsen (PhD in History, University of Hamburg) is a Namibian historian and archivist at the Basler Afrika Bibliographien (Namibia Resource Centre and Southern Africa Library) in Switzerland. He has published widely on Namibia's (visual) history in the nineteenth and twentieth century.

Werner Hillebrecht grew up in Germany. His involvement in the international anti-apartheid movement prompted him to begin documentary work on Namibia in the 1970s. He catalogued Namibia-related material in over 90 European libraries and the United Nations Institute for Namibia (UNIN) in Lusaka, Zambia, creating the foundations for the Namibian bibliographic database (NAMLIT), now housed at the National Library. He worked at the University of Bremen Centre for African Studies, and its Windhoek affiliate CASS (1986-1991), the National Archives of Namibia (1992-1995), the National Library of Namibia (1995-2002) and again at the National Archives from 2002. He retired from the post of Head of Archives in March 2013 but continues to work at the National Archives. He has published many bibliographies and articles on library matters and Namibian history. Email: werner.hillebrecht@gmail.com

Anette Hoffmann (PhD in Cultural Studies, Amsterdam School of Cultural Analysis) is a senior researcher at the Archive and Public Culture Research Initiative at the University of Cape Town, where she works on colonial sound/voice archives. She has published on sound recordings in recent years, and also curated the exhibition 'What We See. Images, Voices, and Versioning', which toured Europe and South Africa and was shown at the Franco-Namibian Cultural Centre in Windhoek in 2013.

Bennett Kangumu Kangumu (PhD in Historical Studies, University of Cape Town) is a Lecturer in the Department of Geography, History and Environmental Studies at the University of Namibia (UNAM), and Director of the UNAM Katima Mulilo Campus.

His research interests are in the areas of political history, cross-border histories, identity formation, historical representations/public history (museums, festivals, memorials), and languages. Email: bkangumu@unam.na

Herbert Kandjimi Karapo (BEd majoring in History, University of Namibia; MA, University of Cape Town) is Principal of Mupini Combined School in Kavango West. He was born in Tsumkwe in eastern Namibia, and schooled at Rupara Combined School, Kandjimi Murangi Secondary, and Rundu Secondary Schools.

Reinhart Kössler is Director of the Arnold Bergstraesser Institute, Freiburg i.B., Germany, and Professor in the Politics Department of the University of Freiburg. Besides a regional focus on Southern Africa, his research includes social and development theory, political sociology, and memory politics. He is author of *In Search of Survival and Dignity. Two Traditional Communities in Southern Namibia under South African Rule* (2005) and a forthcoming book *Negotiating the Past: Namibia and Germany*. Email: reinhart.koessler@abi.uni-freiburg.de

Gilbert Likando (PhD in Adult Education and Community Studies, University of Namibia; MA in Social Science, University of Salford, United Kingdom) is a Senior Lecturer at the University of Namibia (UNAM) and Director of the UNAM Rundu Campus. His research interests are in the area of education and heritage studies, on which he has published many articles and book chapters. Email: glikando@unam.na

Kletus Muhena Likuwa (BA in History and English, University of Namibia; MA and PhD, University of the Western Cape (UWC)) is a full-time researcher with the Land Programme of the Multidisciplinary Research Centre of the University of Namibia. He was born and grew up in the Kavango Region of north-east Namibia, matriculating later from Centaurus High School in Windhoek. He taught at Rundu Secondary School and in the History and Anthropology Departments at UWC. After completing his doctorate, he worked as a researcher on Indigenous Knowledge Systems before his current posting. Email: klikuwa@unam.na

Timoteus Mashuna (BEd, University of Namibia; MA in African Studies, majoring in History and Social Anthropology, University of Basel, Switzerland) is a Curator at the Namibian Ministry of Veterans Affairs, and a freelance journalist writing for the 'Heroes and Heroines' Column in New Era newspaper. Email: tmashuna@gmail.com

Petrus Angula Mbenzi (PhD in Language Studies, University of Namibia) is a Lecturer in Oshiwambo at the University of Namibia. He has authored several Oshiwambo school books. His recent publications include *Oshiwambo common phrases and expressions* and *Oshiwambo for beginners*. *Oshiwambo common phrases and expressions* was translated into Rukwangali, Silozi, Setswana, Otjiherero and Khoekhoegowab. His research interests include Oshiwambo onomastics and Oshiwambo language and culture. Email: pmbenzi@unam.na

Aaron Nambadi (BA in History and English, University of Namibia; MA in Visual and Public History, University of the Western Cape) is the head of the new City of Windhoek Museum, and helped organise a reunion of former residents of the Old Location to gather material for the museum. He served as Vice-Chairperson of the Museums Association of Namibia for a three-year term and is the current Chairperson. He previously worked as a teacher and a researcher for the Archives of Anti-Colonial Resistance and the Liberation Struggle Project, at the National Archives of Namibia. His MA thesis was on the Kavango Legislative Council.

Ellen Ndeshi Namhila (MSc) in Library and Information Science at the University of Tampere, Finland; PhD candidate, University of Tampere) is the University Librarian at the University of Namibia. Educated in Angola, Zambia, The Gambia and Finland, she has published widely and is author of the 1998 Mbapira award-winning *The Price of Freedom* (1997); *Kahumba Kandola Man and Myth: the Biography of a Barefoot Soldier* (2005); *Tears of Courage: Five Mothers Five Stories One Victory* (2009); and *Mukwahepo – woman, soldier, mother* (2013). She worked as Director of the Namibia Library and Archives Service in the Namibian Ministry of Education (1999-2007); Deputy Director: Research, Information and Library Services at the Namibian National Assembly (1995-1999); and as a researcher/librarian at the Social Sciences Division of the University of Namibia (1993-1995). She also served as Vice President of UNESCO's International Advisory Committee of the Memory of the World (2007-2010); Chairperson of the National Heritage Council of Namibia (2005-2010); and prepared the nomination dossier for the Namibian site of Twyfelfontein to be included in UNESCO's World Heritage List. She was an IFLA Governing Board member (2013-2015), and has been on the IFLA Journal Editorial Committee since 2008. Email: enamhila@unam.na or enamhila@gmail.com

Lovisa Tegelela Nampala (MA in History, University of Namibia) is a History teacher at Uukelo Combined School in the Ohangwena Region. Her MA thesis interrogated the impact of Christianity on traditional practices in northern Namibia and a revised version was published in L. Nampala and V. Shighwedha (eds), *Aawambo Kingdoms, History and Cultural Change. Perspectives from Northern Namibia* (2006). She is currently researching the history of Ondangwa and its historical role in the contract labour recruiting system. Email: omwenetuuda@hotmail.com

Pekka Peltola (PhD, University of Helsinki) is a Nordic Africa Institute Associate Special Expert. His doctoral thesis was published as *The Lost May Day. Namibian Workers Struggle for Independence*. In addition to a number of articles published in Finnish, he co-authored the book *Finland and National Liberation of Southern Africa* with Iina Soiri in 1999 and his book *Afrikassa*, on more general issues concerning Southern Africa, including Namibia, was published in 2011. His latest book, *Päätä seinään (Pushing against the Wall. The Life of an Idealist)*, published in 2014 by Into Publishers, Helsinki, discusses aspects of Finnish politics (1963-2005). He is planning a comparative study on Namibia and Botswana – close but interestingly different neighbours. Email: Pekka.peltola@kolumbus.fi

Shampapi Shiremo (BEd, Bachelor of Law, and MA in History, University of Namibia) is Head of Department for Social Sciences at Hochland High School in Windhoek. He was born at Mamono, near Nyangana Roman Catholic Mission Station in north-east Namibia. He did his primary schooling at Nyangana and secondary education at Linus Shashipapo and Rundu Senior Secondary schools. Email: shiremos@gmail.com

Jeremy Silvester (MA, University of York; PhD, SOAS, University of London) is the Project Planning and Training Officer with the Museums Association of Namibia. He previously worked as a Lecturer in the History Department of the University of Namibia. He has published extensively on Namibia's history and heritage, including the following publications: *Dodging Disaster* (2013), *Consuming Culture* (2012), *The Heritage Handbook* (2011), *Posters in Action* (2009), *Words Can Never Be Found: An Annotated Reprint of the Blue Book* (2003), *The Colonising Camera* (1999) and *Namibia Under South African Rule* (1998). Email: silvestj@iway.na

List of Abbreviations

AAB	Anti-Apartheid Bewegung (West German Anti-Apartheid Movement)
AACRLS	Archives of Anti-Colonial Resistance and the Liberation Struggle
AKTUR	Aksienfront Vir Die Beihoud Van Die Turnhalle-Beginsels (Action for the Retention of the Turnhalle Principles)
ANC	Africa National Congress
CANU	Caprivi African National Union
ELCIN	Evangelical Lutheran Church in Namibia
ELOC	Evangelical Lutheran Ovambo-Kavango Church
FELM	Finnish Evangelical Lutheran Mission
FINNIDA	Finnish International Development Agency
FNLA	Frente Nacional de Libertação de Angola (National Front for the Liberation of Angola)
GDR	German Democratic Republic
ISSA	Information Service Southern Africa
MPLA	Movimento Popular de Libertação de Angola (Popular Movement for the Liberation of Angola)
NAN	National Archives of Namibia
NUDO	National Unity Democratic Organisation
OMEG	Otavi-Minen-und Eisebahngesellschaft (Otavi Mining and Railway Company)
PLAN	People's Liberation Army of Namibia
SADF	South African Defence Force
SWA	South West Africa
SWABC	South West Africa Broadcasting Corporation
SWACO	South West Africa Company
SWANLA	South West Africa Native Labour Association
SWAPO	South West Africa People's Organisation
SWATF	South West Africa Territorial Force
UN	United Nations
UNIN	United Nations Institute for Namibia
UNIP	United Independence Party (Zambia)
UNITA	União Nacional para a Independência Total de Angola (National Union for the Total Independence of Angola)
UNSWP	United National South West Party
WNLA	Witwatersrand Native Labour Association
ZANU	Zimbabwe African National Union

Map of Namibia

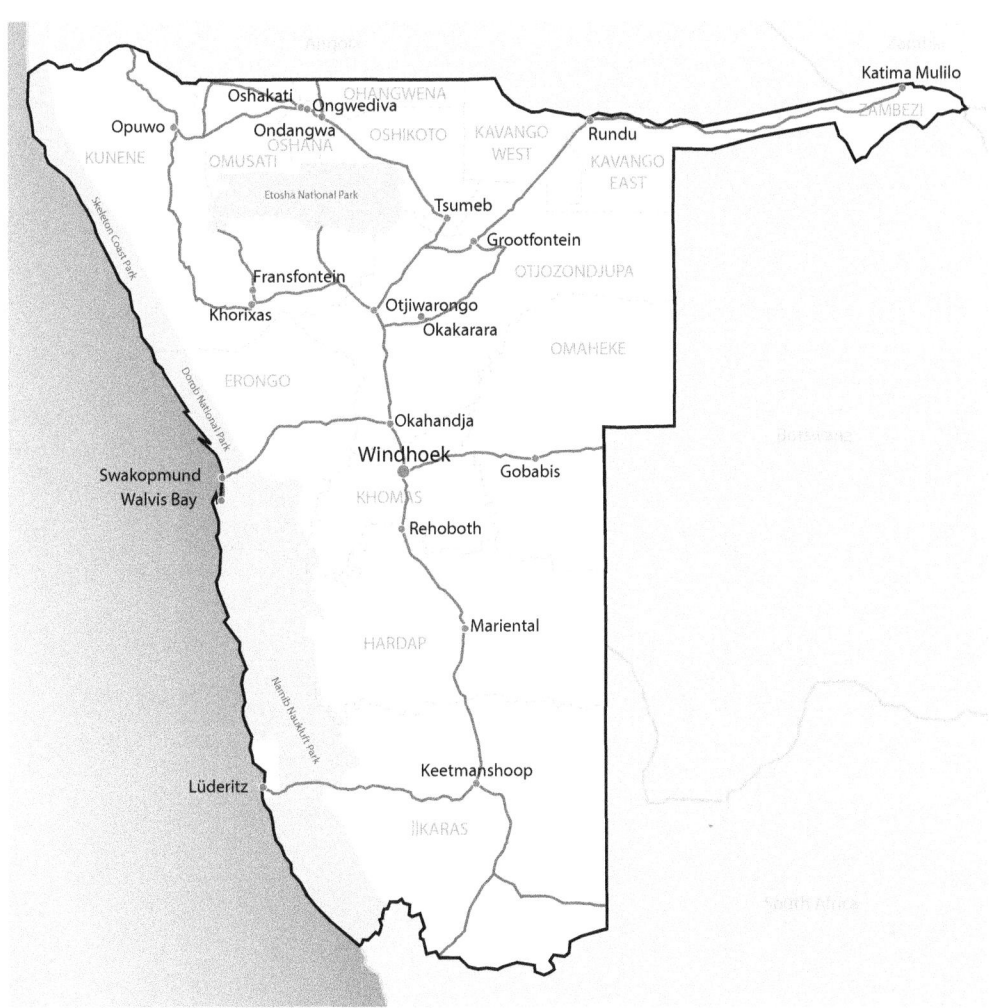

In 2013 the Kavango Region was divided into Kavango East and Kavango West and the Caprivi Region was renamed 'Zambezi'.

Introduction
Re-Viewing Resistance, Liberating History

Jeremy Silvester

Over two decades have passed since the last battles of Namibia's liberation struggle took place in April, 1989 and Namibia finally obtained its independence from South Africa on 21 March, 1990. Today over half of Namibia's population is under the age of 25.[1] When I first taught history at the University of Namibia in the 1990s the majority of my students had strong (and traumatic) childhood memories of the war.[2] Today the majority of students at the university are 'born frees' who do not remember the independence celebrations of 1990, let alone the long, twenty-three year, guerilla war that preceded it.

The majority of the population no longer has strong memories of the liberation struggle, but relies increasingly on the construction of a history of resistance that is reflected in written texts, but more pervasively in the spoken word through public speeches, the radio and TV, in public projects of memorialisation and commemorative public holidays.[3]

History was one of the early conscripts to the nationalist struggle with SWAPO's *To Be Born a Nation* creating a highly influential narrative that interpreted all acts of resistance to German and South African rule as nationalist. In his Foreword to the publication Prof. Peter Katjavivi highlighted the way in which a 'history of resistance' could play a role in nation-building. 'The title is taken from a saying of the Mozambican liberation struggle – "to die a tribe and be born a nation". It encapsulates the drive for unity and the bonds forged through common endeavour and sacrifice that are such vital elements of the national liberation struggle' (SWAPO, 1980, p. iii). The book traced the roots of 'popular resistance' as far back as 1670 and the first meeting between indigenous residents and European travellers on the banks of the Kuiseb River (SWAPO, 1980, p. 151). Independence was thus the culmination of over three hundred years of struggle. Whilst the necessity of discipline and unity was evident during the course of a guerilla campaign against a militarily stronger opponent, this reading of the past reduces the

---

1 The calculations are based on the demographic figures provided by the World Bank's World Development Indicators. <http://data.worldbank.org/data-catalog/world-development-indicators?cid=GPD_WDI>. {Accessed 11 March, 2011}.
2 I was a lecturer in the History Department of the University of Namibia from 1997 to 2005. Since 2005, I have worked as the Project Planning and Training Officer with the Museums Association of Namibia.
3 After independence the commemoration of 'The Day of the Vow' on 16 December was abolished, but Independence Day (21 March), Cassinga Day (4 May), Heroes Day (26 August) and the Day of the Namibian Woman – also Human Rights Day (10 December), were all introduced as public holidays that marked important dates in the struggle for independence.

dynamics of struggle to a simple dichotomy in which characters are presented as either 'Freedom Fighters' or 'Puppets'. The danger is that agency is reduced and the complex political dynamics around issues such as generational conflict, ethnicity, traditional authorities and gender are ignored (Van Walraven and Abbink, 2003, p. 3).

The Archives of Anti-Colonial Resistance and the Liberation Struggle incorporated the nationalist narrative within its lengthy title. The founding premise of the project was the admission that the National Archives of Namibia were dominated by the documentary records of the colonial administrations and that many important oral and written archives that presented oppositional perspectives were absent. The central aim of the project was, therefore, defined as 'filling the gaps' (Namhila, 2004, p. 224). The AACRLS, as it was popularly known, was a joint project between the Namibian and German governments that sought to actively multiply and diversify archival sources and thus 'democratise the archive'. The priorities of the project were to repatriate copies of important archives held beyond Namibia's borders, to support research by young Namibian scholars, to encourage the collection of oral histories of resistance and to support educational projects on Namibian history. The AACRLS achieved a great deal with reference to each of these tasks and it is unfortunate that no comprehensive final report that documented all its achievements was ever produced and made public. Future archivists and historians should also be conscious of Ciraj Rassool's warnings about such documentary projects as documents can become '. . . divorced from their own history of safekeeping, storage, collection and recollection as they had been passed along or transacted into circuits of distribution within which they shed old meanings and took on new ones'.[4] The mission of the AACRLS, to incorporate 'subaltern' groups within the nationalist narrative, may itself have created new layers of silence and exclusion.

On 7-9 December 2009, the AACRLS project organised a conference to mark the dawn of the 20th year of independence and the end of the AACRLS project; it included over 44 presentations. The 19 chapters in this volume have been developed from papers presented at that conference and might be viewed as the raw edge of history production in Namibia. The AACRLS project, based at the National Archives of Namibia, has sought to recover archival materials and support new research in order to reshape both the archives and the history of 'The Struggle'. However, the performance of the conference itself was a seminal moment in the history of discussion about the liberation struggle. Active participants in the liberation war drew on their personal memories to engage with work presented by young historians who had mined the archives. It was for example, perhaps the first public occasion, where details of SWAPO's early involvement with UNITA was discussed.[5] The numerous and extensive interviews conducted by Christian Williams (that provided the foundation for his doctoral thesis) suggest that Namibian leaders are also becoming more willing to present personal perspectives on the struggles within the struggle. The collation of individual insights will provide

---

[4] Ciraj Rassool, 'The Individual, Auto/Biography and History in South Africa' (PhD thesis, University of the Western Cape, 2004), p. 124.

[5] The account presented at the Conference by Comrade Nghiyalasha Haulyondjaba, a former Political Commissar and liaison officer between SWAPO and PLAN. A written account of his version of events can be found in 'Caught in the Eye of a Cold War Hurricane', *Insight*, February 2011.

different views on neglected topics such as the, sometimes tense, relationships between SWAPO and different 'host' nations and liberation movements and a critical appraisal of the operations of the internal security establishment within PLAN that regularly detained SWAPO members (Williams, 2011).[6]

The title of the AACRLS conference, *Moments, Memories and Monuments: Tracing the Footprints to Independence,* suggests a clear linear, chronological, nationalist view of the past as a trail to triumph. History, it presumes, is a series of significant events ('moments') with these events being recalled by participants ('memories') or important historical figures being commemorated ('monuments') to create the footprints that reveal the path to independence.[7] However, as in the conference that took place in South Africa in September 2011, to mark the centenary of the ANC, the AARCLS conference itself marked a moment when a new generation of Namibian historians and historians of Namibia started to explore new views on the past (Soske, Lissoni and Erlank, 2012, p. 30). In a culturally and politically diverse democracy there are bound to be different perspectives on the past. Different historians will prioritise different moments, select different memories and celebrate or demonise different monuments. History will be as plural as the history-tellers.

The conference provided an opportunity to showcase some of the research of new Namibian history-tellers that has been supported by the project over the years and illustrates the emphasis that was placed on supporting the emerging new generation of Namibian historians. Namibians who have recently obtained doctorates in History include Bennett Kangumu, Martha Akawa, Vilho Shigwedha, Kletus Likuwa, Napandulwe Shiweda and Memory Biwa, whilst others such as Helvi Elago, Timoteus Mashuna, Aaron Nambadi, Herberth Karapo, Ndahambelela Alweendo, Naitsikile Iizyenda, Hilma Kapuka, Alma Nankela, Romanus Shiremo, Eliot Mowa, Casper Erichsen, Lovisa Nampala and Inger Nyau have completed MAs in History or Archaeology or the Postgraduate Diploma in Museums and Heritage Studies. All these students have produced significant new research and written work providing new insights and perspectives on Namibia's history and heritage. It would be no exaggeration to state that Namibia is experiencing a renaissance of interest in history and heritage. The new wave of Namibian historians, as architects of the past, are well qualified to work on the wide range of important public history and heritage projects that have emerged over recent years.

One of the challenges facing these Namibian historians has been access to archival materials about the more recent (historically speaking) liberation struggle. Namibia does not have an 'access to information' clause such as is found in South Africa's Promotion of Access to Information Act (No. 2 of 2000). The South African Act enables citizens to request access to archival records that concern them, with the emphasis being placed on

---

6 Christian Williams, 'Exile History: An Ethnography of the SWAPO Camps and the Namibian Nation' (PhD thesis, University of Michigan, 2009).

7 Terence Ranger applied the term 'patriotic history' to the imposition of an unquestionable 'master narrative' as a tool in the construction of a nation in the context of Zimbabwe. Christopher Saunders has expressed the concern that history in Namibia might also be limited to accounts that 'help legitimize the present order' and that 'alternative and critical voices' may be silenced; (Saunders, 2007, p. 26; Ranger, 2004). It is hoped that the present volume indicates that there is actually an ongoing process of historical debate in Namibia within a growing public sphere.

the State to demonstrate to a court of law why a particular file or document should not be made public because, as Richard Callard argues, 'the state must explain and thereby justify its retreat to secrecy' (Callard, 2009, p. 2).[8] The Act has already been used, for example, to ensure that a substantial number of South African documents relating to the attack on Cassinga on 4 May 1978 have been declassified and made accessible to the public. A significant difference also exists concerning the period during which Government records are kept 'closed' to the public. In South Africa, members of the public can view files (that do not have additional security classification) after twenty years; in Namibia the public must wait thirty years.

At present many of the crucial documents relating to Namibia's liberation struggle, such as the archives of the South West African Territorial Force (SWATF), remain in South Africa.[9] Ironically, it is easier for South African, rather than Namibian, historians to access these important records on the Namibian liberation struggle. In Namibia itself SWAPO's own archives are currently housed in a private, party archive and have not yet been fully catalogued. It is for these reasons that historians of the Namibian liberation struggle still tend to rely heavily on interviews with participants, rather than documentary evidence, and this trend is reflected in the chapters in this volume that deal with the more recent history. If the many unwritten histories of the liberation struggle are to emerge, then ways will need to be found to make these major archival collections more accessible to new Namibian historians.

Memories of the liberation struggle for Namibia are being written by ex-combatants and many accounts of the war are emerging. Walking into a typical bookshop in Namibia in February 2011, I found seven books giving personal accounts of the experiences of South Africans who were involved in the 'Border War', but not a single title that provided a Namibian perspective.[10] The point is that whilst all those who participated in the war, on either side, have powerful, if fading, memories of their experiences, not all memories circulate through the same networks. A visit to a bookshop or a surf on the internet (perhaps, today, an even more pervasive medium) will reveal a cacophony of voices and memories that still reflect South African perspectives on the war. Christopher Saunders has noted the surprising point that no Namibian historian has yet critically engaged with this literature and their pervasive argument that the South African military operations against SWAPO were both 'justified' and 'effective' (Saunders, 2007, p. 16).

---

8   Whilst there has not yet been a test case, it does seem possible that Namibians might also be able to seek access to documents through the South African legislation, but in order to do this they need to obtain details of the documents to which they wish to obtain access.

9   The author has, personally, seen extensive shelves of SWATF documents at the South African Army's Documentation Centre in Pretoria, although efforts to locate Koevoet's archives have been unsuccessful to date, as they do not seem to be housed at the South African Police Archives.

10   The seven titles available at the CNA store in Swakopmund on 20 February 2011 were: Cameron Blake, *Troepie: Van Blougat tot Bosoupa* (Cape Town: Zebra Press, 2009); Jannie Geldenhuys, *At the Front* (Johannesburg and Cape Town, 2009); Granger Korff, *19 with a Bullet* (Johannesburg: South Publishers, 2009); Johan Marais, *Time Bomb: A Policeman's True Story* (Cape Town: Tafelburg, 2010); Piet Nortje, *32 Battalion* (Cape Town: Zebra Press, 2003); Tim Ramsden, *Borderlıne Insanity* (Alberton: Galago, 2009); Jacqui Thompson, *Dit Was Oorlog: Van Afkak tot bosbefok* (Cape Town: Zebra Press, 2006).

Oswin Namakalu's publication suggests the wealth of detail that can be drawn from interviews with participants (2004). However, Namakalu did not record his interviews, but used a notebook to record information provided by his sources to create a comprehensive description of the major battles that PLAN combatants were involved in during the struggle. A comprehensive oral history project which would allow surviving participants (who were involved on either side) to record their accounts of the war would be an important legacy project for Namibia and a democratic memorial for future generations of the meaning of the war to those who participated in it. The fact that, in 2007, Namibia signed UNESCO's Convention for the Safeguarding of the Intangible Cultural Heritage means that Namibia has committed itself to developing effective mechanisms for recording indigenous knowledge and collective memories.[11]

The central position of the liberation struggle in the collective consciousness of the nation surely means that significant resources need to be committed to achieve this goal and to continue the work that was started by the AACRLS project. It is commendable that the Ministry of Veterans Affairs has, through its Heritage Directorate, already taken the initiative to establish a collection of audio-visual interviews with ex-combatants and those particularly affected by the war. It should also be noted that one of the positive achievements of the AACRLS was the launch of the 'Footprints' series that sought to make Namibian accounts of the past available to a Namibian readership. It is to be strongly hoped that the National Archives of Namibia will obtain sufficient financial support to sustain and expand this series despite the end of the AACRLS funding.[12]

The chapters in this collection originate from differing points of departure. Some derive from work done for an academic thesis and are thus punctuated with references, whilst others are working papers drawn from shorter research or collection projects supported by the AACRLS. However, all the chapters combine to create a beautiful discord of divergent voices providing alternative perspectives on the past. Richard Callard has argued that the trawling of the archives and the collection of new testimony about past events is important for nation-building: '. . . the digging out of old records is not just of passing academic interest for historians, but also about establishing accountability for past deeds and abuse of power, and that part of the task of establishing accountability in the future is also, therefore, about settling the account of the past' (2009, p. 12). I will, therefore, use the opportunity provided by the Introduction to highlight what, in my view, are some of the most significant points raised by each chapter, but also suggest the ways in which the chapters provide signposts that might lead to further research by young Namibian historians who will continue the important task of debating Namibian history.

---

11   The Convention identifies five main areas (or 'domains') of importance for ICH: 1) Oral traditions and expressions, including language as a vehicle of the intangible cultural heritage; 2) Performing arts; 3) Social practices, rituals and festive events; 4) Knowledge and practices concerning nature and the universe; and 5) Traditional craftsmanship. South Africa has also emphasised the importance of oral history as an additional area of importance, particularly with reference to memories of the anti-apartheid and liberation struggle (Deacon, 2004, p. 9).

12   The three publications produced by the AACRLS in the Footprints Series were Lydia Shaketange, *Walking the Boeing 707* (Windhoek: AARCLS, 2009); Ellen Ndeshi Namhila, *Tears of Courage: Five Mothers, Five Stories, One Victory* (Windhoek: AACRLS, 2009), and a reprint of Vinnia Ndadi's classic account of the migrant labour system and early political mobilisation in Walvis Bay, *Breaking Contract* (Windhoek: AACRLS, 2009).

Ellen Namhila served as Vice-Chairperson of the AACRLS project (which was Chaired initially by Hon. Ben Amathila and then by Hon. Andimba Toivo ya Toivo). Namhila's chapter deals with the process through which she sought to create a new perspective on the liberation struggle by producing a book based on the memories of five women who were intimately involved in the conflict. Namhila's chapter opens this collection by providing an overview of the objectives of the AACRLS project. Namhila previously served as a Director in the Ministry of Education with particular responsibility for the National Archives of Namibia and Namibia's library services and she, therefore, positions the project within the wider context of her ambitions to reconfigure the material content of the National Archives of Namibia which, at independence, was dominated by the documentary paper records of the German and South African colonial administrations. Her chapter reflects on the concept and challenges of creating a 'post-colonial archive' in Namibia.

Namhila's particular interest is in the role that can be played by oral history in addressing silences in Namibian history and absences in the archives. She argues that oral history is essential to address the gender imbalance in the categories of history and the configuration of archives. Yet, she argues further that the recording of narratives is not simply a documentary exercise, but also has a therapeutic and empowering impact on the narrators. Namhila states '. . . I wanted each woman to feel the power of her own voice' through the transformation of the original interviews recorded in Oshiwambo into a translated typed and published narrative. The fact that Namhila repeatedly interacted with the women whose stories she tells over a number of years means that she is extremely conscious of the moral issues raised by her efforts to resurrect painful memories and the importance of building a relationship of trust. Her descriptions of the women's process of remembering during their conversations suggest the potential damage that can be caused by the pillaging of memory by historians who extract interviews, but never return to the speaker.

One might argue that Namhila's chapter reveals very clearly the mediating role of the historian as the creator of a sequential narrative, even though Namhila admits that when she writes the stories of the five women in the book she writes in the first person. The chapter raises interesting questions about the way in which historians often work with oral history, mediate memory and weave a narrative, rather than present the reader with a transcript revealing the original dialogue and the interaction between the distinct voices of the historian and the narrator.[13] In contrast to Namhila's chapter the two chapters (by Shampapi Shiremo and Werner Hillebrecht) that deal with the earliest topics rely far more heavily on archival material.

Werner Hillebrecht writes about two icons of early resistance to colonial rule, Kaptein Hendrik Witbooi and Chief Samuel Maharero. He argues for a denser reading of their roles in Namibian history, rather than a 'cartoon' version of the past that threatens to reduce the complexity of these important historical leaders. Hillebrecht makes it clear that his aim is not 'to tear down monuments', but that historians need to address the

---

13 For an example of a text that conveys the sense of oral history as a dialogue between an interviewer and an interviewee see Elsabé Brink and Gandhi Malungane, *Soweto, 16 June 1976: Personal Accounts of the Uprising* (Cape Town: Kwela Books, 2001).

reasons why both men participated in what (with hindsight) nationalists would view as collaboration with the German colonial forces, by actively assisting in the military conquest of other Namibian communities.

The focus in Hillebrecht's chapter on the Hendrik Witbooi diaries illustrates the way in which archives are constructed and yet, at times, also 'accidental' in their accessioning of documents. Witbooi's chapters were fragmented and scattered, but have, gradually, been retrieved and collated by the National Archives of Namibia. Hillebrecht provides the 'biography' of the books that were the first artifacts of Namibia's documentary heritage to be inscribed by UNESCO on their 'Memory of the World' inventory. Fate has been a factor in the survival and recovery of these fragile notebooks. However it was, of course, the iconic status given to Witbooi and his representation as an honourable opponent of Imperial Germany that gave them recognition and make them 'archivable'.

Whilst it can be argued that the writing of Namibian history as a nationalist narrative which culminates in independence is an important vehicle for nation-building, it can also lead to the marginalisation of histories that may not easily fit into this framework. In 1894, ten years after Namibia was formally colonised by Imperial Germany, a massacre took place which left many Vagciriku dead. **Shampapi Shiremo** argues that one of the reasons the massacre has been 'silenced' from Namibian history has been the failure of Namibian historians to write about internal politics and the friction between neighbouring communities that preceded and transcended colonial rule. Shiremo also argues that a further reason for the absence of the massacre from Namibian history books is that the colonial borders fragmented the archival records that relate to many African communities. The case of the massacre is a good example of one of the central concerns that the AACRLS project sought to address. Whilst the massacre features strongly in the community memory of the Vagciriku living in Namibia, crucial documents relating to the massacre were located in the National Archives of Botswana. Furthermore, Shantjefu, the site of the massacre, is located in Angola, suggesting that further research in the Portuguese colonial archives in Luanda (and Lisbon) might reveal more about the massacre.

Petrus Mbenzi's work highlights, ironically, one of the 'gaps' or 'silences' in the archives of the liberation struggle – and that is the songs that were sung by SWAPO activists, both inside and outside the country. Songs are an important part of the intangible cultural heritage of the struggle and could circulate without the risk of being confiscated (unlike posters or other printed propaganda materials). The singing or, perhaps, even the silent memory of the songs could provide a source of strength within communities facing harassment for their political beliefs and could be, in James Scott's term, one of the 'weapons of the weak' (Scott, 1985). Mbenzi reflects on a collection project conducted with the assistance of students at the University of Namibia which resulted in the documentation of over 2,000 'revolutionary songs'. The translation of the lyrics of the songs provides a new perspective to a wider audience on the political culture of SWAPO and the ways in which the struggle was conceptualised and promoted.

Mbenzi presents his interpretation of the role of songs in the struggle within the broader context of the traditional role of songs in northern Namibia (as the majority of the songs that he has documented are in Oshiwambo). He argues that 'revolutionary songs' drew heavily on themes (and tunes) derived from traditional praise songs or Christian gospel music. Importantly, Mbenzi not only discusses the lyrics of the songs, but also reflects on the media through which they circulated and the extent to which they were sung and heard within and beyond the borders of Namibia. Mbenzi not only provides English translations of songs that were originally sung in Oshiwambo, but also interprets the cultural references made in the songs to belief systems and individuals. One of the challenges that Mbenzi faces in his work and that applies to all forms of intangible cultural heritage is that the music and lyrics of songs often change over time. Mbenzi illustrates the way in which gospel music was recycled with new texts, and future research might use older recordings to reflect on the ways in which the lyrics used by SWAPO also changed over time to reflect changes in the leadership of the movement.[14]

Annette Hoffmann writes about another neglected and disturbing audio-visual collection from the colonial archive. She describes the efforts of Hans Lichtenecker from Germany to 'document' people through the moulding of plaster casts and collection of voice recordings in Namibia in 1931. It seems that Lichtenecker was more interested in the physical sound of the voices that he recorded than the cultural content, with speakers being invited to say 'something' into the recording equipment. Hoffman defines this initiative within a broader Western project, often linked with museums, to create an 'archive of vanishing races' in which artifacts, body castes, photographs, notes and audio-visual recordings were collected to form an ethnographic archive to document a particular community. Such projects pose questions on the shaping of museum collections that parallel those about archiving practices, and suggest that Namibian academics might find it interesting to interrogate the politics of past and present museum collection policies.

Hoffman focuses particularly on Lichtenecker's sound recordings and notes the rarity of recordings of the voices of black Namibians from the early twentieth century. At a time when Namibians were politically voiceless, their voices also, literally, remain unheard. The American activist Allard Lowenstein made clandestine recordings of early nationalist leaders such as Hosea Kutako and Rev. Markus Kooper making statements about their political grievances. However, the important difference was that these speakers were interviewed as important community leaders and were consciously presenting their case to an external audience. Hoffman argues that the Lichtenecker's recordings of people who had been used as models for body castes can also be read as containing subaltern narratives, even though they were composed within a highly controlled situation. The speakers were not leaders and whilst embodied and memorialised through body casting, were disembodied from their individual biographies. Hoffman critically analyses the recordings and highlights traces of agency struggling against the attempt to objectify and classify individuals within a fixed formulaic typology.

---

14 One might consider, for example, the lyrics found on the long playing record *Onyeka = Namibia Will Be Free* (IDAF, London, 1984) which contains praise of the then SWAPO Vice-President, Mishake Muyongo, with current renditions of the same songs that no longer mention Muyongo (who tried to lead a sucessionist movement in Caprivi in 1999 and now lives in exile in Denmark).

One point that Hoffman's work unconsciously highlights is the virtual total absence of academic study of audio-visual sources of more recent Namibian history. Whilst quite extensive work has been done on visual sources, audio recordings and film remain under-researched despite the extensive film archives of the National Archives of Namibia and both sound and film recordings from the South West Africa Broadcasting Corporation and the Namibia Broadcasting Corporation. One important national project would be the establishment of a unified searchable national database providing comprehensive coverage of audio-visual holdings that would help stimulate such research.

In **Kletus Likuwa**'s chapter, the introduction and development of the migrant labour system in the Kavango region is placed within the context of the location of the region at a geographical location which, in the final decades of the nineteenth century, faced the possibility of inclusion within either the Portuguese, German or British colonial spheres of influence. Likuwa argues that the ways in which the residents of the region were economically recruited into the colonial economy requires an analysis of the friction between these competing colonial powers. He also argues strongly that the efforts to establish a Christian missionary presence within different tribal territories within the region should be viewed as laying the foundations for capitalist economic penetration and colonial political occupation. In Likuwa's analysis the missionaries' demands for access and influence and the recruiting agents demands for labour were both perceived as direct manifestations of colonial domination because they directly challenged the authority of traditional authorities.

Likuwa seeks to explain the background to the reasons why, by 1926, male workers from the region were excluded from work on the diamond fields of southern Namibia and recruited instead by the 'Northern Labour Organisation' that focused on providing labour to the copper mine at Tsumeb and other mines in central Namibia, as well as providing labour for commercial farms and urban areas. He argues that one factor that should be considered in the restructuring of the recruiting system was the agency of workers who resisted recruitment to the south because of the negative reports they received about the working conditions there. Likuwa's work complements the work of Patricia Hayes, which looks at the dynamics of the labour recruiting system in the Owambo kingdoms by considering the dynamic between the recruiters and the recruited and, particularly, the role played by traditional authorities in the system.

Whilst these chapters focus on the frictions caused by early encounters with colonialism in Namibia, the chapters by Dag Henrichsen and Bennett Kangumu deal with the transition from engagements at a local level to the development of a broader nationalist political agenda.

On one level **Dag Henrichsen**'s chapter provides an individual biography – the story of Israel Goldblatt whose notebooks documenting his meetings with early Namibian nationalists were recently published by the Basel Afrika Bibliographien (Henrichsen, Jacobson and Marshall, 2010). However, Henrichsen's work also suggests the need for a greater contemplation and problematisation of the racial categories that often form the basis of popular historical analysis in Namibia. Henrichsen asks why there was an absence of a non-racial, liberal tradition in Namibia and considers the factors that generated 'white coherence', rather than taking it as an assumption. Indeed, given the fact that many German-speaking Namibians experienced internment in prison camps for several years during both the First and Second World Wars, the administration's introduction of land settlement schemes that favoured Afrikaans-speaking settlers (such as the so-called 'Angola Boers') and the constant reinforcement of cultural differences between different language groups within the 'white' community, there was also plenty of potential for antagonism and division within the settler community.

Henrichsen argues that the framework for opposition within this community was extremely limited. Advocate Goldblatt engaged with political issues, but essentially viewed problems legalistically through the lens of international law. The chapter provides a new perspective on the attempts to base the campaign for Namibian independence on the principles enshrined in the United Nations Charter, such as universal suffrage, and to seek international intervention prior to the launch of the armed struggle. The chapter emphasises that this form of resistance to the South African occupation of Namibia represented a liberal, rather than a radical, viewpoint. The premise was that reform was necessary to prevent the radicalisation of African nationalist movements and potential threat that this would pose to the existing (racially entrenched) distribution of land and private property. Henrichsen's chapter dissects the political culture of 'settler society' and the boundaries of its imagination that excluded the conception of 'non-racial' political activism.

Bennett Kangumu Kangumu provides two complementary chapters that build on his doctoral research. The first provides an overview of the role played by the Caprivi African National Union (CANU) in the liberation of Namibia. The second focuses on CANU's leader and, later, the Vice-President of SWAPO, Brendan Simbwaye, who was detained by the South African authorities in 1964 and eventually 'disappeared' seven years later in 1971. The first chapter provides a historical overview that provides an explanation of why an opposition movement developed that was explicitly rooted in the Caprivi region, and the way in which the criticism of the colonial administration changed over time, and provides the necessary background to explain CANU's decision to merge with SWAPO. Kangumu's chapter includes interesting observations on the relationship between the nationalist movement and the traditional leadership of the Caprivi and thus highlights the need for a wider consideration of the relationship between traditional authorities and SWAPO during the liberation struggle.

Kangumu's bibliographical chapter on Brendan Simbwaye provides a substantive account of a figure who has been surprisingly neglected in Namibian historiography, perhaps because there does not seem to have been the same type of international campaign to maintain public awareness of Simbwaye as there was with leaders such as Nelson Mandela or Toivo ya Toivo who also 'disappeared' following their arrest. Kangumu's work is characterised by the meticulous care with which he has traced the trail through the Namibian archives. However, Kangumu's research also highlights the fact that many questions from the history of the liberation struggle, such as the sequence of events leading to the presumed death of Simbwaye, will remain unanswered for as long as Namibian historians are not able to easily access and evaluate the South African police and army archives in Johannesburg.

Aaron Nambadi provides the first detailed analysis of the composition and contradictions of 'Homeland' politics through an overview of the history and operations of the Kavango Legislative Council from 1970 to 1979. The chapter is drawn from Nambadi's postgraduate research and is the first work by a Namibian historian since independence that seeks to explore the ways in which the 'Homeland' systems of self-rule impacted on the communities under their authority.[15] Nambadi also attempts to measure the extent to which the system actually devolved any meaningful decision-making powers from the South African controlled administrative structures and the limited political influence of the Windhoek based Legislative Assembly elected by white voters.

Nambadi's chapter is important because it develops an argument regarding the dynamic relationship between 'traditional authorities' and 'nationalist party politics'. The South African political model for the first ethnically based Legislative Councils was built on the foundation of existing traditional political systems. In Kavango, the first members of the Legislative Assembly were all nominated (not elected) by the traditional authorities that represented the five recognised ethnic groups in the Kavango Regions, and the Executive was made up of one representative from each group. The second Council was partly nominated and partly elected. Nambadi avoids a simple nationalist reading of the period that would be drawn towards a critical reading of this political project as a totally inadequate exercise in democratic expression. Instead Nambadi is concerned with suggesting the ways in which the new political structures generated a 'Kavango identity', presented possibilities for changes in political culture, and provided the opportunity to relocate nationalism as an external threat, rather than an emancipatory campaign. The 'Homeland' politics described in Nambadi's chapter provide a useful background to the discussion of the national election that took place in 1978 and which is the subject of the chapter by Timotheus Mashuna.

Up until 1978, only white people were entitled to vote in elections in Namibia. **Timotheus Mashuna** writes about the first election in Namibia, which the South African Administrator-General claimed was 'free', stating that it was based on universal suffrage, and would facilitate the 'transfer of power' to Namibians. Mashuna provides a critical examination of the extent to which the election could be described as democratic and a meaningful development in political culture in Namibia. He notes that the election saw the establishment of the first national electoral roll following a nationwide voter registration campaign, and the first national election campaigns by political parties (although SWAPO and the Namibia National Front held rallies to campaign for support for an election boycott). He argues that the election provided an opportunity for a widespread public debate about the meaning of 'democracy' and the conditions that needed to exist to enable a 'free and fair' election to take place in Namibia, and thus created a forum for political education.

Mashuna's chapter also highlights the significance of the year 1978 in the history of Namibia's liberation struggle. In hindsight, it might be easy to dismiss the 1978 election as a transparent attempt by South Africa to manipulate the democratic process. However, the fact that over 80 percent of the electorate were reported to have voted and

---

15 Nambadi's work provides a much more detailed analysis of the content of 'Homeland politics' than was found in earlier work such as that of Tötemeyer (1978).

that the election followed the adoption of UN Resolution 435, meant that it was crucial for the liberation movement that the international community should not interpret this election as reflecting the democratic aspirations of the Namibian people. The fact that the election took place just over six months after the attack on Cassinga had been a major public relations disaster for the South African Government, which was probably one of the key factors that prevented the international community from accepting the election results as a genuine reflection of the will of the Namibian people. The chapter suggests that there is a need for more extensive research into the propaganda war that took place in the months before and after the election to ensure that the international community refused to accept the South African argument that Namibia had obtained its independence in 1978.

One feature of the years leading up to the 1978 election was a clear escalation of violence in northern Namibia.

The chapter by **Martha Akawa** and myself explains the methodology that we used to try and create the first database that would provide Namibia with a list of the names of all the civilians who were victims of the liberation struggle inside Namibia. We, like Helvi Elago, also discuss the ways in which the past is, or could be, remembered and seek to contextualise our research within the context of the ways in which those who died during the Namibian liberation struggle are remembered today through a variety of memorial projects.

Our work developed a strong public history component when a draft list of the names of all those killed was published in a national newspaper.[16] The chapter raises the issue of the public responsibility of historians, particularly when dealing with sensitive history that involves the, historically speaking, recent death of people. One of the responses to the publication of the list was that a number of adults who had lost one or both of their parents when they were a child contacted us to learn more about their deaths.

The project remains incomplete and the chapter maps out the challenges that faced us and the way in which the project might be expanded if further funding became available. Our research faced the challenge of locating source material that was accessible and that provided the actual names of victims – the evidence provided in the newspaper archives that were consulted by the project presented obvious limitations. However, the chapter argues that the research also faced conceptual challenges as we were confronted on a daily basis with the need to define the boundaries of our subject. What were the geographical and chronological boundaries of the liberation struggle and who might or might not qualify to be defined as a 'civilian'? The chapter simply indicates the choices that we made, but, in doing so, makes clear the subjective nature of the decisions that historians make in the moulding of their narrative texts.

We know that the 1,278 individual cases identified by our research to date do not provide a complete list of those that died during the war and our database is gradually expanding as people contact us with additional names and information. However, in order to make the list as comprehensive as possible it will be necessary to find a way to conduct a comprehensive review of the inquest files in the magistrates courts that

---

16 Jeremy Silvester and Martha Akawa, 'Opening Pandora's Box', *The Namibian*, 5 November 2006.

investigated cases and provided 'cause of death' verdicts in the majority of cases. The chapter also argues that interviews with survivors and the families of victims would also provide more detailed accounts. However, the chapter warns that such research would be likely to raise expectations of compensation that historians are not in a position to directly address. The chapter seeks to present not only some initial research data but also to seriously consider the potential consequences of opening up a new perspective on the past. The chapter's central argument is that history is a narrative about the past that is experienced in the present and, therefore, its impact on the present should always be theorised by the engaged historian. Whilst history sometimes poses as a science, it can never be an innocent activity.

Lovisa Nampala's chapter also deals with the impact of the liberation struggle on people living inside Namibia. However, the perspective that her chapter provides is a case study, rather than a national overview. She focuses on the memories of the war in the village of Okongo in Ohangwena Region, an area that was particularly affected by the war following the construction of an SADF base there in 1973. As she is dealing with memories she focuses on a set of interviews that she conducted with residents of the village. In her chapter Nampala argues that the psychological, social, economic and cultural impact of the war on communities should not just be sought in the 'headline incidents' in which people were killed, but also in the everyday atmosphere of repression, fear and suspicion that permeated society during the war. Military actions such as the violent enforcement of the nightly curfew or the public display of the corpses of dead guerillas left residents traumatised. Nampala argues that a memorial or a museum (or perhaps a memorial museum) would be an appropriate way to deal with this latent social trauma. However, Nampala's analysis of oral histories of the period also reveal that not all memories of the South African presence were negative as, for example, some residents argued that they received good medical treatment from the military hospital.

Nampala's chapter is also significant because she included in her interviews a Namibian who fought throughout the war on the South African side. The demobilisation figures suggest that at least 25,000 Namibians fought in the locally recruited South West Africa Territorial Force (SWATF) and this excludes those who were members of units such as the paramilitary police unit Koevoet or 'Home Guard'. The numbers can be compared to the 42,000 SWAPO members who returned from exile after the end of the war in 1989 of whom 32,000 were 'demobilised' as ex-combatants – meaning, presumably, that the remainder were considered to be civilians (McMullin, 2005). However, few historians have actively interviewed these ex-combatants who could explain the reasons why so many Namibians joined the security forces and provide considerable insight into the ways in which these units operated. Incidents such as the uncovering of the mass graves of unidentified victims of the war at Eenhana, and the role of an ex-soldier in directing the authorities to other mass graves in northern Namibia, illustrate the ways in which such witnesses might provide an alternative perspective of the recent past and provide practical assistance to the mapping of liberation heritage.

Herberth Karapo's chapter provides a second regional perspective that reminds readers of the political complexity of Namibia during the liberation struggle when the limitations of communications and infrastructure (such as the road and rail networks) presented real challenges to young nationalists seeking to weave residents of regions such as the Kavango and Caprivi into a national narrative. Karapo also argues that, given the difficulties of accessing the restricted archival documents of both sides in the liberation struggle, local and regional perspectives are best developed through listening to and documenting oral histories.

Such histories not only provide a sequence of events which are considered to be significant to the oral historian, but also provide insight into the ways in which South African propaganda filtered through society and contributed to what Karapo terms 'a climate of fear'. In one example, the assertion that SWAPO was a communist organisation and therefore hostile to Christianity was visualised in the belief that SWAPO's soldiers might even have 'tails' as the very incarnation of demonic (anti-Christian) forces. The memories that are entwined in Karapo's account of the impact of the war demonstrate the ways in which the banality of violence and the pervasive threat of violence permeated society – the possibility of a landmine explosion on the way to school, unexpected visits by armed men at night whose allegiance was uncertain, or the slap in the face given to a schoolboy by a soldier that still stings decades later!

Karapo's chapter also raises the important issue of the role of the traditional authorities during the liberation struggle, a topic that has been under-researched to date. He argues that traditional leaders were placed in a difficult and ambiguous position. On the one hand, they were responsive to the complaints of their subjects about the abuses of the security forces and the economic grievances of the period. On the other hand, they were also recruited by the South African authorities to serve in administrations of the 'Homelands' that were established as a result of the Odendaal Commission's recommendations, and provided with armed guards.[17] Whilst the impact of the war inside Namibia was considerable many Namibians who went into exile spent most of their time in camps beyond the border.

The presence of a number of former PLAN combatants and commanders was one of the features of the AACRLS conference that added considerable significance and weight to the debates and discussions around the chapters that were presented.

Martha Akawa's research has provoked frank and open discussion about the issue of 'sexual politics' in SWAPO's camps in exile during the liberation struggle. Her chapter tackles the subject from three different perspectives.

The first is her attempt to unpack the social baggage that men and women carried into exile – the conventions and taboos that conditioned gendered relationships and which were framed within the context of both 'traditional' and Christian belief systems. Importantly Akawa does not represent this as a static cultural template, but a contested

---

17   See *Report of the Commission of Enquiry into South West African Affairs, 1962-3* (Odendaal Commission), RP 12/64, Government Printer, Pretoria, 1964.

one, in which the socio-economic intervention of the colonial state through mechanisms such as the imposition of the migrant labour system, which removed men from their homes and families for long periods of time, had had a significant impact on gender relationships.

The second perspective on the experience of women is drawn from the projection of the struggle in the speeches and publications produced by the liberation and solidarity movements in which they presented 'liberation' as having a particular meaning for women involved in the struggle. Akawa seeks to analyse a gendered concept of freedom – who was to be liberated from what when the liberation struggle was over? The third layer in Akawa's chapter is that of personal testimony based on extensive interviews conducted with women and men who lived in the camps, about their own memories and experiences.

In her argument Akawa does not document or claim that there was extensive sexual abuse in the camps, but she uses material from her extensive oral interviews with ex-combatants to open up a debate about the sexual dynamics of the camps and the ways in which relationships were framed within a camp context. The chapter is not only important for the issues that it confronts directly, but also because it opens up a broader discussion about the political culture of the camps and the systems of security and control that were used to manage those who lived in the camps. Whilst the experience of 'exile' continues to be a central reference point in political debate inside Namibia, there has been surprisingly little academic attempt to describe and analyse the camp experience.[18] Akawa explores the 'culture' of the camps by emphasising the militaristic elements of discipline, security consciousness and suspicion and the hierarchical command structures.

Whilst there have been several publications about the Anti-Apartheid Movement and solidarity movement, their focus has tended to be on South Africa, rather than Namibia, and these publications have been difficult to obtain in Namibia.[19] Exceptions have been the excellent six volume series of publications produced by the Nordic Africa Institute covering the roles of Denmark, Finland, Norway and Sweden in the solidarity movement in Southern Africa, which have extensive material relating to Namibia (but which have, to date, not been effectively used by Namibian historians); Vladimir Shubin's work on

---

18   Recent work that has started to provide new insights into the history of SWAPO's camps include Martha Akawaa (2014), *The Gender Politics of the Namibian Liberation Struggle*, and Christian Williams (2009), 'Exile History: An Ethnography of the SWAPO Camps and the Namibian Nation'.
19   For example, on the anti-apartheid movement in the UK, Sweden and the USA see Roger Fieldhouse, *Anti-Apartheid: A History of the Movement in Britain, 1959-1994* (London: Merlin Press, 2005); Hakan Thorn, *Anti-Apartheid and the Emergence of a Global Civil Society* (Basingstoke: Palgrave Macmillan, 2009); William Minter, Gail Hovey and Charles Cobb Jnr. (eds), *No Easy Victories: African Liberation and American Activists Over a Half Century, 1950-2000* (Trenton/Asmara: Africa World Press, 2008).

the role of the Soviet Union; and Christopher Saunders' article on the British-based Namibian solidarity movement.[20]

This publication contains two chapters that provide personal perspectives on the international solidarity movement that campaigned in support of SWAPO for Namibian independence. **Reinhart Kössler** recalls the work of small solidarity organisations in West Germany (as it was at that time), whilst Pekka Peltola provides an insight into the work of Finnish activists, although he focuses more on the ways in which the AACRLS project has attempted to document the history of Finnish support for the Namibian liberation struggle. Ironically whilst the central argument of the Namibian liberation struggle was that Namibia was not a 'Fifth Province' of South Africa, the strategies of many organisations tended to subsume the Namibian struggle within broader anti-apartheid and other issue-based campaigns, and both chapters provide considerable insight into the way in which the solidarity movement in each country intersected with the agendas of other local interest groups and campaigns.

Kössler's chapter, which is based heavily on his personal memories of his own involvement in the solidarity movement, clearly demonstrates the extent to which the solidarity movement included political activists who were often involved in a number of contemporary left-wing campaigns, and this helps to explain why campaigns on Namibia often involved alliances. For example, in the UK in the 1980s, the 'Cancel the Namibian Uranium Contract' (CANUC) campaign enabled the Namibia Support Committee to work with the Campaign for Nuclear Disarmament (CND), which had a much larger membership base, and also with trade unionists organising workers at Liverpool docks who were involved in unloading ships bringing 'yellowcake' (the concentrated uranium powder which is smelted to provide the fuel rods in nuclear reactors) from Namibia. Peltola's chapter also suggest, the different ways in which political dynamics within Finland shaped the form of the solidarity movement there and intersected with wider geopolitical considerations, such as the position of Finland in relationship to its powerful neighbour, the Soviet Union.

Pekka Peltola's chapter provides a systematic explanation of the way in which the Finnish AACRLS Committee approached the process of documentation and offers this as a template for other projects. The proposal should be an important reminder of the need to adequately document the role of other countries, particularly in Africa, such as Ghana, Tanzania, Zambia and Angola, in Namibia's liberation struggle. Peltola highlights the importance of collection and selection in archival work and illustrates

---

20   Iina Soiri and Pekka Peltola, *Finland and National Liberation in Southern Africa*, (Uppsala: Nordiska Afrikainstitutet, 1999); Tor Sellström (ed.), *Liberation in Southern Africa. Regional and Swedish Voices* (Uppsala: Nordiska Afrikainstitutet, 1999); Tor Sellström, *Sweden and National Liberation in Southern Africa. Volume I: Formation of a Popular Opinion 1950-1970* (Uppsala: Nordiska Afrikainstitutet, 1999); Tore Linné Eriksen (ed.), *Norway and National Liberation in Southern Africa* (Uppsala: Nordiska Afrikainstitutet, 2000); Tor Sellström, *Sweden and National Liberation in Southern Africa. Volume II: Solidarity and Assistance 1970-1994* (Uppsala: Nordiska Afrikainstitutet, 2002); Christopher Morgenstierne *Denmark and National Liberation in Southern Africa: A Flexible Response* (Uppsala: Nordiska Afrikainstitutet, 2003); Vladimir Shubin, *The Hot 'Cold War': The USSR in Southern Africa* (Pluto Press, London, 2008); Christopher Saunders, 'Namibian Solidarity: British Support for Namibian Independence', *Journal of Southern African Studies*, 35 (2), (2009).

the need for archivists to be pro-active to shape their collections, rather than being perceived as only cataloguers and storage agents. The archives must be refigured.[21] Whilst the archives are one of the ways in which a nation stores a collective memory of the past, a more publically visible statement is made by the construction of high profile monuments across the landscape.

Helvi Elago's chapter considers the meaning attached to German colonial monuments in 'post-colonial' Namibia with special reference to the 'Equestrian Statue' near the National Museum of Namibia in the centre of Windhoek. She argues that the monument has had 'layers of meaning' attached to it over time and that the decision to move (or even, theoretically to remove) the monument focuses only on the physical presence of the monument and not the intangible cultural significance of the monument to different communities and individuals. She argues that the monument should not be viewed as an uncontested celebration of German colonial might, but an icon that might actually be used to open up public discussion about the past. Elago's arguments suggests the need for further research on the possible plural readings of Namibia's cultural heritage sites, and encourages more multi-vocal interpretative displays reflecting the diverse meanings attached to some of Namibia most iconic heritage sites.[22]

Elago's chapter also starts to open up a debate about the ways in which Namibia's cultural heritage is employed in the branding of Namibia as a tourist destination. She suggests that the packaging of Namibia as a destination with a unique 'German' flavour has been a conscious strategy within the tourism industry and contributes to the fact that Germany provides the largest number of overseas tourists to Namibia. Tourism studies in Namibia have largely been limited to the more practical aspects of the hospitality industry and Elago's arguments suggest the need for greater academic engagement by Namibian historians with the ways in which representations of Namibian history and culture are deployed in the tourism sector. Indeed it might be argued that the exported version of Namibian identity owes more to the pervasive ways in which commercial displays and marketing materials 'package' Namibia than to weighty academic dissertations. Namibian historians must engage with the whole range of ways in which historical narratives are produced and circulated. Since Elago wrote her chapter the statue 'has been moved, and not removed' for a second time (on 24 December, 2013, although the decision had already been announced in August).[23] However, the intense debate on social media and in other forums that surrounded this intervention to reshape

---

[21] For a more expansive argument on the need to refigure the archives see Carolyn Hamilton, Verne Harris and Graeme Reid, 'Introduction', in *Refiguring the Archive*, edited by Carolyn Hamilton, Verne Harris, Jane Taylor, Michele Pickover, Graeme Reid and Razia Saleh (Cape Town: David Philip, 2002).

[22] Whilst Andreas Vogt has provided a comprehensive descriptive account of recognised national monuments prior to independence, there is clearly a need for more research on the meaning of places to people. The National Heritage Council is working towards a more democratic interpretation of heritage significance through programmes such as the 'Heritage Hunt', which could draw on such research (Vogt, 2004). The 'Heritage Hunt' has produced reports on six of the fourteen regions of Namibia, based on residents' proposals of places that they feel are significant.

[23] 'Nujoma to get statue in Windhoek', *Namibian*, 27 August 2013; 'Reiterdenkmal must go – Kaapanda', *Namibian Sun*, 24 September 2013; 'Reiterdenkmal disappears overnight', *Namibian Sun*, 26 December 2013.

the heritage landscape reinforces Elago's argument that the contemporary significance of heritage sites is the opportunity they provide to provoke debate about the meaning of the past, and explore the different perspectives of the past held by individual Namibians within a context where dialogue and increased understanding provide a prerequisite for real post-conflict reconciliation.

André Du Pisani provides a critical commentary on Elago's chapter and a film by Tim Huebschle, *Rider Without a Horse*, which was also screened during the AACRLS conference. Huebschle, visually, argued that the monument might no longer be acceptable in a nation where descendants of those who died fighting the German Schutztruppe drive past the statue on their way to work in the nearby Parliament building. His central argument engages with the question posed by the conference panel. Should monuments that were erected to celebrate colonial victories and achievements be embraced as part of our national heritage or removed as symbolic of values that, with a national constitution enshrining human rights and equality, are now viewed as heresy? Du Pisani notes that conflicts over the way in which the past of a country should be remembered often take the form of battles around the construction or destruction (iconoclasm) of monuments, as this is when competing readings of the past are most often publically performed. Du Pisani's argument is developed further in Gilbert Likando's chapter which argues that heritage should feature more prominently in the school curricula.

Gilbert Likando makes a clear argument about the importance of integrating Namibia's heritage, whether cultural or natural, into our education system. Likando argues that Namibia's rich heritage including its heritage sites, oral traditions and museum objects, should be seen as important educational resources. Heritage education, he argues, can help Namibians to gain greater knowledge of (and respect for) the country's cultural diversity and biodiversity and thus play an important role in nation-building. However, Likando also highlights five potential dangers that might emerge during the process of integrating 'heritage' into the curriculum.

One of the threats that Likando highlights is the 'romanticism' of the past that has been one of the common criticisms of the 'heritage industry'. His argument implies that heritage as well as heritage education must allow for alternative readings of past events. Stuart Hall has argued that heritage shapes the nation, but that the nation is an 'ongoing project, under constant reconstruction. We come to know its meaning partly through the objects and artefacts which have been made to stand for and symbolize its essential values' (Hall, 2008 p. 220). Heritage education would, therefore, be at the forefront of the constant debate over the significance and meaning of Namibia's natural and cultural heritage and, therefore, at the very centre of the process through which Namibia's identity is forged and interrogated.

Re-Viewing Resistance in Namibian History seeks to question categories that create a simplified 'cartoon' version of the past. The chapters employ new empirical evidence to suggest new perspectives on the past. As a whole, the chapters present an alternative to a history that focuses on a few individuals at the expense of a wider understanding of the notion of resistance that is more inclusive, by providing regional perspectives in the tradition of 'history from below'. However, it is hoped that the book will not only write 'forgotten' people into history, but also serve to provide a reading of the past that reflects the tensions and competing identities that pervaded 'the struggle' and created ambiguity regarding those who remained peripheral to it or opposed to it. If readings of the past provide the windows through which society addresses the present, then the ways in which we package the past will be indicative of the way in which we deal with the present.

References

Akawa, M. (2014) *The Gender Politics of the Namibian Liberation Struggle*. Basel: Basel Afrika Bibliographien.

Blake, C. (2009) *Troepie: Van Blougat tot Bosoupa*. Cape Town: Zebra Press.

Brink, E. and Gandhi Malungane, G. (2001) *Soweto, 16 June 1976: Personal Accounts of the Uprising*. Cape Town: Kwela Books.

Callard, R. (2009) Illuminating the Politics and the Practice of Access to Information in South Africa. In Allan, K. (ed.) *Chapter Wars: Access to Information in South Africa*. Johannesburg: Witwatersrand University Press.

Deacon, H. (with Luvuyo Dondolo, L., Mrubata, M. and Prosalendis, P.) (2004) *The Subtle Power of Intangible Cultural Heritage: Legal and Financial Instruments for Safeguarding Intangible Heritage*. Cape Town: Human Sciences Research Council.

Eriksen, T. L. (ed.) (2000) *Norway and National Liberation in Southern Africa*. Uppsala: Nordiska Afrikainstitutet.

Fieldhouse, R. (2005) *Anti-Apartheid: A History of the Movement in Britain, 1959-1994*. London: Merlin Press.

Geldenhuys, J. (2009) *At the Front*. Johannesburg and Cape Town: Jonathan Ball Publishers.

Hall, S. (2008) 'Whose Heritage? Un-settling "The Heritage", re-imagining the post-nation'. In Fairclough, G., Harrison, R., Jameson, J. and Schofield, J. (eds). *The Heritage Reader*. London and New York: Routledge.

Haulyondjaba, N. (2011) 'Caught in the Eye of a Cold War Hurricane', *Insight*, February 2011.

Hamilton, C., Harris, V., Taylor, J., Pickover, M., Reid, G. and Saleh, R. (eds). (2002) *Refiguring the Archive*. Cape Town: David Philip.

Henrichsen, D., Jacobson, N. and Marshall, K. (eds). (2010) *Israel Goldblatt, Building Bridges: Namibian Nationalists Clemens Kapuuo, Hosea Kutako, Brendan Simbwaye, Samuel Witbooi*. Basel: Basel Afrika Bibliographien.

Korff, G. (2009) *19 with a Bullet*. Johannesburg: South Publishers.

McMullin, J. (2005) 'Far from Spontaneous: Namibia's Long Struggle with Ex-Combatant Reintegration'. In Fitzgerald, A. M. and Mason, H. (eds). *From Conflict to Community: A Combatant's Return to Citizenship*. Shrivenham: Global Facilitation Network for Security Sector Reform.

Marais, J. (2010) *Time Bomb: A Policeman's True Story*. Cape Town: Tafelberg.

Minter, W., Hovey, G. and Cobb, C. Jnr. (eds). (2008) *No Easy Victories: African Liberation and American Activists over a Half Century, 1950-2000*. Trenton/Asmara: Africa World Press.

Morgenstierne, C. (2003) *Denmark and National Liberation in Southern Africa: A Flexible Response*. Uppsala: Nordiska Afrikainstitutet.

Namakalu, O. (2004) *Armed Liberation Struggle: Some Accounts of PLAN's Combat Operations*. Windhoek: Gamsberg Macmillan.

Namhila, E. N. (2004) 'Filling the Gaps in the Archival Record of the Namibian Struggle for Independence', *International Federation of Library Associations (IFLA) Journal*, 30 (3).

Namhila, E. N. (2009) *Tears of Courage: Five Mothers, Five Stories, One Victory*. Windhoek: AACRLS.

Ndadi, N. (2009) *Breaking Contract*. Windhoek: AACRLS.

Nortje, P. (2003) *32 Battalion*. Cape Town: Zebra Press.

Onyeka = Namibia Will Be Free (1984) Long playing record. London: International Defence and Aid Fund.

Ramsden, T. (2009) *Borderline Insanity*. Alberton: Galago.

Ranger, T. (2004) 'Nationalist Historiography, Patriotic History, and the History of the Nation: the Struggle Over the Past in Zimbabwe'. *Journal of Southern African Studies*, 30 (2).

Rassool, Ciraj. (2004) 'The Individual, Auto/Biography and History in South Africa', PhD thesis, University of the Western Cape.

Report of the Commission of Enquiry into South West African Affairs, 1962-3 (Odendaal Commission), RP 12/64, Government Printer, Pretoria, 1964.

Saunders, C. (2007) 'History and the Armed Struggle: From Anti-colonial Propaganda to "Patriotic History"?' In Melber, H. (ed.) *Transitions in Namibia: Which Changes for Whom?* Uppsala: Nordiska Afrikainistitutet.

Saunders, C. (2009) 'Namibian Solidarity: British Support for Namibian Independence', *Journal of Southern African Studies*, 35 (2).

Scott, J. (1985) *Weapons of the Weak: Everyday Forms of Peasant Resistance*. New Haven and London: Yale University Press.

Sellström, T. (ed.) (1999) *Liberation in Southern Africa. Regional and Swedish Voices*. Uppsala: Nordiska Afrikainstitutet.

Sellström, T. (1999) *Sweden and National Liberation in Southern Africa. Volume I: Formation of a Popular Opinion 1950-1970*. Uppsala: Nordiska Afrikainstitutet.

Sellström, T. (2002) *Sweden and National Liberation in Southern Africa. Volume II: Solidarity and Assistance 1970-1994*. Uppsala: Nordiska Afrikainstitutet.

Shaketange, L. (2009) *Walking the Boeing 707*. Windhoek: AACRLS.

Shubin, V. (2008) *The Hot 'Cold War': The USSR in Southern Africa*. London: Pluto Press.

Silvester, J. and Akawa, M. (2006) 'Opening Pandora's Box', *The Namibian*, 5 November 2006.

Soiri, I. and Peltola, P. (1999) *Finland and National Liberation in Southern Africa*. Uppsala: Nordiska Afrikainstitutet.

Soske, J., Lissoni, A. and Erlank, N. (2012) 'One Hundred Years of the ANC: Debating Struggle History after Apartheid'. In Lissoni, A, Soske, J., Erlank, N., Nieftagodien, N. and Badsha, O. (eds). *One Hundred Years of the ANC: Debating Liberation Histories Today*. Witwatersrand/Cape Town: Witwatersrand University Press/South African History Online.

SWAPO (1980) *To Be Born a Nation*. London: Zed Press.

Thorn, H. (2009) *Anti-Apartheid and the Emergence of a Global Civil Society*. Basingstoke: Palgrave Macmillan.

Thompson, J. (2006) *Dit Was Oorlog: Van Afkak tot bosbefok*. Cape Town: Zebra Press.

Tötemeyer, G. (1978) *Namibia old and new: Traditional and modern leaders in Ovamboland.* London: C. Hurst & Co.

Van Walraven, K. and Abbink, J. (2003) 'Rethinking resistance in African history: An introduction'. In Abbink, J., de Bruyn, M. and van Walraven, K. (eds). *Rethinking Resistance: Revolt and Violence in African History.* Leiden: Brill.

Vogt, A. (2004) *National Monuments in Namibia – An inventory of proclaimed national monuments in the Republic of Namibia.* Windhoek: Gamsberg Macmillan.

Williams, C. (2009) 'Exile History: An Ethnography of the SWAPO Camps and the Namibian Nation', PhD thesis, University of Michigan.

Williams, C. (2011) 'Living in Exile: Daily Life and International Relations in SWAPO's Kongwa Camp', *Kronos* No. 39.

1 Transforming the Traumatic Life Experiences of Women in Post-Apartheid Namibian Historical Narratives

Ellen Ndeshi Namhila

Introduction

This chapter is based on the experience of interviewing five women, and writing and publishing their stories in a book with the title *Tears of Courage: Five Mothers, Five Stories, One Victory*.[1] That book was published with the financial support of the Archives of Anti-Colonial Resistance and the Liberation Struggle (AACRLS) Project. The project was jointly funded by the Federal Republic of Germany and the Government of the Republic of Namibia and administered under the auspices of the National Archives of Namibia. Published in 2009, the book brought out for the first time the hidden and untold sufferings of ordinary village women's experiences at the hands of the apartheid military, police and prison guards, during the formative years of the liberation struggle. Namibian women played a pivotal role in the struggle against colonialism and apartheid as they fed, clothed, nursed, and acted as a shield for the freedom fighters. The women whose stories are in the book were all arrested by the apartheid police. One was beaten until she had a miscarriage, another imprisoned in Pretoria where she had to give birth in jail, another had her house destroyed and burnt to the ground and her husband killed, another was beaten and tortured when the police could not find her brother (who was on the police's list of wanted persons), and the last was sentenced to a jail term in Pretoria along with her two brothers.

In the epilogue of the book, John Otto Nankudhu, Commander of Omugulugwoombashe, SWAPO's first military camp inside Namibia, which was attacked by the South African military in August 1966, stated: 'It is gratifying to see the story of these women written down. They carry a history of our country we cannot afford to lose. I know some of these women very well because it was mainly due to them that we survived in northern Namibia and escaped arrest from the apartheid authority for a long time.' As Beth Goldblatt and Sheila Meintjies argue, 'Our society constantly diminishes the women's role and women themselves then see their experiences as unimportant' (1996). Indeed at the launch of the book, one of the five women who spoke said: 'It

---

[1] Significant sections of this chapter are drawn directly from my previous publication, *Tears of Courage: Five Mothers, Five Stories, One Victory* (Windhoek: AACRLS, 2009) with the permission of the National Archives. However, I felt it was important to expand here on the issues that were raised by the research process that led to that publication.

never occurred to me that our past experiences mattered to anyone or to the history of our country and that it is worth recording and writing.'

What the book did for these women is that it made their contribution known so that it could be shared with the whole country. Afterwards, school children, teachers and film makers approached them in their communities wanting to know more about their experiences. In turn, they felt valued, appreciated and acknowledged, which has helped them in the healthier way in which they are now able to relate to their past experiences and retell their stories without having an emotional breakdown. Seemingly, sharing their experiences was a therapeutic experience.

In this chapter I will outline the importance of the AACRLS project that sponsored the production of the book, highlight my specific research experiences interviewing these five women, and indicate the historical significance of the stories told by the women to broaden policy research on gender and development in Namibia and on the way 26 August is celebrated and commemorated in Namibia every year as National Heroes day. The chapter argues that the book *Tears of Courage* helps remind both the public and historians that amongst those heroes that we celebrate on National Heroes' Day there are also heroines. The narratives of these ordinary village women are a great contribution to the history of women in Namibia, placing their stories in the national historiography of the liberation struggle alongside those of men.

The AACRLS Project

The National Archives of Namibia has, since the country's independence on 21 March 1990, attempted to document Namibia's long underground history of resistance to colonialism and apartheid. Actually, far-sighted individuals at the helm of the Archives already started with such activities before independence, under the obvious constraints of the prevailing political climate of the apartheid regime.

Nevertheless, progress was rather slow, and a substantial boost to such efforts came only about ten years after independence, when two factors came into play. One was the relocation of the National Archives to house Namibia's most important documents and audio-visual records in new purpose-built accommodation, a proud symbol of independent Namibia and a stark contrast to the dusty, tiny old dungeons which the old colonial archives had inhabited since 1955. The other factor was that the first colonial power to rule over Namibia, Germany, was persuaded to contribute substantial financial support to a special project to document the entire historical heritage of resistance, from the early uprisings against German rule, through the long years when South Africa seemed to rule with absolute power, to the modern liberation struggle, which led to independence.

This special project, had the long-winded name the 'Archives of Anti-Colonial Resistance and the Liberation Struggle' Project or, not much shorter, the AACRLS. In its early beginnings in 2001, it was resolved that it did not make sense to create a separate archives for this material but to let it contribute to the holdings of the National Archives or the National Museum as appropriate, so that all funds could be focused on securing the heritage, instead of creating and maintaining a new institution. In doing this, it is also emphasised that there is a single history of a united Namibia, in the sense of the slogan of the liberation movement 'One Namibia – One Nation', and not a compartmentalised history in compartmentalised institutions.

The main impact of the AACRLS Project was that it made it possible for an independent body, the National Steering Committee of the project, to focus additional financial support to key areas where the National Archives was hampered by insufficient funding, insufficient staffing, and a bureaucracy with very inflexible and time-consuming procedures. The most important areas were:

1. The collection of oral history, through encouraging and enabling volunteers to interview resource persons and deposit the results centrally;
2. The collection of existing scattered documents, including photographs and sound and video documentation, both from Namibia and from abroad;
3. The popularisation of struggle history, especially in the education sector;
4. Capacity building for the National Archives to store, document and preserve the material.

The AACRLS Project dealt with dispersed, displaced, entangled, hidden, and destroyed archives.

Dispersed Archives

Archives are dispersed, because a central record-keeping facility for the liberation movement did not exist. Correspondence, reports and publications can be found scattered worldwide in the archives of supportive governments, solidarity organisations and individuals, as well as United Nations bodies. For example, no single archives or library has a complete set of the liberation army's journal *The Combatant*. However, such a set can be pieced together physically by collecting donations, and digitally by scanning at various repositories.

Displaced Archives

Wars and the actions of occupation forces can displace archives. This is not only a phenomenon of developing countries. Europe is still grappling with the legacy of cultural heritage displaced by the Second World War. Namibia suffered the removal of archival records to South Africa during the transition to independence. Fortunately, the new South Africa is willing to restitute these archives, and has already done so with several important collections, such as the records of the South African Administrator-General in Namibia.[2] The return of military records of the former 'South West Africa Territory Force' (SWATF) and Koevoet, which were removed to Pretoria on the eve of Namibia's independence, is however still outstanding.

---

2 'Those records were created in SWA-Namibia; they reflect a core aspect of the country's constitutional and socio-political history, and they constitute an integral part of the archival heritage of the people of Namibia.' A statement issued on 20 August 1997, by the South African Minister of Arts, Culture, Science and Technology, Lionel Mtshali.

Entangled Archives

Archives can be seen as entangled by being an inseparable part of one country or organisation's archives, yet also being of central importance to another country. In such a case, it should be feasible to ask for copies in whatever format. Namibia can lay claim to many entangled archives, and the AACRLS was quite successful in obtaining relevant copies. Outstanding examples of this were the donation of microfilms of the entire records of the German Colonial Office, which were handed over by the German Foreign Minister in 2003, as well as the microfilms of the Namibian and South African records in the archives of the former Rhenish Mission, now VEM, in Wuppertal (Germany), and digital copies of the United Nations Security Council documents concerning Namibia (including resolutions, official documents and letters covering the period 1960-1990). Bilateral co-operation with the National Archives of Botswana under the general cultural co-operation agreement of both countries is expected to yield another important set of copies. The collection of entangled records has, probably, been the most successful part of the project.

Destroyed Archives

Uncaring custodians or disasters can destroy archives. The AACRLS has, in its quest to secure records from organisations involved in the liberation struggle, come across several instances where the entire central records of an organisation have been carelessly destroyed, because the custodians did not realise their importance. In such cases, the quest for surrogate records extracted from individual members and from correspondents, such as foreign solidarity organisations, can be quite successful, but it is work-intensive and professionally challenging to piece together and reconfigure an archive.

Hidden Archives

Archives can be hidden in the memories of those who witnessed history, but whose memories have not been recorded. The AACRLS encouraged interested individuals to research and record oral interviews with people from all walks of life who witnessed historical events of our colonial past or custodians of oral traditions about past events. It also attempted to collect and centralise oral history recordings, which had already been collected for academic theses and other purposes, and are now gathering dust in the private custody of researchers. 'Oral history gives history back to the people in their own words. And in giving a past, it also helps them toward a future of their own making' (Thompson, 1978, p. 20). Uncovering the 'hidden archives' contained in oral histories and tradition can, therefore, be seen as an important contribution to the larger objective of reconfiguring the colonial archive.

The focus of this chapter will be on the challenges faced in attempting to salvage one set of these hidden archives. The reflections made here are based on the oral history research that resulted in the publication of *Tears of Courage: Five Mothers, Five stories, One Victory* by the AACRLS. The evidence presented in that book was based on an intensive series of individual oral history interviews, group discussions and recordings, with five women ex-prisoners, torch-bearers of the Namibian liberation struggle, over a period of ten years.

Tears of Courage: Five Mothers, Five Stories, One Victory

The book was written with the firm belief that oral history needs to be a central tool for Namibian historians, but also with the recognition that:

> if oral history is to be a reliable research tool, if it is to be respected historical evidence, and if it is to justify a national association in its name, then those who produce oral history, the scholars that use its product, and the institutions that finance its projects must have some means of understanding its proper role and of evaluating what is being done in the field. We need to know more about the place of oral history in the system of historical analysis, and we need to understand better the contribution that oral history can make to the writing of history (Moss, 1977 p. 429).

This chapter will also argue that there has been a male gender bias in history writing in Namibia and that this distortion of the past has implications for our perceptions of the present, particularly with reference to the narrative of Namibia's liberation struggle. Cheryl McEwan writes that 'if black women are denied a presence and agency in the stories of national liberation, black women's belonging and citizenship in South Africa is compromised in the process of nation building' (2003, p.740). Although this statement referred to women in South Africa in their attempt to deal with their past traumatic experiences with apartheid, the same argument applies to Namibian women.

If their stories are not brought forward so that they can be taken into account and create an impact on gender policy research and development, ordinary women's rights to services and privileges as citizens of a free Namibia may be compromised. Research by van der Merwe and Gobodo-Madikizela reveals that 'the act of individuals talking about their personal experiences does not imply an end to all pains and sufferings, but rather facing and working through trauma, so that the tragic loss caused by trauma is balanced by a gain in meaning' (2008 p.viii). Whilst Alessandro Portelli's work has stressed that memory is as much about 'creating meanings' of the past as reconstructing 'what happened' (Field, 2008, p.146).

I interacted closely with these women, especially the youngest of the five, who lost her husband in a tragic shooting when the South African military attacked their home in search of SWAPO guerrillas. After publishing and launching *Tears of Courage,* I observed a significant improvement in the three ladies who were still alive as they, subsequently, spoke more openly about their life experiences. Although they do not have money, they each phoned me from time to time from a relative's phone, just to ask how I was doing and to tell me about their school children and their teachers, or that a journalist had visited their home to ask them more about their experiences after reading their story in the book. The experiences and memories were ones they would not easily share at the time I did the first interviews. Once they had told their stories and they had been written down and shared with a wider public, the public responded in sympathy, understanding, and total solidarity as they shared in their pain and suffering. Through the stories which the five women shared with each other, they bonded, and each realised the strength this solidarity brought them.

I wrote these stories in the first person because I wanted each woman to feel the power of her own voice as represented in the text by her own words. I know now that this was the right thing to do because writing in any other way would have reduced the impact these stories now have on the women themselves and on readers. Whilst verification of authenticity and integrity of the source with persons who took part in the same event, and searching court records, church records, newspaper articles of the time, was an important part of collecting these stories, I took a deliberate decision to write up the stories in the women's own voices. This is important to engage the reader directly with the women and to capture the stories in the uninterrupted voices of these women. I also decided not to make cross references to court records because I do not know the context under which these court procedures and recordings were made. However, the evidence available from the Supreme Court records in Pretoria was crucial in helping me establish the authenticity of the story I was hearing and that these things really happened. I too had my own preconceived ideas. For example, I thought it was impossible for any system, no matter how gruesome, to arrest a pregnant woman from Namibia, jail her in Pretoria, South Africa and provide no support when she went into labour. Seeing her name in the court transcript was more than enough verification to prove that the source I was working with had integrity and deserved the detailed recording and documentation of her voice. The court records were an important source and were thoroughly explored to verify some factuality in the story and authenticity of the sources. Another valuable source utilised in the research collection and writing were the church records. As the dates of events were not always remembered, church registers became an important archival source to verify the dates of events such as births, deaths, marriages and trial dates.

I considered the five village women as the creators of archives in their own right and 'the question of who has the power to make, record and interpret history' is answered in the story of these five women, making them the makers of those 'laws of what can be said' (McEwan, 2003, p. 742). History from below is 'people's history' and connected with 'people's power' and empowerment. 'These localised re-presentations of the past are of fundamental importance in producing unsanitised versions of history that allow previously marginalised groups, especially black women, agency in their own representation' (McEwan, 2003, p. 747). The construction of history is not just simply about the reconstruction of the past, but also about representation in the present.

Recording Hidden Stories and Writing *Tears of Courage*

Tears of Courage was born out of an interview with Meme[3] Priskila Tuhadeleni in December 1999. Meme Priskila was the widow of one of Namibia's historical legends and national heroes, Tate[4] Eliaser Noah Tuhadeleni, popularly known as 'Kaxumba

---
3   A term of respect for a woman older than the speaker.
4   A term of respect for a man older than the speaker.

kaNdola'. Tate Kaxumba was one of the pioneers of Namibia's liberation struggle. He was an active mobiliser who raised popular consciousness of the need for people to stand up and fight for their rights, for freedom and justice. I did not know Kaxumba personally in my youth, but I heard many fascinating historical tales about his life and how he gave the colonial government a tough time when they tried to implement apartheid in Namibia.

It was around 1972 when I got to know of Kaxumba through the stories of his bravery, as a fearless fighter and defender of the people,[5] but also that he had seemingly supernatural powers to evade capture. The apartheid government wanted Kaxumba dead or behind bars. As a small child of about eight/nine years old, I did not understand why the colonial government wanted a good man dead. Eventually, Kaxumba was arrested and detained by the apartheid police in 1967 and, together with many of his comrades, he was secretly removed from Namibia to South Africa, and sentenced to life imprisonment on Robben Island.

This myth about Kaxumba remained with me until 21 March 1990 at the Windhoek Stadium on Independence Day when his name was mentioned in official speeches. My interest and curiosity was aroused again and, in 1996, I went to northern Namibia to look for Tate Kaxumba. I found him, but he was too busy working with the social issues of the local community and I was only able to speak to him for a very short period. My next attempt to schedule an interview did not materialise because he was already ill, and in 1997 his asthma became worse and he died.

It took me a while to decide what to do next and how to pursue my interest, so I visited Meme Priskila, his widow, at their home at Endola in 1998, to ask her permission to continue my research. She gave me the permission, and one of the most striking stories she told me was how the first six SWAPO combatants arrived from Tanganyika at their home at Endola in July 1965, to mobilise the Namibian people for the independence struggle. In addition, she suggested a number of other resource persons, political friends of her husband and many supporters of the struggle. In return, each respondent led me to others. I then started recording and writing Tate Kaxumba's biography, which was published in 2005, and was largely based on what I was told in interviews by his family, friends, neighbours, prison inmates and comrades (Namhila, 2005).

One of the respondents Meme Priskila pointed out to me was Meme Drothea Nikodemus, a sister to the late Immanuel Shifidi who was one of Tate Kaxumba's political friends, a comrade with whom he shared many painful years of incarceration on Robben Island. Meme Priskila told me that on one of her visits to her imprisoned husband in the Robben Island prison, off Cape Town, South Africa, she went with the mother of Tate Andimba Toivo ya Toivo and Meme Drothea Nikodemus. She said 'I will take you to Drothea's house right now if it fits your schedule.' I accepted the offer and we immediately took off to Meme Drothea's home. When we got to the house, her poverty nearly drove me to tears, but since I was there to do my job I had to fight back those tears.

---

5   1972 was the time thousands of striking workers were deported to northern Namibia, where I lived and there was a lot of unrest. Workers were sent from the mines and factories in the 'Police Zone' to 'Owamboland' where they organised meetings. The local people associated the struggle of the workers with the earlier struggles waged by Kaxumba in the 1960s and recalled his name in conversations when the 'Boers' came to arrest the local young men in our village.

The Shifidi Family

I interviewed Meme Drothea to find out what she knew about Kaxumba kaNdola. While she narrated the story she also mentioned her brother Immanuel Shifidi and many other people from Namibia who were arrested and sentenced to imprisonment on Robben Island. Meme Drothea told how, following the attack in 1966 on Omugulugwoombashe, her brother arrived with seven of his comrades and stayed for several days at her house. She explained how her brother would come with his comrades and she would prepare food for them. Meme Drothea spoke of the dramatic measures taken by the apartheid government against people who were supporting the comrades. She felt that the police wanted the comrades to starve. Many women, herself included, were arrested and exiled to prisons in South Africa.

Meme Drothea shared the story of her experiences in a South African jail and this led me to the stories of two other Namibian women with whom she had been imprisoned, namely, Meme Justina Amwaalwa and Meme Selma Amputu. Meme Justina Amwaalwa was arrested whilst pregnant. Meme Drothea described the strong character traits of Meme Justina, who had to put up with harsh prison conditions and the ruthlessness of the prison guards and, even after all these hardships, Meme Justina still gave birth to a healthy baby boy. I was fascinated by the story of Meme Justina even though it did not have direct links to Kaxumba. While I was working on the Kaxumba story, I always kept Justina at the back of my mind. I tried hard for two years to trace the two women without any success. After two years of searching through friends and acquaintances from those areas, I finally found out that Meme Selma Amputu had passed away but after a long search I found Justina.

How the Research Expanded

In 2001, I undertook a trip to go and interview Meme Justina. I visited her again in 2002 and with the support of the AACRLS project I visited her in 2003 to clarify and check certain facts. From the interview with Drothea I learned for the first time that Namibian women were also arrested and held in prisons in South Africa, alongside men. After recording the stories of these two women I started transcribing them and read them over and over. Drothea and Justina have many things in common. Firstly, they were both married women who were arrested and taken from their homes by the apartheid police for providing food and shelter to SWAPO combatants who had retreated southwards following the attack on Omugulugwoombashe. Both were humiliated by their arrest in front of their small children and were forced to spend time in prison in Pretoria, leaving their children at home without maternal care and support. They were both kept for nearly a year in a South African prison and shared the experience of detention, trial and release. While Justina provided shelter and food to Immanuel Shifidi in the spirit of solidarity and comradeship, Drothea was Shifidi's biological sister.

The stories of Drothea and Justina compelled me to look out for similar stories whenever I travelled to villages and local communities. I always carried a recorder, empty cassettes, batteries, note pads and a camera when I went to weddings and funerals just in case I met a person with similar experiences. In December 2003, I went to Okahao for official duties. As we often finished our official business around 17.00. I was left with plenty of time in the evening and did not know what to do. So, I started talking to the workers at the lodge where I was staying and asked them about historical events and persons that had played an exceptional role in the struggle for independence. They said:

'Go to Uukwalumbe village. You will hear the story of gwaMumbandja gwaShitumwa and his children.'

Who is gwaMumbandja? I asked.

'Oh, you don't know? Hmm, the Boers used to hang them in that big baobab tree in Okahao and beat them up.'

The Tragedy of the gwaMumbandja Family

Meme Aune Ndadi, the owner of the lodge, offered to take me to Uukwalumbe about 4km west of Okahao. We found Meme Lahja, daughter of Mumbandja gwaShitumwa. Meme Lahja was a sister to Patrick Iyambo, popularly known by his combat name 'Lungada'. Lungada is the name of a local bird known in English as the fork-tailed drongo. According to Owambo tradition this bird signifies alertness or vigilance. The lungada is always patrolling the sky as it can fly up high and can see further than all other birds and so can alert other birds and other animals of any approaching danger. The name 'Lungada' is associated with a person who is vigilant – always alert, a visionary – someone who is able to see far and away, and be a guard-protector of others from dangers. This is very well suited with the philosophy of the liberation struggle as combatants name themselves after someone or something from which they draw wisdom and inspiration. Lungada was one of the first group of six SWAPO combatants who returned to Namibia in 1965 and stayed at the household of Tate Kaxumba kaNdola, the husband of Meme Priskila. Patrick Iyambo was the only one of the six comrades who escaped arrest by the police. All the remaining comrades were caught in the South African police net along with their supporters and trainees. They searched for Lungada without success and, when they failed to arrest him, they directed their anger and frustration on his family.

I interviewed Meme Lahja Iyambo and listened to the story of her family's struggle to survive the persecution of her family by the South African army and police and to live a normal life under their watchful eyes until the end of the struggle for independence. The story of Lahja is in a way similar to that of Drothea, Justina and Priskila in that it revolves around another SWAPO combatant who was wanted by the South African police following the battle of Omugulugwoombashe. Patrick, like Immanuel Shifidi and Kaxumba kaNdola, survived the battle and their families were watched, followed and suspected by the apartheid army and police. The struggle for independence even cost the Mumbandja family the life of a family member. Meme Lahja told me the tragic story of her family including the attack on her brother's house on the night of 23 June 1968 by the South African forces, which resulted in the death of her brother, Ushona. She also told me that her sister-in-law had witnessed her husband being assaulted and killed by the apartheid military and police. At that time her sister-in-law, Meme Aili Andreas Itula was the only civilian survivor of this tragic incident. Hence, after completing the story of Meme Lahja, I realised the need to get evidence from Meme Aili Andreas, who was actually there when their house was attacked.

Dealing with Unresolved Trauma

In 2005, I again returned to Okahao to find Meme Aili Andreas Itula. Having considered the sensitivity and possible unresolved emotions around the matter, I asked Meme Lahja to accompany me to the house of her sister-in-law and to introduce me to her in person. Meme Lahja and two of her brothers agreed and they all accompanied me to Meme Aili's home. As Meme Lahja introduced me and the reasons for my coming, Meme Aili exclaimed 'Hmm' and, looking at me directly, she said: '*Owali peni ano, oshilongo shamanguluka naaanaale, ndele opotoya paife*' meaning, 'Where have you been, the country got independence long, long ago and you are coming only now.' I could not respond to Meme Aili's question because Meme Lahja was still explaining why I had come to see her.

As soon as Meme Lahja mentioned the incident of that fateful night of the raid on their home, I saw Meme Aili's face changing, her body became very tense and she burst into tears and cried and sobbed saying 'Why, oh why, oh why.' I too became emotional. Silently, I started asking myself, why have I come to torture this woman, to remind her of painful things she fought for many years to try to forget. I blamed myself for not planning this trip more tactfully or being more sensitive to her needs. I felt she was not ready for us. So, I advised Meme Lahja that we must not dwell any further on this matter. It was best that we stop all the discussions on this issue and just listen sympathetically to what she was saying. We sat for about half an hour with Meme Aili sobbing and her brother in-law trying to diffuse the situation by asking about other things. We left that house without seeing Aili smile.

I was worried about Meme Aili. The attack on the house took place in 1968 and that day in 2005 she reacted as if it had been only yesterday. What did that tell us? I could not stop wondering. Was it morally correct just to leave her alone? What was my responsibility as a researcher to my respondent, whose memories I had stirred so vividly and emotionally? After pondering on this matter, I decided to return to Meme Aili two days after the first visit. This time, I went alone. When she saw me, she looked me in the eye and, said: '*Oweya nduno!*' meaning, 'So, you came!' Without knowing what to expect, I smiled and said, 'Yes Meme, I have come.' She took me to a room, right in the interior of her home, and there we spoke nicely. I started by telling her everything that was possible to know about who I was and why I wanted to know her story. Slowly, I came to the subject of my research.

This time Meme Aili was calm and she agreed to tell me what had happened. The interview was long and intensive as she related her story and cried nearly throughout the whole interview. Without realising it, I found myself crying with her. The good thing was that it was recorded on tape because I would not have been able to make any notes during that interview. It was clear to me that I must not rush her. If she was crying I would stop asking questions, I would not humiliate her by asking her to stop crying or walking away while she was crying. I sat next to her and consoled her when it was appropriate to do so.

Methodological Issues

I did not have a research plan when I started interviewing these women, except that I had wanted to diversify the historical sources of our National Archives, of which I was the Director at the time. I interviewed these women at different times because I worked full-time and the only opportunity I had was when I went to the north during holidays, weddings, funerals or when I combined the interviews with official trips. I recorded these stories out of personal interest without a plan about what to do with the products. I recorded these stories on tapes as they were told to me orally in Oshiwambo, which is the mother tongue for all five women.

One of the women, Meme Justina, would not talk to me when I first visited their home unless her husband was with her. After recording her first interview, I wrote it up and brought it to her with the photographs I had taken of her family and her during the previous visit. I wanted her to read the text or give it to her children to read it to her. After this, I seemed to have earned her trust and when I returned for further interviews, we got on with it without anyone to witness what she was telling me. Life stories, especially from village women, are honest and reflect the fact that they did not always fully understand the politics behind questions such as 'Why did the apartheid police arrest me for feeding my brothers' (Namhila, 2009, pp. 73-74). The interviews reflect the importance of family loyalties in the struggle and their role as a support network.

Meme Aili broke down and sobbed during our interviews, I felt I could not walk away from her during the breakdowns which were sparked by the interview questions. It would be totally inhumane. People find it hard to talk about personal traumatic experiences if they have not yet fully dealt with the situation and made peace with it. A researcher in this situation needs to phrase her questions in such a way that they allow the victim not to feel judged or that her feelings had not been respected.

Oral history collectors have to face these challenges but what I recommend is that a respondent should not be rushed. If the respondent is not ready to be interviewed, the researcher must not force matters. Collecting people's memories is a challenge that cannot be taken lightly. It may depend on the subject matter and whether the respondent is a direct survivor or a secondary source. Nevertheless, in a country such as Namibia in which the history of the majority of the population exists only in an oral format, oral history writing must be given urgency and become an utmost priority for historians. It would also be constructive to explore the ways in which oral history might be more effectively integrated into the school curriculum as a practice as well as a source. Concrete initiatives have already been undertaken to do this in South Africa which also has an active Oral History Association (Kros and Ulrich, 2008).

When a person has given her right to a researcher to unlock her privacy, this is a privilege and an honour and researchers must realise this. If someone has opened up her whole life to you, it is an act of trust, and therefore care and sensitivity on the part of the researcher is critical. How many of us are willing to share stories of our lives with others? Some tragic occurrences seemed very severe and leave wounds that cut so deeply that they may take a lifetime to heal or may never heal at all. Maturity, humour, tact and cultural sensitivity are required in such instances.

I verified the stories by talking about them to the persons who were involved in these events. I also checked through existing documents, archival sources and newspapers to find out about what was written about these women or the events they described. As soon as I had established the authenticity of each story, I transcribed and translated it from Oshiwambo to English and wrote it up. I gave each woman the opportunity to read her own story and to verify whether the text accurately represented what she had told me orally. Considering that these stories were written in English and these women do not read or speak fluent English, I left the written drafts with them and asked them to give these stories to relatives or their own children who spoke and read English.

I heard their own stories being read to them by their grandchildren with pride and compassion, and witnessed the solidarity these stories generated within the families who felt that the recognition it provided restored family honour. I agree with van der Merwe and Gobodo-Madfikizela (2008, p. viii) when they wrote that:

> Trauma victims have a contradictory desire to suppress their trauma as well as to talk about it. To talk about it, would mean an extremely painful reliving of the event – so, for inner survival, they normally suppress the memory. Yet, paradoxically, it is precisely confrontation of the suppressed memory that is needed for inner healing.

I am just glad that whilst the women were still alive they were able to make peace with the legacy of their traumatic past and knew that they had been able to share this heritage with succeeding generations to learn from their experiences. It has even been claimed that oral history, like court testimony, is empowering as 'the voice of the witness is paramount' (Wieder, 2004: p. 13)

It is interesting how in April 2010, when I briefly met Meme Priskila Tuhadeleni, the first question she asked me was: 'To which of your kids did you pass on your talent of writing?' I was not prepared to give her an answer and now she has died, so maybe her question was really implying that I should train more Namibians to become the authors of their own life stories. In my experience, interview sessions can be rather dramatic and emotional, but the reward comes from public response, positive feedback from the public and more understanding at the family and community level, and the praise the women receive for what they have done for our country's freedom and independence

Systematising the Data Collection

Each woman gave me the telephone number of a relative or neighbour whom I could call to find out whether there was anything they would like changed or added. In one case the manuscript was given to a selected member of the community to read through and, apart from the spelling of some peoples' names and places, all five women accepted the written stories as a true reflection of what they had told me.

Each of these women was interviewed at least three or four times and every time I repeated the interview new information, which had not been told to me during the first interview, emerged. In the case of Meme Aili, on the day I visited her together with Meme Tuhadeleni, she openly spoke to me about her family including her parents' struggle to obtain permission from the apartheid government to travel to Windhoek to mourn their son. This was very critical information which explained the social impact of the apartheid system on the socio-cultural lives of the community. Meme Justina spoke more openly about the circumstances that lead to Shifidi's arrest and how a person regarded as a confidant betrayed their trust, valuable information which she had not felt able to give during my first two visits. After this vigorous data collection process, I started writing up the stories in the voices of these women. In the end I was really surprised how these stories turned out to be of great quality. What I also think played a role is the fact that I always tried to arrive early at my respondent's home and to stay there talking to them informally. If she was ploughing I would go in the field with her and if she was cooking I would follow her to the kitchen, take photographs and sometimes just talk and show an interest in what she was doing. All five ladies were very photogenic and became even more interested when I brought them the photos taken during previous visits. If she was in the field I could not just stand there talking, so I would also pick up the mahangu (pearl millet) or participate in what she was doing even in a marginal way. This brought me closer to the ladies and they spoke more openly than when we were seated in a semi-formal question and answer interview session. These informal conversations provided the foundation for the more formal interview.

Why Publish?

So, I asked myself, what should I do with these stories? I felt that keeping them as an accession in the stack room of the National Archives of Namibia in the hope that one day a researcher might discover them and use them was not enough. This would be the same as keeping them in my head, hidden from the general public. These stories needed to be heard. They needed to be shared. I had to find a way to tell and retell these powerful stories of these mothers of the Namibian struggle. This is especially important to our children who were born after independence or those who were too young to understand the struggle, or to anyone who wishes to understand the Namibian independence struggle

I felt I had a responsibility to share these stories with the general public. I felt that they could contribute to national reconciliation. These stories are carried by wounded souls that still need healing. They are mirroring our society, which is crying out for peace and reconciliation. It has not been easy for me to record these stories, to listen the whole day to stories of pain and torture and to transcribe and write them down. I am deeply honoured and feel greatly privileged that these five women have allowed me to listen to their life stories, which I proudly shared with the rest of the world. It is in the spirit of solidarity with those who gave their lives and selflessness to the liberation of our country that these stories were given the honour they deserve.

So, eventually, the AACRLS Project agreed to publish the stories that I had written based on the oral history interviews. A long process of consolidating the many disjointed fragments of interviews into a coherent story followed. They were recorded at different times and viewed the events through the eyes of different people. As it is with oral history, not everybody remembers in the same way, and new questions came up that had to be asked and resolved, sometimes telephonically, but in the end the pieces came together. Archival evidence turned up that nobody had expected. Meme Justina's incredible story about how she was interviewed in Pretoria after giving birth in prison was a tough nut to crack, because she could not remember the name of the journalist or the newspaper, and it took the mobilisation of a network of contacts of historians and archivists to unearth this piece of evidence. Finally, an archivist at the University of South Africa identified the article, complete with a photograph of the mother and her baby, in a short-lived small newspaper called *The World* in its issue of Wednesday, 13 September 1967.[6]

The title of the book *Tears of Courage: Five Mothers, Five Stories, One Victory* portrayed the bravery and strength of the inner spirit of these five mothers who fought heroically in the struggle for the liberation of their motherland. They were arrested, detained, beaten, tortured, humiliated, abused, endured the loss of life of family members and personal property. Despite all this, they stood firm until victory on 21 March 1990, when Namibia gained its independence from the apartheid colonial regime.

The Importance of Personal Motivation

My interest in documenting women's stories started in 1995 when I wrote my own autobiography *The Price of Freedom* that was published by New Namibia Books in 1997. This was followed by *Kaxumba kaNdola Man and Myth: A Biography of a Barefoot Soldier* published by Basler Afrika Bibliographien in 2005.

In 1999, I attended the memorial service of Tate Gotlieb Nathaniel Maxuilili in Windhoek and his burial in Walvis Bay. Tate Maxuilili was one of the icons of our liberation struggle, who served a prison term in South Africa and had been confined to housearrest for several years under apartheid. After listening to all the speeches that were given and all the condolence messages that were read, I felt so bad that I cried. I cried not so much because Maxuilili had died, but more so because I felt history had been lost. I stood there, feeling helpless, as we buried an encyclopaedia of our history. I was part of the crowd, witnessing archives being buried deep in the ground, without leaving a trace of evidence for future generations. Maxuilili had so much to tell about our past, and now he was dead. I stood there and watched history being buried. We did not tap his life experience. We did not document his political struggle. Now he is gone and buried with an important part of the history of our country; a history that would have reminded our present and future generations of who we had been as a country and people; a history that could help direct our future vision.

After Tate Maxuilili's burial, I reflected quite a bit and recalled the funerals of Tate Moses Garoeb in 1997, Tate Simeon Namunganga and others. I realised thinking does not help, because, as I was thinking and worrying, and not acting, the list of heroes of our history who have passed on was getting too long. How is history going to judge us for watching the heroes and heroines of our struggle die one after the other without leaving evidence or traces that document their contribution? My guilt in not recording grew more and more. Every day a brave cadre during the liberation struggle passed

---

6   University of South Africa (UNISA) Archives, Newspaper clippings.

away and it was no longer possible to watch in silence. With the assistance of many like-minded and committed comrades, friends and colleagues, we worked hard to obtain the political and practical support of the Namibian Government.

Conclusion

It therefore must be emphasised that a few individual efforts to collect these stories are not sufficient to tell the full story of what happened to the people of Namibia during apartheid. While the existing biographies and books on our struggle are significant, more recording needs to be done, more personal stories need to be captured, and the memories of this long and bitter struggle need to be preserved for posterity.

Recording these stories has not been easy. There were times when I felt rejected because a respondent was holding back information from me, which they perhaps considered confidential and could not just entrust to a stranger. However, through experience, I have learned to accept what I was given at a particular time and to continue working with respondents until they learnt to trust me and to tell me their whole story.

I have learnt through this oral history recording process that private stories are very difficult to share publicly. People have been keeping these personal stories to themselves and they become suppressed secrets that must be forgotten. It is the right of each person to tell their stories or to refuse to tell them. When they decide to tell, we must be very grateful.

A number of research projects are now brought to a wider audience. The AACRLS Project created the 'Footprints' Publication Series and *Tears of Courage* is the third volume in this series. There is great potential for us to continue with the AACRLS Oral History research and projects such as the *Tears of Courage* demonstrate that we have just scratched the surface of Namibia's oral history archive.

I have focused on the contribution of oral history, because I feel this is an area which needs particular attention, and it does not mean just putting a microphone under somebody's nose and requesting them to talk. It requires prior planning and familiarisation with the subject matter and the community in which the respondent lives, as well as an understanding of the context of a particular incident.

Finally, it must be stated that the struggle was the process by which many of us formed our identity. Therefore, if the history of the struggle gets lost, we will have nothing to help us understand who we really are, what we were during the struggle and what we have become after independence. I strongly believe that in order to understand ourselves, we need to look back along our 'memory lane'. If we lose these stories that document the continuity between the different phases of our lives, we lose not only our history, but also ourselves. Memory helps us to define who we are because of who we have been and when memory is lost, people become lost. It is for these reasons that I am looking and searching for myself, for my history and identity, so that I can secure my survival and that of the people who share this history.

A significant outcome of this book is that all the living women in *Tears of Courage* are now recognised by the Namibian Government with the status of 'heroine of the liberation struggle', and have enjoyed the benefits of this status since 2012.

References

Cross, C. and Ulrich, N. (2008) 'The Truth of Tales: Oral Testimony and Teaching History in Schools'. In Denis, P. and Ntsimane, R. *Oral History in a Wounded Country: Interactive Interviewing in South Africa.* Scottsville: University of KwaZulu-Natal.

Denis, P. and Ntsimane, R. (2008) *Oral History in a Wounded Country: Interactive Interviewing in South Africa.* Scotsville: University of KwaZulu-Natal.

Field, S. (2008) 'What can I do when the interviewee cries?' In Denis, P. and Ntsimane, R. *Oral History in a Wounded Country: Interactive Interviewing in South Africa.* Scottsville: University of KwaZulu-Natal.

Goldblatt, B. and Meintjes, S. (1996) *Gender and the Truth and Reconciliation Commission: A submission to the Truth and Reconciliation Commission.* Johannesburg: University of the Witwatersrand.

Kros, C. and Ulrich, N. (2008) 'The truth of tales: Oral testimony and teaching history in schools'. In Denis, P. and Ntsimane, R. *Oral history in a wounded country: Interactive interviewing in South Africa.* Scottsville: University of KwaZulu-Natal.

McEwan, C. (2003) 'Building a postcolonial Archive? Gender Collective Memory and Citizenship in Post-apartheid South Africa', *Journal of Southern African Studies*, 29 (3).

Moss, W. W. (1977) 'Oral History: An Appreciation', *The American Archivist*, 40 (4).

Namhila, E. N. (1997) *The Price of Freedom.* Windhoek: New Namibia Books.

Namhila, E. N. (2005) *Kaxumba kaNdola Man and Myth: The Biography of a Barefoot Soldier.* Basel: Basler Afrika Bibliographien.

Namhila, E. N. (2009) *Tears of Courage, Five Mothers, Five Stories, One Victory.* Windhoek: AACRLS.

Norrik, N. R. (2006) 'Humour in oral history interviews', *Oral History*, 34 (2).

Thompson, P. (1978). *Voices of the Past: Oral history.* New York: Oxford University Press.

Tonkin, E. (1986) 'Investigating Oral traditions', *The Journal of African History*, 27 (2).

Schneider-Kempf, B. (2009) Translated by C. Gantert, 'Dispersed Musical Treasures – the Music Autographs of Beethoven and Bach at the Berlin State Library', 75th IFLA General Conference and Council, 23-27 August 2009, Milan, Italy.

Van der Hoeven, H. and Van Albada, J. (1996) 'Memory of the World: Lost Memory – Libraries and Archives destroyed in the Twentieth Century', prepared for UNESCO for IFLA and ICA, Paris: UNESCO, 1996.-ii, 70 pp.; 30cm.-(CII-96/WS/1).

Van de Merwe, N. C. and Gobodo-Madikizela, P. (2008) *Narrating our Healing Perspectives on Working through Trauma.* Cambridge: Cambridge Scholars Publishing.

Wieder, A. (2004) 'Testimony as Oral History: Lessons from South Africa', *Educational Researcher*, 33 (6).

Archival sources

University of South Africa (UNISA) Archives
Newspaper clippings from '*The World*', 13 September 1967.

2 Hendrik Witbooi and Samuel Maharero: The Ambiguity of Heroes

Werner Hillebrecht

Figure 2.1 Hendrik Witbooi
(Deutsch-Südwest-Afrika: Kriegs und Friedensbilder, 1907)

Figure 2.2 Samuel Maharero
(Deutsch-Südwest-Afrika: Kriegs und Friedensbilder, 1907)

Hendrik Witbooi and Samuel Maharero are two familiar icons. Both of these portraits were probably taken in the same style, but on different occasions, by the Windhoek photographer Lange. Both men started their careers as leaders in a controversial way, Hendrik by rebelling against his father, Kaptein Moses Witbooi; Samuel by succeeding his father Maharero in violation of traditional succession rules. Both led their people in the struggle against German colonial rule. Witbooi died from a German bullet in 1905. He was buried in a secret, forgotten grave near Vaalgras, which has not been rediscovered. Maharero died in exile in Bechuanaland in 1923, eight years after German rule ended, and seventeen years after he had left; indeed he only returned to Namibia for his reburial in Okahandja. Both are remembered to this day by their respective communities in an annual commemoration, and both had a history of fighting against each other, and side by side, both for the Germans, and against the Germans.

This chapter focuses on Hendrik Witbooi, as it is mainly based on research of his correspondence, but Samuel Maharero also appears again and again, as their stories are inextricably linked. The chapter should not be understood as an attempt to tear down monuments. In any case, although he deserves a monument, Witbooi does not have one, just an empty grave at Heroes Acre, Windhoek, and a memorial stone in Gibeon. In my personal opinion, Hendrik Witbooi is a hero for a number of reasons, and that he died from a German bullet is but the least of them. But this chapter is a reminder of the complexity of history and that 'heroes' are rarely as flawless as popular versions of history would like to portray. Contemporary images of cartoon and 'Hollywood Heroes' create expectations that run the risk of obscuring histories that contain different and discordant perspectives. History is rather a patchwork, like those tapestries sewn together by Nama women in Gibeon and elsewhere.

The Hendrik Witbooi Papers

Apart from being a war leader of his people (the Witboois or |Khowesin of Gibeon) as well as of a wider Nama alliance, Hendrik Witbooi is known for his prophetic insights into the nature of colonialism, which he documented in his various writings. It is for these writings that he is known world-wide. The largest portion of his papers are kept at the National Archives of Namibia. Much of it has been published – once in the original text and several times in English and German translations – and these papers are deemed so important that they have been awarded the prestigious status of being listed on UNESCO's international 'Memory of the World' inventory of the most important documentary heritage of humanity.[1] They consist of four books, where Witbooi and his scribes,[2] entered incoming and outgoing diplomatic and administrative correspondence, treaties and proclamations – mostly in Cape Dutch, which served as the lingua franca between different linguistic communities in nineteenth century Namibia.

    I want to sketch briefly the complexity of the story of these papers since it illustrates the background against which the AACRLS Project was created and provides a good example of the way in which Namibia has had to reconstruct archives that have been fragmented, scattered and, now, recovered from abroad. The most famous item is the so-called 'diary' (although it actually contains only two diary entries, whilst the rest consists of recorded correspondence). It was captured by the German forces when they attacked the Witbooi settlement of Hoornkrans in 1893; the leader of the attack, Kapitän Curt von François, later took it with him to Germany, and it is still not clear how it returned to Namibia, but in 1918 it was at the disposal of the South African administration and it was cited when the latter compiled the famous 'Blue Book' (François, 1895, p. 227, Administrator for South West Africa, 1918). It was then kept by the SWA Department of Education, and soon after the National Archives was established, in 1939, it was deposited in the Archives (Hoernlé, 1987).[3]

---

1   http://www.unesco.org/new/en/communication-and-information/flagship-project-activities/memory-of-the-world/register/full-list-of-registered-heritage/registered-heritage-page-5/letter-journals-of-hendrik-witbooi/; see also: http://www.unesco.org/new/fileadmin/MULTIMEDIA/HQ/CI/CI/pdf/mow/nomination_forms/letter_journals_of_hendrik_witbooi.pdf

2   The texts are in different handwritings. Through comparison with other signed texts, Samuel Izaak, Petrus Jod and Hendrik Witbooi junior (Klein-Hendrik) have been identified as scribes. Although fully literate, Hendrik Witbooi was handicapped in writing because he had lost the thumb on his right hand.

3   Although no accession date is recorded, it was listed as Private Accession no 2 in the Archives.

The compilation of the first published edition of Witbooi papers (in 1929) unfortunately led to the disappearance of another important section of Witbooi's papers. The German administration's files on the Witboois contained many letters from Witbooi, and against all archival rules, the compiler (a certain Mr Bruchhausen) was allowed to remove all the original files from the archives. He took them to South Africa and never returned them, and to this day they remain lost.[4]

Two more books with copies of Witbooi's correspondence after 1893, and some loose papers, were found by the German trader August Wulff when he (with other Germans) searched the deserted village of Gibeon after Witbooi's declaration of war in late 1904. Wulff, who had apparently been on friendly terms with Witbooi,[5] kept his find secret from the German authorities and took the papers to his native Bremen, where he sold them 30 years later to the *Ueberseemuseum* in Bremen – and where they were subsequently forgotten, and only rediscovered around the time of Namibian independence in 1990.[6] To the credit of the Museum and the State of Bremen, it must be said that they did a perfect restoration of the original books, and returned them to Namibia, only keeping a microfilm.

A fourth book with copies of Witbooi's last known correspondence (after Witbooi's declaration of war in October, 1904) was apparently found by the German troops when they captured Witbooi's base at Rietmond, which was, presumably, taken apart.

A substantial part of this book with three important letters reappeared in private hands in Germany after 1990 (Goebel, 2000, pp.1-21). The AACRLS Project and the German Embassy were able to ensure that it was repatriated to Namibia.[7] A fifth letter-copy book was reportedly donated to the National Archives in 1963, but was not accessioned and disappeared without a trace.[8]

Apart from the books, there are further letters from and to Witbooi scattered in various places in Namibia, Germany, Botswana and South Africa. Fragments of Witbooi's correspondence were taken by the German officer Schwabe during the Naukluft War in 1894 (see Figure 2.3), and resurfaced in a museum in Freiburg, and at least digital copies of these letters were returned to Namibia.[9] Several other original letters were lost, but have been documented through the publication of contemporary transcriptions or translations. The cataloguing, transcription, translation and collation of these scattered letters in a central register at the National Archives of Namibia is far advanced, but not yet entirely completed.[10]

---

4   Repeated attempts by the Director of Education (H. H. G. Kreft) to recover the files from Bruchhausen are documented in NAN SWAA A 50/71 Native Affairs. Hendrik Witbooi's diary.
5   He took several photos of Witbooi, some of which show them together in a rather informal setting. NAN photo collection 14102, 14103, 14104.
6   Letter from Wulff to the Ueberseemuseum Bremen dated November 1934, NAN A. 650, folder H.
7   NAN Accession AACRLS.117.
8   The donation by one Mrs O. Lampe is reported in the South West Africa Administration's 'White paper on the activities of the different branches for the financial year 1963-1964', p. 10.
9   NAN Accession AACRLS. 199.
10 NAN Accession AACRLS. 238.

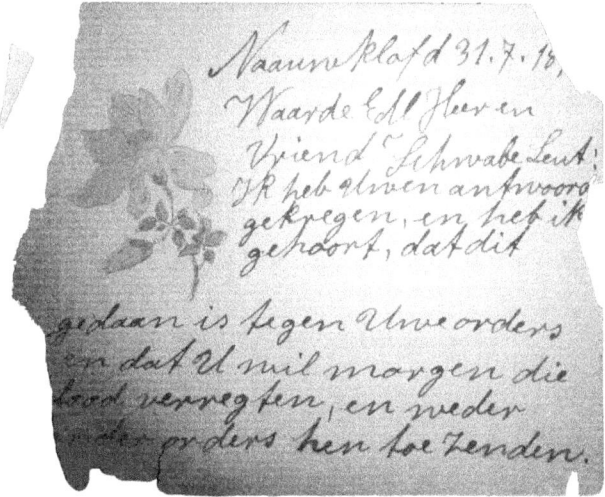

Figure 2.3 Fragment of a letter from Witbooi to Lieutenant Schwabe during the Naukluft War, dated 31 July 18[94]
(NAN AACRLS. 199 Schwabe Papers)

The Pre-Colonial Background

A popular myth about pre-colonial history has it that pre-colonial Namibian history is characterised by continuous tribal wars between mutually hostile ethnic groups, with the missionaries continuously, but unsuccessfully, attempting to broker peace, and the German occupation finally bringing peace and development to the country. This is the version that was popularised by missionary and historian Heinrich Vedder, in his monumental work *South West Africa in early times* and in many articles and schoolbooks (Vedder, 1966). It has long been debunked by historians, especially Brigitte Lau (1995), but is still lingering in books for the tourist market.[11]

The reality is much more complex, as it must be realised that 'pre-colonial' Namibia was already a colonial frontier zone, much influenced by colonial South Africa, where white settlers had grabbed land and displaced indigenous communities, which had then moved northwards across the Orange River, trying to maintain their independence, yet already dependent on the colonial market for trade and for the weapons and ammunition which they needed to assert their sovereignty. An unequal and unsustainable trade with ostrich feathers, ivory and cattle, which were exchanged for arms and consumer goods, led to a volatile period of conflict, and this created the opportunity for the colonising power to come in and 'divide and rule' under the pretext of providing 'protection' (Lau, 1987).

---

11 Although the crude Vedderian version is no longer popular, the brief historical outlines in most travel guides refer to pre-colonial Namibia as an era of violent conflict.

Realising the Danger

The Witbooi Papers illustrate how clearly Hendrik Witbooi saw through the smokescreen of the German claim that the primary aim of its involvement in Namibia was to provide 'protection'. The relevant passages from his letters are well-known and have been cited so many times, but let me repeat some key statements. Witbooi wrote to Maharero Tjamuaha, the father of Samuel Maharero, on 30 May 1890 after Maharero had concluded a protection treaty with imperial Germany:

> You will eternally regret that you have given your land and your right to rule into the hands of White men. For this war between us is not nearly as heavy a burden as you seem to have thought when you did this momentous thing,

and further,

> I doubt that you and Herero nation will understand the rules and laws and methods of that government, and will accept them in peace and contentment for long.

I have cited just two short passages from two powerful and prophetic sections of this letter, but in between these passages is an equally eloquent passage (which is usually left out) where Witbooi insults Maharero and his people for having a murderous disposition:

> Inhumanely you hack others to death, slit the throats of living people, and dig out bodies from their graves; murder women and children, as you did last year, when you arrived in my absence to kill my women and children.

Witbooi surely felt that way, as he had been outraged at the Herero attack on Gibeon during his absence in September 1889 (only a little over six months earlier), but this is hardly the language with which you persuade someone to become an ally against a more dangerous enemy. It was Witbooi's weakness, shown in much of his correspondence, that he saw himself as God's weapon against what he perceived as other unjust and murderous leaders, who had to be punished first before they could see the light, repent and ally themselves with Witbooi. This is even repeated after the death of the old Herero leader, Maharero, in 1890, when he wrote a brusque ultimatum to the Herero (see Figure 2.4):

'i. Do you still intend to go on fighting?

ii. Are you still unwilling to understand?

iii. Are you still unwilling to repent?

iv. Are you still unwilling to seek peace?'[12]

---

12   NAN A.2 Witbooi to Samuel Maharero, 20 May 1891, pp. 119-120.

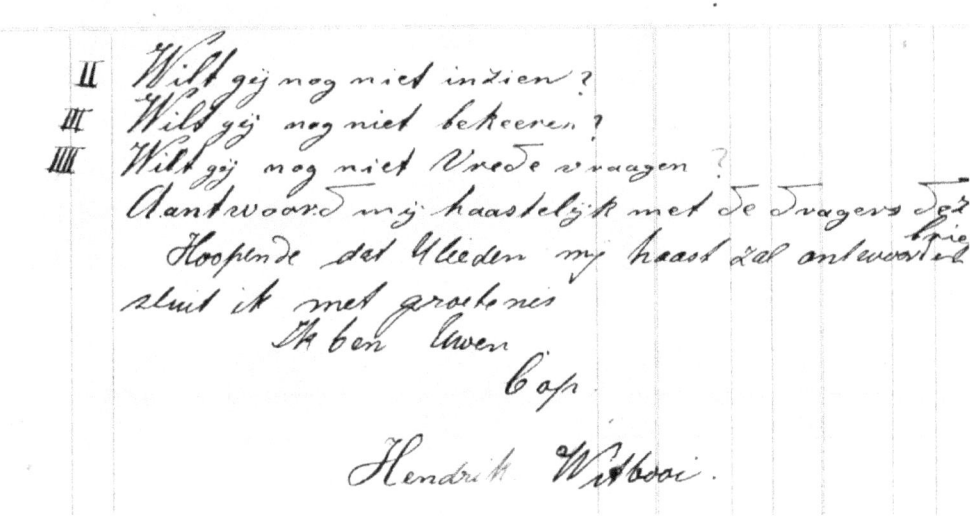

Figure 2.4 The ending of Witbooi's letter to Samuel Maharero, dated 20 May 1891
(NAN A.2 p. 120)

It is not surprising that Samuel Maharero, who, in the meantime, had taken over in Okahandja, answered in a mocking tone,

> 'If you are tired of war, you can always ask for peace. You are Christians and educated. Can't you come to your senses?'[13]

Thus the long series of Witbooi's raids on Herero cattle continued, with the Herero retaliating whenever they could.

Samuel Maharero and the Germans

Of course Samuel Maharero's equally provocative answer must be seen against the background that he had come to power with tacit German support, especially from the missionaries, against stiff opposition from other Herero leaders and against the strong claims (under traditional law) of Nikodemus Kavikunua (Kambahahiza) and Asser Riarua (Gewald, 1997, pp. 47-55). However, no direct German military support was forthcoming, and some German settlers even joined in the frequent raiding and counter-raiding and robbed Samuel Maharero of the cattle he had just taken from Witbooi. In April 1892, therefore, he started to take Witbooi's peace offers seriously.

---

13   NAN A.2 Samuel Maharero to Witbooi, 20 June 1891 p.197.

Several rounds of negotiations took place between Hendrik and Samuel, with the Rehoboth Basters as intermediaries. Witbooi was eager to come to an agreement, because a German arms embargo threatened him directly. As he wrote to his friend and ammunitions supplier Duncan,

> I can't understand exactly what the Germans are planning to do. They tell the chiefs of this country that they come as friends to prevent other powerful nations to take their land away from them. But it looks to me as if they are the ones who are taking the land.[14]

In a letter to the German military commander, Curt von François, he clearly advocated the sovereign rights of African leaders:

> An independent and autonomous chief is chief of his people and land – because every ruler is chief over his people and country, to protect it and himself against any danger or disaster which is threatening to harm himself or his land.

And further:

> If a danger threatens one of us which he feels he cannot meet on his own, then he can call upon a brother or brothers among the Red chiefs, saying: Come, brothers, let us together oppose this danger which threatens to invade our Africa, for we are one in colour and custom, and this Africa is ours. For the fact that we various Red chiefs occupy our various realms and home grounds is but a lesser division of the one Africa.[15]

If Samuel Maharero shared similar sentiments, he did not communicate them, but he had seen enough to realise the danger that the German arms embargo also posed to the Herero. The common threat of Boer settlement added to the urgency (François, 1999, p. 159). So in November 1892, both sides came to an agreement, and there are no further reports of cattle raids. As Samuel wrote to Hendrik,

> The most urgent task for me just now is to ensure that all of our land is occupied by our nation, and that we push this powerful and strong nation back from our country with energy and force, lest we lose it by default.[16]

---

14   NAN A.2 Witbooi to Robert Duncan, 28 June 1891, pp.183-184.
15   Witbooi's minutes of the negotiations with Curt von François, 9.6.1892, as translated in Witbooi (1995, pp. 85-86). Original text in NAN A.2, pp. 209-218. The 'Red Chiefs' refers to the leaders of the different Khoekhoegowab-speaking Nama communities with territories north and south of the Orange (Gariep) River in the northern Cape and southern 'Namibia'.
16   Samuel Maharero to Hendrik Witbooi, 1 November 1892, as translated in Witbooi (1995, p. 116). Original text in NAN A.2, pp. 276-277: '*laat elke plaats kan maar onze Natie zelf wonen, en laat maar de machtigen en sterksten Natie voor ons maar in onze grond met kracht maar uitstoten*'.

German Attack

The new alliance between Hendrik Witbooi and Samuel Maharero was threatening enough for von François to take action. He had secured military reinforcements from Germany, and immediately after their arrival attacked Witbooi at Hoornkrans, without any provocation, on 12 April 1893. The attack turned into a massacre of women and children, which was reported to Berlin by von François as a great victory, while most Witbooi fighters escaped. They began a guerrilla war which soon found the Germans helpless and immobile in Windhoek, as Witbooi had managed to capture most of their horses. Samuel Maharero remained neutral in this conflict.

François' unsuccessful war was not received kindly in Berlin, and the German government sent new troop reinforcements under Major Leutwein to replace von François. Leutwein, a much cleverer strategist, first left Witbooi alone and set out to force the other two remaining independent Nama communities, the Kai|Khauan of Gobabis and !Khara Khoen (Simon Kooper's community) of Gochas, into a protection treaty. Then he turned against Witbooi, who had retreated into the Naukluft Mountains, and soon realised that his military force was still too weak to defeat him. Leutwein then concluded a truce whilst he waited for further reinforcements, all the time maintaining a lively correspondence with Witbooi about the terms of a possible permanent treaty.

This correspondence was held in the German files about Witbooi, which disappeared in the 1920s. However, we have two independent sources from which it can be reconstructed: the transcriptions which were made by Bruchhausen from the missing files and published in 1929,[17] and Witbooi's journals 2 and 3 (the ones that were taken to Bremen) where his drafts of the letters to Leutwein, as well as copies of some of Leutwein's letters, were written down.[18] When the reinforcements came, Leutwein ended the truce, and a war began which was harsh on both sides. Eventually, Witbooi agreed to sign a treaty, while Leutwein had to make substantial concessions. Probably the most important concession in Witbooi's eyes was that they were allowed to keep their weapons. Leutwein also had to drop his condition that Witbooi should retire into exile, and be succeeded as Kaptein by his son. He had to justify this to Berlin, and later admitted that the German troops were as exhausted as the Witboois, and that he would not have been able to prevent them from breaking out of the Naukluft to continue the war elsewhere. Witbooi himself had to consider the desperate situation of the women and children. The Witboois had to agree to settle in Gibeon with a German garrison, and to give military assistance to the Germans.[19]

The 'Ten Year Peace' (1894-1903)

The substantial diplomatic and philosophical correspondence of Witbooi dries up at this point. Witbooi was worn out, sick, and lacked his previous zeal. His communications with German officials revolve around health problems. Quite characteristic is a small

---

17   Witbooi (1929).
18   NAN A.650.
19   NAN ZBU W.II.d.16, 83-86.

note from Witbooi to Leutwein, found in a German file: 'May you, as you may wish, help me with a little brandy, if you have some. I am very tired.'[20] This coming from Witbooi who had previously been known as a strict teetotaller, very much in contrast to Maharero!

The two 'Bremen' journals and loose papers contain interesting information about this period. They demonstrate the efforts Witbooi made to keep up a civil administration with record-keeping, as he had done before at Hoornkrans. There are lists of officials, birth and death registers, records of court cases, and letters documenting his efforts to earn money through the establishment of a transport business (see Figure 2.5).

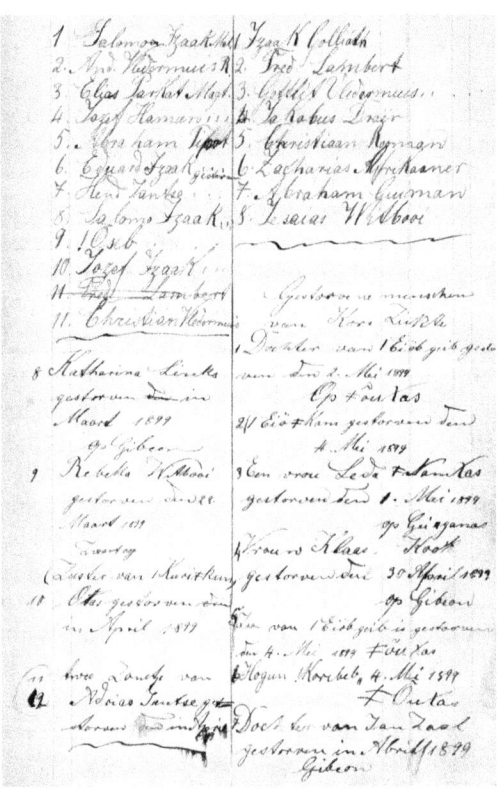

Figure 2.5 List of officials in the Witbooi Government, and death register for 1899, in the Hendrik Witbooi Papers
(NAN A.650,1 p. 11)

A few very cautiously worded letters to other leaders indicate that, under the overwhelming German presence, he did not trust in writing anymore but preferred mouth-to-mouth communication.

But the bulk of documents signed by Witbooi over the next ten years can be found in the German files in the form of land sale contracts. They show the fast process of land alienation, into which the Witboois were forced due to their rising debts to traders. The

---

20   NAN ZBU D.IV.c, fol.253 Witbooi to Leutwein, undated, about June/July 1896.

same process occurred among the Herero, and quite obviously was the driving force behind their readiness, in 1904, to rise against the Germans. The parallel nature of the process in both communities disproves the contemporary German explanation, that the Nama were unproductive and had previously lived from robbing the Herero, so that now they could not sustain themselves by honest work and had to sell their land to survive. Why then did the same happen among the Herero, who were now, supposedly, 'protected' from the Nama cattle raids? An economic analysis of the practices and terms of trade for this period is still outstanding, although the material for such an analysis exists in the form of contemporary cash books and trade statistics, whilst the Witbooi journals also contain ample economic evidence.

The Ten-Year War

Instead of naming the ten-year period from 1896 to 1903 the 'peace years', as is common in German colonial literature, they should, more aptly, be termed 'war years'. Almost every year from 1896 to 1903 saw a German military expedition against 'rebelling tribes' (Drechsler, 1980, pp. 92-105). With the exception of the far north, Leutwein used the period to forcefully demonstrate that he would not tolerate any dissension from German rule, and in almost all cases, he did this with the assistance of Witbooi, Okahandja Herero, and Rehoboth Baster soldiers, as agreed in their respective treaties. The first of these, and the most ruthless and bloody campaign, was the war against the united Kai|Khauan and Mbanderu in 1896. It was triggered by the Germans and Samuel colluding to expand German settlement at the expense of the Mbanderu, and Samuel's erstwhile rival as paramount chief, Nikodemus. In this war, Hendrik Witbooi and Samuel Maharero personally participated, as is documented in a famous photo taken after the battle of Otjunda (Figure 2.6).

Figure 2.6 Witbooi, Leutwein and Maharero during the war against the Mbanderu, 1896
(Leutwein, Elf Jahre Gouverneur in Deutsch-Südwestafrika, 1906, p. 113)

Leutwein sent a copy of this photo to Witbooi, remarking: 'This is a very valuable photo, as it proves our unity, through which we succeeded to re-install the peace properly.'[21]

After the war Nikodemus Kavikunua and the Mbanderu chief and prophet Kahimemua were court-martialled and executed at Okahandja. Hendrik Witbooi, Samuel Isaak, and two Okahandja Herero selected by Samuel Maharero were part of the jury and agreed to the death sentences.[22]

This war had a rather perverse echo in the Witbooi papers – Witbooi's conversion from the main symbol of anti-colonial resistance to a German ally, as shown by his participation in the Mbanderu War. The conflict was widely reported in German newspapers, and as a result, he received what, in current terminology, we would describe as 'fan mail'. The loose Witbooi papers from Bremen contain two postcards from Germany – and there is reason to believe there were more of this kind – with best wishes for the brave new German ally.[23] Witbooi was also frequently asked to autograph postcards that people were sending to Germany – the Rhenish Mission even made a business out of selling such signed postcards (Figure 2.7).

Figure 2.7 Postcard signed by Hendrik Witbooi and Samuel Izaak in 1900
(NAN A.650, J)

How comfortable Witbooi felt with this sudden celebrity status is difficult to tell. But it is quite certain that he had little choice. Should we call him a puppet and collaborator for this? His efforts to create a united front to stop the German strategy of protection treaties had failed, and it took a period of ten years under effective German rule to show

---

21   NAN ZBU W.II.d.16, fol.1 Leutwein to Witbooi, 31 December 1896.
22   NAN A.786 (Vedder Quellen), vol. 29a, p. 49.
23   NAN A.650, G, no.8 and D, no.10.

all the 'protected' communities what colonialism meant in practice. He had done his part, and lost the argument. As he remarked with dry humour to Leutwein, when he helped to quell some unrest in the far South among other Nama communities: 'These Kapteine did not know what they signed. But I knew, and that is why I made war *before* [I signed].' (Leutwein, 1906, p. 154. Emphasis in the original).

From Mercenary to Guerilla

When the nationwide uprising started with a local incident at Warmbad in late 1903, the Witboois had once again joined the Germans to force the Bondelzwarts into a new treaty. But the concentration of the German military in the South to fight the Bondelzwarts, depleting central Namibia of German troops, was also, apparently, one of the factors which triggered the Herero uprising in January 1904.[24]

Although Samuel Maharero sent two letters to Witbooi, asking him to join the uprising in January 1904, Witbooi never received them as they were kept by the Rehobother messenger who was entrusted with their delivery. Samuel wrote:

> all our obedience and patience towards the Germans are killing us, because every day they shoot someone for nothing. And my brother, do not consider your first response and stay away. Stand up, and let whole Africa fight against the Germans, and not die from wastage and prison and all that.[25]

Nobody can tell whether Maharero's plea would have been successful if it had reached its addressee. If Hendrik Witbooi had joined the uprising at this stage, it would have dramatically changed the early course of the war, but he kept to the terms of his treaty with Leutwein and continued to supply the German military with auxiliary troops who served them until after the Battle of Ohamakari, when a number of them deserted and found their way back to Gibeon.[26] While the remainder of the Herero forces, together with their women and children, fled through the Omaheke towards Bechuanaland, Witbooi made up his mind, sent letters to all the other Nama leaders inviting them to join him, and formally declared war on the Germans. He wrote to Leutwein (see Figure 2.8):

> I have for ten years stood in your law, under your law, and behind your law – and not I alone, but all the chiefs of Africa. For this reason I fear God the Father. [Because of]

---

24 Jan-Bart Gewald (1996) maintains that the beginning of the uprising was not prepared beforehand, but a self-fulfilling prophecy, triggered by German settler and military paranoia. Be that as it may, it is certain that there was a general readiness to fight against German rule, otherwise the fast and wide spreading nature of the uprising would not have taken place.

25 NAN ZBU D.IV.1.2, vol.2: *'want al gehoorsaamheit, en geduldigheit van onz, aan den Duitsters, die maak onz gedaan, want helle schiet elke dag een man vor niet. En laat myn broeder niet zyn eerste woord denken en af staan, Staan op; en laat Helle Africa Vechten tegen de Duisters laat onz liewerder gedaan dood, en niet staan dood met morserij met Dronk en ale manieren'.*

26 It has been speculated that their reports about German warfare might have played a role in the decision by Hendrik Witbooi to fight the Germans again.

All the souls which have for the last ten years perished from all the nations and from among all our chiefs, without guilt or cause, without open war in peace and under treaties of peace, the reckoning that I shall have to God our Father in Heaven is very great.[27]

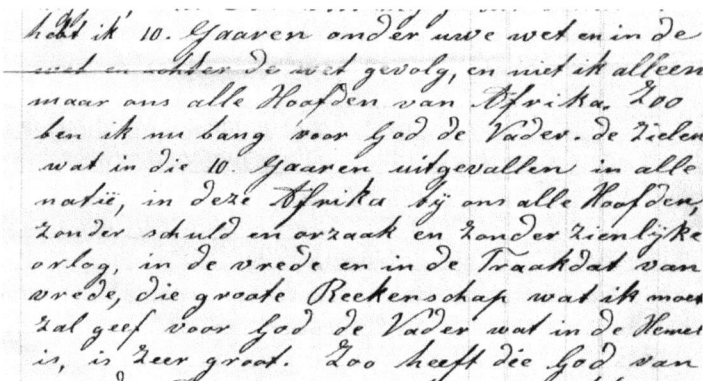

Figure 2.8 Letter from Hendrik Witbooi to Theodor Leutwein dated 3 November 1904
(NAN AACRLS. 117, p. 11)

The Herero had allowed the Germans to encounter them in large battles that were decided by their superior fire-power. Thus, this part of the war was largely over within eight months. Witbooi and other Nama units in the South relied on guerilla tactics, and it took the Germans four years and immense reinforcements until they could quell all armed resistance. Once again, Hendrik Witbooi was able not only to lead the uprising, but also to express the reasons behind it a succinct and moving way in a letter written as a response to the German district officer Schmidt:

> It is true and I agree with what you say to me, about your might and abundance in everything, and I also agree with you that I am very weak. But you have not told me what you want me to say; you only boast of your might which I only know too well. You also mention the price on my head; so now I am an outlaw. As for your grievous concern for my nation, I do not share that. Because I did not create men, nor did you, but God alone. Thus I now sit in your hand, and peace will be at one and the same time my death and the death of my nation. For I know that there is no refuge for me under you.
>
> To your remarks on peace I reply, don't lecture me like a schoolchild on your peace. You know very well that I was right there with you many times during your peace, and have come to see in it nothing but the destruction of all our people. For you have got to know me, and I have got to know you, through the hard experience of my life. (Schmidt, 1934. pp. 54-55).

---

27   NAN AACRLS.117 Witbooi to Leutwein, 3 November 1904, p. 11.

In similar vein to the Herero extermination order, von Trotha issued a bombastic declaration to the Nama, putting a price on the head of Hendrik Witbooi and other leaders.[28] However, this did not work as none of the mentioned leaders were ever captured or killed due to betrayal by a member of their own community. Hendrik Witbooi eventually fell from a German bullet near Vaalgras on 29 October 1905. He was hastily buried by his troops in a secret and unmarked grave, maybe partly because they were being pursued and had little time, maybe partly because they wished to spare his remains the fate of being dug up and sent to Berlin. The oral history of this event has been lost through the subsequent traumatic experience of the Witboois who were not only decimated through internment on Shark Island, but also through deportation to Cameroon, from where only a few survivors would return in 1913 (Hillebrecht and Melber, 1988, pp.132-151).

The Legacy Lives On

What survived is the memory of the great Kaptein, who was so small in stature that it earned him the nickname 'Kort', which could be translated as 'Shortie'. It has not yet been properly researched when the community at Gibeon started to commemorate his death in an annual festival, but this has become a regular and lively event that is rarely missed.

In contrast, the annual Herero Festival (Red Flag Day) at Okahandja can be precisely dated to the reburial of Samuel Maharero in 1923 (he died in Bechuanaland on 14 March, 1923 and was buried there before arrangements were made for the return of his body). Samuel had lived rather quietly in Bechuanaland in exile after the flight through the Omaheke in 1904. For some time, he also made a living in the Transvaal by brokering exiled Ovaherero as contract labourers to the South African mines. Now, after his death, he became important again as a rallying point for the rebuilding and restructuring of the Herero community in Namibia. His burial was the first public manifestation that they would not be content forever as a subservient underclass under a South African regime that proved no better than German rule, and refused to restore their land.

In a photo from this burial (Figure 2.9 overleaf), we see for the first time Hosea Kutako on a public platform. Twenty-five years later, Chief Hosea Kutako and Kaptein David Witbooi, and later on Hendrik Samuel Witbooi who succeeded David as Witbooi Kaptein, would join in petitioning the United Nations.

At the Heroes Acre near Windhoek, history has concluded a full circle, and Hendrik and Samuel are commemorated side by side in symbolic graves. They started out fighting each other, then made peace, then fought side by side together under German command, then fought against each other – one for, one against the Germans; and finally again on the same side against the Germans. Their memory has been an inspiration throughout the liberation struggle of Namibia. Heroes? One cannot say they never wavered in fighting colonialism. Yet they did what they did according to their knowledge and understanding of the circumstances. There can be no doubt they deserve their place of honour.

---

28   NAN BKE B.II.74.d.7 Proclamation dated 23 April 1905, 'Aan de oorlogvoerende Namastamme'.

Figure 2.9 Herero notables gathering at the Okahandja Location for Samuel Maharero's funeral, 23 August 1923. In centre (standing): Hosea Kutako
(NAN photo 18600, donated by E.S Tjirimuje)

References

Administrator for South West Africa (1918) *Report on the natives of South-West Africa and their treatment by Germany*. London: HMSO.

Deutsch-Südwest-Afrika: Kriegs- und Friedensbilder; 100 Original-Aufnahmen von Friedrich Lange. Windhoek 1907.

Drechsler, H. (1980) *'Let us die fighting': the struggle of the Herero and Nama against German imperialism (1884-1915)*. London: Zed Press.

François, Hugo von. (1895) *Nama und Damara. Deutsch-Süd-West-Afrika*. Magdeburg: Baensch.

François, Curt von. (1899) *Deutsch-Südwestafrika: Geschichte der Kolonisation bis zum Ausbruch des Krieges mit Witbooi April 1893*. Berlin: Reimer.

Gewald, J. B. (1996) *Towards redemption: A socio-political history of the Herero of Namibia between 1890 to 1923*. Leiden: CNWS.

Goebel, K. (2000) 'Ein Fund im Hause Hendrik Witbooi in Rietmond 1904. Zur Entstehungsgeschichte des Witbooi-Aufstandes'. In *Deutsch-Südwestafrika. Mitteilungsblatt / Traditionsverband ehemaliger Schutz- und Überseetruppen*, no.86, pp.1-21.

Hoernlé, W., Carstens, P., Klinghardt, G. and West, M. E. (1987) *Trails in the thirstland: The anthropological field diaries of Winifred Hoernlé*. Rondebosch, South Africa: Centre for African Studies, University of Cape Town.

Hillebrecht, W. and Melber, H. (1988) 'Von den Deutschen verschleppt. Spurensicherung'. In: Mbumba, N., Patemann, H., Katjivena, U., Angula, N. and Tjitendero, M. (eds) *Ein Land, eine Zukunft: Namibia auf dem Weg in die Unabhängigkeit*. Bremen: Hammer.

Lau, B. (1987) *Southern and Central Namibia in Jonker Afrikaner's Time*. Windhoek: National Archives.

Lau, B. (1995) '"Thank God the Germans came". Vedder and Namibian historiography'. In: *History and Historiography*. Windhoek: National Archives.

Leutwein, T. (1906) *Elf Jahre Gouverneur in Deutsch-Südwestafrika*. Berlin: Mittler.

Schmidt, K. A. (1934) 'Hendrik Witbooi's letzter Aufstand und Tod'. In: *Deutsche Rundschau*, vol. 240.

South West Africa Administration. White Paper on the Activities of the Different Branches for the financial year 1963-1964.

Vedder, H. (1966) *South West Africa in Early Times. Being the story of South West Africa up to the date of Maharero's death in 1890*. London: Cass & Co.

Witbooi. H. (1929) 'Die dagboek van Hendrik Witbooi, Kaptein van die Witbooi-Hottentotte, 1884-1905. Bewerk na die oorspronklike dokumente in die Regeringsargief, Windhoek'. Cape Town: Van Riebeeck Society.

Witbooi, H. (1995) *The Hendrik Witbooi Papers*. Translated by A. Heywood and E. Maasdorp, annotated by B. Lau. Windhoek: National Archives of Namibia. 2nd edition.

Websites

http://www.unesco.org/new/en/communication-and-information/flagship-project-activities/memory-of-the-world/register/full-list-of-registered-heritage/registered-heritage-page-5/letter-journals-of-hendrik-witbooi/

http://www.unesco.org/new/fileadmin/MULTIMEDIA/HQ/CI/CI/pdf/mow/nomination_forms/letter_journals_of_hendrik_witbooi.pdf

Archival sources

National Archives of Namibia (NAN)

A.2 Hendrik Witbooi Journal I

pp. 119-120. Witbooi to Samuel Maharero, 20 May 1891

p.197. Samuel Maharero to Witbooi, 20 June 1891

p.183-184. Witbooi to Robert Duncan, 28 June 1891

pp. 209-218. Witbooi's minutes of the negotiations with Curt von Francois, 9 June 1892

pp. 276-277. Samuel Maharero to Hendrik Witbooi, 1 November 1892

A.650 Witbooi Bremen Papers

Folder D, no.10. Postcard from "Germanen im Goldenen Engel", Hildesheim, to H. Witbooi, 1896

Folder G, no.8. Postcard from Rüdt, Mannheim, to H. Witbooi, undated

Folder H. Letter from Wulff to the Ueberseemuseum Bremen, November 1934

Folder H, no.12. Postcard with Witbooi signature, sent by Wulff to Bremen, 1900

A.786 Vedder Quellen

vol. 29a, p. 49.

AACRLS Archives of Anti-Colonial Resistance and Liberation Struggle
AACRLS.117 Hendrik Witbooi Journal IV
AACRLS.199 Kurd Schwabe Papers
AACRLS.238 Hendrik Witbooi Correspondence Transcriptions

BKE Bezirksamt Keetmanshoop
B.II.74.d vol.7 Proclamation dated 23 April 1905, "Aan de oorlogvoerende Namastamme".

Photo Collection
nos. 14102, 14103, 14104

SWAA South West Africa Administration
A 50/71 Native Affairs. Hendrik Witbooi's diary

ZBU Zentralbüro das Kaiserlichen Gouvernements
D.IV.c, fol.253. Witbooi to Leutwein, undated, about June/July 1896
D.IV.l.2, vol.2. fol.74-76. Samuel Maharero to Witbooi, undated
W.II.d.16, vol.3, fol.83-86. Protection treaty
W.II.d.16, vol.5, fol.1. Leutwein to Witbooi, 31 December 1896

3 The Vagciriku-Lishora Massacre of 1894 Revisited

Shampapi Shiremo

Introduction

One day in March or April 1894,[1] the Vagciriku community of the Kavango Region in Namibia and Cuando-Cubango Province in Angola lost almost all its able-bodied men. This happened after a force of armed BaTawana men on horseback, commanded by *Kgosi*[2] Sekgoma, which had travelled from Botswana, shot in cold-blood all the able-bodied Vagciriku men at a place called Shantjefu.[3] *Hompa* Nyangana of the Vagciriku, his son, Mbambo, women and children were captured and taken into captivity in Ngamiland. The BaTawana army also confiscated all the Vagciriku cattle, guns and horses as booty.

Compared with colonial massacres in Namibian historiography such as the Hornkranz Massacre of 1893, the Old Location Massacre of 1959 or the Cassinga Massacre of 1978, the Lishora Massacre of 1894 is relatively unknown. The small body of literature about the Lishora Massacre of 1894 is generally one sided and situated outside the 'colonial narrative'. In Vagciriku oral history, *Hompa* Nyangana's despotism is usually blamed for the Lishora Massacre of 1894 as it is described as being a response to the conflict between *Hompa* Nyangana and the section of the Vashambyu led by *Hompaghona* (Prince) Kanyetu. *Hompa* Nyangana is sometimes remembered as an authoritarian leader who used violence to settle scores with his rivals. The view that *Hompa* Nyangana played a direct role in the Lishora massacre has never been critically questioned, because the existing secondary literature and oral narratives ignored the primary and archival sources kept in Botswana's National Archives. It appears evident that in the past, Namibian researchers on the Vagciriku-Lishora Massacre of 1894 remained totally unaware of the

---

1   In August 2008, I found a document in the Botswana National Archives and Record Services which showed that the Vagciriku-Lishora Massacre took place in March or April 1894 (I will refer to this document in detail later in this chapter). Previously I had believed that the massacre took place in 1893, thus my BA mini-thesis was entitled 'The Lishora Massacre of 1893 and its effects on the Vagciriku Community'.
2   *Kgosi* is the title given to the hereditary leader of the BaTawana community. The title *Hompa* is used by the traditional leader of the Kwangali, Mbunza, Shambyu and Gciriku communities in the Kavango Regions of Namibia today, whilst the term *Fumu* is used by the Mbukushu leader.
3   Shantjefu is a village found in the Cuando-Cubango Province of Angola near the Kwito River in the Gciriku area. It was at this village where the Vagciriku men were assembled by *Kgosi* Sekgoma and later on massacred in cold blood. After the massacre, Shantjefu became known as Lishora. It appears that in the old Rumanyo language, '*kushora*' also meant to shoot. In contemporary Rukavango a powerful shot in soccer/football is called '*lishora*', so Lishora could mean 'a place of shootings' or 'a place of death.'

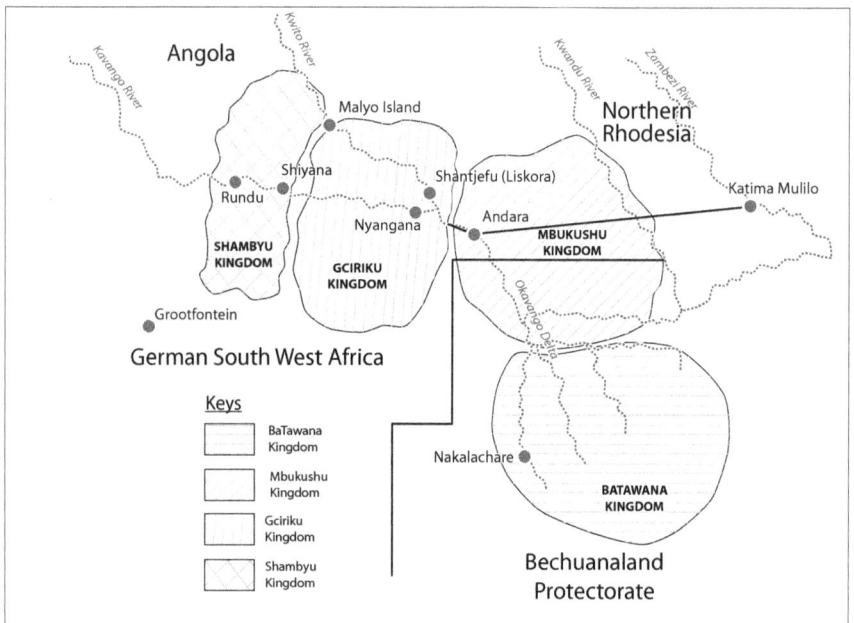

Figure 3.1 Map of the Gciriku, Batawana, Mbukushu and Shambyu Kingdoms in the 1890s

availability of archival sources on the topic in Botswana's National Archives.[4] Thus, it is not surprising that though John Mutorwa was exposed to the local oral written sources on the causes of the Lishora Massacre, he concluded his work by calling for further research into the matter as, he argued, the causes of the Lishora tragedy are not altogether known (Mutorwa, 1996, p. 11). However the main focus of Mutorwa's research was not to investigate the causes of the Vagciriku-Lishora Massacre, but to focus on another aspect of Vagciriku history.

This chapter focuses on important, newly discovered, contemporary documents produced by BaTawana and the European officials who were tasked to investigate the causes of the Vagciriku-Lishora Massacre of 1894 and highlights the differences between these contemporary written accounts and oral tradition in the region.[5] Whilst the oral tradition focuses on the internal politics of the kingdom and the tensions in its relationships with neighbouring states, the archival evidence locates the conflict within the context of contemporary imperial rivalries.

Written accounts of the Vagciriku-Lishora Massacre are found in both primary and secondary sources. The primary sources appear in the form of correspondence and

---

[4] This author was alerted to the existence of this material in around June 2008 by Dr Jeremy Silvester and Werner Hillebrecht who compiled a list of historical files that are relevant to Namibian history held by the Botswana National Archives.

[5] BNARS (Botswana National Archives and Record Services). HC 144. Correspondence on Ngamiland Affairs and the Ghanzi District and Lake Ngami Police detachment. Boer Trekkers, Isaac Johan Bosman acting on behalf of the BSACo, and papers relating to the murder of a German subject, Phillip Wiesels and a British subject, Robert Arthur Faraday, by Nyangana and the capture of Nyangana by Sekgoma's men (1894-1898).

statements from the Bechuanaland British Protectorate's colonial officials during the period 1893 to 1896. These officials had written down contemporary accounts by the BaTawana. *Kgosi* Sekgoma and other prominent BaTawana appear to have given statements to the Bechuanaland British Protectorate Administration. Secondary sources that refer directly to the Lishora Massacre are found in a book and an article that were published nine and ten years after the incident. The book is by Major Hill Gibbons (1904) entitled Africa: From the South to North through Marotseland, and the article is entitled 'Die Mambukuschu' by Professor Siegfried Passarge (1905). Whilst these two publications date from 1904 and 1905, the two authors state that they recorded their accounts between 1898 and 1900, only a few years after the massacre, when memories of the event were still fresh. There are a few other publications that make reference to the Lishora Massacre, with an article called 'Die Diriku' by August Bierfert (1913) and another entitled *Founding a Protectorate: History of Bechuanaland, 1885-1895* by A. Sillery (1965), being the most significant.

Friction with White Traders

Two white traders, Phillip Wiesel (or Weise) and Robert Arthur Faraday, were killed in 1892 – at a historical moment when colonial powers were attempting to define the boundaries of their territorial claims in the wake of the Berlin Conference of 1884. The kingdoms in this part of Africa were on the periphery of the expanding territorial claims of three European powers – Germany, Britain and Portugal. One might argue that *Hompa* Nyangana's orders to kill the two European traders were an effort to assert his local autonomy and a direct challenge to the imposition of colonial rule and foreign control over long-distance trade. It appears that the shooting of the two traders was a decision taken at the Vagciriku King's council after extensive debate. At this meeting, some relatives and Vagciriku council members were reported to have advised *Hompa* Nyangana against this course of action with one arguing: 'that is not good, the white men will turn on us and the Lake natives.' *Hompa* Nyangana replied to this, 'I don't know much about the white men, but I am sure the Lake natives [i.e. Sekgoma's community] will be satisfied'.[6]

Before 1892, the Vagciriku were involved in two other incidents in which they killed European traders. The first incident took place shortly before 1878 and involved Portuguese traders, and the second incident took place on the 27 July 1878 and involved the killing of an American trader, Charles Thomas. The second incident provoked a retaliatory attack from a force led by European traders based in the region. Though putting up a spirited resistance, the Vagciriku were defeated as about 22 Vagciriku men were reportedly killed and many more wounded (McKiernan, 1954, p. 176). At that time *Hompa* Nyangana fled his kingdom to Ukwangali where he was given asylum for a short period before he returned to his kingdom. Many of the Vagciriku homesteads, including *Hompa* Nyangana's own palace, were burned in this attack (McKiernan, 1954, p. 168).

---

6 BNARS: HC 144. A letter dated 10 December 1895 by Lieutenant Barre Phipps to the Resident Commissioner.

The American trader, Gerald McKiernan, one of those operating in the area in the 1870s, described the European trader and Boer trekker community as: 'European civilization that was spreading over the interior, far in advance of real colonial power'. Referring to the shooting of Charles Thomas by the Vagciriku, McKiernan continued that 'the more intelligent natives saw what was coming; way back on the Okavango when one chief warned another in 1878 not to attack white people if he did not want to bring bad consequences upon himself' (1954, pp.12-13). The statement by McKiernan can be translated to mean that those Africans who resisted Europe's 'civilising mission' were 'less intelligent' and were fighting a losing battle against the colonial power. It is clear, that *Hompa* Nyangana and his people were labelled as 'less intelligent' at that time. McKiernan adds that the necessity to maintain feelings of allegiance to the *Hompa* Nyangana among the (native) population explains the unanimous response to the call for a commando, after the death of Charles Thomas.

Despite the devastation that *Hompa* Nyangana and his people experienced as a result of the firepower of the white traders and Boer trekkers, the Vagciriku were reported to have made a vow that they would never allow another white man in their country because of the 1878 Thomas incident. Aurel Schulz and August Hammar who were trading in the Hambukushu area were strongly advised not to travel through the country of the Vagciriku. They were informed that it was impossible for them to go that way, as some white people had killed a chief near Darico (Gciriku) on the river (Schulz and Hammar, 1897, p. 243). As *Hompa* Nyangana was fully aware of the likely consequences of killing white traders it is interesting that he would order such action in 1892. Professor Wilhelm Möhlig argues that *Hompa* Nyangana was consistently hostile to European traders and missionaries until 1910 when the Roman Catholics established a mission station on their seventh attempt (2008, p. 81).

If it had not been for the traders' refusal to sell firearms to the BaTawana and the Vagciriku, they would have probably have remained alive. The written records show that their refusal to sell Martini-Henry Rifles was the motive behind the killings.[7] The prohibition of the sale and import of firearms to Africans was proposed at a conference of European colonial powers at Brussels in 1889-90. When this law was enforced in the former Bechuanaland British Protectorate and German South West Africa (GSWA) in 1891 and 1892 respectively, it caused a lot of resentment amongst the African communities. In fact, *Landeshauptmann*[8] Curt von François wrote that the enforcement of this law in GSWA caused considerable tension and described the relationship between Herero and German traders in the years 1892 and 1893 as 'intolerable' (1899, p.163). The efforts of the imperial powers of Europe to impose controls on the arms trade in Africa provide an important background to the BaTawana account of the Lishora Massacre.

Professor Siegfried Passarge (1905) and Major Hill Gibbons (1904), who both lived in Ngamiland at the time, asserted that in 1894 or 1895 a European trader lost his life in Gciriku territory on the orders of *Hompa* Nyangana. Gibbons explicitly claimed that because of the murder of the European trader, 'Weisel' at the order of *Hompa* Nyangana,

---

[7] BNARS: HC 144. A letter dated 10 December 1895 by Lieutenant Barre Phipps to the Resident Commissioner.

[8] German for 'State Captain'. The title was used by the German empire for governors during the early stages of its colonial rule over South West Africa (1893-1898).

whites living at Lake Ngami encouraged the Tawana chief, Sekgoma, to send a punitive expedition against the Gciriku (1904, pp. 212-213).

Professor Siegfried Passarge clearly states that the murder of a Boer, 'Wiese', by Nyangana was the cause of the war between the BaTawana and the Gciriku (Wilmsen, 1997, p. 286). The alleged killing of two European traders on the orders of *Hompa* Nyangana in 1892 and the claim that encouragement was given by the white community of Ngamiland to *Kgosi* Sekgoma to attack the Vagciriku are now both corroborated by archival evidence. There is little doubt that the two traders were killed in *Hompa* Nyangana's territory, as he confirmed this. In 1894, while in captivity in Ngamiland, *Hompa* Nyangana is quoted to have said: 'Yes, I have killed white men, but I only did so by the command of my paramount Chief, Sekgoma'.[9] The borders between the German colony of Deutsch-Südwestafrika and the British Protectorate of Bechuanaland were freshly negotiated and had still to be given tangible meaning on the ground. Yet the imposition of colonial authority by the Germans and the British impacted on the existing relationships between African polities in which the BaTawana sought to assert their authority over the Gciriku, and the Vagciriku sought to assert their authority over the Vashambyu of Kanyetu.

Evidence presented at the Inquiry into the deaths of the traders shows that in late 1895, John Macdonald 'discovered' that *Kgosi* Sekgoma had ordered *Hompa* Nyangana to kill Wiesel and Faraday, because they had refused to sell Martini-Henry rifles to Sekgoma in 1891.[10] It is significant that of the four white men who spoke to *Kgosi* Sekgoma about the murder of the German trader, two were of German origin, Georg Reinhardt and Frederick Scheepers. On 30 January 1895, Georg Reinhardt sent a statement to the German colonial authorities in Windhoek. He reported the murder of Phillip Wiesel and Robert Arthur Faraday and the subsequent actions that *Kgosi* Sekgoma took against *Hompa* Nyangana and his people. *Kgosi* Sekgoma and *Hompa* Nyangana blamed each other for the death of the two traders.

Georg Reinhardt was camping at *Kgosi* Sekgoma's palace at the time of the Vagciriku-Lishora Massacre. The evidence shows that two months before the Massacre Georg Reinhardt questioned *Kgosi* Sekgoma about the death of the German trader. In late December 1893, Reinhardt and his three colleagues pressed *Kgosi* Sekgoma to sign a 'treaty of friendship' with the BSACo in order to 'defend' the BaTawana. They told *Kgosi* Sekgoma that the German army in GSWA was preparing for war with the BaTawana, because *Kgosi* Sekgoma and *Hompa* Nyangana had been reported to the Cape by Franz Müller, who claimed that they had murdered a German trader. Reinhardt's assertion strengthens the claim made by both Passarge and Gibbons that *Kgosi* Sekgoma was encouraged to carry out a punitive expedition against Nyangana by the white BSACo agents in Ngamiland.

However, in her article entitled 'The Tawana's Military Campaign into Kavango' Dr Maria Fisch rejects the claim by Gibbons and Passarge, stating that no instigation of *Kgosi* Sekgoma by these white BSACo agents ever took place. Rejecting the account

---

9   BNARS: HC 144. Statement dated 4 September 1894 sent by Sekhome, Chief of the Batawana, Lake Ngami, to Bathoen, Chief of the Banwaketsi, p. 4.
10   BNARS: HC 144. A letter dated 10 December 1895 from Lt. Barre Phipps to the Resident Commissioner.

from Ngamiland, Dr Fisch does, however, note that: 'Sekgoma defended his Kavango foray by saying that he intended to punish Nyangana for the murder of white traders' (2007, p. 122). Yet, Fisch claims that the only recorded murder was the case of an American trader, Charles Thomas, whom the Gciriku killed in 1878, 15 years before the Lishora Massacre. Fisch argues that after this incident in 1878, the white community at Lake Ngami tended to attribute all disappearances to Gciriku violence, but that, even if such allegations were true, they were not the main reason for the Tawana's campaign against the Kavango people, but merely a pretext (2007, pp. 122-123). Dr Fisch supports the position found in the oral history of the Vagciriku and the Vashambyu, which identifies *Hompa* Nyangana as the main cause of the Lishora Massacre, which is cast as a legitimate, punitive raid of a defiant subject.

The BaTawana Version of the Lishora Massacre

A substantive BaTawana account of their military campaign against the Vagciriku and the Vashambyu along the Kavango and Kwito rivers is contained in an important statement that was written down by a Sergeant Edwin Lloyd. The BaTawana statement was sent to Cape Town to Dr Rutherford Harris, who was then Secretary of the British-South African Company (BSACo). It is entitled 'Statement sent by Sekhome, Chief of the BaTawana, Lake Ngami to Bathoen, Chief of the BaNwaketsi'.[11] The statement is said to have been made by Bäetsile who was *Kgosi* Sekgoma's personal messenger. It becomes evident in the statement that Bäetsile was himself a participant in the massacre of the unarmed Vagciriku men. As the statement was taken down by the BSACo officer, Sergeant Edwin Lloyd, it is possible that *Kgosi* Sekgoma and his messenger Bäetsile prepared the statement to persuade the officer that they were a strong military force and clever strategists.

The fact that a statement meant for *Kgosi* Bathoen of the BaNwangetse was also sent to the Secretary of the BSACo, Dr Rutherford Harris, suggests that the chartered company had a particular interest in the whole matter. The BSACo had been formed in 1889 by Cecil Rhodes as a vehicle for the economic and colonial penetration of Africa and this suggests the wider framework within which the incident must be placed. The BaTawana statement indicates that *Kgosi* Sekgoma and Baetsile believed that *Hompa* Nyangana was not responsible for his people's massacre as some oral sources suggest. Unlike, the Vagciriku and Vashambyu versions of the causes of the Lishora Massacre, which seem to place all the blame on *Hompa* Nyangana, the BaTawana's statement actually describes him as innocent and even naïve about the *Kgosi* Sekgoma intentions.

The BaTawana statement does not make any reference to the claim made in local oral tradition that *Hompa* Nyangana invited *Kgosi* Sekgoma to attack *Hompaghona* (Prince) Kanyetu of Shambyu because the latter had stolen his wife Katiku kaSheshere. The version drawn from oral tradition argues that the Massacre should be seen within the context of a historical tension between *Hompa* Nyangana and *Hompaghona* Kanyetu, based on their feud over a woman and Nyangana's insecurity regarding a possible challenge to his

---

11 BNARS: HC 144. Statement dated 4 September 1894 sent by Sekhome, Chief of the Batawana, Lake Ngami, to Bathoen, Chief of the Banwaketsi, p. 1.

rule by his own maternal relatives. Before 1890, Hompa Nyangana was alleged to have sought assistance from the BaTawana ruler, Moremi, to attack *Hompaghona* Kanyetu. Dr Fisch's Gciriku and Shambyu sources for her article (2007), claimed that the conflict over Katiku kaSheshere was the root cause of the Lishora Massacre. The attack was, therefore, meant to complete the defeat of *Hompaghona* Kanyetu and his followers.[12] However, in the oral accounts, the BaTawana attack on *Hompaghona* Kanyetu was repulsed with heavy losses and, therefore, *Kgosi* Sekgoma attacked the VaGciriku (Möhlig, 2001, p. 196). In the end, many of *Hompaghona* Kanyetu's followers were killed, including Kanyetu himself. In Kgosi Sekgoma's statement the BaTawana only acknowledged three casualties on their part in the battle.

The BaTawana statement does not indicate that *Hompa* Nyangana encouraged their attack on his own kingdom. *Kgosi* Sekgoma is quoted as responding to a challenge from *Hompa* Nyangana about the presence of his armed men by saying: 'we are not an army; we are passing on to hunt; you must lend us boats to cross the river'.[13] The statement also undermines the popular oral tradition of the Vashambyu and the Vagciriku that *Hompa* Nyangana collaborated with *Kgosi* Sekgoma to exterminate the Vashambyu led by *Hompaghona* Kanyetu at Malyo. The BaTawana statement claims that as he was suspicious of the BaTawana's intention in the area, *Hompa* Nyangana actually sent messengers to the village of *Hompaghona* Kanyetu to warn him about the BaTawana's approach. The same statement claims that, because of *Hompa* Nyangana's message, the people at *Hompaghona* Kanyetu's village were actually prepared and ready to defend themselves against the BaTawana.

The statement suggests a completely different motivation for the military campaign by the BaTawana. The statement indicates that the BaTawana had orders to execute able-bodied Vagciriku men and to capture *Hompa* Nyangana. *Kgosi* Sekgoma is quoted as having urged his soldiers to kill *Hompa* Nyangana. According to the statement, *Kgosi* Sekgoma suggested this plan to his soldiers as they were marching back to Ngamiland with their prisoners, but was prevented from executing it by one of his men named Chaune who reminded Sekgoma about the reason for their campaign. Chaune intervened by saying: 'No, is he not your witness? Will you not point to him as the man who killed white people, and tell the white people "here he is"?'[14] Chaune's intervention implies that white people had been killed by *Hompa* Nyangana, but that *Kgosi* Sekgoma had

---

12   According to Dr Fisch's sources, the woman in question was identified as 'Kashekere' and not as 'Katiku'. Amongst the Vagciriku, the name Katiku means 'a girl born at night'. It is the same name as Kasiku amongst the Vakwangali, Kathiku amongst the Hambukushu, Namasiku amongst the Aluyi and Nausiku in Oshiwambo. Katiku was her own name, whereas 'kaSheshere' explains 'whose daughter she was'. Thus, in this case Katiku kaSheshere means 'Katiku, the daughter of Sheshere'. The preposition 'ka' which precedes the name Sheshere means 'the child of'. Dr Fisch based her account on interviews and five of her informants were more than 90 years of age when she interviewed them in 1977-79 and 'all were still blessed with the gift of recollection.' Her informants also included the then ruling *Hompa* Linus Shashipapo whom she had interviewed in 1966. In this chapter the woman is referred to as Katiku kaSheshere.

13   BNARS: HC 144. Statement dated 4 September1894 sent by Sekhome, Chief of the Batawana, Lake Ngami, to Bathoen, Chief of the Banwaketsi, p.1.

14   In appreciation of Chaune's advice, *Kgosi* Sekgoma gave him a portion of the spoils of the battle, 5 women and 4 oxen. BNARS: HC 144. Statement dated 4 September 1894 sent by Sekhome, Chief of the BaTawana, Lake Ngami, to Bathoen, Chief of the Banwaketsi.

been implicated in those murders and that *Kgosi* Sekgoma needed evidence to challenge the allegation that he was the murderer.

Kgosi Sekgoma was later interviewed by Major Hamilton Goold-Adams, who after an earlier spell in the territory became the Resident Commissioner of Bechuanaland (1897-1901), regarding the death of the two traders, Phillip Wiesel and Robert Arthur Faraday, and about his attack on the Vagciriku (Main, 1996). On the 9 July 1896, Major Goold-Adams was, allegedly, informed by *Kgosi* Sekgoma that the BaTawana had decided to punish *Hompa* Nyangana because he had killed the two traders and some of his own people, the Vagciriku.[15] There is also a letter which quotes a German man, Georg Reinhardt, as stating that he was staying at *Kgosi* Sekgoma's place when Sekgoma came back from his Kavango campaign and that he saw everything that the BaTawana brought from there.[16]

Whilst the BaTawana blamed *Hompa* Nyangana for the murder of the white traders it is clear that a number of pieces of evidence (that appeared before the Vagciriku-Lishora Massacre) implicated *Kgosi* Sekgoma in the deaths. One was a letter written by a 'native' evangelist, Khukhwi Mogodi of Ngamiland, to John Moffat, an Assistant Commissioner of the Bechuanaland British Protectorate, who was stationed at Palapye. In the letter (dated 29 December 1893), Mogodi reported on a meeting at which he had been present. At the meeting, *Kgosi* Sekgoma was accused of having killed some white people by a German trader in Ngamiland, Franz Müller, who also claimed to have reported the case to the Cape Colony. Both *Kgosi* Sekgoma and *Hompa* Nyangana were implicated by Müller as having been involved in the murders.[17]

The Choreography of Power

Despite, or perhaps because of, the allegations that *Kgosi* Sekgoma was responsible for the death of the traders, he was persuaded to sign a treaty with the BSACo of Cecil John Rhodes. The archival narrative of the massacre thus becomes entangled with the history of competing colonial claims as a range of political actors sought to present indicators of power. Whilst the Bechuanaland Protectorate was extended to include Ngamiland and the BaTawana on 30 June 1890, colonial officials were not posted there until 1894. In October 1894 Headman J. Mashabbi of the BaTawana swore before Magistrate Walsh that the BSACo's agents had warned them that the Germans were going to come to ask for the heads of the white people that Nyangana had killed.[18] Faced with this threat, an alliance with the BSACo would provide 'protection'. However, in the statement *Kgosi* Sekgoma refuted claims by BSACo agents (Isaac Johan Bosman, Mathys Andries Joubert, Georg Reinhardt and Frederick Scheepers) that he had granted exclusive land

---

15   BNARS: HC 144. Major Hamilton Goold-Adams to Resident Commissioner.
16   BNARS: HC 144. A letter dated 20 June 1895 by Sir Percy Anderson from the British Foreign Office to Sir Edward Fairfield in the Colonial Office.
17   S. Shiremo, 'The Reign of Hompa Nyangana over the Vagciriku, Relations with Neighbouring Kingdoms, Politics and Challenges to his Leadership: An Era of Hostility and Violence, 1878-1924', (MA thesis, University of Namibia, 2010), pp. 110-111.
18   BNARS: HC 144. Affidavit sworn by J. Mashabbi to Magistrate, A.B. Walsh on 4 October 1894, at Nakalachwe.

and mineral concession rights in Ngamiland to the BSACo. He swore that when the BaTawana signed the papers they were under the impression that they were only signing a 'treaty of friendship' with the BSACo.[19]

Kgosi Sekgoma admitted that the BSACo agents had presented him with 'five' firearms and a wagon as gifts, which he had initially refused to accept but was eventually pressurised to take. At the time, no trader or European was allowed to trade guns and ammunitions to Africans without obtaining a licence/permit from the relevant government. The Bechuanaland British Protectorate's Proclamation to control the trade in guns and ammunition specified harsh punishments and fines to any trader who did not observe the ban. For example, Clause 37 of the High Commissioner's proclamation dated 9 May 1891 reads as follows:

> No person shall deliver to any other person any gun or pistol, any lock, stock, barrel, or other part of a gun or pistol, or any percussion caps, or any gunpowder or cartridges, or any lead, without the written sanction of a Resident Commissioner, Assistant Commissioner or Magistrate, under a penalty not exceeding five hundred pounds sterling, or under pain of imprisonment for any period not exceeding seven years.[20]

On 6 February 1894, shortly before the Lishora Massacre, the Assistant Commissioner, John Moffat, complained to the High Commissioner about Bosman and his colleagues' conduct in giving Martini-Henry breech-loading rifles to Sekgoma. He wrote '...the giving of breech-loading rifles is a breach of the Brussels Convention. I do not think that Messrs Reinhard and Bosman had a permit from the office of the Bechuanaland Protectorate.[21] At the time Bosman and colleagues entered Ngamiland, the import of weapons and ammunition was forbidden. Every wagon going from Bechuanaland to Ngamiland was searched for weapons, and whites could only bring a limited number of hunting weapons into the territory for their own personal use (Wilmsen, 1997, p. 240). However, Moffat made it very clear in his letter that the wagon of Bosman and colleagues was never searched for weapons as they had smuggled the guns into Ngamiland. He wrote that: 'Bosman and Reinhard passed through Kanye in October last – took the desert road to the Lake. My Informant here states that Bosman gave to Sekhome five breech loading rifles, which he himself saw'. When news of this criminal conduct reached the High Commissioner's office, the Chairman of the BSACo, Cecil John Rhodes, defended the actions of Bosman and his colleagues.[22]

The documentary evidence, therefore, suggests that the archival narrative of the 'massacre' of 1894 is entangled with that of economic imperialism, but the paper trail perhaps understates the complexity of the political relationships between the Vagcirku, Shambyu and BaTawana. In the late 1960s and early 1970s, Professor Thomas Tlou also

---

19   BNARS: HC 144. Affidavit sworn by Kgosi Sekgoma to magistrate A.B. Walsh on 4 October 1894 at Nakalachwe.
20   Bechuanaland Protectorate and B.S.A Company's Territory: High Commissioner's Notices & Proclamations, pp. 33-34.
21   BNARS: HC 144. A letter dated 6 Februrary 1894 by the Assistant Commissioner, John Moffat at Palapye to the High Commissioner at Cape Town.
22   BNARS: HC 144. A letter dated 9 March 1894 by Secretary of the BSACo to the High Commissioner.

gathered some oral evidence amongst the BaTawana regarding *Kgosi* Sekgoma's military campaign against the Vagciriku. According to the oral testimony of the BaTawana, *Kgosi* Sekgoma decided to launch the attack because he intended to extend his territory and capture the cattle of the Vakwangali and Gciriku (Tlou, 1985, p. 125).

Evaluating the Extent of the Massacre

In attacking the Vagciriku at Shantjefu, *Kgosi* Sekgoma used trickery to achieve his plans. Both oral and written versions on Lishora agree that through *Hompa* Nyangana, *Kgosi* Sekgoma managed to convince all the Vagciriku men to disarm completely, before he ordered his soldiers to open fire on them leading to the event being remembered as a 'massacre'. The reason for pretending to come with peaceful intentions and disarming the Vagciriku seemed to replicate the tactics of a Boer Commando Unit that had attacked the Vagciriku a few weeks earlier. *Kgosi* Sekgoma told Major Hamilton Goold-Adams that 'the Boers' had attacked the Vagciriku shortly before his forces arrived:

> On arrival there (they) found that the town had already been raided and burned by a party of Boers from their settlement in the Portuguese territory of Mossamedes, probably carried out to punish him for the aforesaid murder of the white men. Nyangana, on Sekgoma's arrival, being a refugee on the far side of the Okovango [sic].[23]

It appears that in this particular case, the Vagciriku men opened fire on the Boer Commando Unit first as they were suspicious that they had ill intentions. Axel Eriksson who led the Boer Commando Unit to Mossamedes in Angola related that when the Commando, consisting of 20 wagons, was crossing the river, 'the natives' (Vagciriku) opened a fierce fire towards them, but fled afterwards. The Boer Commando, however, burned five homesteads belonging to the Vagciriku' (Johansson, 2007, p. 68). As they anticipated retaliation, after having killed the two traders in 1892, the Vagciriku were alert. Although, the Boers burned some homesteads, not a single Mugciriku man or woman is reported to have been killed in this attack, as most of them retreated and took cover. However, when *Kgosi* Sekgoma's army approached it pretended to be a hunting party. At the time *Kgosi* Sekgoma and *Hompa* Nyangana seem to have enjoyed a close relationship. After the military encounter with the Boer Commando a few weeks before, *Kgosi* Sekgoma is reported to have promised 'bullet proof special medicine' to *Hompa* Nyangana – an apparently attractive offer.[24]

Whilst there are conflicting explanations of the cause of the Lishora Massacre, there seems to be unanimity about the extent of the casualties that the Vagciriku suffered. Both written and oral sources agree that the Vagciriku men were exterminated at Shantjefu by the BaTawana. Sekgoma's statement claimed 'all the Vagciriku men' came as requested and, upon instruction, 'they were killed to a man'. The statement supports the claim in Vagciriku

---

23   BNARS: HC 144. Major Hamilton Goold-Adams's report dated 9 July 1896 to Resident Commissioner.
24   BNARS: HC 144. Statement dated 4 September 1894 sent by Sekhome, Chief of the Batawana, Lake Ngami, to Bathoen, Chief of the Banwaketsi, p. 1.

oral history, which also states that almost all Vagciriku men were killed and that only a few survived.²⁵ Although, this incident occurred in 1894, the BaTawana used modern firearms, in particular Martini-Henry rifles. Unlike the old Muzzle-loaders, Martini-Henry breech-loading rifles could fire several shots in rapid succession. The impact of the shooting was greater because the attackers were mainly armed with these rapid fire rifles and only a few magazine-loading muskets (Tlou, 1985, p. 78). In a newspaper article in Botswana in 2001, it was claimed that for that expedition, Sekgoma mobilised a relatively small mobile force consisting of a few hundred horsemen all armed with modern rifles.²⁶ The article argued (without citing sources) that after surrendering their arms and capturing *Hompa* Nyangana, 'the BaTawana ambushed the now all defenceless Bagcereku [Vagciriku], whose resulting defeat was complete'.²⁷ It is against this background that the said event is best categorised as a massacre rather than as a *war* or a *battle* as some observers have labelled it. The people who were killed were defenceless and innocent, as they were under the impression that the BaTawana had come with peaceful intentions.

As there are no demographic statistics available about the population of the Vagciriku at the time, it is difficult to estimate the number of men who were killed. But, one can speculate that since the BaTawana army consisted of a few hundred mounted men and was armed with modern rifles, the casualties suffered by the Vagciriku men may have been in the hundreds. In 1878, Gerald McKiernan, who described the killing of his fellow American hunter and trader, Charles Thomas, by the Vagciriku wrote that in that attack *Hompa* Nyangana had between 200 and 300 hundred men (McKiernan, 1954, pp. 166-167). By 1894, this number could have increased to between 300 and 600 men. *Kgosi* Sekgoma persuaded all the Vagciriku men to come out because he claimed to have a special medicine that would make them bullet-proof. Gordon Gibson (1981, p. 164) pointed out that in 1898, through the intervention of a British Magistrate stationed at Maun (the capital of Ngamiland District in Bechuanaland), 1,200 Gciriku were freed, most of them women and children, suggesting that not less than 40 per cent of the original population perished in the Lishora Massacre, according to my estimates of the total Gciriku population at the time.²⁸

The Response of the British, German and Portuguese Colonial Powers

When the killing of the two European traders took place the current boundaries of Namibia, Botswana and Angola had been recently mapped by the Germans, British and Portuguese. A military response against the perpetrators was necessary to give substance to these boundaries which existed on paper only. Phillip Wiesel was a German subject and Robert Arthur Faraday was a Scot and thus a British subject. The two traders were killed in February or March 1892 in the Vagciriku area within the borders of German

---

25 George Mukoya (Interview:1989).
26 'Builders of Botswana', BOPA, 7 September, 2001. http://www.gov.bw/cgi-bin/news.cgi?d=20010907.
27 Ibid.
28 R.S. Shiremo (2002) 'The Lishora Massacre of 1893 and its effects on the Vagciriku Community' (BA research thesis, University of Namibia), p. 34.

South West Africa.[29] However, the BaTawana were British subjects and in 1894 when they attacked the Vashambyu and the Vagciriku, who were German and Portuguese colonial subjects respectively, they transgressed colonial borders. *Kgosi* Sekgoma of the BaTawana claimed that his people had attacked the Vagciriku to punish them because they had murdered the two European traders.

In 1894, the colonial powers had not established 'effective colonial control' over what are known as the Kavango Regions of Namibia, but were seeking to persuade traditional authorities to acknowledge their sovereignty. *Landeshauptmann* Major Curt von François, with a unit of German soldiers, visited the eastern Kavango in 1891. This visit took place only a year before the shooting of the two traders and three years before the Lishora Massacre. Surely, his visit was not only to give a message to the local inhabitants about German control of the territory but also to counter the possible influence of other foreign powers in the area? His visit immediately followed the proclamation in 1890 by the British of Ngamiland as part of the Bechuanaland Protectorate, although this was not immediately accompanied by the arrival of any British officials.[30] British officials only arrived in Ngamiland in 1894, as a direct response to *Kgosi* Sekgoma's expedition into Kavango in Namibia and Angola, which took that expedition through territories then claimed by the Germans and Portuguese. Before 1890, Ngamiland was outside British control but the BaTawana who ruled in the area had extended their own sphere of influence' deep into present day eastern Kavango in Namibia and Angola. However, the area was divided between the German and Portuguese colonies as stipulated in the German-Portuguese Boundary Treaty of 30 December 1886 (Hangula, 1993, pp. 19-20). The treaty stated that the course of the Kavango River would form the borderline between the two powers.

The killing of Wiesel and Faraday on the orders of *Hompa* Nyangana in German territory offended both the Germans and the British. Germany was offended because Phillip Wiesel was a German subject. Mogodi's letter provides evidence that traders told the BaTawana that the Germans were preparing to wage war against them in response to the murders.[31] The killing of subjects under German 'protection' could be interpreted as a sign of insubordination on the part of *Hompa* Nyangana and his people.

At the time of the Vagciriku-Lishora Massacre in 1894, Andries Lambert, Chief of the Kai-/Khauas Khoi in the Gobabis area, was executed by a firing squad led by *Landeshauptsmann* Major Theodor Leutwein, who was supported by BaTawana soldiers. Amongst other charges made against Chief Lambert, was the accusation that he had murdered a German trader and robbed a BaTawana settlement (Hillebrecht, 2002, p. 11). *Hompa* Nyangana's act of ordering and participating in the killing of Phillip Wiesel would have been seen as a similar crime. On the 28 June 1895, after *Hompa* Nyangana had been released from captivity by *Kgosi* Sekgoma, Sir Edward Fairfield from the Colonial Office in London wrote:

---

29   BNARS: HC 144. A letter dated 11 May 1896 by H. J. Poynton, trooper in charge at Rietfontein, to the Cape Police D.2 at Mafeking.
30   http://www.gov.bw/cgi-bin/news.cgi?d=20010907.
31   BNARS: HC 144. A copy of an extract from a letter dated 29 December 1893 of Khukhwi Mogodi to John Moffat, the Assistant Commissioner stationed at Palapye.

It seems probable that the murder took place within the German Protectorate, and, if so, the proper course would seem to be to send Nyangana, if he is still in Sekhome's custody, to the German authorities on the Damaraland border, if they can arrange to receive him, so that his alleged crime may be inquired into and dealt with.[32]

The British were offended by *Hompa* Nyangana's actions as Robert Arthur Faraday was a British subject. Anthony Sillery argues that despite this, the British Government was not willing to take action in case it sparked an international diplomatic incident. The British were not prepared to enter territories controlled by other colonial powers as this would mean the violation of international agreements and this might lead to military conflict. One can also speculate that the Germans found themselves in the same dilemma, as *Kgosi* Sekgoma, a Britsh subject, was also accused of involvement in the killing of Wiesels. In a letter dated 7 May 1895, William Goodenough, Acting British High Commissioner, stated that the British administration proposed measures to 'restrain' *Kgosi* Sekgoma's activities against the inhabitants of the German Protectorate (Sillery, 1965, pp. 187-188). The letter was clearly a response to *Kgosi* Sekgoma's attack on the Vashambyu and Vagciriku in German and Portuguese territories.

Though it appears evident that the authorities in German South West Africa would also have conducted their own enquiries regarding the killing of the two traders, the relevant reports and correspondence have yet to be located. In May 1896, W. Faraday, a brother of the late Robert Arthur Faraday, used a newspaper article from the *Western Daily* to raise the case:

> The German authorities are now instituting inquiries into the murder of a German named Weisel and of an Englishman named Faraday. They are supposed to have been murdered and robbed by a native chief to the north of Lake Ngami.[33]

He complained that the British authorities had been slow to investigate the death of his brother; however, the absence of any actual police presence by any of the colonial powers in the region at this date means that there was no effective investigation mechanism. The author of an article by the Botswana Press Agency (BOPA) in 2001 argued that the archival evidence is suspect because:

> In fact, like the British, at the time neither the Germans nor the Portuguese had any genuine administrative presence in the region. This resulted in confused correspondence between Berlin, Lisbon and London as to what exactly had occurred, with the hapless Nyangana initially being seen as the aggressor.[34]

---

32   BNARS: HC 144. A letter dated 28 June 1895 by Sir Edward Fairfield from the Colonial Office to Sir Percy Anderson of the Foreign Office.
33   BNARS: HC 144. *Western Daily* newspaper article (Exact date unknown).
34   'Builders of Botswana', *Daily News*, 7 September, 2001. < http://www.olddailynews.gov.bw/cgi-bin/news.cgi?d=20010907>. {Accessed on 10 April 2013}.

The argument might also explain why evidence regarding the massacre of the Vagciriku in 1894 from the side of the Portuguese has yet to be found. Shantjefu, the place where the Vagciriku men were assembled and massacred by the BaTawana, was actually inside 'Portuguese territory', in present-day Angola. Thus, the massacre was a clear violation of Portuguese territory by subjects of the British Bechuanaland Protectorate. One assumes that the Portuguese must, therefore, have commented on the issue, but these archival documents have also still to be obtained.

Conclusion

The case of the Vagciriku-Lishora Massacre provides a good example of the way in which the history of an African community has been fragmented between the archives of three colonial powers. The different versions of events indicate the different perspectives and agendas of those creating both the oral and the written sources. The Massacre has been largely ignored in Namibian historiography, perhaps because the popular account of events does not locate it within the dominant historical nationalist narrative of anti-colonial resistance and the independence struggle. However, this chapter has argued that an analysis of the causes of the Massacre must take account of the colonial context.

The killing of Wiesel and Faraday by the Vagciriku in 1892 should not be seen as having been simply motivated by robbery, but also as a response to European colonialism and colonial efforts to control the arms trade in order to maintain their technological military advantage. The oral tradition reduces the Massacre to the consequence of a domestic dispute. Access to the archives in Botswana and the new documentary evidence there enables a different interpretation that draws on the statement of the BaTawana and the colonial authorities. The different versions of the account of the Massacre can be best understood in terms of the negotiation of sovereignty between rival 'pre-colonial' African states and rival colonial powers. One of the attractions of history is that it can, and should, always be revisited.

References

Bierfert, A. (1913) 'Die Diriku'. In Voigt., B. (comp.) *Lesebuch Zur Heitmakunde von Deutsch Südwest Africa.* Stuttgart: Strecker and Schröder.

Fisch, M. (2007) 'The Tawana's Military Campaign into Kavango'. *Namibia Scientific Society.* Vol. 55.

Gibbons, H. (1904) *Africa: From the South to North Through Marotseland.* Massachusetts: Norwood Press.

Hangula, L. (1993) *The International Boundary of Namibia.* Windhoek: Gamsberg Macmillan.

Hillebrecht, W. (2002) How the Kai-lKhauas were robbed of their Land, *The Namibian,* 31 May.

Johansson, P. (2007) *The Trader King of Damaraland: Axel Eriksson, A Swedish Pioneer in Southern Africa.* Windhoek: Gamsberg Macmillan.

Main, E. (1996) *Man of Mafeking: The Bechuanaland Years of Sir Hamilton Goold-Adams 1884-1901.* Gaborone: The Botswana Society.

Mberema, K. P. S. (1988) *Gciriku Orthography.* Windhoek: Department of National Education.

Möhlig, W. (2001) 'From Oral History to Local History Textbook: Two Examples from Kavango Region, Namibia'. In Harniet-Sievers, A. *A Place in the World: New Local Historiographies from Africa and South Asia.* Leiden: Brill.

Möhlig, W. (2008) 'Naming Modern Concepts in RuManyo (Bantu Language of the Kavango)'. In Limpricht, C. and Biesele, M. (eds) *Heritage and Cultures in Modern Namibia-In-depth Views of the Country*. A TUCSIN Festschrift. Windhoek: Klaus Hess Publishers.

Mutorwa, J. (1996) *The Establishment of the Nyangana Roman Catholic Mission Station During the Reign of Hompa Nyangana.* Windhoek: Gamsberg Macmillan.

Passarge, S. (1905) 'Die Mambukuschu' *Globus*, Vol. 87, no 13.

Schulz, A. and Hammar, A. (1897) *The New Africa: A Journey up to the Chobe and down the Okavanga Rivers, A Record of Exploration and Sport.* London: William Heinemann.

Sillery, A. (1965) *Founding a Protectorate: History of Bechuanaland, 1885-1895*. London: Mouton & Co.

Shiremo, R. S. (2002) 'The Lishora Massacre of 1893 and its effects on the Vagciriku Community'. BA thesis. University of Namibia, Windhoek.

Shiremo, R. S. 2010. 'The Reign of Hompa Nyangana over the Vagciriku, Relations with Neighbouring Kingdoms, Politics and Challenges to his Leadership: An Era of Hostility and Violence, 1878-1924'. MA thesis. University of Namibia, Windhoek.

Tlou, T. (1985) *A History of Ngamiland 1750 to 1906: The Formation of an African State.* Gaborone: Macmillan Botswana.

Von François, C. (1899) *Deutsch Südwest Afrika: Geschichte der Kolonisation bis zum Ausbruch des Krieges mit Witbooi, April, 1893*. Berlin: Reimer.

Wilmsen, E. (ed.) (1997) *The Kalahari Ethnographies (1896-1898) of Siegfried Passarge.* Frankfurt: Rudiger Koppe Verlag.

Websites

http://www.gov.bw/cgi-bin/news.cgi?d=20010907

http://www.olddailynews.gov.bw/cgi-bin/news.cgi?d=20010907 *Daily News*, 'Builders of Botswana', 7 September 2001. {Accessed on 10 April 2013}.

Archival sources

Botswana National Archives and Record Services (BNARS)

Bechuanaland Protectorate and B.S.A Company's Territory: High Commissioner's Notices & Proclamations, pp. 33-34.

HC 144. Correspondence on Ngamiland Affairs and the Ghanzi District and Lake Ngami Police detachment

Copy of an extract from a letter dated 29 December 1893 of Khukhwi Mogodi to John Moffat, the Assistant Commissioner stationed at Palapye.

Letter dated 6 February 1894 by the Assistant Commissioner, John Moffat at Palapye to the High Commissioner at Cape Town.

Letter dated 9 March 1894 by Secretary of the BSACo to the High Commissioner.

Statement dated 4 September 1894 sent by Sekhome, Chief of the Batawana, Lake Ngami to Bathoen, Chief of the Banwaketsi.

Affidavit sworn by J. Mashabbi to Magistrate A.B. Walsh on 4 October 1894 at Nakalachwe.

Affidavit sworn by Kgosi Sekgoma to Magistrate A.B. Walsh on 4 October 1894 at Nakalachwe.

Letter dated 20 June 1895 by Sir Percy Anderson from the British Foreign Office to Sir Edward Fairfield in the Colonial Office.

Letter dated 28 June 1895 by Sir Edward Fairfield from the Colonial Office to Sir Percy Anderson of the Foreign Office.

Letter dated 10 December 1895 by Lieutenant Barre Phipps to the Resident Commissioner.

Letter dated 11 May 1896 by H.J. Poynton, trooper in charge at Rietfontein, to the Cape Police D.2 at Mafeking.

Major Hamilton Goold Adam's report dated 9 July 1896 to Resident Commissioner.

Western Daily Newspaper article (Exact date unknown).

4 Revolutionary Songs as a Response to Colonialism in Namibia

Petrus Angula Mbenzi

Introduction

Traditional songs in Africa were often used as a weapon against indiscipline in a society (Finnegan, 1970). Transgressors were ridiculed and shamed through singing when boys and girls met for social dancing in an open space (which usually took place in the evening) and vulgar language was hurled against the offender. Misdemeanours and the shameful acts of certain people were also criticized through action songs. On these occasions, the names of 'alleged' offenders were mentioned as well as the offences they had committed. These songs were also performed when people did teamwork for threshing, weeding and so forth.

During the struggle for independence, the same strategy was applied. Ruth Finnegan (1970, p. 273) argues that it would be a mistake to assume too easily that there is necessarily a complete break in continuity between traditional political poetry and that of modern politics. Songs were used to sensitise the oppressed to their plight and to expose the iniquities of the old regime. The proponents and protagonists of the apartheid system were criticised and Namibians were encouraged to resist oppressive laws. To boost their morale and demonstrate their indefatigable quest for emancipation from the yoke of colonialism, the People's Liberation Army of Namibia (PLAN) fighters composed various revolutionary songs.

With the attainment of independence, the popularity of these songs has dwindled. They are sung on rare occasions and it is feared that some songs may vanish with time if they are not properly recorded and documented to ensure their survival. As a result the historical events inherent in these songs may drift into obscurity. This chapter investigates the functions of revolutionary songs in the Namibian independence struggle and identifies their most important themes. The main aims of the chapter are to highlight the historical value of the songs and gauge their significance during the colonial era.

Theoretical Framework

There are other scholars who have investigated the role of songs in dismantling the shackles of colonialism in Africa. Finnegan (1970) investigates the role of songs in several African countries such as Rhodesia (now Zimbabwe), South Africa and Kenya and examines the content and form of such songs. She illustrates how these songs were performed to sensitise the oppressed to their plight. She also reveals the strategies used to perform these songs in order to avoid conflicts with the Government of the day. The approach used by Finnegan is employed in this chapter to analyse the role of revolutionary songs in Namibia. Chijere (2001) analyses the role of songs in the colonial and post-colonial era in Malawi. He points at the way in which songs were used to denigrate the apartheid regime and to glorify the then President of Malawi, Kamuzu Banda. In this chapter the concepts of the 'glorification' and 'denigration' of individuals, as applied by Chijere, are used to chronicle events which happened before the demise of colonialism in Namibia.

Methodology

The songs referenced in this chapter were collected between 2002 and 2004, with the help of Oshiwambo-speaking language students, when a total of 2000 songs were collected. A previous collection of songs had been made by Sabine Zinke (1992) who had travelled from East Germany to be a teacher in SWAPO's camps at Kwanza Sul, Angola. It was easy to obtain songs as many of my students had been politically active and could themselves remember most of the songs. Each student had to interview several people who were eager to impart their knowledge of songs. However, some people who were interviewed were reluctant to give the exact words of some songs claiming that they did not promote the new spirit of national reconciliation. The interpretation of songs also proved somewhat problematic as the composers of the songs were unknown. There seems to be very limited literature which deals with the role of songs in the liberation struggle in Namibia. In interpreting the messages of these songs I, therefore, had to rely heavily on my own personal experience.

Political Songs Expressing Suffering and How They Were Popularised

Namibians who worked on the contract labour system as farm labourers or mine workers were brutalised and exposed to incessant horrors. Those who survived the experience and returned to their place of origin told stories of the harsh treatment that had been meted out to them by their employers. Rumours circulated widely of workers who had disappeared without trace, and of people who had been killed and fed to pigs. (Nujoma, 2001, p. 23). The Founding Father, Sam Nujoma, argues that when he heard these horror stories of the exploitation of blacks by white farmers he used to sing a revolutionary song that he had learnt from other boys when they were herding cattle: 'I am going to make a problem with the whites'. (2001, p. 23).

In 1957, the Owambo contract labourers in Cape Town formed the Ovamboland People's Congress (OPC). They were inspired by their African National Congress counterparts. OPC's aim was to fight the exploitative contract labour system and the policies of the South West Africa Native Labour Association (SWANLA). The OPC was later renamed OPO (Ovamboland People's Organisation) which culminated in the formation of the South West Africa Peoples' Organisation (SWAPO) in 1960 – a name that was more inclusive as it covers the whole spectrum of Namibians. SWAPO used various strategies to sensitise the masses to their plight. One of the strategies was to use revolutionary songs to express various themes such as suffering or the need for revolt, or as an intercession for peace.

To express the suffering of Namibians at the hands of the White South Africans, various political songs were composed referring to specific events:

Ove li peni nava aluke
MuNamibia tu va mone
Twa hal'okumona omilongo nhatu
Kahumba kaNdola naMaxuilili
Ove li peni tu va mone...

(Where are they, they must return
We want to see the thirty [people]
Where are Kahumba KaNdola and Maxuilili?
We want to see them)[1]

This song makes a reference to thirty people who were arrested in 1966 and detained on Robben Island. They were found guilty of high treason under the Terrorism Act and sentenced to various sentences ranging up to life imprisonment. People who languished in jails were subjected to harsh treatment. Songs were composed to reveal the suffering the prisoners went through:

Aamwameme ya dhipagwa
Yamwe ya lemanekwa
Ya fikwa nomalusheno
OmolwaNambia
Li n' okawe nongopolo
Li n' omapya niimuna
Li n' efuta li n' omvula nomakuti go opola

(Our brothers are killed
Some are maimed
They are given electric shocks
For the sake of Namibia
It has diamonds and copper
It has fields and livestock
It has sea, rain and beautiful jungle)

While this song focuses on the atrocities committed against blacks, it also includes an ode to Namibia. Namibia is praised for her mineral wealth, natural resources and so forth. It was believed that Europeans had 'scrambled for Africa' in search of wealth in order to enrich their countries. This argument is clearly stated in the following verse:

---

1   Eliaser Tuhadeleni (known as Kaxumba kaNdola) was Accused Number One in the 1968 Terrorism Trial. Nathaniel Maxuilili was a SWAPO leader in Walvis Bay who was another of the accused in the trial.

Ouyamba womevi lyetu
Tawu tutwa mo
Ngaashi okawe nongopolo
Momina yaShomeya

(The wealth of our country
Is transported away from our country
Such as diamonds, and copper
From Tsumeb mine)

Songs also made references to important political events in the liberation struggle such as the Cassinga massacre, and forceful removal of blacks from the Old Location in Windhoek. According to Sabine Zinke in 'Songs of the Liberation Struggle':

> Songs are historical documents of the struggle of the Namibian people, under the leadership of SWAPO. Again and again the significant events and dates, for instance, the 26th August, the Kassinga massacre and others are sung. Thereby it is in no case a matter of a simple chronicle, but a partisanship received clearly in the artistic processing of facts. And again and again, in songs memorials are erected to the Namibian patriots (Zinke, c.1986, p. 25).

It is true that songs serve as a reservoir of historical records. There are still various events which are reflected in songs. Some of these events appear in songs only. The names of those who contributed to the liberation struggle and of those who opposed it are reflected in songs. The entire history of the liberation struggle can, in some ways, be chronicled in songs.

The songs expressing suffering were performed despite the ban placed on political activities by the colonial regime. There were forums for articulating the aspirations of the people through these songs. One of the forums was the radio service. Although South West Africa Broadcasting Corporation (SWABC) was strictly controlled by the colonial regime, songs were performed on the Radio under the flimsy pretext that they were traditional songs. In fact, often traditional songs were interpolated as political songs. Individual Oshiwambo traditional singers such as Iita yaKadha and Ndatoolomba yaLuwayo included revolutionary songs in their collection. In one of his songs, Iita yaKadha, sings:

Veta yiilumbu ahi dhipaga aantu
Shongola ngee kwe ya na mangiwe
Mangwe neembale a he nadho koohina

(The law of whites kills the people
If Shongola comes he should be tied
Be tied with palms leaves and return with
them to his motherland)

Here Iita yaKadha stresses the severity of the laws of the colonial regime. Shongola (the one with a whip) was a nickname for the Native Commissioner for Owamboland, Cocky Hahn, who had retired at the end of the Second World War after more than twenty five years in his post. He was given this name because he used to whip the natives in Ondangwa. The expression 'Tying a person with palm leaves' in Oshiwambo means that one must be killed.

Ndatoolomba yaLuwaya also criticises the deceit and cunning of a white man and calls for stringent action against him:

Yeeyee iilumbu ye tu kengelela
Yeeyee iilumbu ye tu enda meendunge
Yeeyee mauta etu naa ka lwe

(Yeeyee whites have deceived us
Yeyee whites have pulled tricks on us
Yeeyee our weapons should be used to fight)

The songs of both Iita and Ndatoolomba were played on the radio without being censored. It is not known whether the Owambo Administration was pleased with the performance of such songs or whether it did not take it seriously. White people were probably not aware of this widely broadcast criticism. Finnegan (1970, p. 284) argues:

> In a colonial situation in which political power was ultimately in the hands of foreigners, many of whom could not speak the local language, songs and poems had the double advantage of being ostensibly nothing to do with politics at all (unlike say, newspapers) and of being unintelligible to many of those in authority.

Apart from songs broadcast on SWABC, songs were also popularised through the 'Voice of Namibia' radio service. According to a SWAPO publication entitled *Namibia: Culture and the Liberation Struggle*:

> Some songs are sung in the various indigenous Namibian languages, some are sung in English, but they are all popularized through the Voice of Namibia radio programs which is beamed to Namibia daily, for hours from the national radio stations of Angola, Congo, Ethiopia, Tanzania, Zambia and Zimbabwe. As a result, the songs are well known and widely sung by the broad masses of our people in all parts of Namibia (SWAPO, c. 1986).

The other places where political songs could also be performed without any significant danger were churches and schools. In the colonial era one period a week in schools was allocated to music. Learners had to sing religious songs. However, what started as religious songs were often turned into political songs. These religious songs were parodied to suit the political agenda of the learners and also to conceal the true nature of the revolutionary songs. It was not easy for the teachers to stop the learners because this period was not supervised. Several teachers were also staunch supporters of SWAPO. It was also difficult to distinguish between some political songs and religious songs as some songs were a mixture of politics and religion:

Penduk' Mukwetu okwa sha eluwa lyetu tendela
Onena muupika tse tu ze, tal' omathimbo tu ga na
Uudhigu nomaluhodhi yakwetu moondholongo ye li
Iihuna notaa hepekwa
Madhengo notaa monithwa ×2
Omukwetu tu galikane, kuKalunga omunankondo
A kwathe yakwetu mbo wo moondholongo ye edhililwa

(Comrade wake up, the day has broken, dawn has broken
To get out of slavery today, watch the times we are in
Of difficulties and sorrow, our comrades are in jail
They are being tortured
They are subjected to beatings
Comrade, let us pray to God, the Almighty
To help our comrades who are kept in jail)

The Evangelical Lutheran Church in Namibia (ELCIN) even included political songs in its hymn book *Ehangano*, (ELCIN, 1985, p. 695). One song was popular and sung every Sunday:

Tate Kalunga, Tal' Oshigwana shetu
Neho lyolukeno Omuwa tu sil'ohenda

Mevi ndi lyetu maluhodhi tu ga na
Mbinzi oya tika Omuwa tu sil'ohenda
Tate lotitha iihuna mevi lyetu
Nkugo yetu uva Omuwa tu sil'ohenda

Tate u tu shi otse aadhinwalela
Mokati kiigwana, Omuwa tu sil'ohenda
Tate dhima po mayonagulo getu
Twa yono kungoye Omuwa tu sil'ohenda

(God, our Father have mercy upon our nation
With a merciful eye, Lord have mercy upon us

In our land we have sorrows
Blood has been shed, Lord have mercy upon us
Father, cease the iniquities among us
Hear our cry, Lord have mercy upon us.

Lord you know we are the downtrodden
Among the nation, Lord have mercy upon us
Father forgive our trespasses
We have sinned against you)

This song was accompanied by a prayer for peace and the cessation of hostilities, and the safe return of the then exiled people to their motherland. Some collaborators in the Owambo administration called for the banning of this song because it was political in nature, but the church stood its ground and argued that the song was aimed at calling on God to end the suffering and atrocities in Namibia. Writing on political songs in South Africa, Finnegan (1970, p. 283) states:

> In certain circumstances hymns can have similar overtones. Some of the religious verses of the South African separatist churches founded by Shembe express political aspirations and ideals that are difficult to communicate through more formal political channels. More explicitly political are some of the performances of the originally Methodist inspired hymn *Nkosi sikele iAfrica* (God bless Africa) which is used as a political song in meetings of the African National Congress and other political contexts, the Mau Mau hymns and the way in which during Nkrumah's imprisonment by the colonial authorities, political protest was expressed by the singing of Christian hymns…

Songs as a Response to Colonial Regime Propaganda

The colonial regime carried out propaganda activities against SWAPO. Both the print and electronic media were used to spread propaganda. Through the propaganda machine SWAPO was portrayed as a communist organisation which was against Christianity. It was also reported on the South West Africa Broadcasting Corporation (SWABC) that the people in exile suffered from hunger and had no food reserves. Materials containing South African Defence Force (SADF) and South West Africa Territorial Force (SWATF) propaganda stated that:

> Communists don't believe in God or in our immortal soul inside us. They persecute religion. With that they deny the three first commandments: Thou shall not have a strange God before me; thou shall not take God's name in vain; Thou shall keep the Sabbath holy (Namakalu, 2004, p. 149).

In response to this propaganda, songs were composed to refute these false allegations:

Shiwana shetu sha kala nale
Sha lombwelwa omapuko noipupulu
Vati fy' ovadipai neetelelosha
Vati ohatu ly' omwiidi
Twa fa oinamwenyo
Omu moSWAPO ihashi ningwa

Shapo okoAmerica
Itashi ka ningwa

(Our nation has been told
Wrong things and lies
Allegedly we are murderers and terrorists
Allegedly we eat grass
Like animals
That is never done in SWAPO
Maybe it is done in America
It will never be done [in SWAPO])

The song refutes the allegations levelled against SWAPO by the colonial regime and depicts the Americans as the ones who commit the atrocities they are accused of. The statement made by Bishop Dumeni of the Evangelical Lutheran Church in Namibia (ELCIN) during a conference at St Peter's in Minnesota in 1987 is one of many by Namibian clergymen that asserted that SWAPO was not opposed to the church:

> SWAPO has churches in their refugee camps. The churches send chaplains to preach to the people in exile. Many SWAPO freedom fighters have been baptized and confirmed in the military camps. Does this sound like communism? (Dumeni, 1987)

The Americans were regarded as staunch supporters of the colonial regime; hence they are attacked in songs. In 1974 it was claimed on the radio by the former head of the Owambo administration, Fillemon Elifas, that hunger afflicted SWAPO:

> SWAPO attracts a large number of people, but does not have food for the people. SWAPO should return people to their motherland where there is plenty of food (South West Africa Broadcasting Corporation, Oshiwambo Service, 1974).

Claims that the residents of SWAPO camps were forced to eat grass was not the only propaganda made against SWAPO, there were also rumours that PLAN fighters used to turn into *omapumputu* (ground hornbills) and anthills. Such propaganda prompted the colonial forces to shoot the *omapumputu* dead in its attempt to eliminate SWAPO. Pseudo cultural youth organisations run by the army such as ETANGO, EZUVA, EJUVA and NAMWI in Owamboland, Hereroland, Kavango and Caprivi respectively conducted shows for the children in which they tried to indoctrinate them (Namakalu, 2004, p. 146).

The South African colonial administration attempted to establish a number of internal political structures based on ethnicity as an alternative to the nationalist politics of SWAPO and these culminated in the establishment of an interim government in Namibia. The establishment of the interim government was lampooned in songs:

Oukoloni medu letu inatu hala
Aawe nande
Aawe nande aawe nande
Kapangelo kopakathimbo inatu hala
Naka mbombwe naka tyanghulwe nolukaku
Opo se tuha pangelwe komadjailongo

(We do not want colonialism in our country
Not at all
Not at all, not at all
The interim government must be bombed
It must assaulted, it must be kicked with a shoe
So that we are not ruled by foreigners)

It must be noted that the members of the South West African Territorial Forces (SWATF), that contained the local Namibian recruits and fought with the South African forces against PLAN, composed counter-revolutionary songs. They thus parodied the songs of the liberation struggle to strengthen their position. In one of the songs Cornelius Ndjoba, who was the Chief Minister in the Ovamboland Legislative Assembly from 1975 to 1980, was depicted as the President of Namibia. This was copied and adapted from a liberation song which depicted Sam Nujoma as the President of Namibia.

The Denigration of Opponents and Glorification of SWAPO Leaders

During the liberation struggle the proponents of the apartheid system were denigrated through political songs. Some songs were peppered with destructive remarks and vulgar language. The protagonists of the apartheid system were targets of destructive criticism and lampooned to turn the masses against them, whilst the leaders in the liberation movement were flattered and extolled in several ways. Members of the Owambo administration were called names and abusive language was common in songs:

Ei ya topa mOshikuku otai londwele
Oshikumbu Mupekaka, hawe inamu tila
Opulana otai lu
Ei ya topa mOngwediva otai londwele oinyakwi yaKandove

(The gun fired in Oshikuku warns
The whore, Mupekaka, no, do not be afraid
The PLAN is fighting
The gun fired in Ongwediva warns
The tatters of Kandove)

Mupekaka was a female member of the Ovambo Legislative Assembly and Kandove was a senior army officer in Koevoet. In Oshiwambo the word *Oshikumbu* is used in reference to a woman who sleeps around or to a prostitute. It is not true that Mupekaka was a whore. The negative word was simply used to tarnish her image and encourage her to abandon her political ideology. Kandove was a head of the Koevoet unit which was notorious for hunting down PLAN fighters. Soldiers under his command were referred to as *oinyankwi* (worthless things). This derisive song was directed against specified people to tarnish their image. Similar abusive language is evident in a song in which Cornelius Ndjoba and Fillemon Elifas were ridiculed and attacked:

Lombweleni Ndjoba nomusi Elifas
Tatu ya tu ya longithe
Omudhimba Ndjoba
Nomusi Elifas
Otatu ya tu ya longithe

(Tell Ndjoba and the deceased Elifas
That we will teach them a lesson
The corpse Ndjoba and the deceased Elifas
We will teach them a lesson)

It is a taboo among Aawambo, where the two leaders hailed from, to refer to someone as deceased or a corpse while he/she is still alive. The lines attack the two leaders in the Owambo administration, Cornelius Ndjoba and Fillemon Elifas. The latter was the Prime Minister of Owambo while Ndjoba was the Minister of Education who later became the Prime Minister of Owambo after the assassination of Fillemon Elifas in 1975. It must be pointed out that members of the Owambo administration were also notorious for using vulgar language against SWAPO. The PLAN fighters were called *ookaandje* (jackals) and *omahwiyu* (owls) in the speeches of the leaders in the Owambo administration and propaganda posters depicted SWAPO as a hyena (Silvester, 2009, pp. 194 & 201).

Ndjoba and Fillemon Elifas (often locally known as 'Shuumbwa') were criticised for welcoming the establishment of homelands. The South African regime employed the divide and rule tactic and Namibia was divided into Bantustans according to the Odendaal Plan of 1964. Owamboland, for instance, was declared an independent state in May 1973 and in the ensuing years; the other homelands in Namibia were also declared 'independent states'. It was clear that many Namibians never accepted the homelands:

Uuyuni wonena tawu kongo omboloto
Tawu landitha po oshigwana
Shuumbwa ne nandjomba tamu tu topagula
Ts' inatu hala omavugumbo

(The world is after the bread
Selling out the nation
Shuumbwa and Ndjomba we do not want homelands
We are fighting for Namibia)

The message in the song was directed against the same two leaders. The innocuous remark in the first line makes reference to the fact that Shuumbwa and Ndjoba were accused of being more interested in their salaries and not concerned about the plight of the suffering nation. The South African President was vehemently criticised:

Shigwana shetu sha tukagulwa kuBotha
Momavigumbo shi shiwe
Shi kolonyekwe

(Our country is cut up by Botha
into homelands
So that it can be colonised)

The SWATF counteracted the opposition of SWAPO to the establishment of homelands by composing songs that praised the new developments:

Vambolanda oshilongo shi
Vambolanda evi ndi
Oshilongo oshiholike
Mu mwa kala ootate noomeme
Vambolanda evi ndi

(Vamboland is a country
Vamboland is a beloved country
In which our fathers and mothers live
Vamboland is a country)

This song was often sung during the military parade and was also performed during the opening ceremony of the Owambo Legislative Assembly. The Owambo administration had its 'national anthem', *Omuwa u yambeke evi lyetu* (Lord bless our land). It was taken from the ELCIN hymn book, formerly known as *Omaimbilo* (now *Ehangano*). President Botha was severely criticised in songs and depicted as an animal with a tail (in response to South African propaganda images that represented SWAPO's President, Sam Nujoma, as a hyena and other animals):

Botha paife otu li kwete momushila
Shila waBotha otwe wu teta ko

(We are holding Botha by his tail
We have cut off Botha's tail)

In this song Botha is depersonalised. It was a common practice to use zoomorphism to liken the supporters of the colonial regime to animals. To cut off someone's tail and hold it is also an Oshiwambo saying which means one's enemy is totally defeated.

The proponents of the colonial regime were likened to dogs as was the case with the members of the multiparty conference. This was an attempt by the South African regime to establish an internal settlement in Namibia in the mid-1980s. Those who betrayed the liberation struggle were called snakes. To call someone a snake means he was a traitor, treacherous, unreliable, a witch and, that, therefore, people should not socialise with him/her. One of the songs that was composed to denounce the attempts by the colonial regime to install the multi-party conference claimed:

Oombwa membwinda
Dha ngwangwana
Kadhi wete ko
Oshiwana kashi va hole
Sha loloka okulandithwa po

(The dogs in the multi-party conference
Are confused
They have lost vision
The nation does not like them
It is tired of being sold out)

This song refers to the members of the multi-party conference which included political parties such as the Democratic Turnhalle Alliance (DTA), SWANU (South West Africa National Union) and others who are referred to as 'dogs'. To call someone a dog is one of the worst swear words in Oshiwambo.

The establishment of the multi-party conference was a strategy used to show the world that democracy was at work in Namibia. An invitation was extended to SWAPO to join this conference, but SWAPO vehemently rejected this call and the institution was therefore criticised and satirised in songs. Writing on the functions of songs in Africa, Finnegan (1970, p. 276) states that derisive songs are often directed against unpopular individuals who are attacked in the lyrics of the songs. Such a trend is also typical of Oshiwambo traditional songs:

Selima gwaMulamba Selima
Selima omulali gweendingosho
Selima nani omukumbu gwowala

(Selima of Mulamba
Selima spends nights in shebeens
By the way Selima is a whore)

Finnegan (1970, p. 276) also argues that the faults and customs of others are ironically commented on or their accents are parodied and ridiculed.

Whereas the proponents of apartheid were attacked in songs, the leaders of SWAPO were extolled in songs for their bravery and determination to fight the colonial regime:

Olye ngoka te ende kombanda yomeya ×3
Halilwa Sam Nauyoma
Olye e tu p'ondjembo onene yombazuka
Hailwa Sema Nauyoma
Olye ta yamukul'omapulo getu Hilwa Sam Nauyoma

(Who is walking on the surface of water?
Comrade Sam Nauyoma [the variant form of Nujoma]
Who has given us Bazooka?
Comrade Sam Nauyoma
Who answers our questions?
Comrade Sam Nauyoma)

Originally this was a religious song based on the biblical text about the ability of Jesus to walk on water. It was thus converted into a political song to glorify Sam Nujoma as a leader of SWAPO. Nujoma was portrayed as the source of inspiration for the liberation struggle. The lyrics of one of the most popular songs in the liberation struggle were:

Sema ou li peni.
Yelula epandela.
MolwaNamibia

(Sam where are you?
Hoist the flag
For the sake of Namibia)

This song depicts Nujoma as the one who is able to lead Namibians to victory. This song is still popular amongst SWAPO supporters in independent Namibia. Apart from Nujoma, other heroes of Namibia are also exalted in songs:

Nehale okwe li kondjela
Mandume okwe li sila
Iipumbu okwa s'omupongekwa
Maherero naJannie Jonker oye li sila
Kutako okwe li kondjera...

(Nehale fought for it
Mandume died for it
Iipumbu died in captivity
Maherero and Jannie Jonker died for it
Kutako fought for it)

In this song there is a reference to Nehale lyaMpingana, the leader of eastern Ondonga, whose warriors attacked and defeated the Germans at Amutuni on 28 January 1904. There is another reference to King Mandume of the Aakwanyama who resisted the conquest of Oukwanyama by Portuguese, and there are references to the Herero and Nama leaders, Maharero and Jan Jonker Afrikaner. Samuel Maharero secretly planned and carried out a revolt against the Germans that started on 12 January 1904, and Jan Jonker Afrikaner also fought against the Germans. Hosea Kutako was the first black Namibian to petition the UN for the independence of Namibia in 1946. These leaders are exalted in songs because they resisted the occupation of Namibia by white South Africans and Germans. Singing about these early resistance leaders played an important role in creating a sense of a 'national' struggle for independence involving leaders (past and present) from all regions of Namibia. The song also created the sense of a historical continuity to the struggle in a similar fashion to the way in which ZANU (Zimbabwean African National Union) framed their struggle as the 'Second Chimurenga' in reference to the popular name 'Chimurenga' given to the first phase of resistance to colonialism in the late nineteenth century (Martin, 1981).

The song placed SWAPO within a historical narrative of resistance that claimed earlier local acts of resistance as part of the nationalist struggle against colonialism. The leaders of other countries who supported the cause for liberation of Namibia were also praised. The then President of Zambia, Kenneth Kaunda, and the President of Angola, Eduardo dos Santos, as well as Fidel Castro, the then president of Cuba, feature prominently in songs. It has to be noted that Zambia and Angola acted as host countries for Namibian refugees during the liberation struggle, hence the praise for the leaders of those countries. The Cuban forces in Angola carried out an onslaught against the colonial forces together with the PLAN fighters. Whilst those countries are extolled in songs, the USA and particularly its former President, Ronald Reagan, was derided in songs:

Reagan wedhu, wedhu
We tu lombwela Aakuba
Namibia ke shi Angola wedhu

(Reagan shame on you, shame on you
You told us about Cubans
Namibia is not Angola)

The United Nations (UN) adopted Resolution 435 in 1978 to pave the way for the independence of Namibia. However, the South African regime set a condition that the resolution could only be implemented if the Cuban troops withdrew totally from the Angolan territory. The linkage of the Cuban forces' withdrawal from Angola was supported by the Reagan Administration. It is for this reason that Reagan is attacked in songs.

Songs as a Unifying Force

Songs were used to promote national unity among the suffering masses in Africa. There was a call for the people to unite against a common enemy. Various slogans promoting unity often preceded these songs. Writing on liberation songs in Malawi, Chirwa (2001, p. 1) states:

> The target was the colonial system and those who collaborated with it. Surprisingly the names of the administrators, chiefs (who were regarded as agents of the colonial system) and those politicians who collaborated with the regime featured prominently in most of the songs. There was not much emphasis on Banda as a person though he was frequently mentioned in the songs. Wherever he was mentioned it was in connection with the nationalist struggle and the making of the Malawi nation, the pride of the people of the Malawi and their victory and not with Banda's personality as such. The name of the political leader was placed within the context of the collective process of the struggle and its achievement. The collective nationalist spirit was also reflected in the slogans that the majority of Malawian people could identify with. The cockerel and the slogan kwacha meaning dawn, which symbolized the coming of a new nation and a new political dispensation was stressed.

A similar situation also developed in Namibia during the liberation struggle. The name Nujoma was used frequently in songs to emphasise unity and collective responsibility and not to personalise the liberation movement. The slogan *Kwa yela kwa sha* ('The day has broken') was popular in Owambo in the 1960s, symbolising that it was high time to challenge the colonial authorities. Slogans such as 'One Namibia, One Nation; One Namibia, One Leader' (that being Sam Nujoma) were also popular as well as songs which were aimed at strengthening unity among Namibians:

> Let us unite
> Let us unite
> In the name, Namibia

The song was translated into various indigenous languages such as Otjiherero, Oshiwambo and Khoekhoegowab and so forth. It was sung when Namibians marched, and during political rallies. Similarly, the song: *Nkosi sekelel'iAfrica* (God bless Africa) also became widely popular in Africa and it was translated into several languages. It became the ANC's (African National Congress) party anthem. The melody of this song was also adopted by SWAPO for her anthem. Preaching unity was not confined to songs only, because the former President of Namibia, Dr Sam Nujoma, often stressed the significance of unity in dismantling the shackles of colonialism at political rallies, arguing that a united people striving for the common good of all people in the society would always emerge victorious. The popular slogans of SWAPO testify to the fact that unity was the core message in the political arena during the liberation struggle in Namibia: 'United we stand; Divided we fall'; 'A people united shall never be defeated'.

Music played an important role in SWAPO's camps in exile to create unity amongst recruits who had often never met 'Namibians' from other regions of the country, such as the Caprivi. Minette Mans argues that:

During the liberation struggle, the performance of *omaimbilo emanguluko* (freedom songs) and *uudhano wopankondjelo* (dance plays with liberation texts) in the exile camps was an important way of confirming and affirming ideology and maintaining patriotism (Manns, 2003b, p. 125).

Incitement and Revolt

The Macmillan English Dictionary defines 'incitement' as something that encourages people to be violent or commit crimes or the deliberate act of encouraging violence or crime. Incitement is one of the themes in the songs of the liberation movement. For example, there was a call to assassinate the colonial masters and their proponents:

Shigwana shaNamibia Vorster na Dhipagwe
Gwomwele, gwomwele
Gwondhimbo, gwondhimbo
Gwegonga, Gwegonga nogwekatananee

(People of Namibia, Vorster must be killed
One must take a knife
One must take a club
One must take a spear
One must take a panga)

This was a call to Namibians to take drastic measures against the colonial regime. John Vorster was singled out because he was the President of the South African regime at the time this song was being sung. The lyrics of the songs were subsequently updated to reflect changes in the leadership of the party and their opponents. Namibians were encouraged during the liberation struggle to use any means at their disposal to harm the colonialists and those perceived as collaborators. In one of the songs there was a serious, gendered, call on men to join the armed struggle:

Aana yaNamibia
Oshike ano mwa nik' onkulukadhi
Ne mwaa shi aakulukadhi
Thikameni tu kondjeni
Tu kondjitheni aatondi
Ye ya mevi lyetu Nambia

(Children of Namibia
Why do you behave as women
Yet you are not women
Stand up and fight
Let us fight the enemy
Who came in Namibia)

This song was directed to Namibian men to take up arms against the colonial regime. In Oshiwambo for example, a cowardly man is likened to a woman. Traditionally women were not expected at the battle front. This was not regarded as an allegation of female cowardice among women, but as a way of encouraging men to turn away from their cowardly behaviour. It was believed men become aggressive once they are likened to women. This was therefore a good strategy to encourage more men to join the liberation struggle. But it does not mean women never participated in the armed struggle. Their role in the decolonisation process cannot be ignored as some women were more active than men at the battlefront.

The high morale and fighting spirit among PLAN combatants were apparent from their freedom songs and other revolutionary songs known as '*Omayimbilo gomokahonde,* (literally meaning 'Songs that PLAN fighters sing having engaged with the enemy and caused enemy blood to flow'). The use of songs as an encouragement tool cut across Africa. Guma (1977) argues that songs are the dramatic poetry of many communities in Africa and that they are descriptive of the joys, sorrows, hopes and aspirations of individuals. Revolutionary songs reflect all the themes adumbrated in the preceding sentence. When the PLAN fighters gained victory over their enemies, songs were sung to signal victories:

Omutondi otwe mu ulikile moKwito quanavale
MoKwito okwe ya keengolo.

(We taught the enemy a lesson at Cuito Cuanavale
We brought him to his knees at Cuito Cuanavale)

It is widely believed that the enemy forces suffered heavy casualties at the battle of Cuito Cuanavale and that this battle forced the enemy to agree to the ceasefire process which culminated in the full implementation of the UN Resolution 435 (Maria Nahole, 2009: personal communication).

Conclusion

This study has shown that songs were used as an effective weapon against colonialism. These songs cannot be divorced from culture as Africans traditionally used songs to criticise their opponents. The suffering and torture carried out against Namibians during the war were criticised through songs. The leaders in the liberation movement SWAPO were often glorified in songs. Namibians were also motivated to fight colonialism with vigour and determination through songs.

Songs appear to have been a more powerful and diffusive form of propaganda than leaflets or newspapers, as they reached both literate and non-literate peoples and SWAPO's radio service, the Voice of Namibia, could be used to teach and spread songs of resistance. These revolutionary songs performed various functions to accelerate change in Namibia. Writing on the role of liberation songs in South Africa, Gray (2004, p. 99) argues that:

Liberation songs should be seen as a powerful building block to the past as they are a concrete form that echoes a collective cry of discontent by Black South Africans between 1912 and 1994. They are unique to South Africa and are part and parcel of the country's history. As such they are valuable educational tools which allow for a greater understanding of the liberation struggle and traditional culture.

The same argument could be applied to the important (and still growing) archive of Namibian liberation songs.

References

Chijere, C. W. (2001) 'Dancing Towards Dictatorship: Political songs and Popular Culture in Malawi', *Nordic Journal of African Studies* 10 (1).

Dumeni, K. (1987) 'The Cry of the Churches in Namibia'. Speech delivered at the National Namibia Conference, St. Peter, Minnesota, 20-22 March 1987.

ELCIN (1985) *Ehangano* hymnbook formerly known as *Omaimbilo*.

Finnegan, R. (1970) *Oral Literature in Africa*. Nairobi: Oxford University Press.

Gray, A-M. (2004) 'The Liberation Songs: An Important Voice of Black South Africans from 1912 to 1994', *Journal of Education*, 10 (33).

Guma, S. (1983) *The Form, Content and Technique of Traditional Literature in Southern Sotho*. Pretoria: Sigma Press.

Macmillan English Dictionary for Advanced Learners (2002) Oxford: Macmillan.

Manns, M. (2003a). *Music as Instrument of Unity and Diversity: Notes on a Namibian Landscape*. Uppsala: Nordiska Afrikainstitutet.

Manns, M. (2003b) 'State, Politics and Culture: The Case of Music'. In Melber, H. (ed.) *Re-examining Liberation in Namibia: Political Culture since Independence.* Uppsala: Nordiska Afrikainstitutet.

Martin, D. and Johnson, P. (1981) *The Struggle for Zimbabwe: The Chimurenga War*. Harare: Zimbabwe Publishing House.

Namakalu, O. (2004) *Armed Liberation Struggle. Some Accounts of Plan's Combat Operations*. Windhoek: Gamsberg Macmillan.

Namhila, E. N. (2005) *Kaxumba kaNdola: Man and Myth. The Biography of a Barefoot Soldier*. Basel: Basel Afrika Bibliographien.

Nujoma, S. (2001) *Where Others Wavered. The Autobiography of Sam Nujoma*. London: Panaf Books.

Silvester, J. (2009) 'The Struggle is Futile' – A Short Overview of anti-SWAPO Visual Propaganda'. In Miescher, G., Lorena Rizzo, L. and Silvester, J. (eds). *Posters in Action: Visuality in the Making of an African Nation*. Basler: Afrika Bibliographien.

SWAPO (c. 1986) *Namibia: Culture and the Liberation Struggle*. Luanda: Department of Information and Publicity.

Zinke, S. (c. 1986) 'Songs of the liberation struggle'. In *Namibia: Culture and the Liberation Struggle*. Luanda: SWAPO Department of Information and Publicity.

Zinke, S. (1992) *Neue Gesänge der Ovambo: musikethnologische Analysen zu namibischen Liedern*. Hauptbd, Volume 1. Humboldt-Universität.

5 Of Storying and Storing: 'Reading' Lichtenecker's Voice Recordings

Anette Hoffmann

No need to hear your voice when I can talk about you better than you can speak about yourself.
(bell hooks, 1990, p. 241)

Introduction

With the invention of the phonograph – or sound/voice writer – by Thomas Alva Edison in 1877, the human voice could become an object. What so far had been the elusive, ephemeral effect of sound waves could be captured and stored on Edison wax cylinders. As an object the voice could at once be separated from its source and social setting, become transportable, but also indexical to its absent referent. The phonograph, writes Erika Brady, 'was distinctively the product of 19th century scientific and social preoccupations' (1999, p. 11) of which the collecting of (exotic) objects was certainly one. The voice, conserved on wax cylinders, could become part of 'accumulative, item-centered, indexic' collections that were treasured by museums, academic institutions, as well as medical collections (1999, p. 14).

The new technology of voice-recording was almost immediately introduced to the study of folklore and to anthropology. Shortly after the recording of voice had become possible, its storage was institutionalised. In Berlin the Phonogramm-Archiv was founded in 1900. Erich von Hornbostel, the Director of the Archive between 1905 and 1933, saw the aim of the archive as creating a collection of musical phonograms of all peoples of the world. The recordings were thought to provide comparative material of modes of expression – both in language and in music – that were deemed key to the cultural character of peoples.[1] Today the Phonogramm-Archiv in Berlin is one of several archives in Europe that host immense historical sound and voice collections from many formerly colonised countries.[2] To ensure the accumulation of such a comprehensive collection, it was the strategy of the archive to equip German researchers and travellers with a phonograph and wax cylinders. The German artist Hans Lichtenecker was one of them.

Hans Lichtenecker (1891-1988) went to Namibia (then South West Africa) in 1931 with the explicit aim of creating an 'archive of vanishing races'.[3] The target group for this archive were people Lichtenecker called '*Buschmänner und Hottentotten*'.

---

1 Until 1923 the Phonogramm-Archiv was associated to the Institute of Psychology.
2 See Ziegler (2006) and the portal *dismarc*, in which one can search for sound recordings in European archives <http://www.dismarc.org/> {Accessed on 15 March, 2011}.
3 Namibia Scientific Society. Hans Lichtenecker's Diary, (unpublished), page 1.

During his expedition he produced life-casts, photographs, registers of skin and hair colours, hair samples, a travelogue, and voice recordings on 57 wax cylinders.[4] Lichtenecker's recordings of voices in Namibia did not follow the preoccupations of linguistics or musicology; instead, he had the idea to *collect* the voices of 'natives' (*Eingeborenenstimmen*) as a supplement to their alleged 'racial features'. Lichtenecker regarded himself as an artist. Although he was commissioned by the German raciologist Eugen Fischer to take photographs in Rehoboth[5] and had learned to make casts from Theodor Mollison at the University of Munich, he did not have the direct support of an academic institution in Germany. His idea was to reproduce the 'Face of Southwest' ('*Das Gesicht von Südwest*', which is also the title of his photo album).

---

[4] Not all of what the voices had to say can be retrieved. Some of the cylinders did not survive their journey to Leningrad – where they were taken as spoils of war by Russian soldiers during the last days of World War II – and only returned to the archive in 1990. Some of the cylinders became mouldy and the delicate wax relief that carries the voices has been destroyed. Of the 57 recorded cylinders that Lichtenecker brought back from Namibia, 41 are still intact. Transcribing and translating the recordings in Namibia was hard work for Memory Biwa, Levi Namaseb, Renathe Tjikundi and Rhyn Tjituka, who did the translations from Khoekhoegowab and Otjiherero in 2007-8. This was not only due to the background noise, the sometimes old-fashioned way of speaking, and the often obscure situation of the recordings, but also because of the 'pain in the voice' of some speakers, as Memory Biwa described it to me. I am deeply grateful for the dedicated work of translating and transcribing Memory, Rhyn, Levi and Renathe invested in the project. The digitising was funded by the Archives of Anti-Colonial Resistance and the Liberation Struggle (AACRLS) project in Windhoek and the Mopane Foundation in Windhoek. I am very grateful for their generous support, without which the digitalisation, reworking of the sound quality, and the translation and transcription of the recordings would not have been possible. Most of the translations and transcriptions can be found in Anette Hoffmann (2009) (ed.). *What We See. Reconsidering an Anthropometrical Collection from Southern Africa: Images, Voices and Versioning*. My own research was made possible by a postdoctoral fellowship at the Programme on the Study of Humanities in Africa, at the University of the Western Cape, South Africa. I am deeply grateful for having been granted this fellowship and excellent research and learning experience at UWC in 2007-8, and for being able to produce the exhibition 'What We See' from there. I also thank the Namibian Scientific Society for allowing me to use the photographs and diary of Hans Lichtenecker.

[5] Mollison and Fischer were raciologists. Fischer advised the National Socialists in questions of race and was one of the architects of the Nuremberg Laws (he was also actively involved in the sterilisation of the so-called '*Rheinlandbastarde*' – children whose parents were German women and African soldiers of the French Army). Lichtenecker saw Fischer as his mentor; he took photographs in Rehoboth for Fischer, who had conducted anthropometric research in the POW camps in Namibia and in Rehoboth in 1908. The photographs were used for Fischer's article 'Neue Rehobother Basterstudien. 1. Antlitzveränderung verschiedener Altersstufen bei Bastarden' (1938, see also Lichtenecker 1964). Lichtenecker travelled at his own expense, the casts he took were, to my knowledge, not delivered to Mollison, but were shown at the 'Kolonialausstellung' of the National Socialists in 1934 in Köln. Lichtenecker tried later to sell the casts, and the 'heads' he had produced from the casts. One of the 'heads' is held by the Naturkundemuseum in Vienna. Most of the casts were sold to the National Museum in Windhoek in the 1980s.

The collection produced by Hans Lichtenecker in Namibia in 1931 includes the recorded voices of people who were photographed, measured, and cast.[6] The life-casts he produced in Namibia, imprints of faces, heads, hands and feet, consisting of a wax-like substance,[7] were thought to realistically represent the features of 'racial types' (*Rassentypen*). In many cases people spoke into the phonograph immediately after they had gone through the suffocating and often terrifying procedure of cast-making. Especially in the recordings that were produced in the police station in Keetmanshoop, where most of the casts were made, the process of the cast-making resonates.[8] Lichtenecker did not understand these recordings as cultural expressions in terms of music or language,[9] and much less as part of a conversation. Knowing that he did not understand what they were saying, the people who were recorded at times spoke more freely than, no doubt, he realised.

---

[6] The photo-album Hans Lichtenecker produced of his expedition also has a photograph showing the 'digging up' of 'supposedly a Bushman grave' in the Namib, (*'ein vermeintliches Buschmangrab'* in the original caption), and a photograph of a skull. The original caption identifies it as the photograph of a *'Buschmannschädel aus der Namib'* (a bushman skull from the Namib). The skull does not appear in any of the parts of the Lichtenecker collection in Windhoek or in Berlin. It is not clear to me what happened to it. (All photographs and the diary are kept by the Namibian Scientific Society in Windhoek.) It was, however, not Lichtenecker's aim to collect human remains. The researchers from the German-speaking countries who 'collected' (in many cases this meant digging up graves, taking human remains from prisons, camps, etc.) skulls, heads, and other human remains in South Africa and Namibia, were mainly Eugen Fischer, Felix von Luschan, Gustav Fritsch, and Rudolph Pöch (Rudolph Virchow also conducted research on human remains he had ordered from South Africa). Most of the skulls seem to be held today at the Charité in Berlin. Complete human heads from Namibia were 'discovered' in the cellars of the University of Freiburg in 2009, and had probably been sent there for Fischer's research. However, if one considers the extent of the activity of 'collecting' and the institutions involved, one might still find more collections of human remains in museums in Germany. For an overview on the discussion on the collections, and questions of their return see: <http://www.freiburg-postkolonial.de/Seiten/anthropologische-schaedelsammlungen.htm>. {Accessed 8 April, 2011}.

[7] The material Lichtenecker used for the life-casts is called Negocoll.

[8] I have argued that the cast-making in the police station in Keetmanshoop worked with a 'performance of terror' that forced people to submit to the anthropometrical praxis. Interestingly, apart from 'working with' prisoners (which was also the strategy of Wilhelm Bleek for his research on 'Bushman' languages), Felix von Luschan had taken casts and produced recordings in the pass offices in Kimberley and Johannesburg in 1906. One might, therefore, link the racist practices of research in the twentieth century not merely to military subjugation (see Rassool and Legassick, 2009, p. 185; Hoffmann, 2011) but also to the systematic control of mobility and an ever-perfected system of surveillance.

[9] The Phonogramm-Archiv aimed at vocal or musical recordings as a representation of culture (see also Britta Lange, 2007, p. 318).

The Voice and the Archive

The right to opacity, which Glissant claims, is more fundamental than the right to difference, it is a right not to be understood.
(Celia M. Britton, 1999)

The colonial archive, as Premesh Lalu and others have argued, has the potential to organise the readings of historians (2008, p. 62). The division of Lichtenecker's collection that follows the logic of archival conventions, as well as the colonial politics of storage and collecting, are a case in point. According to the distinction of disciplines and the strategies of the archive in Berlin to accumulate examples of musical expression from all over the world, the recordings were stored as a collection of (voice-) objects in the Phonogramm-Archiv Berlin. The casts, together with the anthropometrical materials and registers, were sold to the National Museum in Windhoek in the 1980s, where they are stored today. The recordings were thus separated from the alleged 'archive of races' to which they speak. Especially in the voice recordings, different, and highly specific politics of accumulation, storing – but also storying – converge, and so do different narrative strategies that frame, conserve and give accounts of the expedition of 1931.[10] Lichtenecker's diary and the photo album narrate the tale of a journey to a former German colony as an adventurous endeavour of producing an 'archive of races'. The recorded voices are more difficult to read. Not only does the situation in which people were speaking often remain obscure, but the strategies of narrative and poetic framing are complex, metaphorical, and difficult to decode. Still, the accounts and speech acts of people who were recorded create interventions: allowing for the eruption of critique that reveals the irreconcilability of different attempts to frame or narrate the events of making casts in Namibia in 1931. In many cases, the people who were recorded immediately after their casts were taken, spoke directly of and to the experience of the cast-making. Their accounts give insights into the immediate violence of the project. Friedrich Blauw from southern Namibia, for instance, is cited in Lichtenecker's catalogue as follows:

> *Ich wurde heute morgen von einem Polizisten geholt und hierher gebracht. Hier wurde mir und einem anderen Jungen Zeug ins Gesicht geschmiert, das genau so aussieht wie ich, bloss es kann nicht reden.*

> I was fetched and brought here this morning by a policeman. Here another boy and I had this stuff smeared on the face that looks like me but cannot speak.[11]

---

10 The photographs and diary are held by the Namibian Scientific Society in Windhoek, and, in a digital version, at the Basler Afrika Bibliographien.
11 From Lichtenecker's original report at the Phonogramm-Archiv in Berlin, transcript of cylinder no. 26, the sound recording has been destroyed by water damage (translations from German: Anette Hoffmann).

In several other cases the speech acts or performances that were recorded seem to abscond from the immediate situation of the recording and refer to a larger colonial context of which the cast-making is but one situation.

If, as Lalu has argued, 'one cannot hope to retrieve a silence[d] subject […] by way of the colonial archive', and if the subaltern consciousness, voice, or agency cannot be retrieved through colonial texts (2008, pp. 62-63), what could the position of the recorded voice be?

This question touches upon the extensive debate on subalternity (a Gramscian term) and whether or not the archive, read against the grain, will yield a 'subaltern subject'. Since Gayatri Spivak's influential essay 'Can the Subaltern Speak?' (1988) and the founding of the Subaltern Studies Group (of historians) in India (1982) this debate has been of immense importance to postcolonial studies and historiography. Scholars of orature have often misinterpreted Spivak's question and stressed the ability of performers of orature to speak from and with specific genres.

Lichtenecker's recordings seem to speak to both points: on the one hand, the recordings (often entailing discernable fragments of oral archives) *did not* speak to Lichtenecker or any of his contemporaries (or 'the Germans' to whom they were at times explicitly addressed), because they were not in the position to do so and thus could neither be heard nor understood (and were neither translated nor made public in any way until 2009). At the same time, people did speak from within the position that the genres of orature allow for: in the encoded, opaque mode that did not need to be invented for the situation of the recordings, but was readily available from within the genres. Edouard Glissant's notion of opacity (1997) is essential here: it allows us to read the inscrutable utterances (of some of the recordings) not as muteness (the inability to speak) but as a strategy of defence against the objectifying investigation that was operative in this case. Speaking in an opaque manner allows the person who is the designed 'object' of research to give in to the epistemic violence only up to a certain point, by withdrawing into the position of an incomprehensible, unreadable *image*. He or she becomes the object of the investigative gaze, and *only* this, not merely because she or he is not granted the position to speak (back) but because his or her utterances are irreducibly dense to the point of complete inscrutability. In other words: Haneb's utterances (and those of other speakers) retreat into the rich (and for Lichtenecker unknown) repertoire of allegoric orature permitted to speak without engaging with the aggressive investigator. In this way, comments *were* articulated and can be discussed within the framework and discourse of recent postcolonial scholarship (see Sonderegger, 2009; Hoffmann, 2009a, 2009b, and 2011).

Clearly, the speaking voice relates differently to the person who speaks than, say, the minutes of a trial that write of or about a person. At the same time the voice we hear today often cannot be read as an uncomplicated indicator of personal subjectivity or agency. Let me explain: the recorded voices of Lichtenecker's collection are highly mediated, first, in terms of the rationale that has brought about the praxis of recording – the anthropometrical practice that did indeed silence the voices, for it did not allow for a conversation – but also by means of recording technique, situation, and context. Additionally, people – as in the case of Wilfried Tjiueza – often spoke in specific, often highly opaque genres of orature (praise poetry, or *omitandu* belong to those genres) that do not transmit a clear position of authorship. Still, we deal with a situation that differs from the taking of photographs both in terms of position and in regard of the possibilities of the person to structure and create the recording: the speaker utters, and therefore (at least to a certain extent) controls the words and the tone of the words that are spoken. He or she hears him/herself while speaking (whereas one usually cannot see oneself while being photographed). The recordings do not merely transmit speech or songs, they transmit voices, with all aspects of prosody, sequence, dialect, rhythm, (even of breathing), mood, and the generic features of the speech acts or performances. However, this palpable presence of the bodily or personal trace of the speaker does not alleviate the reading or understanding of the specific speech act.

It is within the genres of speech that the 'storying', which is also a culturally specific praxis of storing, occurs. The recordings transmit hints or fragmentary comments encapsulated in stories or poetry, which allow for a tracing of people's assessments of the situation of cast-making. Storied in narrations or poetry, those hints are smuggled into the colonial archives, thereby transgressing the usual flow of information.

Fragments

The fragments of stories and historiology one can find in Lichtenecker's recordings speak to the project of racial classification, which was the reason and rationale for their production. These traces allude to, but do not tell this other story. Listening to those recordings today one does register an absence, the disappearance of stories or (at that time) contemporary discourses, but it is not within the scope of scholarly licence to *create* the stories that we search for – that is the work of literature. Often speaking to the anthropometrical project, the recorded voices bear witness to the absence, or disappearance of subaltern narrations, to stories that remained outside the (colonial) record and cannot be retrieved.

What makes the conserved voices appear uncanny is, therefore, not only their disembodied quality, as 'mere' voices, and the fact that they speak but do not explain, but also their reference to the traceable absence of stories which appear as dismembered sonic remains (and reminders). Reading the fragments that the recordings provide, one faces a complex exercise of identifying genres, rhetorical figures and tropes that lie outside the immediate context of the recordings. As in any other historiographic or historiologic narrative, attention to the generic properties and features of the speech acts are vital for any close reading of the recordings.[12]

People who spoke into the phonograph applied different strategies of storying or emplotment,[13] tapping into different archives of oral and written texts. The genres of speech vary from citations of praise poetry, to fragments of, or complete versions of

---

[12] For a lucid reading of the politics of evaluating oral texts and recent debates on orature and historiography, see Hamilton, 2002.

[13] Hayden White's notion of emplotment is very useful here; it can also describe the narrative encodation of experiences, narrated episodes of peoples' lives, or past experiences. At the same time his idea of the universal archetypes of emplotment (romance, satire, tragedy and comedy) does not hold when one deals with African modes of narrative or poetry, which create and transmit (historical) events (see White, 1973 and 2006).

stories, and personal memories. In the following I will look into two people's accounts that were given in different recording situations during Lichtenecker's expedition in 1931.

Petrus Goliath. Explaining the experience of cast-making:
'I could not breathe with my mouth...'

Figure 5.1 Petrus Goliath and Willem (no surname mentioned) look at
a cast shown to them by Hans Lichtenecker
(Photo from Lichtenecker's Photo Album. Courtesy of the Namibian
Scientific Society in Windhoek)

Petrus Goliath spoke into the phonograph in the police station in Witpütz, where he had undergone the procedure of being measured, photographed, had been asked about his genealogy, and had been cast in August 1931. He gives the following account (wax cylinder 23):[14]

---

14 The transcription reads as follows: *O xū-e ||nâu tama i tsî mûde ǂgan tsî |nāti nēpa ra |ō xūn hoan nēn ge... Tātse ta ams !nâsa |om ||oa. ǂGaede ǂgan, ǂgaede, mû|û, mû|û ti ra hî. ... Tsî ta go |aesen, |â aosenni xa |â. Tsî ta go nēsisa a ||khowa-aihe o ta ge nēsi toxopa go |omsa go hō.*
  |Gui !nâsa ta ge !Garib !nâ go tsâ. !Apu-e ta ge ||khāti ūhâ i. O ta ge !gam ||gammi !nâ goman xa ||gôa-ūhe tsî ge tsâ. O ta ge gomaǂareb ai ge !khō tsî ta ge !apu-e ge ||nāxū. Tsî ta ge mûs |guisa ge hîta. Tsî ta ge gomab xa ge... tsî ta ge a ||nā o ta ge gomaba ǂareb ai !khō ob ge gomaba nēpa uri. O ta |khomtse gomaba ǂoaxa o ta ge tita ge ǂgâ. Tsî khom ||nāti gere nēti dīgu, dīgu, dīgu, dīgu... Tsî ta ge ||nā dommi ai !Khūb xa a ūǂuihe... tsî ta ǂgao tama, tsî ta dī ||oa. Hî-î |ū ta a xū-i ge dī ||oa ta a-e xawe... End (transcribed by Levi Namaseb).

I did not hear anything, my eyes were blocked, and what was being played... but I could not breathe with my mouth, ears were blocked, ears were sore, sore, sore, sore, that is how it was and I sweated, wet, wet, wet from my sweat (laughing), and when it was lifted from my face, I was able to get my breath back.

One day I was swimming in the !Gariep,[15] I had a gun and the cows led me into deep waters and I swam and I held to the tail of the cow and let go of the gun...and the cow...and when I went in and held onto the cow's tail, the cow jumped, and when the cow came up, I went down and that is how we...and in that manner God took me out...I cannot do something that I do not know, but people... [16]

In the first part of the recording, Petrus Goliath gives a detailed report of his experience of the cast-making that he had just gone through. His laughter in-between seems to express relief after a stressful situation that had caused fear: 'I was able to get my breath back.' In the second part of his speech he elaborates on his figurative description – this time he speaks of nearly drowning in the !Gariep. In the mode of narratively leaving the situation he finds himself in and reaching into the past, Petrus Goliath intensifies his description, explaining the sensation of suffocation in the procedure of cast-making. Linking this experience to a situation in his life when he had nearly drowned, Petrus Goliath tapped into his 'personal archive' so as to make sense of and communicate a situation that had caused fear, pain, and loss of control. Telling this story to Willem (see footnote 16), and maybe, to an imagined audience,[17] Petrus Goliath shared his experience and made this rather unusual event accessible by means of the comparison to a more common experience – the suffocating sensation of almost drowning. Instead of blaming Hans Lichtenecker, Petrus Goliath puts his own experience of the anthropometric praxis at the centre of his account and thereby transmits his understanding of the situation to his audience.

---

15   The river on the southern border of Namibia that was named the Orange River in 1779 by an official of the Dutch East Indies Company.
16   Translation by Memory Biwa. Lichtenecker's catalogue says that this recording is a conversation between Petrus Goliath and Willem (no surname mentioned); it seems as if Petrus is telling the story to Willem, since there does not seem to be a second speaker.
17   Hein Willemse, a scholar working on orature in South Africa, has remarked at a conference in Namibia ('1904-2004 – Decontaminating the Namibian Past', University of Namibia, 2004) that in most cases he experienced people who spoke into a video camera or recording device, *expected* listeners and therefore addressed their performances or speech acts to an imagined audience. Without the presence of an audience any performance would be useless. In the case of Lichtenecker's recordings, there were several moments in which 'the Germans' or people in Germany were addressed (see Hoffmann, 2009).

Haneb. Comparing to Make Explicit:
'Oh my sister, my back is burning and I am powerless!'

The story does not express a practice.
It does not limit itself to telling about a movement. It makes it.
(Michel de Certeau, 2011, p. 81)

Figure 5.2 The hands of Haneb and Jatura are cast
(Photo from Lichtenecker's Photo Album. Courtesy of the Namibian
Scientific Society in Windhoek)

Haneb, for whom we have no surname, was working on the farm where Lichtenecker's journey through Namibia commenced. He was a Damara speaker, 17 years old, and came from Vaalgras in southern Namibia and, like most of the speakers, no other information about him could be found in Lichtenecker's record.[18] His recordings were produced when Lichtenecker tested his equipment on the farm where Haneb worked at the time. It might be for this reason that he appears on several recordings, but it is also possible that he liked speaking into the phonograph. Apart from telling the story of the Jackal and the Sun on two cylinders (3 and 4), he sings a song, which (as I learned only

---

18   In some cases we were able to identify people because they were well known, like for instance Isaak Witbooi and Andreas Goliath. In the case of Wilfred Tjiueza, we had the exceptional luck to meet his family (after circulating his photograph on Okahandja Day in 2007), especially his niece Rosa Kandanga, who was able to identify her uncle and was willing to speak about him (see Hoffmann 2009, p. 110). I thank Mr and Mrs Kandanga for sharing their time and memories with us.

recently) is part of a story.[19] Let me start with the 'Jackal and the Sun'. This is a story of a *mèsalliance* with no apparent solution: Jackal falls in love with the Sun and carries her on his back. When the Sun is burning his back he desperately tries to get rid of her, but cannot shake her off:

> ...Then the Jackal came where the Sun was sitting. And said: 'Oh what a pretty girl!'
> And he said: 'Come let me carry you on my back, my daughter!'
> And he took her. Then the Jackal carried the Sun and went. Then, after he carried the Sun she burned him. Then he said: 'O, my daughter, in the name of God let me go, so that I can take you off. Get down first I want to go and urinate.' He said like that. Then the Sun said: 'No, I was sitting on the ground.'
> Then the Jackal said: 'Please get down I want to go and defecate.'
> Then she said: 'I was sitting on the ground.'
> Then the Jackal ran and went under a tree. And he dug around the root of the tree. And he went in. Then the Sun said: 'No, I will not get off. You carried me on your back.'
> Then he said: 'Oh, my sister, my back is burning out and I am powerless.'
> Then the Sun at that moment said: 'No, I was on the ground. As I am there my brothers never carry me on their backs. Now, you fell in love with me and carried me on your back.'
> Then the Jackal said: 'Oh, my sister, I carried you on my back just because of love, but I now realize something about you, so get down from me first.'
> At that moment the Sun replied to the Jackal and said: 'No, I will not get off. I will sit on your back. You carried me on your back. As I am here when my brothers carry me, they don't ask me to get off their backs. They take me off their backs. Am I not a pretty girl of yours? Why do you want to take me off now? Let us get to your home.'[20]

'Jackal stories' are numerous and wide-spread in southern Namibia and South Africa. A version of the story has been written down by Wilhelm Bleek; this version appears to be an explanation for the 'scorched' (darker) fur on the back of the Jackal (1864). In most stories the figure of the Jackal is a trickster, the 'clever one, the arch-deceiver' (Maingard 1937, p.226), the one who manages to outwit (and actually *ride*) Hyena, Lion and Wolf, tricks the 'Baas' (Guenther 1999, p. 99) and is generally characterised as triumphing by means of 'guile and cheating' (Steinmetz 2007, p.179). Schmidt writes that the Jackal, being so clever, but also 'only human' – that is, sometimes being outwitted himself – appears to be a role-model within the societies that made him popular figure in stories. At the same time, Hendrik Witbooi was characterised by Herman Alverdes (1906), a German soldier in the colonial war as 'the Jackal of Jackals', which conveys a certain respect, but also refers to cheating and lying.[21]

---

[19] I thank Sigrid Schmidt for generously sharing her knowledge with me and sending me a written version of the story she had recorded with Christina Garises in 1993 (see Schmidt, 2001, pp. 108-111).

[20] Translation and transcription by Levi Namaseb.

[21] These entangled, mutual borrowings and characterisations are difficult to read. Sigrid Schmidt argues that southern African story-tellers borrowed from European 'Reynard the Fox' stories that had arrived at the Cape with the settlers. On the other hand, Khoekhoegowab speakers, who are said to have positively identified with the Jackal, are also identified with the Jackal by Germans and at the same time criticised for identifying with it (see Steinmetz, 2007, pp. 178-179; Schmidt, 1986, p. 180).

Interestingly the metaphor of the 'burning burden' that cannot be shaken off, which appears in this story, had been used before by Hendrik Witbooi in a letter to Samuel Maharero (May 1890). In this letter Witbooi warns against signing the 'protection treaty' with the Germans.[22] He writes: 'But what you have done now, surrendering yourself over to the government by another, by White people, thinking it is wisely planned: that will become to you like carrying the sun on your back' (Lau 1995, p. 55). Clearly Haneb and Hendrik Witbooi make use of the allegories of a shared archive of orature in Khoekhoegowab. The use of this story in the case of Haneb is much less explicit than the warning issued by Hendrik Witbooi. Owing to Haneb's status as a young man, his speech act is invested with much less authority than the 'voice' of Witbooi's letter. Did Haneb use the metaphor to refer to colonialism as a burden, or to define the socio-political situation in which he lived (or both)? Did he quote Hendrik Witbooi to give weight to his comparison? Was this quote a well-known (contemporary) rhetoric figure of reference to the predicament of colonialism? To whom did Haneb speak?

On cylinder no. 6, Wilfred Tjueza, who also worked on the farm Lichtenstein at the time, seems to reply to Haneb's story. He, too, tells the story of the Jackal and the Sun – but in his version, in Otjiherero, the Jackal manages to shake of his burden and run away. Did the farm workers speak mainly among themselves? Or did they envisage another audience?

Haneb's situation of being subjected to Lichtenecker's cast-making project speaks of the power relations of the time, and so do the stories he presents.[23] The pictures above show him having his fingerprints taken, and with his hand covered with the wax-like material from which the casts were made. The song Haneb chose to sing into the phonograph gives further hints for a possible reading of his attitude to and assessment of Lichtenecker's project. What sounds like a cheery little song actually transmits a text that refers to an experience of cruelty. This song was recorded on cylinder 52.

Some of them (male persons) said
Some of them said…
Some of them said: let's kill him
Some of them said…
Some of them said: what has this Damara said?
Some of them said he he he he
Some of them said…
Some of them said…
Some of them said: he he he he
Some of them said: let's beat him to death
Some of them said: what has this Damara said?

---

22   I asked Memory Biwa whether this story could be read as a comment on the colonial situation. She told me that Hendrik Witbooi had used this metaphor in the letter to Maharero. I thank Memory for sharing this insight.
23   The conditions of the production of the casts varied considerably, in different places, at different times and with different people. The making of casts on the farm might have been less forceful than for instance in the police station in Keetmanshoop, where most of the casts were produced in August 1931 (see Hoffmann, 2009).

Some of them said: let us kill him
Some of them said: what has this Damara said?
(lines repeated several times)[24]

Fortunately Sigrid Schmidt heard the song that was part of the exhibition 'What We See'[25] (shown in Cape Town and Basel in 2009) and was able to identify the singing as a fragment of a song that appears in a story called *The Poor Little Son and the Warriors*. The story goes as follows: a little Damara boy is left alone at home, while the women are in the *veld* to gather food and the men are hunting. The boy's name is !Hansoroxatsoab, which refers to his marginal (social) position, meaning 'the one who sits with his anus in the skins of veld onions' (Schmidt 2001, p. 172). In the story a group of Nama warriors arrive, with the intention to spy out the space because they are planning a night attack. It is their debate – whether or not to kill the little witness – that is transmitted in the song. The boy, who is not asked to give an account, sings the song to attract the women's attention on their return. Schmidt writes that this story exists in several versions; in all of them the protagonist is a neglected, sometimes orphaned child.[26]

The song is encapsulated in a story and it accounts for a strategy of enunciation from a rather subordinate position: the child, who is not asked to give an account of something that happened to him, is able to transfer information and describe a perilous situation as well as a threat to his family, and thus manages to rescue the group. His singing merely offers the information to the women, it does not directly address them. On a very basic level, the story conveys the position of a child in a dangerous situation and his witty response to it. Further, it speaks about smuggling messages of danger. Let me pause on the attempt to inform – or smuggle a message – for a moment. There were several instances, where people in southern Namibia tried to speak to 'the Germans' as a potential audience of the recordings.[27] In one case a complaint was issued: a man named Peterson (or Pieterse?) informs listeners that 'he had done service in the German army during the entire war, and they still owe him 50 Mark salary'.[28] Further, three men in white uniforms, Kapitein Andreas Goliath, Friedrich Goliath and Daniel Goliath came to the police station in Keetmanshoop – not to be cast, and they were not cast – but explicitly wishing to send their regards to Germany (see Hoffmann 2009). They spoke into the phonograph, and each had one photograph taken, in full uniform, wearing German 'Südwester' hats.[29] Their recordings (on cylinder 42) speak of the challenges of life in the south, of managing to teach children in schools and trying to

---

24 Translation by Memory Biwa.
25 The exhibition 'What We See' is based on Lichtenecker's visual, written and acoustic archive. The exhibition was first shown in the Slave Lodge (IZIKO Museums) in Cape Town, from February to end of May 2009 and from there it travelled to the Basler Afrika Bibliographien in Basel, Switzerland, to Vienna, Osnabrück and Berlin and was shown in Windhoek in August-September 2013 (see Hoffmann, 2009).
26 Sigrid Schmidt refers to versions of the theme/story that were written down by Dorothea Bleek (1929, p. 301), Matthias Guenther (1989, p. 152), and Roger Hewitt (1986, pp. 69-70).
27 Since none of the recordings was translated before 2007, the messages did not arrive at their addressee. Today, the recordings can also be heard at the National Archives in Windhoek.
28 From Lichtenecker's catalogue, transcription of cylinder 28 (destroyed), my translation.
29 Whereas others (also the women) were forced to bare their heads for the camera and for casting.

survive permanent hardship. Taken together, the messages appear like an attempt to open a conversation with a potential audience, thereby transgressing the boundaries that were set up by the anthropometrical endeavour that sought to turn the speech acts into examples of 'voices of natives' (that were to supplement Lichtenecker's 'archive of races'). This conversation did not take place (see also Hoffmann, 2009a and 2009b; Sonderegger, 2009).

Singing this song, (but choosing not to tell the story?), Haneb seems to perform or incorporate the role of the child as a witness, who is able to convey a warning. This appears to be a very elaborate strategy of articulation: 'playing' the child, he, too refers to a situation he is not asked to account for, since he was not asked to comment on what had happened to him in the situation of the recording. He (like everyone else who has been recorded)[30] was just requested to sing or speak into the phonograph. Like the boy in the story, Haneb uses the specific potential of voice and song to convey, or almost smuggle a message. Haneb 'stories' his assessment of the cast-making, as well as his own experience, by means of making use not only of the contents of a vast oral archive in Khoekhoegowab, but also of the strategies of articulation it allows for. He thus frames his own experience and produces meaning with the song's reference to a story that is known to him, but not told in this moment. What audience did he imagine? Are his Jackal story and song directed to an imagined audience or rather a clandestine communication with the people who were present during the recording (and who, apart from Lichtenecker was actually present)?

As with many of the cases of this collection, the actual 'scene' of recording cannot be reconstructed. Thus, there will be no exhaustive understanding of what exactly happened during Lichtenecker's journey, what people thought about it, or what exactly they tried to convey. Still, even staying with the fragments, a subaltern position and strategies of articulation from within this position emerge. Taken together, Haneb's speech acts refer to a burden, and to imminent danger. Haneb can also be seen as staging himself as a witness, who could only speak from the margins – since he was not asked to give an account of what happened to him, let alone what it felt like. Together with the speech acts of Friedrich Blauw and Petrus Goliath, who tell us what happened to them (being fetched by a policeman), and how it felt to be cast (suffocating, scary), we are listening to experiences that were not transmitted in Lichtenecker's adventurous travelogue.

These strategies of enunciation are intrinsically linked to the act of speaking in an opaque manner and to the archive of orature of which they make use. This archive allows the young man to borrow from the weight of Hendrik Witbooi's voice, and the significance of his allegoric image that operates as a warning. At the same time, Haneb manages to refer to the colonial situation without naming it. The codification of the song that comes with a story (which is not told at this moment) allows him to hint at imminent danger without explicitly specifying the threat.

My reading cannot account for the prosodic features of voice – that would be the work of scholars who speak Khoekhoegowab and are able to 'read' the tone, rhythm, and mood of the voices. Listening to these recordings as fragments, it becomes clear

---

30 Apart from the three men in white uniforms, Andreas, Daniel, and Friedrich Goliath, who came to send messages to Germany.

that they are not simply a supplement to Lichtenecker's narrative that is told by means of casts, photographs and a travelogue. Instead of rounding off the story told by Lichtenecker, the recordings disturb his narration, and thus complicate and expand our understanding of what happened during the recording and cast-making sessions. What is told on the recordings points towards considerably *other* experiences, specific readings of the situation, but also interpretations of history and moments of theorising (see Hoffmann, 2009b). Some recordings speak of colonial wars or even request reparations for the injuries of the colonial war (2009b, pp. 135-143).

Though the recordings do not convey uncomplicated or unmediated positions, listening and 'reading' historical sound recordings might, not unlike the interpretation of photographic archives, reveal a vast treasure of new sources for research into African histories. What can be read in many cases is not so much subjective agency or a specific position, but rather a use of discursive elements, genres, strategies of speech and acute assessments of specific events. More research into historical sound recordings, especially when done with a command of the languages in question, will allow for informed readings of historical discourses that are difficult to trace in the written or visual archives.

References

Alverdes, H. (1906) *Mein Tagebuch aus Südwest*. Oldenburg: Stalling Verlag.

Bleek, D. (1929) *Comparative Vocabulary of Bushman Languages*. Cambridge: Publication of the School of African Life and Language.

Bleek, W. H. I. (1864) *Reynard the Fox in Africa, or, Hottentot Fables and Tales*. London: Trübner.

Brady, E. (1999) *A Spiral Way. How the Phonograph Changed Ethnography*. Jackson: University Press of Mississippi.

Britton, C. M. (1999) *Edouard Glissant and Postcolonial Theory. Strategies of Language and Resistance*. Charlottesville and London: University of Virginia Press.

De Certeau, M. (2011) *The Practice of Everyday Life*. Berkeley: University of California Press.

Fischer, E. (1938) 'Neue Rehobother Basterstudien. 1. Antlitzveränderung verschiedener Altersstufen bei Bastarden'.

Glissant, E. (1997) *The Poetics of Relation*. Ann Arbor: University Press of Michigan.

Guenther, M. (1989) *Bushman Folktales: oral traditions of the Nharo of Botswana and the |Xam of the Cape*. Studien zur Kulturkunde 93. Stuttgart: Franz Steiner Verlag.

Guenther, M. (1999) *Tricksters and Trancers: Bushman Religion and Society*. Bloomington: Indiana University Press.

Hamilton, C. (2002) 'Living by Fluidity: Oral Histories, Material Custodies, and the Politics of Archiving'. In Hamilton, C. et al. (eds) *Refiguring the Archive*. Cape Town and Doordrecht: Springer.

Hewitt, R. (1986) *Structure, Meaning and Ritual in the Narratives of the Southern San*. Hamburg: Buske Verlag.

Hoffmann, A. (2009a) 'Widerspenstige Stimmen – Unruly Voices'. In Hoffmann, A. (ed.) *What We See. Reconsidering an Anthropometrical Collection from Southern Africa: Images, Voices, and Versioning.* Basel: Basler Afrika Bibliographien.

Hoffmann, A. (2009b) 'Finding Words (of Anger)'. In Hoffmann, A. (ed.) *What We See. Reconsidering an Anthropometrical Collection from Southern Africa: Images, Voices, and Versioning.* Basel: Basler Afrika Bibliographien.

Hoffmann, A. (2011) 'Glaubwürdige Inszenierungen. Die Produktion von Abformungen in der Polizeistation in Keetmannshoop im August 1931'. In Berner, M., Hoffmann, A. and Lange, B. (eds.). *Sensible Sammlungen. Aus dem anthropologischen Depot.* Hamburg: Fundus Verlag.

hooks, b. (1990) 'Marginality as a Site of Resistance'. In Ferguson, R. et al. (eds) *Out There: Marginalisation and Contemporary Culture.* New York: The New Museum of Contemporary Arts.

Lange, B. (2007) 'Ein Archiv von Stimmen. Kriegsgefange unter ethnographischer Beobachtung'. In Maye, H. et al. (eds.). *Original/Ton.* Konstanz: UVK Verlagsgesellschaft.

Lalu, P. (2008) *The Deaths of Hintsa. Postapartheid South Africa and the Shape of Recurring Pasts.* Cape Town: HSRC Press.

Lau, B. (1995) *The Hendrik Witbooi Papers.* Translated by A. Heywood and E. Maasdorp. 2nd edn. Windhoek: National Archives.

Lichtenstein H. (1812) *Travels in southern Africa in the years 1803, 1804, 1805 and 1806.* Schomburg Collection of Negro Literature and History. London: Henry Colburn. Republished by the Van Riebeeck Society, Cape Town, in 1930.

Lichtenecker, H. (1964) 'Meine Handlangerdienste.' In *Newsletter of the S. W. A. Scientific Society.* Vol. V, Nr. 6-7, Windhoek.

Lichtenecker, H. (1964) 'Warum Abformungen von Lebenden?' In *Newsletter of the S. W. A. Scientific Society.* Vol. VI, Nr. 9. Windhoek.

Maingard, L. F. (1937) 'The ǂKhomani Dialect, its Morphology and other Characteristics'. In Jones, J. D. R. and Doken, M. (eds). *Bushmen of the Southern Kalahari. Papers reprinted from Bantu Studies Volume X, no. 4 and Volume XI no. 3.* Johannesburg: University of Witwatersrand Press.

Namibia Scientific Society. Hans Lichtenecker's Diary (unpublished).

Rassool, C. and Legassick, M. (2009) 'South African Museums and Human Remains'. In Hoffmann, A. (ed.) *What We See. Reconsidering an Anthropometrical Collection from Southern Africa: Images, Voices, and Versioning.* Basel: Basler Afrika Bibliographien.

Schmidt, S. (1986) 'Tales and Beliefs about Eyes-on-His-Feet: the Interrelatedness of Khoisan Folklore'. In Biesele, M. et al. (eds) *The Past and the Future of !Kung Ethnography. Critical Reflections and Symbolic Perspectives. Essays in Honour of Lorna Marshall.* Hamburg: Helmut Buske Verlag.

Schmidt, S. (2001) *Tricksters, Monsters and Clever Girls. African Folktales, Texts and Discussions.* Köln: Rüdiger Köppe Verlag.

Sonderegger, R. (2009) 'What one does (not) hear. Approaching canned voices through Rancière'. In Hoffmann, A. (ed.) *What We See. Reconsidering an Anthropometrical Collection from Southern Africa: Images, Voices, and Versioning.* Basel: Basler Afrika Bibliographien.

Steinmetz, G. (2007) *The Devil's Handwriting. Precoloniality and the German Colonial State in Qingdao, Samoa, and Southwest Africa.* Chicago: The University of Chicago Press.

Spivak, G. C. (1988) 'Can the Subaltern Speak?' In Nelson, G. and Grossberg, L. (eds) *Marxism and the Interpretation of Culture*. Urbana: University of Illinois Press.

White, H. (1973) *Metahistory: the Historical Imagination in Nineteenth-Century Europe*. Baltimore: Johns Hopkins University Press.

White, H. (2006) 'Historical Discourse and Literature Writing'. In Korhonen, Kuisma (ed.) *Tropes for the Past. Hayden White and the History/Literature Debate*. Amsterdam and New York: Rodopi.

Ziegler, S. (2006) *Die Wachszylinder des Berliner Phonogramm-Archivs*, Berlin: Veröffentlichungen des Ethnologischen Museums Berlin.

6 Colonialism and the Development of the Contract Labour System in Kavango [1]

Kletus Muhena Likuwa

Introduction

The contract labour system in Namibia was a colonial invention and needs to be explored in the context of colonial historiography. Many scholars have written on the contract labour system in Namibia. However, while there is a general understanding of the system, the Kavango as a supplier of contract labour is neglected, as the historiography has largely focused on the supply of labour from the region that was labelled 'Ovamboland' (Clarence-Smith and Moorsom, 1977; Cronje and Cronje, 1979; Hishongwa, 1992; Kane Berman, 1972; McKittrick, 1998; Moorsom, 1989; Cooper, 2001). However, the area known today as the regions of Kavango East and Kavango West has a significant role in the history of migrant labour in Namibia and there is an opportunity to reassess the system using a different regional context.

Although labour recruitment in the Kavango had been on-going prior to 1925, it was unorganised with limited numbers of recruits collected by colonial officials, and it was only after 1925 that the South African administration finally managed to formalise labour recruitment. The formalisation of the contract labour system in the Kavango occurred with the formation of the Northern Labour Organisation (NLO) and Southern Labour Organisation (SLO) in 1925. These were later amalgamated into the South West Africa Native Labour Association (SWANLA) which recruited labourers from the Kavango and Ovambo in the early 1940s until the collapse of the contract labour system in 1972.

Using qualitative research methods to gather and analyse data, this paper employs oral interviews, archival and written sources to explain the encounters of the Kavango population with colonialism and asks why both German (1885-1915) and South African (1915-1989) colonial authorities needed labourers from Kavango, and what strategies the colonial administration used to extract labour. It explains why, despite the creation of a market for consumption of European goods in Kavango, fewer men went for contract work during the German colonial period than during the South African colonial period. Understanding the impact of colonialism on these communities provides the necessary background to explain the challenges colonial authorities faced with regard

---

[1] I would like to thank the Carl Schlettwein Foundation of Basel, Switzerland, for the financial support for my PhD studies at the University of the Western Cape. I also thank Professor Uma Dhupelia Mesthrie, my PhD supervisor, for her academic guidance and support for this chapter. I thank the Dean of Research Office of the University of the Western Cape for granting me funding for a writing fellowship.

to extracting labour from the Kavango for the colonial economy. The chapter underlines the importance of colonialism in the development of the contract labour system in the Kavango.

Colonialism in Kavango

Colonialism in Kavango, as in the rest of Namibia, did not begin with the German conquest of the country in 1885 but with the earlier activities of European travellers, hunters, traders and missionaries who paved the way for that conquest. Kavango encountered the first wave of colonialists in the form of European and American explorers, hunters and traders who had penetrated the area by the early 1850s.[2] By the time Germany claimed Namibia as a colony in 1884, European and American hunters and traders, therefore, had a long history of exploiting and destroying the natural resources, the wild life and the social and political lives of the communities of the Kavango. The introduction of European goods in the Kavango by European traders laid the foundation for a new western economic lifestyle among the Kavango as the European goods became the same type of goods men from the Kavango aspired to acquire during the contract labour system period.

In spite of the creation of the new colony of 'German South West Africa', the presence of the German imperial authorities in the Kavango was limited to visits by a handful of colonial officials to the area. Curt von François was the first official of the German administration in Namibia to explore the Kavango in 1891.[3] The German authorities faced infrastructural problems due to the lack of proper roads to travel to the Kavango, as well as the resistance of the local population, who were reluctant to accept a permanent colonial administration in their area. It might be argued that in most parts of Namibia, the nature of colonial control was first, European hunters and traders who introduced market capitalism that resulted in the economic control of the local population, while missionaries pacified the local inhabitants and undermined existing cultural and spiritual systems, with the final phase of colonialism being the permanent military occupation of an area by the German authorities. In the case of the Kavango, although European hunters and traders had attempted the first stages of economic exploitation, the arrival, acceptance and establishment of missionaries proved difficult. The people rejected the evangelists from Botswana many times, for example in 1883, King Diyeve of the Hambukushu refused to allow them to enter his territory (Magadla and Voltz, 2006, p. 65). As early as 1896, the German colonial authorities urged the Catholic Church to expand their mission establishment to the Kavango and support their endeavours.[4]

---

2   Records of traders to the region include Johan August Wahlberg who visited the Kavango around 1855 and Charles Andersson who was trading in the region in 1859.
3   Other prominent German colonial figures who 'explored' the Kavango included Lieutenant Otto Eggers (1899), Paul Jodka and Dr Gerber (1902), Richard Volkmann (1903), Captain Victor Franke (1906), Streiwolf (1906), Seiner (1908), Schultze (1908), Zawada (1909), Fischer (1909), von Heydebreck (1911) and von Zastrow (1911).
4   S. Shiremo (2005), 'The Role of Kavango Kings in the anti-colonial resistance: 1903 the year of unity and resistance'. Unpublished paper presented at a conference at Rundu College of Education.

The interest of the German administration in the establishment of missions was apparent when it appointed two fathers for the Windhoek station in 1896.[5] The task of the two Catholic missionaries in Windhoek was to find a way to expand into the Kavango, and in 1903, Father Josef Filliung and Father B. Hermann of the Windhoek mission station set off on their third expedition to the northern part of Namibia, accompanied by Father Ludwig Hermandung, Brother Joseph Bast and Brother Anselm Reinhard, and successfully reached the Kavango River at Nkurenkuru.[6] However this expedition was also a failure. The missionaries relied on an agreement that had, allegedly, been made by a German colonial official with the Kwangali *Hompa*,[7] Himarwa Ithete, earlier (in 1902), but when the missionaries arrived at Himarwa the following year, the *Hompa* denied any knowledge of such an agreement (Budack, 1976).

In anger and desperation for a mission settlement among the Kavango, the Fathers summoned a patrol from Grootfontein under *Oberleutnant* Volkmann, which arrived at the river on 12 April 1903. However, rather than generating 'shock and awe', the patrol only succeeded in placing the Chief in a more defiant mood. Volkmann, with the direct personal involvement of the two Roman Catholic missionaries, Hermandung and Nachwey, attacked and burned down the village of Uukwangali *Hompa* Himarwa, which resulted in casualties amongst the Vakwangali people. An attempt to establish a mission station with Chief Nampadi of the neighbouring Mbunza tribe also failed and the missionaries had to abandon their mission (Budack, 1976).

The Catholic missionary expeditions to Kavango were not merely spiritual missions but were directly connected to the agenda of the German imperial government to extend their political power over the Kavango populations (Hunke, 1996, p. 10). These initial encounters between the Kavango people and the German missionaries and troops in 1903 created a bad reputation for both the Catholic mission and the German colonial administration among the Kavango people. The collaborative attack by the German colonial troops and the Catholic missionaries on the Vakwangali in 1903 and later, the German attack on the Vashambyu suggested a collaborative effort by the German colonial administration, the Catholic missionaries and the white farmers. The people of Kavango did not distinguish between them. By 1910, Roman Catholic missionaries were accepted in Kavango only among the Vagciriku, thanks to Klemens Mbambo,[8] the son of *Hompa* Nyangana, who convinced his father to accept a missionary, as Shidonankuru[9] explained in an interview:

---

5   K. Dierks (2005), Colonial period: German rule, http://www.klausdierks.com/Chronology/contents.htm>
6   Oblates of Mary Immaculate, 100 years of OMI history in Namibia 1896-2005. <http://www.rcchurch.na/omi/History.htm>
7   *Hompa* is a term in a singular form, used by the people in the Kavango to refer to the traditional head of their ethnic group; the plural form would be *Vahompa*.
8   Klemens Mbambo was the first-born of *Hompa* Nyangana from his senior wife Nkayira. In the early 1890s, he was taken captive with his father by King Sekgoma of the Batawana. While in Botswana he attended a mission school where he learnt English. Although his father returned later in 1897 to Kavango, he remained in Botswana at the mission school and returned only later.
9   Shidonankuru's mother Tunapu and Klemens Mbambo were both children of *Hompa* Nyangana. This means, therefore, that Klemens Mbambo was the uncle of this interviewee (Shidonankuru) and that *Hompa* Nyangana was her grandfather.

Mbambo was the one who accepted our Djami and Pater Kuiverte [Bierfert] who later went to Mbukushu. He said 'I beg you dear father, do not chase the missionaries who have come with the wagon to come and teach the children, do not refuse. Allow them to begin a school to teach our children'. If it was for Nyangana alone, they [the missionaries] would have been slaughtered [Shidonankuru is laughing].[10]

The first establishment of the Roman Catholic mission station in Kavango is, therefore, credited to Klemens Mbambo rather than to *Hompa* Nyangana. The oral account supports the claim that *Hompa* Nyangana was personally extremely hostile to a missionary settlement in his kingdom. Even after allowing the Catholic missionaries to settle in his area, *Hompa* Nyangana had doubts about the presence and intentions of the missionaries, as Father Bierfert indicated:

One day he came to me and said that there was something that worried him a lot [literally: that he had something heavy on his mind], and asked for our help. Thereupon he narrated amply that some years ago, after the unfortunate war with the Germans, numerous Vaherero passed through his land and warned [cautioned] him of missionaries and that one day he would be experiencing the same as they experienced. They too used to accommodate missionaries, but then soldiers came, and these had now taken away their land. At this Njangana used an expression which in former times was frequently heard in Hereroland: 'The horse (the wagon) has destroyed the Herero people' (Bierfert, 1938, p. 23).

Thus, *Hompa* Nyangana was aware of the plight of the Herero people in central Namibia which came about from accepting missionaries, who in turn, collaborated with the German colonial troops to subdue the Herero nation. It shows *Hompa* Nyangana's concern that accepting missionaries in his area might be a stepping stone that would lead to a physical colonial presence and the eventual loss of power over his land and people, and submission to German colonial dominance. The German authorities established military posts in Kavango only in 1911 after the Catholic missionaries had established a settlement in 1910 (Van Tonder, 1966, p. 30). The chronology confirms the nature of German colonial settlement patterns in Namibia as described by Guido Weigend:

The missionaries made the natives dependent on the stations, the trading practices selectively favoured certain tribes and the missionaries urged natives to submit to German rule. The missions were a gruesome reality of colonialism in Namibia (Weigend, 1985, p. 161)

Weigend argues that, at that time, we cannot separate missionaries from colonialism as they were the vanguard of German colonialism in Namibia. This view is reinforced by the following words of one of the founding fathers of Catholic Mission scholarship, J Schmidlin, who argued:

---

10 Interview by the author with Shidonankuru, 15 June 2003, Gumma village.

The mission is one that spiritually conquers our colonies and assimilates them internally. The state may have the power to conquer and annex the protectorates at the external level; yet the deepest goal of colonial policy, the internal colonization, must be implemented with the help of the missions. The state could well enforce physical obedience through punishments and laws, yet it is the mission's duty to bring the natives to spiritual submission and devotion. In this context we may reverse the phrase pronounced by the secretary for the colonies, Dr. Solf, at the Reichstag, 'to colonize is to do mission work' into 'to do mission work is to colonize' (quoted in Hunke, 1996, p. 10).

The above statement is proof that when the Catholic mission came to Kavango it formed part of the early stages of German imperialism because to do mission work was to colonise, just as to colonise was to do mission work – a relationship encapsulated in the expression 'the civilising mission'. Little progress was therefore made with colonial labour extraction and migration in the absence of the missionaries.

During the early months of World War I (1914-1918), the German magistrate of Outjo and other German officers were shot at the Portuguese Police Post of Naulila and the Portuguese maintained that the first shots were fired by the Germans.[11] The result was the dispatch of a punitive expedition into Portuguese Territory in November 1914 under Col. Francke and the complete defeat of the Portuguese at Naulila. When the reports of the shooting of the German officers reached the administration,

reprisals were immediately authorised from the German Headquarters on the various Portuguese Police Posts on the border which were attacked without warning and their occupants killed. Amongst other posts, that at Fort Cuangar was attacked and the garrison killed. The Portuguese assert that the Germans were assisted by the Chief Kandjimi and his followers.[12]

Simon Kandere also alludes to the joint attack by the Germans and *Hompa* Kandjimi Hawanga on the Portuguese along the Kavango River:

The Germans came to fight the Portuguese. Hawanga told them 'let me first go across the river and encircle their ammunition store room before you start to shoot your weapons. He told them that 'when you will hear my gun shot you should also start shooting with your guns. The Portuguese will be running for their weapons and then I will kill all of them'. He went there and then shot his gun in the air. He indeed finished them off, every time a Portuguese came out he shot him with a bullet and only the Mullatos[13] were spared. All the Portuguese who were there were finished off. The graveyard you see at Nkurenkuru, who do you think killed them? It was Hawanga. He finished them off. You should have seen how the heavy guns were being shot from

---

[11] NAN ADM 30, file 243/3, vol. 2, 16 November 1917, Windhoek, SWA Administrator to Minister of Defence 'Administration of Okavango area: S.W.A. protectorate'.
[12] NAN ADM 30, file 243/3, vol. 3, Windhoek. Report entitled 'Patrol to Nkurenkuru' dated 16 January 1917 by Frank Brownlee to the Administrator of S.W.A.
[13] A mulatto refers to a person of mixed blood: Portuguese and black.

across [pause] ... the Germans were shooting from across the River while Kandjimi was on the camp busy killing the Portuguese. No bullet touched him.[14]

The Portuguese colonial officials, reportedly resented *Hompa* Kandjimi as they strongly believed: 'He had assisted in the German attack upon, and capture of Fort Cuangar in 1915 and had looted from the Portuguese certain arms, stock and goods.'[15]

The German victory over the Portuguese along the Kavango during the First World War was short-lived. Shortly afterwards, the South African troops under Lieutenant Lawson reached the Kavango and defeated the Germans in 1915. The first South African Military Regiment (S.A.M.R) that dislodged the German authorities' control of the Kavango in 1915 did not permanently occupy the former German posts and the Kavango was left as it had been since 1902 and continued to form part of the administrative district of Grootfontein.[16] The absence of a permanent South African colonial military structure along the Kavango left some former German officials still roaming around at liberty within the Kavango and continuing to trouble the local people, which prompted the return of South African troops under Major Brownlee to the Kavango on 23 August 1916, with the aim:

> to re-assure the natives who it was alleged were being tampered with by German agents and to deal with any German who might be found residing in that area and to establish relations with the Portuguese authorities on the border.[17]

The South African colonial officials made arrangements with the Portuguese officials (who had, since the defeat of Germans by South African troops, returned to their former colonial outposts) to control the Kavango population.[18] The arrangements allowed the people on both sides of the Kavango River to have free use of the river for the purposes of boating, fishing, watering of stock, etc.[19] It also allowed the people on either side of the Kavango river to cross and re-cross the river freely for visiting, business or other lawful purposes with no pass being necessary for such a crossing.[20] It was also agreed that no person from the Portuguese territory would be permitted to reside on the Protectorate side of the Kavango without the permission of the Portuguese authorities and *vice versa,* and that any person proceeding from one territory to the other for unlawful purposes or without a pass would be returned to the territory in which he

---

14 Transcribed interview by Shampapi Shiremo with Simon Nzamene Kandere, Rundu, Nkarapamwe, 31 July 2005, pp.12-13.
15 NAN ADM 30, file 243/3, vol. 3, Windhoek. Report entitled 'Patrol to Nkurenkuru' dated 16 January 1917 by Frank Brownlee to the Administrator of S.W.A.
16 NAN ADM 30, file 243/3, vol. 2, Windhoek. Letter from the Administrator of SWA to the Minister of Defence in Pretoria dated 16 November 1917 titled Administration of the Okavango area: SWA Protectorate.
17 Ibid.
18 NAN ADM 30, file 243/3, vol. 3, Windhoek. Report by Major Frank Brownlee titled 'Resumé of arrangements concluded between the Commandant Fort Cuangar and the Military Magistrate Grootfontein district on the 27 September 1917'.
19 Ibid.
20 Ibid.

or she resided by the authority of the other territory.²¹ Despite this arrangement for co-operation, the two colonial authorities had a lot of issues to settle to improve their relations. The South African colonial authorities demanded that the German colonial agents who had fled from the Namibian side of the Kavango to the Angolan side should be handed over to stand trial, but in response, the Portuguese demanded that before they would do this *Hompa* Kandjimi Hawanga of the Vakwangali should be captured and handed to them to stand trial for his attacks on the Portuguese during World War I.²² The persistent failure of effective co-operation between the South African and the Portuguese colonial authorities strained both their relationship and attempts at mutual political control over the Kavango.

The mistrust and lack of co-operation between the Portuguese and the South African colonial officials presented the *Vahompa* of the Kavango with an opportunity to manoeuvre around the Portuguese proposal for the creation of separate kingdoms on both sides of the Kavango River. The incumbent *Vahompa* resisted colonial advances that were against the idea of their existing status as rulers of both banks of the Kavango River and found ways to play one colonial power off against the other as a technique to maintain their *status quo*. In 1917, for instance, a Portuguese official who had not succeeded in convincing the *Vahompa* of Kavango to leave the Namibian side of the Kavango River and settle on the Angolan side, carried out an expedition to appoint some new *Vahompa* on the Angolan side of the Kavango. However, he encountered opposition and deception from the incumbent *Vahompa* who were resident on the Namibian side of the Kavango River. In the Vagciriku area, *Hompa* Nyangana convinced the Portuguese official that he would like to continue to be the *Hompa* on the Angolan side of the Kavango also.²³ *Hompa* Nyangana explained that the fact that he did not reside in Portuguese territory was because he had been forced to live near the Catholic mission station and that formerly the Germans had demanded this and now the South Africans were making the same demand.²⁴ *Hompa* Nyangana proposed sending some men to the protectorate authorities and asking for permission to return to his old abode on the Portuguese side of the border with part of his people and to leave the rest of his tribe with a new *Hompa* in the Protectorate.²⁵ *Hompa* Nyangana, however, did not mean a word that he said to the Portuguese official as he later admitted to a Portuguese official:

> You have on two occasions tried to get me to trek over the river to live in Portuguese territory. I again tell you that I will not do as you wish me to do. I shall remain in British territory.²⁶

---

21 Ibid.
22 NAN ADM 30, file 243/3, vol. 3. Report by Frank Brownlee to the secretary for the protectorate titled 'Patrol to Nkurenkuru' dated 16 January 1917.
23 NAN ADM 30, file 243/3, vol. 2. Letter from LTNT Col. Jose Carregado Vianna to the Military Magistrate of Grootfontein, 10 December 1917.
24 Ibid.
25 Ibid.
26 NAN ADM 30, file 243/3, vol. 2. Statements under oath attached to a letter of report by Major Frank Brownlee to Lieut. Hahn of Ovamboland administration, dated 24 April 1918.

In the Mbukushu area, *Fumu*[27] Disho on the Namibian side of the border warned the Portuguese official that if another *Fumu* was going to be appointed on the Angolan side of the Hambukushu he was going to fight that Portuguese-appointed *Fumu*.[28] Major Brownlee, a South African official, complained about Portuguese attempts to reconfigure traditional authorities: 'I conclude from the former letter that the Portuguese authorities at Cuangar are looking for trouble and that they are constantly irritating our natives.'[29] The case is a good example of the way in which the imposition of colonial boundaries fuelled political tension within traditional authorities that sought to maintain their own boundaries of authority, which transcended the new definitions of territory that were imposed on them.

The above indicates that the South African colonial authorities opposed the Portuguese strategy and were not ready to condone it. After 1917, a detachment of the South African army occupied a post at Nkurenkuru along the Kavango River and introduced regular military patrols along the river establishing a measure of political control over the area. The patrols indicate the competition between the Portuguese and South African colonial administrations for control of the population along the Kavango River. It is also clear that the traditional rulers in Kavango felt their power over their territory was threatened. The strategy of the kings was to align with one of the colonial powers as a means of continued survival and this meant supporting the colonial needs for the extraction of men from their area as contract labourers.

Colonial Economy and the Need for Labour from Kavango

During the period of the German conquest of Namibia, minerals were discovered which led to the development of infrastructure requiring lots of local labour (Kohler, 1958). The colonial authorities constructed harbours, such as the port at Swakopmund in November 1889, and from 1892 there was copper mining at Otavi carried out by the South West Africa Company (SWACO), whose mining rights were later given to OMEG (the Otavi-Minen-und Eisebahngesellschaft). The construction of a railway line in South West Africa started in 1898 and the railway line to Otavi was completed by 1906. Copper mines were in operation at Guchab and Khan from 1906 and diamond mining followed at Lüderitz after 1908.

The increase in white farm settlers in the police zone after 1908 also added to the increased demand for African labour (Stals, 1967, pp. 190-194). The new farm settlers needed labourers to work for them, but the war of 1904-1907 where local communities confronted the German colonial state decimated potential Herero and Nama labourers and the administration therefore looked to the Kavango and Ovambo regions to procure migrant labourers.

---

27 *Fumu* is a singular term in the Mbukushu language for a hereditary traditional head of the ethnic group, of which the plural form is *Hafumu*.
28 Letter from LTNT Col. Jose Carregado Vianna to the military magistrate of Grootfontein, 10 December 1917.
29 NAN ADM 30, file 243/3, vol. 2. Letter by Major Frank Brownlee to the Secretary for the protectorate titled 'Affairs at Nkurenkuru', dated 26 January 1918.

Labour recruitment from Kavango was small, but encouraged by the visiting German colonial officials to the area. By 1902, Dr Gerber had already attempted to reach agreements with the Kavango kings to encourage men to report for contract labour, but was unsuccessful, as these traditional leaders did not sign the agreement (Beris, 1996, p. 215). In 1909 German and the Portuguese colonial officials held discussions on how they could co-operate to encourage more contract labourers from the Kavango.[30] After 1908, the German colonial administration intended to make land available for German settlers in the Kavango with the hope that this would encourage the people of the Kavango to come forward in search of work on the farms and in mines and, for this reason, they ordered a straight road to be cleared from Nurugas to Casamas.[31] Indications are that men from Kavango were recruited as labourers only in 1909, during the final years of German colonial rule in Namibia.[32]

The people's reaction towards the colonial extraction of labour from the Kavango was based on their economic situation and their relations with the colonial authorities. The economic situation of the Kavango people had been influenced by European and American travellers, hunters and traders, the Vimbari and Arab slave traders, both before and after the German colonial conquest of Namibia in 1884. A market for the consumption of European goods had long been established in the Kavango, but despite this, most people were discouraged from going and working as labourers during the German colonial period. There are reasons for this lack of interest. Despite the ban on the slave trade by Britain and other European nations, slave trading continued in Kavango up to the end of German colonial rule in Namibia and the Kavango people continued to acquire European goods such as clothes and blankets, which they needed, without having to go and work as migrant labourers.[33] Well aware of the exploitation of their wildlife by the European hunters and traders, and the ensuing pest epidemic of the 1890s that killed their cattle, Kavango people were still in control of their natural resources and made a living from them. Although the epidemic infected and killed many cattle in the Kavango, the population refused to have their cattle vaccinated, and killed a squadron of soldiers that was sent to convince them. The epidemic infected even wild animals that provided meat for people, as Mangondo recalled:[34]

---

30 A. Eckl (2004) 'Konfrontation und kooperation am Kavango (nord Namibia) von 1891 bis 1921', PhD thesis, University of Cologne, Germany, p. 117. A meeting was held between Von Zastrow of the German and De Almeida of the Portuguese administration at Namutoni on 9 September 1909 to discuss the Kavango as a source of contract labourers.

31 Beris, A. 1996., *From mission to local church: one hundred years of mission by the Catholic Church in Namibia,* p. 215. Windhoek: Roman Catholic Church.

32 A. Eckl (2007), 'Reports from beyond the line: the accumulation of knowledge of Kavango and its peoples by the German colonial administration 1891–1911', *Journal of Namibian Studies,* 1, p. 22.

33 Rey argues that the Hambukushu of Kavango suffered from the slave trade as late as 1912. C. F. Rey (1932),'Ngamiland and the Kalahari: a paper read at the evening meeting of the society on 6 June 1932', *Geographical Journals,* Vol. 80, No. 4, October. p. 305.

34 R. Kampungu (1965), 'The concept and aim of Okavango marriage customs', Romae, Pontifica Universitas Urbaniana, pp. 239-240. Mangondo, a member of the Vakwangali royal family, born in 1878, was the daughter of Nasira who, in turn, was the maternal granddaughter of King Himarwa Ithete of the Vakwangali. By April 1956, when Mangondo was interviewed by Romanus Kampungu at a mission station in Tondoro, she was already old and blind. She narrated to Kampungu her personal experience of the epidemic of the 1890s in the Ukwangali area of Kavango.

Numbers of them were found everywhere even along the river lying dead. The sick animals would be found everywhere easy to kill even by a child. The plague provided meat for the people who were suffering the loss of their cattle. Those of Gciriku were attacked by this disease at '*epemba*' (harvest) at the season of the new fruit and those of Ukwangali during winter. (Kampungu, 1965, pp. 352-353).

The Kavango people continued to hunt game which became easy prey during the epidemic; they ate their crops, and dug and collected wild fruit from the forest and were therefore able to survive, without turning to recruitment into the colonial labour force as a necessary option.

During the South African colonial period, kings exerted an important influence on the labour supply in Namibia. The approach of the South African administration was to co-opt the traditional leadership and rule indirectly through them. Colonial officials presented gifts to the Kavango kings and brought a message of goodwill from the Administrator of South West Africa as a way to buy the friendship of the kings and their people. The colonial officials carried the message about the establishment of a new colonial administration to the kings, who in turn, responded to the Administrator.[35] Apart from the colonial officials recruiting labour during their visits to the Kavango, kings were encouraged to send men for contract work. Remuneration by colonial authorities to kings was a useful colonial strategy to extract migrant labour. Some kings visited the administrative centres of Grootfontein and Tsumeb personally to claim their monthly remuneration. The colonial officials had good opportunities to obtain more labourers from the Kavango and ordered an eye to be kept on the men who were reporting for work to ensure their proper treatment so that they would take back a good report of labour conditions. The administration requested more labourers from the Kavango and remunerated kings who responded to the request.[36] These kings continued to send labourers in small numbers who were distributed to mines and farms, as the following extract indicates:

> I have the honour to inform you that today 16 Ovambo [Mbunza] labourers arrived here for work, having been sent down by Chief Karupu. As Karupu is not in receipt of pay from the administration he has been supplied with goods to the value of 10/- as a reward for his services and to encourage him to send further batches of labourers.[37]

The strategy of remunerating the kings to encourage them to send labourers was a common feature in southern Africa. In Malawi, for instance, the colonial administration exploited the traditional customs through the form of paying head money to the chiefs,

---

35 NAN ADM 30, file 243/3, vol. 3. Frank Brownlee to the Secretary of the Protectorate 'Patrol to Nkurenkuru'. 16 January 1917.
36 NAN ADM 95, file 2794/8. Frank Brownlee to the Secretary for the Protectorate, 'Ovamboland labourers from Okavango'. 21 May 1917.
37 NAN ADM 95, file no 2794/8. Acting Military Magistrate to the Secretary for the Protectorate 'Ovamboland labourers from Okavango'. 20 June 1917. The word 'Ovambo' in the text above is corrected to 'Mbunza' as King Karupu was the King in the 'Mbunza area' along the Kavango River and also to show that the use of 'Ovambo' was a common colonial misrepresentation of the people from the Kavango which makes the statistics about labour recruitment problematic.

either the traditional ones or those installed by the colonial power, to ensure that they made their subjects available for use by the colonists.

From the 1920s, Kavango kings who had resisted colonial domination began to die,[38] and the colonial administration replaced them with more amenable ones who could be deposed by the Native Commissioner at any time, in terms of Proclamation No. 15 of 1928 which dealt with installing and deposing of chiefs. This made kings helpless and dependent on the Native Commissioner and this helped to centralise the commissioner's power and control over the Kavango population. As a result of the extended powers of the commissioner, the kings in Kavango became controllable. They were used by the authorities to pass on information and apply colonial laws to their subjects and compel them to sign up for contract labour. Their loss of power to (and control by) the commissioner made them depend on co-operation as a means of survival. In return for remuneration from the recruiting organisations, the kings assisted the commissioner in a number of ways. They helped collect the tribal tax fund which all young men were expected to pay and they built grain storage facilities in their kingdom where the recruiting organisation stored grain to give as rations to contract labourers going to the south of Namibia.

Despite the kings of the Kavango sending labourers, the mines still experienced a large shortage in the supply of labourers and the administration thought African messengers could entice labourers from the Kavango to come south.[39] By 1918, the number of labourers from the Kavango was reported to be sufficient with some to spare, and the colonial authority expressed the view that a regular supply would be a valuable asset and should be encouraged by every reasonable means.[40] The colonial authorities spread reports about the Portuguese authorities mistreating the local people as a means of justifying the settlement of the Kavango from the Angolan side to the Namibian side as 'fugitives', and thus increasing their pool of contract labourers. The South African administration, therefore, was not interested in returning the population from their side to Angola as this would have diminished the supply of contract labour.

The South African colonial administration finally posted a Native Affairs Commissioner to the Kavango at Nkurenkuru village in 1921.[41] The arrival of a permanent Native Affairs Commissioner in the Kavango was a turning point in the relationship with the local population as his activities and implementation of colonial policies changed the lives of the Kavango people forever. The first settled colonial representative to the Kavango, Rene Dickman, locally known as *Kasamane* [Old One], arrived at the time when men from Kavango were reluctant to proceed to the 'Police

---

38 NAN SWAA, 2083, A. 460/19. Native Commissioner. The following kings died during the 1920s: Kandjimi Hawanga on 19 March 1923, Nyangana waMukuve on 23 December 1924, Ndango waShimbenda in November 1925.
39 NAN ADM 95, File 2794/8. Frank Brownlee to the Secretary for the Protectorate, 4 June 1917.
40 NAN ADM 95, file 2794/8. Frank Brownlee to the Secretary for the Protectorate 'Ovamboland labourers from Okavango'. 11 Mar.1918.
41 NAN ADM 30, file 243/3, vol. 3. Secretary of South West Africa to the superintendent for native affairs at Nkurenkuru 'Recruiting of native labour' 11 March 1921.

Zone'[42] because of the bad reports they had received from returning labourers about an epidemic which had resulted in many deaths. The Commissioner dismissed this as rumour, as the following report indicates: 'The returning labourers from Mbunza and Ukwangali areas spread rumours to the effect that an epidemic had broken out in the south and that seven natives had died at the Grootfontein copper mines.'[43] In fact in 1919, there were repeated outbreaks of the influenza epidemic and these were preceded by measles that swept the diamond fields with appalling suddenness and severity and resulted in a death toll of 20 per cent amongst the workers at some sites.[44] Returning labourers in both Kavango and Ovamboland spread reports about conditions on the diamond mines and this increased fear there and resulted in fewer men reporting for contract labour during the 1920s.[45] In his tour of the Kavango in the Shambyu and Gciriku areas in 1923, the Native Commissioner was unsuccessful in recruiting local men because most of them hid in the forest as he approached their villages. The commissioner was convinced by the women's explanation that most men were away in the bush to collect *veldkos* and this was in spite of the fact that they had had good rains and a good harvest the previous year.[46]

Previously, most men from Kavango who were recruited at the recruiting depot in Tsumeb had been posted to work in the Lüderitz mines, but after 1923, men from the Kavango demanded to be recruited by the Grootfontein depot as a way to avoid being sent to Lüderitz, where they feared that workers were dying from disease. The new Commissioner reported that any attempts to force the men to go to the Tsumeb recruiting depot presented a great risk of the men refusing to proceed to the south altogether, with a consequent drop in recruitment, as there were fears that they might actually be sent to the far south.[47] Faced with the protest of Kavango men against being recruited at Tsumeb depot for the Lüderitz area, the office at Tsumeb was moved to Ondangwa and it was agreed that all the labourers from the Kavango would in future be employed in the Tsumeb/Grootfontein area only and that the magistrate of Grootfontein would be responsible for their medical examination, recruitment and distribution.[48] The administration encouraged the Native Commissioner of Kavango to make this new arrangement widely known to all the kings and headmen and to instruct all future recruits from Kavango to report to the magistrate of Grootfontein. While this was simply a new strategy of labour extraction by the administration, it was certainly a victory for the Kavango labourers. It points to the ways in which people could shape recruiting practices.

Throughout the 1920s there were fewer labour recruits from both the Kavango and Ovamboland, which led to a serious labour crisis between 1923 and 1925 (Emmett,

---

42 The 'Police Zone' was a term that referred to the central and southern part of Namibia where contract labourers from Kavango and Ovamboland went for work and where there were stringent police controls over Africans.
43 NAN ADM 30, file 243/3, vol. 3. Native Affairs Commissioner R. Dickman to the Native Commissioner of South West Africa 'Labour: Okavango district', 1 Dec. 1923, Windhoek.
44 NAN South-West Protectorate. Report of the Administrator of South-West Africa. 1919, p. 6).
45 NAN Territory of South-West Africa. Report of the Adminstrator 1921, p. 12.
46 Ibid.
47 NAN ADM 30, file 243/3 vol. 3. R. Dickman to the Native Commissioner of South West Africa, 1 Dec. 1923.
48 Ibid.

1999, pp. 174-175). The diamond mines in Namibia, especially, complained of labour shortages, but the colonial administration lacked the infrastructural capacity to extract more labourers from the Kavango. The administration was not prepared to take the sole responsibility of recruiting and their alternative, in view of this problem, was to stop recruiting from the Kavango altogether.[49] On 6 September 1923, the Administration convened a meeting in Windhoek with the representatives of the mines, who recommended that a representative of the mines visit the Kavango area for the purpose of investigating the roads, water supply and most likely centres for obtaining recruits.[50] However, despite efforts by the Lüderitz Chamber of Mines and the Otavi Minen und Eisenbahn Gesellschaft (OMEG) to implement the proposal for an expedition to Kavango, it did not take place, apparently on the grounds that:

> The number of natives in that area is very limited, and even supposing the expedition was successful in combing out one or two hundred more labourers, this would not materially affect native labour supply and unless a good case can be made out, it is regretted the permit applied for cannot be granted.[51]

The above seems to indicate that the reason behind the refusal of permission was that the population of Kavango was too small, but such a conclusion excludes other factors, such as the lack of interest in recruitment and the protests by the Kavango men. The men from Kavango, therefore, continued to be allocated only to the mines in Tsumeb and Grootfontein, while the diamond mines in the south received Ovambo workers exclusively in order to meet the wishes of the local people of Kavango. As the general manager of a mine explained, 'If the very same boys are allocated to the copper mines and Ovambos thereby released for the diamond mines, everyone, including the natives themselves, has all reason to be satisfied'.[52]

The Formation of the Northern Labour Organisation (NLO) and its Operations, 1925-1943

Since the labourers from the Kavango after 1923 were no longer in favour of working at the diamond areas of Lüderitz in the south of Namibia, the authorities in Namibia had to consider this boycott and come up with a new strategy for ensuring a continued supply of labourers for the diamond mines in the south, and so they recruited labour from South Africa, Bechuanaland and Basutoland (Emmett, 1999, pp. 176-177). An outstanding feature of the first ten years of South African rule in Namibia (1915-1925) was the ability of the northern areas (Kavango and Ovamboland) to resist the

---

49   NAN SWAA 2407, file no. A 521/10. The Secretary of South West Africa to the Administrator of S.W.A, 'Native labour recruitment-Okavango natives', 2 July 1926.
50   NAN SWAA 2407, file no. A521/10. Sgd. M Otzen to the Inspector of Mines, 23 February 1924.
51   NAN SWAA 2408, file F/521/11. The Secretary for South West Africa to the Secretary for Lüderitz Chamber of Mines, 'Investigation of native Labour resources: Okavango', 31 March 1924.
52   NAN SWAA 2408, file F/521/11. The General Manager of Lüderitzbucht to the Secretary of South West Africa, 'Re: native labour', 27 November 1924.

pressure of the colonial state to extract a migrant labour force (Emmett, 1999, p. 79).[53] The colonial administration, therefore, needed to find internal solutions to the labour demands of the diamond areas and white farmers. The colonial administration finally invited all the major stakeholders in the economy to a conference in 1924 to address the labour supply crisis.

The outcome of the conference was the formation of two recruiting organisations, the Northern Labour Organisation (NLO) and the Southern Labour Organisation (SLO) in 1925, which began the officially organised recruitment of contract labourers from the Kavango and Ovambo respectively. The ethnic and economic rivalry between the German-owned copper mines in Tsumeb and the coastal diamond mines, owned by British/South African capital, was part of the reason for the creation of the two (NLO and SLO) recruiting organisations which supplied labour to the copper and diamond mines respectively (Silvester, Wallace and Hayes, 1998, p. 38). However, it is important to recognise that this rivalry accommodated the 1923 demands by Kavango men not to be recruited to the dangerous diamond mines of the south. The SLO agreed with the diamond mines of the south to draw contract labourers from Ovamboland, while the NLO received permission from the administration to supply African labour from the Kavango to northern mines, industrial concerns, and farmers in the territory.

The NLO undertook the first expedition to the Kavango in December 1925 to establish rest camps on the migrant routes (these were the Gciriku–Muramba–Matako–Nuragas– Karukuvisa–Grootfontein route and the Nkurenkuru–Grootfontein or Nkurenkuru– Ntsintsabis–Tsumeb routes). A representative of NLO, E. Schoenfelder (locally known as *Katjire*), who was sent to report on labour conditions in the Kavango, returned in 1926, and by 1927, Bertrand of the NLO reported that they were obtaining all the recruits that they could possibly expect to get from the Nyangana area.[54] Although the NLO obtained men from Angola and Northern Rhodesia (Zambia) as contract labourers, the administration did not support this.[55] The labour organisation was therefore experiencing problems in identifying and recruiting people who were domiciled only on the South West African (Namibian) side of the Kavango, and this impacted negatively on their recruitment process.[56] In view of this threat of migration and loss of potential labourers, stringent control over the labour supply was necessary and the colonial authority in Namibia passed the Northern and Extra Territorial Native Control (NETNC) Proclamation No. 29 of 1935, which finally allowed control and recruitment of labour outside Namibia and indicated a change of heart towards their earlier policy of refusing the NLO permission to recruit outside Namibia.[57]

The administration's policy aimed at preventing the detribalisation of the Kavango and Ovambo people. In accordance with this policy, such Africans were normally to return to their homes periodically. Proclamation No. 29 of 1935 required all Africans

---

53   Ibid p. 79.
54   NAN SWAA, 2426, A521/26 (V.5). The Northern Labour Organisation'.
55   NAN NAR, file 11/1/2. 'Illegal recruiting, Administrator to the Managing Secretary of NLO', 14 December 1935.
56   NAN NAR, file 11/1/2. 'NLO Managing Secretary to the Secretary for South West Africa', 28 November 1935.
57   NAN NAT [20], file 25. 'Circular on Control of Extra-Territorial and Northern Natives' 8 January 1936.

from Kavango and Ovamboland to possess an identification pass to enable them to be recruited in the Police Zone and discouraged further issuing of visiting passes to them. Visiting passes were no longer issued to Africans in order to limit their movements to the urban areas to employment purposes only, and thus control the Africans as a colonial labour reserve. Metal tube containers (as used in Northern Rhodesia) were issued to the African labourers to carry their identification passes. The series of colonial regulations that were passed in 1935 not only prevented Africans from Kavango and Ovamboland from moving permanently to the city but helped to channel migrant labour at reduced wages. These Africans were recruited mainly by companies such as SWACO and OMEG of Tsumeb, Otavi and Grootfontein areas.

Act No. 32 of 1937 declared the Kavango a Native Territory and introduced a tribal fund tax to be paid by any man who belonged to the 'Kavango Native Territory'. The tribal tax fund was a colonial strategy for labour recruitment, which targeted only mature men who were in good health to report as contract labourers for the colonial economy.

The Native Commissioner continued to be a central recruiting agent and did all in his power to ensure a large supply of contract labourers. He created a camp in each of the areas of the five ethnic groups where he used to convene meetings to inform people of colonial policies. In his meetings in 1937, he provided men with certificates in metal tubes to identify them for tax payments. He levied and collected a tribal tax at a rate of 5/- on all males over the age of eighteen years, which was due on the 1 October every year.[58]

The system of administration in the Kavango was quite different from that in Ovamboland. There were no headmen or sub-headmen, and the administration therefore had to create new 'tribal' administrative structures. The colonial administration divided the Kavango into six tribal administrative units, each with appointed native recruiters (also known as 'labour headmen'), whose services might be withdrawn if they were given notice.[59] The kings usually recommended their next of kin for positions as 'native recruiters' who were subject to the orders of the Native Commissioner and their kings.[60] These native recruiters did not have a fixed salary but were remunerated depending on the number of recruits they enlisted and escorted to the Police Zone. Native recruiters, therefore, created their own links within communities for more potential labourers to report to them for work. Since some of the potential labourers had to cross from Angola, they needed boats to be able to cross the crocodile-infested Kavango River. The NLO did not have boats to ferry potential recruits across the Kavango River and depended on local boat owners. NLO remunerated boat owners for each recruit ferried by deducting small amounts from the salary of the designated labour headmen, and this caused conflicts between the local boat owners and the labour headmen.[61] The native

---

58   NAN NAR, file N4/3/2. 'The Chief Native Commissioner in Windhoek to the Assistant Native Commissioner of Rundu', 23 January 1938.
59   By 1939 the following were the native recruiters: Phillipus Mudiro for the reserve area, Shivanda for Kwangali, Kasiki for Mbunza, Frans Kashasha for Shambyu, Linus Shashipapo for Gciriku and Muyatwa for Mbukushu area.
60   NAN NAR, file 11/1/2. Declaration by Langhans Kanyinga, 02 January 1936.
61   NAN NAR, 11/7. Report on the conflict between native recruiter for Sambyu area, Kashasha and Mbandje, a boat owner at Rundu, in, 'native recruiter, Sambio area'.

recruiters, or labour headmen, became well-respected figures within their communities and some, like Langhals Kanyinga, accumulated wealth.

The NLO enjoyed the sole role of recruiting in the Kavango and Angola until this role was challenged by an Anglo-American recruitment association known as the Witwatersrand Native Labour Association (WNLA) which recruited men for the South African gold mines and the tobacco farmers of Southern Rhodesia (Zimbabwe). WNLA had a recruitment office at Shakawe in Botswana where Mr. Matthias Davis was their recruiting agent. When WNLA began its recruitment operations in Angola and Kavango in the late 1930s, more Kavango men chose to be recruited by WNLA for the South African mines and the Zimbabwe tobacco farms. The WNLA native recruiters in Kavango were seen actively looking for more people to recruit in Kavango and this increased the concern of the NLO in Namibia. The NLO feared that WNLA paid higher wages than the NLO and labourers would, therefore, choose WNLA over the NLO, which would possibly lose control over their recruiting area. The recruiting activities by WNLA in the Kavango were seen as illegal since WNLA had no formal agreements, as the Assistant Native Commissioner of Rundu indicated.[62] The NLO's pool of labour was, therefore, threatened and it had to consider new strategies for labour recruitment. The administration, on behalf of the NLO, finally reached an agreement with WNLA that the NLO would limit its recruitment to Namibia while WNLA would limit its recruitment operations to Angola.[63] Despite the agreement with WNLA, the NLO continued to lose labourers as more men preferred jobs in South Africa to those in Namibia. This threat to the pool of labour from the Kavango forced the NLO to expand its recruitment among the Ovambo for the northern mines and the farms of Grootfontein, Otavi and Tsumeb, and not to limit the Ovambo labourers to the diamond mines of the south, as was previously the practice. These advances of the NLO into Ovamboland led to complaints and demands from the SLO who wanted to expand recruitment for farm and mine labourers from Kavango, and this encouraged new talks about the possibility and necessity of forming a recruiting organisation that would operate in both Kavango and Ovamboland to recruit for the mines and farms of South West Africa.[64]

In Ovamboland, labour migration is related to the process of pauperisation combined with severe shortfall in the colonial economies (Clarence-Smith and Moorsom, 1977, p. 71; McKittrick, 1996, p. 120). In the Kavango, lack of clothing was the main problem and was a central motivation in the labour recruitment process. The love of clothes had been introduced to the Kavango people by colonialists (European hunters, traders, etc.) and accessibility to traded goods was curtailed by the Commissioner and police. The mission stations in the area did not provide clothes and the colonial prohibition on killing animals reduced accessibility to animal skins for traditional clothing. People were, therefore, left with only the option of working on contract, not so much to supplement food supplies as they always had food in abundance, but to acquire money to purchase clothes. Labour migration from Kavango during the German occupation period was

---

62 NAN SWAA 2407-A521/10/2. 'Native labour recruitment-Okavango natives'.
63 NAN SWAA, 2426, A521/26 (V.5). 'Rest camps on the Okavango River', 28 June 1944.
64 NAN SWAA, 2426, 521/26, V.5. 'Suggested revision of agreement between NLO and SLO for the recruitment in Ovamboland and the Kavango'.

low and totalled only 122 men from 1910 to 1913,[65] in contrast to Ovamboland which recorded 9,295 labourers in 1911, 6,076 in 1912 and 12,025 in 1913.[66] While not a comprehensive statistical compilation, the table below shows the extent of the disparity in migration from the Kavango and Ovamboland in the 1920s, the 1940s and 1950s. It shows that, despite the operations of NLO and later the South West Africa Native Labour Association (SWANLA), the number of men reporting for recruitment from the Kavango remained low. However, the table also indicates that recruitment of men by SWANLA (1943-1972) was higher than its predecessor NLO (1925-1942).

Table 1 SWANLA recruitments

Compiled from, 'The annual report of SWA Administrator of 1938-40 on labour recruitments from Kavango', (AKA 552, N1/15/6-2) from the sub-chapter 'Native Affairs' in the 'Report of the Adminstrator of South-West Africa' for the years 1925 and 1926, and from SWAA, A 521/26 (v. 5).

Year	Kavango	Ovamboland
1924	346	3,273
1925	243	3,269
1926	355	4,033
1941	639	4 060
1942	351	3,137
1943	539	6,659
1959	1,033	14,960

This trend continued for the whole period of the contract system and by 1971, whilst there were 43,000 contract labourers in Namibia, only 3,000 were from the Kavango and the rest were from Ovamboland or 'Extra-Territorial' – mainly from Angola (Kane-Berman, 1972, p.5). The statistics for labour migration indicate that the response to labour migration in the Kavango was not the same as in Ovamboland and there was never the same value attached to contract labour migration in the Kavango as in Ovamboland.[67]

---

65   A. Eckl, (2004) 'Konfrontation und kooperation am Kavango (Nord Namibia) von 1891 bis 1921' (PhD thesis, University of Cologne), p. 120.
66   M. J. Olivier, (1961) 'Inboorlingheid en administrasie in die mandaat gebied van Suid Wes- Afrika' (PhD thesis, University of Stellenbosch), p. 253.
67   Ibid.

Conclusion

The introduction of European goods through European hunters and traders in the Kavango laid a foundation for the integration of the Kavango Region into the contract labour system of Namibia in the colonial period. Men entered the contract labour system to acquire money to purchase European goods. Various mineral deposits that were discovered in Namibia from the 1890s required African labour to extract them. The Herero and Nama, who had previously formed part of the labour force of the colonial economy, were hugely reduced in numbers by the national wars of resistance (1904-1907) and the Kavango became an area of colonial interest for the supply of labour.

After 1902, the Kavango formed part of the administrative district of Grootfontein. Although, by 1908, the German colonial administration intended to make land available for German settlers in the Kavango, with the hope that this would encourage the people of the Kavango to find their way to the centre in search of work on the farms and in mines, this did not materialise (Beris, 1996, p. 215). The German administration lacked an adequate administrative infrastructure and faced hostility and resistance from the Kavango people. It took until 1910 for the Catholic missionaries to establish a permanent settlement in the Kavango (40 years later than the establishment of the first mission station in Ovamboland and a century after the establishment of the first mission station in southern Namibia). The German administration did not have any permanent recruiting agents to facilitate labour extraction from the Kavango during most of the German colonial period.

During the South African military occupation, the South African authorities did not enjoy good relations with the Portuguese administration across the Kavango River because each wanted to attract the sparse population of the Kavango as a source of labour. The South African administration even began to remunerate *Vahompa* for each recruit that came from their area as a means of encouraging them to send more men as labourers to the south.

The *Vahompa*, who feared the notorious Portuguese officials of southern Angola, were therefore compelled to align themselves with the South African administration and felt duty bound to support the South African administration's demand for contract labourers. Despite this collaboration between the administration and the *Vahompa* with regard to labour extraction, the contract labourers protested about being sent to the dangerous diamond fields in the south and this compelled the administration to convene a labour conference to address the issue. The conference led to the formation of NLO and SLO, the recruiting organisations which, from 1926, operated in the 'Kavango' and 'Ovambo' respectively to recruit labourers. The competition between the NLO and SLO finally necessitated merging the two organisations and, by 1943, the South West Africa Native Labour Association (SWANLA) was formed and recruited labourers in Namibia until its demise in 1972.

References

Beris, A. (1996) *From mission to local church: One hundred years of mission by the Catholic Church in Namibia with special reference to the development of Archdiocese of Windhoek and the Apostolic Vicariate of Rundu*. Windhoek: Roman Catholic Church.

Bierfert, A. (1938) *25 Jahre bei den Wadiriku am Okawango*. Hünfeld: Verlag der Oblaten.

Budack, K. F. R. (1976) 'The Kavango: The Country, its people and History'. *Namib und Meer, Band 7*: Swakopmund.

Clarence Smith, W. G. and Moorsom, R. (1977) 'Underdevelopment and Class Formation in Ovamboland, 1844-1917'. In Palmer, R. and Parsons, N. (eds) *The Roots of Rural Poverty in Central and Southern Africa*. Berkeley: University of California Press.

Cooper, A. D. (2001) *Ovambo Politics in the Twentieth Century*. Lanham: University Press of America.

Cronje, G. and Cronje, S. (1979) *The workers of Namibia*. London: International Defence and Aid Fund for Southern Africa.

Dierks, K. (2005) Colonial rule: German period. <http://www.klausdierks.com/Chronology/contents.htm> {Accessed on 20 June 2011}.

Eckl, A. (2004a) 'Serving the Kavango Sovereigns' Political Interests: The Beginning of the Catholic Mission in Northern Namibia', *Le Fait Missionaire*, No. 14.

Eckl, A. (2004b) 'Konfrontation und kooperation am Kavango (nord Namibia) von 1891 bis 1921', PhD thesis, Universitat zu Köln, Germany.

Eckl, A. (2007) 'Reports from beyond the line: the accumulation of knowledge of Kavango and its peoples by the German colonial administration 1891 – 1911', *Journal of Namibian Studies*, 1.

Emmett, T. (1999) *Popular Resistance and the Roots of Nationalism in Namibia, 1915-1966*. Basel: P. Schlettwein Publishing.

Fleisch, A. and Möhlig, W. (2002) *The Kavango Peoples in the Past: Local Historiographies from Northern Namibia*. Cologne: Rüdiger Köppe.

Hunke, H. (1996) *Church and State, the political context of 100 years of Catholic mission in Namibia*. Windhoek: Roman Catholic Church.

Hishongwa, N. (1992) *The contract labour system and its effects on family and social life in Namibia*. Windhoek: Gamsberg Macmillan.

Kampungu, R. (1966) *The Concept and Aim of Okavango Marriage Customs Investigated in the Light of Ecclesiastical Legislation*. Roma: Pontifica Universitas Urbaniana.

Kane Berman, J. (1972) *Contract Labour in South West Africa*. Johannesburg: South African Institute of Race Relations.

Kohler, O. (1958) *A Study of Karibib District, South West Africa*. Union of South Africa, Department of Native Affairs, Ethnological publication No. 40. Pretoria: Government Printers.

Magadla, T. and Voltz, C. (eds) (2006) *Words of the Batswana, letters of Mahoko a Becwana, 1883 to 1896*. Cape Town: Van Riebeeck Society.

McKittrick, M. (1996) 'The burden of young men: generational conflict and property rights in Ovamboland', *African Economic History*, Vol. 24.

McKittrick, M. (1998) 'Generational struggle and social mobility in western Ovambo communities, 1915-54'. In Hayes, P. et al. (eds) *Namibia under South African rule, mobility & containment, 1915-46*. Oxford: James Currey.

Moorsom, R. (1989) 'The Formation of the Contract Labour System in Namibia, 1900-1926'. In Zegeye, A. (ed.) *Forced Labour and Migration: Patterns of Movement within Africa*. London: Haus Zell.

Oblates of Mary Immaculate. 100 years of OMI history in Namibia 1896-2005. <http://www.rcchurch.na/omi/History.htm> {Accessed 14 June 2011}.

Olivier, M. J. (1961) 'Inboorlingbeleid en administrasie in die mandaad gebied van Suid Wes-Afrika', PhD thesis, University of Stellenbosch, South Africa.

Rey, C. F. (1932) 'Ngamiland and the Kalahari: a paper read at the evening meeting of the society on 6 June 1932', *Geographical Journals*, Vol. 80, No. 4, October.

Shiremo, S. (2005) 'The Role of Kavango Kings in the anti-colonial resistance: 1903 the year of unity and resistance'. Unpublished paper presented at a conference at Rundu College of Education.

Silvester, J., Wallace, M. and Hayes, P. (1998) 'Mobility and containment: an overview, 1915-1946'. In Hayes, P. et al. (eds) *Namibia under South African rule, Mobility & Containment, 1915-46*. Oxford: James Currey.

Stals, E. (1967) *Die aanraking tussen blankes en Ovambos in Suid Wes Africa, 1850-1915*, PhD thesis, Universiteit van Stellenbosch, South Africa.

Van Tonder, L. L. (1966) *The Hambukushu of the Okavango land: an anthropological study of South Western people in Africa*, PhD thesis, Port Elizabeth University, Eastern Cape, South Africa.

Weigend, G. (1985) 'German settlement patterns in Namibia', *Geographical Review*, American Geographical Society, vol. 2.

Archival sources

National Archives of Namibia (NAN)

ADM Secretary for the Protectorate [30]

File 243/3, vol. 3, 16 January 1917. Report entitled "Patrol to Nkurenkuru" by Frank Brownlee to the Administrator of S.W.A.

File 243/3, vol. 3, 16 January 1917. Frank Brownlee to the Secretary of the Protectorate "Patrol to Nkurenkuru".

File 243/3, vol. 3. Report by Major Frank Brownlee titled "Resumé of arrangements concluded between the Commandant Fort Cuangar and the Military Magistrate Grootfontein district on the 27 September 1917".

File 243/3, vol. 2, 16 November 1917. Letter from the Administrator of SWA to the Minister of Defence in Pretoria titled "Administration of the Okavango area: SWA Protectorate".

File 243/3, vol. 2, 10 December 1917. Letter from LTNT Col. Jose Carregado Vianna to the Military Magistrate of Grootfontein.

File 243/3, vol. 2, 26 January 1918. Letter by Major Frank Brownlee to the Secretary for the Protectorate titled "Affairs at Nkurenkuru".

File 243/3, vol. 2, 24 April 1918. Statements under oath attached to a letter of report by Major Frank Brownlee to Lieut. Hahn of Ovamboland administration.

File 243/3, vol. 3, 11 March 1921. Secretary of South West Africa to the Superintendent for Native Affairs at Nkurenkuru.

File 243/3, vol. 3, 1 December 1923. Native Affairs Commissioner R. Dickman to the Native Commissioner of South West Africa "Labour: Okavango district".

ADM Secretary for the Protectorate [95]

File 2794/8, 21 May 1917. Frank Brownlee to the Secretary for the Protectorate, "Ovamboland labourers from Okavango".

File 2794/8, 4 June 1917. Frank Brownlee.

File 2794/8, 20 June 1917. Acting Military Magistrate to the Secretary for the Protectorate "Ovamboland labourers from Okavango".

File 2794/8, 11 March 1918. Frank Brownlee to the Secretary for the Protectorate "Ovamboland labourers from Okavango".

NAR Native Affairs Rundu

File 11/7, undated. Report on the conflict between native recruiter for Sambyu area, Kashasha and Mbandje, a boat owner at Rundu, in, "Native Recruiter, Sambio area".

File 11/1/2, 28 November 1935. "NLO Managing Secretary to the Secretary for South West Africa".

File 11/1/2, 14 December 1935 "Illegal recruiting, Administrator to the Managing Secretary of NLO".

File 11/1/2, 02 January 1936. Declaration by Langhans Kanyinga.

File N4/3/2, 23 January 1938. "The Chief Native Commissioner in Windhoek to the Assistant Native Commissioner of Rundu".

NAT Native Affairs Tsumeb [20]

File 25, 8 January 1936. Circular on Control of Extra-Territorial and Northern Natives.

SWAA South West Africa Administrator

File AKA 552, NI/15/6-2 'The Annual Report of SWA Administrator of 1938-40 on Labour Recruitments from Kavango', from the sub-chapter 'Native Affairs' in the 'Report of the Administrator of South-West Africa' for the years 1925 and 1926.

SWAA [2083]

File no. A. 460/19. Native Commissioner.

SWAA [2407]

File A521/10/2. "Native labour recruitment-Okavango natives".

File A521/10, 23 February 1924. Sgd. M. Otzen to the Inspector of Mines.

File A 521/10, 2 July 1926. The Secretary of South West Africa to the Administrator of S.W.A, "Native labour recruitment-Okavango natives".

SWAA [2408]

File F/521/11, 31 March 1924. The Secretary for South West Africa to the Secretary for Lüderitz Chamber of Mines, "Investigation of native Labour resources: Okavango".

File F/521/11, 27 November 1924. General Manager of Lüderitzbucht to the Secretary of South West Africa, "Re: native labour".

SWAA [2426]

File A521/26 (V.5). Suggested revision of agreement between NLO and SLO for the recruitment in Ovamboland and the Kavango.

File A521/26 (V.5). The Northern Labour Organization.

File A521/26 (V.5), 28 June 1944. "Rest camps on the Okavango River".

South-West Protectorate

Report of the Administrator of South-West Africa for the year 1919, p. 6.

Territory of South-West Africa

Report of the Administrator for the year 1921, p. 12.

7 Liberals and Non-Racism in Namibia's Settler Society? Advocate Israel Goldblatt's Engagement with Namibian Nationalists in the 1960s[1]

Dag Henrichsen

Introduction

Namibia's settler society has a very weak, indeed almost non-existent tradition of advocacy of non-racism. Up to the early 1970s, none of the settlers' political parties postulated principles of non-racism – that is individually based citizenship and democratic rights as well as legal, economic and social opportunities irrespective of apartheid's racial designations and ascriptions. This is in contrast, for example, to political parties in 'white' South Africa or Zimbabwe (See Hancock, 1980; Marks, 1995; Rich, 1984; Vigne, 1997).[2] South African visitors to Windhoek in the early 1960s, whether Ruth First, the radical left-wing journalist and writer or the Vice-President of the South African Liberal Party, Randolph Vigne, were either appalled or expressed grave disillusionment with respect to the prospect of any European non-racial political activity in this South African colony. Ruth First stated in 1963: 'It remains a frightening fact that not a single white political leader in South West Africa has ever advocated a non-racial democracy' (1963, p. 54). Two years earlier, Randolph Vigne had summed up his talks in Windhoek with, amongst others, Advocate Israel Goldblatt and African nationalists like Clemens Kapuuo, Levy Nganjone or Zedekia Ngavirue by stating: 'If Goldblatt is right, and it is an impossibility to build bridges at this stage [in early 1961], the best hope of bringing about a non-racial group inside SWA and avert[ing] a racial clash, is to afford travel and study to some of the young African leaders …'[3]

---

1 This paper provides in part a summary of arguments presented in the book *Israel Goldblatt. Building Bridges. Namibian Nationalists Clemens Kapuuo, Hosea Kutako, Brendan Simbwaye, Samuel Witbooi*, edited by Dag Henrichsen, Naomi Jacobson and Karen Marshall, Basel, 2010. In the following, I refrain from providing detailed references to the Goldblatt papers and notes, most of which are quoted at length in the book and housed (as copies) at the archives of the Basler Afrika Bibliographien (BAB), PA.7, Israel Goldblatt. The viewpoints presented in this paper are my own and do not necessarily reflect those of the other co-editors of the book.
2 This literature discusses the various liberal, progressive and more radical positions in 'white' southern African societies and provides useful introductions to definitions of concepts, ideologies and paradigms, which I cannot deal with here.
3 NAN AACRLS 096, R. Vigne: 'Confidential Report', 1961.

The literature on the formation of apartheid society in Namibia provides no coherent argument for the notable absence of political thought and practice of non-racism in settler society. Rather, it provides an array of dynamics and arguments for the very rigid entrenchment of racism on all levels of society. In general, as André du Pisani has phrased it, 'white politics was for all practical reasons seen to be a mere extension of the white South African political scene' after World War II, by which he, in particular, meant 'the degree of ideological congruency between the ruling National Party in South Africa and the majority of whites inside the Territory', that is, Namibia (du Pisani, 1986, pp. 141, 144). The main reason for this, as he points out, was the 'legal dispute between South Africa and the United Nations' and its domestic political repercussions (1986, p. 141), an opinion supported by Martin Eberhardt (2007, p. 512ff). Indeed, in Namibia, any advocacy of non-racism was obviously connected to the future of not only the political but also the legal status of the country, that is, the question of its incorporation by or independence from South Africa, and the particular role of the United Nations in this respect.

Namibia's legal status as a Class C Mandated territory after World War I was highly contested by South Africa. It argued until the 1970s that the Mandate over 'South West Africa' had lapsed with the dissolution of the League of Nations and its transformation into the United Nations Organisation in 1946 and that the UN, therefore, had no say in the affairs of Namibia. Consequently, South Africa strove to incorporate Namibia as a fifth province into its own legal and political system of apartheid, so it could also capture a larger number of 'white' voters in its colony. It was supported by the local National Party of SWA, the ruling white political party, which, given the increasingly beleaguered settler society in the wake of Africa's decolonisation, by 1960 dominated the political system and culture in the colony. Among the local white opposition parties, the United National South West Party (UNSWP) argued that the Mandate over SWA was still valid, but that the UN did not become the legal successor of the League of Nations, and thus the party expressly 'supported the South African Government in its refusal to place South West Africa under UN Supervision'.[4] Its leader, Advocate Niehaus, had nevertheless suggested greater autonomy for Namibia from South Africa since the early 1950s. The shortlived South West Party (SWP, 1960-1963) of Japie Basson, Ferdinand Lempp and Marga Vaatz also opposed the placing of Namibia under a Trusteeship of the United Nations, while at the same time trying to attract from among the local 'white' electorate, voters with any anti-incorporation sentiments. The party propagated the principle of 'self-government' for Namibia, and a federal association with South Africa, albeit with little success. In fact, the SWP was mainly concerned with the unity of the three European language groups (English-, Afrikaans- and German-speaking) and as such also, like the other 'white' parties, fostered ethnic building blocks (Eberhardt, 2007, p. 504ff).

Apart from the intense extension of South African rule inside Namibia after World War II in the wake of African decolonisation, including the rapid extension of its apartheid and homeland policy and legislation, other general factors contributed to racial entrenchment in Namibia. Important was the rapid economic growth in the colony from the 1950s onwards, accompanied by a steady increase of the settler

---

4   Quoted from the UNSWP political manifesto of 1954, in Du Pisani, 1986, p. 143.

population (1921: 19,432; 1958: 66,000) and as such the rapid extension of European settler farming and, on a political level, the expansion of apartheid votes (Emmett, 1999, p. 261ff). The conservative 'white' vote also had much to do with the intense occupation amongst the settler society to 'reconcile' the important German-speaking voters after their 'dissident' Nazi politics during the 1930s and now, after World War II the accommodation (and naturalisation) of many Germans within the National Party (Eberhardt, 2007).

Whilst all these developments fostered 'white coherence', factors explaining the absence of any liberal political activities relate, in turn, to the smallness of the settler society, in contrast to South Africa and Zimbabwe and as such implying rigid (informal) measures of social and political control. The very nature of the colonial economy, in turn, could explain the notable absence, for example, of left 'white' trade union activities in Namibia.[5] Thus, not surprisingly, non-racism as political thought and practice in Namibia and, as such, also any dissident and more radical anti-colonial activities amongst the settlers, were virtually absent. It seems that the first non–racial political party in Namibia was the Federal Party, formed in the mid-1970s and led by Advocate Bryan O'Linn (O'Linn, 2003, pp. 65f, 88ff, 129). Whilst this did not mean the absence of any critical (public) discussions,[6] these remained during the 1960s, mostly relegated to the private sphere. Any public non–racial or radical positions amongst Europeans in the 1960s, it seems, came from a few clergymen like the Anglican Bishop Robert Mize or a couple of German pastors. They all, like the Rev Michael Scott who was internationally active on behalf of the Herero Chiefs' Council, came from outside the country, and were only temporarily based in Namibia, and several faced deportation.[7]

This chapter reflects on the endeavours of Israel Goldblatt (1897-1982), a legal practitioner from Cape Town residing and practising in Namibia since the early 1920s and being by 1964 the most senior advocate in the whole of Namibia and South Africa, to contribute towards a non-racial vision for Namibia in the 1960s. Whilst Goldblatt deliberately chose what he regarded as a non-political approach, and as such clearly emphasised the limits of his engagements, his endeavours nevertheless provide the wider context in which any articulations and actions of settler non-racism or, to phrase

---

[5] These issues would definitely warrant in-depth research. Amongst the German population, an *Arbeiterverband* did exist, though its history and political credo is not known (Eberhardt, 2007, p. 156). Scant details are also known about a group of German-speaking anarchists in the late 1920s. Pers. info. from Giorgio Miescher (Basel).

[6] Apart from O'Linn's work (2003) and its many references to the different political opinions amongst Europeans in the 1960s and 1970s, see also the detailed analysis of Eberhardt (2007, p. 506ff) and the few references to any non–racial thought as expressed, for example, by Marga Vaatz. It should be noted that neither she nor other SWP leaders maintained, as far as is known, regular contacts with African politicians.

[7] Various mission church bodies became important radical advocates of change after World War II, though mainly through the influence of African clergymen (for example Bishop Auala) and, to a lesser extent, through clergymen from outside the country (such as Rev. Michael Scott from the late 1940s onwards, or, from the 1960s, various young West German clergymen and clergywomen, for example Pastor Wienecke). On the very conservative European leadership for the various Rhenish Mission congregations in Namibia until the early 1970s, and 'rebels' like Wienecke, see Gockel (2010). On the progressive position of the Anglican Church in the 1960s, see my comments with reference to Bishop Mize in this chapter.

it differently, dissenting political positions vis-à-vis mainstream 'white' politics took and could take place.

Israel Goldblatt and his vision for an independent Namibia

It is perhaps not surprising that it was the shooting at the Old Location in Windhoek on Thursday 10 December 1959 that spurred Israel Goldblatt to reflect on the future of Namibia. As is well known, on that day, simmering protest in the Old Location, Windhoek's main African township, burst into open conflict when a group of European officials, confronted with a large number of protesters, called in the police, with grave consequences. By the next morning, approximately 12 men and one woman had been shot dead and more than 50 people injured.[8] Society at large, its African majority as well as its minority settler society, was deeply shocked by such brutal violence which for many, not only Africans, was regarded as having been deliberately provoked.[9] For the African political parties and bodies, that is SWANU, which had been founded in the Old Location only three months before the shooting, in September 1959, the slightly older worker's movement, OPO, formed in April 1959, as well as the then dominant African political body in the colony, the Herero Chiefs' Council (HCC), 10 December became a national day of mourning and resistance. 'To the memory of those who were murdered by the forces of Apartheid. Their blood will sink in, not in vain, and will inspire others', read the inscription of a commemorative tombstone which was erected on the initiative of leading politicians of the Old Location, only to be instantly demolished by unknown forces (Goldblatt, 2010, p. 54).

Israel Goldblatt did not become directly involved, as a lawyer and advocate, in the official Commission of Enquiry instituted after the shooting and presided over by its sole member, Justice Cyril Hall. He was briefly consulted by Rev. Bartholomew Karuaera of the Herero Chiefs' Council when their legal representative, the South African lawyer and Deputy President-General of the ANC, Oliver Tambo, was barred from entering Windhoek in January 1960.[10] As Sam Nujoma, a leader in the Old Location conflict who was faced with a deportation order and whom Tambo was also to represent, remembered, the 'magistrate did not want to be confronted by a black lawyer'.[11] In Namibia at the time there was not a single African lawyer.

---

8   The first reliable list of the victims was published by the *South West News* (SWN), the newspaper issued in 1960 by activists and journalists in the Old Location, in its first issue, 5 March 1960, Vol. 1, No 1, p. 4.
9   See the comments by Dan Minnaar of the *Windhoek Advertiser*, as quoted by Vigne in his 'Confidential Report' 1961, in NAN AARCLS 096.
10   According to Rev. Karuaera in a conversation with DH, 2006.
11   Tambo was hired to defend those accused of organising the resistance in the Old Location in December 1959, amongst them Sam Nujoma and Nathaniel Mbaeva. Nujoma himself, who since late December had faced deportation, had initially approached the lawyer Lucian Goldblatt, Israel Goldblatt's son (Nujoma, 2001, p. 80; Ngavirue, 1997, p. 270). After the refusal to allow Tambo to enter Windhoek, the attorney Wentzel, on the suggestion of liberal politicians in South Africa and funded by Michael Scott's Africa Bureau in London, made submissions to the Hall Commission, which, according to Vigne, were ignored (1997, p. 185).

In early 1960 Israel Goldblatt considered matters which *he* considered as being at the heart of the matter, namely the overall legal and political future of South West Africa as a South African colony and, simultaneously, a Mandate of the United Nations Organisation. As is well known, the legal dispute revolving around the status of South West Africa had reached a climax in the 1950s when the United Nations allowed the Namibian petitioners to the UN, Mburumba Kerina and Jariretundu Kozonguizi, and also Rev. Michael Scott, to directly report to the Fourth Committee of the UN General Assembly. The Herero Chiefs' Council and other Namibian politicians, often jointly, had already been organising a very successful petitioning of the Committee for over a decade. Goldblatt regularly studied the proceedings of the Committee, including the Namibian statements and petitions.

Six weeks after the Shootings in the Old Location, amidst a general climate ridden with fear, and a few weeks before British Prime Minister Harold Macmillan's 'Wind of Change' speech to the South African Houses of Parliament in Cape Town with its vision of decolonisation and modest criticism of apartheid, Goldblatt wrote to the World Federation of United Nations Associations (WFUNA) in Geneva to propose the establishment of a United Nations Association in Namibia. The WFUNA from 1946 onwards intended to promote, as its mission reads, 'tolerance, understanding, solidarity and co-operation among men, women and children throughout the world without distinction as to race, sex, language, religion or political orientation'. Its national associations aimed to 'contribute to the removal of obstacles to peace, to work for justice, security and disarmament' and 'to strive for the recognition of and respect for human rights and fundamental freedoms throughout the world'. Goldblatt obviously was well aware of these intentions and it was probably disappointing for him that the Secretariat in its prompt answer pointed out that 'the position of a UNA in South West Africa might well prove to be extremely delicate. ... The only way out in such circumstances sometimes is the establishment of an association composed of leading black and white personalities who have previously agreed on a common program to spread objective information'.[12] Goldblatt did not regard the circumstances in the aftermath of the Old Location shooting conducive to form such a 'mixed' group of leading personalities and had articulated this opinion to Randolph Vigne in March 1961. He now opted for a less ambitious step by establishing what he called the 'Study Group', a non-political, informal[13] body comprised of interested European acquaintances, in order 'to educate ourselves' on the role of the UN in the South West Africa dispute. Given the general opposition amongst the settler society at large to any role or involvement of the UN, his undertaking, modest as it was, can be read as a serious attempt by a tiny group of 'whites' in Windhoek to move beyond South African propaganda.

---

12   BAB, PA.7: Sec. of the World Federation to Goldblatt, 5 February 1960 (letter incomplete). A UNA branch had been established in Johannesburg by the late 1950s.
13   As he explains in his notes, he did ask at a later stage for official permission to have such a gathering (Henrichsen et al. 2010, p. 69)!

The 'Study Group'

The 'Study Group' established itself in early 1960 and included Europeans only. Amongst them was the former editor (until early 1960) of the German daily, the *Allgemeine Zeitung*, Ferdinand Lempp, who had been dismissed by the press owners, the Meinert family, for his modestly critical reporting on the shooting in the Old Location. Another initial member was the local politician Marga Vaatz whom Goldblatt had befriended and who in mid-1960 formed, together with Lempp and Japie Basson, the shortlived South West Party, leading them to resign from the Study Group. Other members were farmers, lawyers, medical doctors and businessmen, mostly German-speaking, like the lawyer Dr Meyer, or Dr Kiwi, a general practitioner, or the Secretary of the Karakul Board, Ernst Rudolf Scherz, who was the pioneer in the study of local rock art, and Mrs Gebhardt, one of the few women in the group and known for her 'non–conformist' lifestyle (Henrichsen et al., 2010, p. 4ff).

Most of the members were, as Randolph Vigne observed, 'of irreproachable unpolitical character and integrity'. They might not have viewed themselves as liberals, or, for that matter, as advocates of non-racism though they seemed to have shared concerns about South Africa's efforts to incorporate Namibia. Meeting at the home of Goldblatt in Schwerinsburgweg and studying the UN documents, Goldblatt's intention was, as Vigne phrased it, 'to keep himself and this group out of politics in any form, in the hope that one day they may be able to make a statement of unquestioned authority and sincerity, which could influence events towards peaceful change-over'. He added that to him it seemed that 'As an amateur political philosopher, Goldblatt believes in universal franchise (I wonder if he is the only white man in SWA who does so?) and he cheerfully accepts the inevitability of the changeover. As with every white liberal I met, I urged him to make contact with non-whites...' Vigne also noted that amongst the 'white' politicians, lawyers and journalists whom he thought 'could help in the changeover in South West', like Lempp and 'perhaps' Marga Vaatz, or the barrister Joachim Berker or Dan Minnaar from the *Windhoek Advertiser*, the barrister Bryan O'Linn 'as a possible man of action in future SWA politics ...' impressed me more than anyone ...' (O'Linn, 2010, p. 19). O'Linn, who started his legal career in Windhoek in early 1961, had apparently expressed critical ideas about the apartheid system in Namibia as early as the late 1950s, and in the 1960s as a member of the UNSWP attempted to move this 'white' opposition party into more progressive politics, with little success, as he himself had to concede (Henrichsen et al., 2010, p. 19).

In November 1960, Goldblatt in his personal capacity published the first of two publications on the findings of the Study Group. The 'pamphlet', as he termed it, was entitled *The Conflict between the United Nations and the Union of South Africa in regard to South West Africa*, and was followed in 1961 by a more elaborate analysis the so-called 'booklet' entitled *The Mandated Territory of South West Africa in Relation to the United Nations*. Both publications attracted the interest, much to the surprise of Goldblatt, of Clemens Kapuuo and Rev. Karuaera and led them to contact Goldblatt in late 1961. Goldblatt wrote after their first encounter: 'The Herero leaders had read my pamphlet – and appeared to have confidence in me' (Henrichsen et al., 2010. p. 19). It was, as we shall see, Goldblatt's unambiguous position in his publications on the crucial importance of the UN's role in the SWA dispute, that generated confidence amongst a group of politicians who had been petitioning the UN for years.

Israel Goldblatt was the only legal representative in Namibia of the early 1960s who took a keen interest in the future of the South African colony by studying the legal role of the United Nations in the so-called SWA dispute. In fact, he was regarded as the UN expert in the country, based on his publications. In his 'pamphlet', he rejected, after a careful analysis, the legal claim of South Africa over Namibia and emphasised instead the role of the United Nations in bringing about development and independence for *all* of Namibia's inhabitants.

This opinion was the opposite of the political mainstream of white politics and white popular thinking in the colony, and that of the South African administration and their legal representatives. As he explained in the introduction to the pamphlet, it was intended as 'a warning to the people of South West Africa to do some serious thinking. It is intended, too, as a warning to the political parties in the Territory to stop thinking in terms solely of white votes, and to come down to the realities of the situation in South West Africa' (Henrichsen et al., 2010, Foreword). Goldblatt argued that 'the only way' to end the conflict between the Union of South Africa and the United Nations 'can be ... by the Union Government's recognition of the supervision of the United Nations' and the 'transition [of SWA] into the [UN] Trusteeship System' (Henrichsen et al., 2010, p.30). As such he effectively argued for the direct and intervening role of the United Nations in the administration of the territory whose 'supervision of this Territory embraces all the inhabitants of South West Africa' (1960, Foreword). These arguments had been voiced over and over again since at least 1947 by the Herero Chiefs' Council and other African petitioners in Namibia, but not by a member of the settler society (Goldblatt, 1960, p. 30).

In his 'booklet' of 1961 Goldblatt succinctly summed up his views:

> Year after year, in South Africa and in South West Africa, possibly for party political reasons or possibly from sheer ignorance, we have had the same argument repeated that the power to administer South West Africa as an integral portion of the Union and the power to apply its laws to the territory in some way conferred independent rights upon the Union. Once and for all let that ghost be laid. ... The power to administer South West Africa as an integral portion of the Union and the power to apply its laws, are mere authorities granted to the Mandatory Power [i.e. the United Nations] ... Not the dominant consideration, but the only consideration is the interests of the inhabitants of South West Africa. The interests of the Union play no part whatsoever (1961, p. 24).

These were strong views indeed! Importantly, he accused South Africa's politics as promoting 'hostile and uncontrolled African forces', by which he meant the newly independent African states. Evoking the familiar images of the time in the white press, he predicted an 'unrestrained and extremely aggressive attitude of these nations which will develop, if the Union of South Africa were to continue to ignore the United Nations' (1961, p. 24).

His analysis left no room for ambiguity. He argued that 'a Trusteeship Agreement with the United Nations' would allow 'an orderly development of this Territory, to a stage when a peaceful transition can take place from Trusteeship status to self-government or independence, by agreement between all interested parties, in which property and political rights can be safeguarded'. He too, like many Southern African commentators at the time, warned against 'mounting hostile action by African independent states, which all are bound to stir up the Africans within the Territory and which may, in the final result, when moods are ugly, and temperatures are high, sweep away all political and property rights presently enjoyed by the Whites in the Territory'. Goldblatt's position obviously reflected key principals of liberalism, notably with respect to individual (property) rights and concerns, similar to, for example, Randolph Vigne, concerning a 'racial clash'.

From the perspective of readers in Windhoek of the early 1960s, his analysis, and its publication, was a pronounced political intervention amidst the tightening bid of the colonial power to incorporate SWA. The South African government had to realise that one of its most senior advocates renounced publicly the claims of the government over Namibia, and explicitly warned its white electorate against the political manoeuvres of the government. The electorate had made up its mind already in the Referendum of 1960 on the question of South Africa becoming a Republic outside of the Commonwealth: 62 per cent of the 'white' electorate in Namibia (but only 52 per cent of the electorate in South Africa itself!) had voted for the formation of a Republic and, as such, for an even closer incorporation of Namibia into South Africa and the continuation of Apartheid (Eberhardt, 2007, p. 508). This clearly shows how far mainstream 'white' politics opted not only for the *status quo* but also for an increasing alignment with apartheid South Africa and thus against UN trusteeship, against independence and against non-racism.

Given this context, Goldblatt's views can be regarded as 'radical', as John Dugard, the 1960s Advocate of the Supreme Court of South Africa and Professor of Law at Witwatersrand University in Johannesburg, emphasised. 'His voice', Dugard remembered in 2007, 'was a lonely and brave voice from Namibia'.

> There was little discussion among lawyers of the issue [of UN authority over SWA]. Goldblatt was the only lawyer who presented a pro-UN position. Later, when I did [so myself] I also felt the disapproval of the establishment. So Goldblatt was certainly unique at that time. Both in respect of the contacts he maintained with black Namibians and in respect of his views on the legal status of SWA.[14]

Another close colleague of Goldblatt, the Cape Town based Judge and Senator to the South African parliament, Henry Fagan,[15] had this to say in 1961 after having read Goldblatt's manuscript of the 'booklet':

---

14   Dugard to Henrichsen, e-mail dated 6 October 2007. See also Dugard (1973).
15   On Fagan, who as a Judge chaired the Native Laws Commission in 1949/50, and also, between 1957 and 1959 was Chief Justice and, from 1962, Senator to the South African Parliament until his death in 1963, see especially M. D. Southwood, 'Fathers and their children on our Bench'. In *Consultus*, April 1990, p. 30.

It gives one a picture of a long story in which South Africa's representatives seem to fare very badly. As one who sees their difficulties and sympathises with their side,[16] I keep asking myself, as I read the proceedings recorded shortly in your pages: ' Is it wise to let so much go by default and where they deign to state our case, why do it so provocatively?' It certainly makes me feel very nervous indeed about the matters now pending before the International Court of Justice [ICJ].[17]

As is well known, the ICJ from the early 1960s was drawn into the legal battle between South Africa and the United Nations over the administration of South West Africa. Goldblatt's position, it seems, remained a lonely one and even international legal experts seemed not be aware of his analyses.

It is not known how members of the 'Study Group' discussed Goldblatt's position. Nor is it known when the 'Study Group' disintegrated. During the visit in mid-1962 of Victorio Carpio, the UN emissary to Namibia, Goldblatt, like many African politicians, patiently waited in the Foyer of the Grand Hotel in downtown Windhoek to be allowed to talk to him, as Rev. Karuaera remembered in 2006.[18] Like most Namibians, he, too, could not do so. It might well be that Goldblatt's attempt to meet Carpio was also, like his publications, endorsed by the 'Study Group' and it seems likely that after the failure to meet Carpio the 'Study Group' dissolved. In fact, developments by then had already taken a different course for Israel Goldblatt. It was the African politicians like Clemens Kapuuo and Rev. Karuaera who, from late 1961, increasingly engaged him in matters of more immediate concern, for example the rights of those Old Location residents who continued to resist removal by the municipality. Out of their meetings generated an unusual engagement across the colour lines (discussed later).

Goldblatt's 'Study Group' was not the only study group at the time in 'white' Windhoek. Another one, the 'S.W.A. Political Group' was led by Joachim Berker and Ferdinand Lempp. Their group also included the Vaatz couple as well as Dan Minnaar. It did not have, as Vigne observed in 1961, 'the intellectual stature of Goldblatt's group'.[19] A lecture which Berker's group organised with the renowned South African writer Alan Paton in Windhoek in July 1960, caused a stir when three African men, including Zedekia Ngavirua from the 'only non-racial newpaper in the territory', the *South West News*, were barred from attending the lecture.[20] After having talked to an array of African and European politicians and intellectuals in Windhoek, Vigne came to the conclusion that

> I can see a real purpose, though perhaps not a political purpose, in Goldblatt's group, but none in Berker and Lempp's, except that perhaps they will agree on a course of independent action and their association with like-minded people inside political parties is healthy. But I feel it is significant that there are two such groups [that] have come

---

16 Fagan, a friend and university colleague of Goldblatt, was a 'Nationalist', i.e. member of the National Party of South Africa.
17 BAB, PA.7: Fagan to Goldblatt, 9 June 1961.
18 Rev. Karuaera to Henrichsen, pers. comm., 2006.
19 NAN AACRLS 096: Vigne, 'Confidential Report', 1961.
20 See the report in the *South West News* No 6, p.1, and Henrichsen, 1997, fn 82.

together almost simultaneously with SWAPO and SWANU [in 1959/60], and in them does lie some hope for inter-racial co-operation in the future.²¹

How modest the endeavours of a few Europeans have come to be valued becomes clear from Ruth First's assessment of the 'Study Group'. Without naming any particular body, she observed during her Windhoek visit of mid-1962, and after having socialised with Israel Goldblatt and his family, that there existed

> a scattering of South West Whites ... who are breaking from White supremacy politics ... They are trying to get to grips, in discussions among themselves, with African grievances, and by looking into the facts of the mandate's history they are adjusting themselves to the idea that the U.N. cannot be dismissed as dangerously meddlesome ... But this group is still very small and has not ventured to make public its existence (First, 1963, p. 53).

As the next section outlines, it was the approaches of Clemens Kapuuo and some other African politicians towards Goldblatt from late 1961 that changed Goldblatt's view of the impossibility 'to build bridges'. In fact, for the next few years to come, this is what Goldblatt attempted to engage in – building bridges, albeit 'on my own responsibility'²² and not within the framework of an organisation, a formal group or political party.

Encounters with the Namibian Nationalists

From late 1961 onwards Israel Goldblatt met (at times outside the legal consultations and on a more private basis) a group of young African politicians who were all actively involved in not only the Old Location conflict but in the formation of modern African political parties and the development of modern Namibian nationalism. Most of the men belonged to the then dominant African political body inside Namibia, the Herero Chiefs' Council presided over by Chief Hosea Kutako, or, more precisely, to the *Ozohoze*, Kutako's group of younger activists (Ngavirue, 1997, p. 210; Emmett, 1999, p. 299). Some of the men are to be regarded as crucial figures of modern Namibian nationalism as it developed in the late 1950s and early 1960s and a few became crucial politicians inside Namibia in the 1970s. Amongst them, and most prominent in Goldblatt's papers, was the eloquent Clemens Kapuuo, then the Deputy Chief and designated successor to the veteran of modern Namibian nationalism, Chief Hosea Kutako, who was then over 90 years old. Another was Levi (actually, Levy) Nganjone, then a member the Herero Chiefs' Council and at the same time the Publicity Secretary of SWAPO, the party founded in mid-1960, which would soon develop into Namibia's most important liberation movement. Another was Rev. Bartholomew Karuaera, a pastor of the independent AME Church and simultaneously the influential Secretary-General of the Chiefs' Council. These and other men belonged to the small African

---

21   NAN AACRLS 096: Vigne, 'Confidential Report', 1961.
22   NAN AACRLS 096: Goldblatt in a letter to Vigne, 5 August 1961.

intelligentsia of Windhoek. They were often teachers by education and profession and some, like Kapuuo, Nganjone and Karuaera, had been politically active in various political and cultural bodies that had sprung up in the Old Location in the 1950s like the African Improvement Society or the South West Africa Progressive Association.[23]

Through his at times very regular encounters with these men, Israel Goldblatt was to meet in due course also prominent African politicians from other parts of the country, amongst them the southern Namibian Kaptein Hendrik Samuel Witbooi, like Hosea Kutako a veteran politician and prominent petitioner to the UN in New York. He also would meet, through Kapuuo, the Caprivian politician Brendan Simbwaye, then already under police surveillance or imprisoned, and to whom he would provide legal counsel on an irregular basis for a couple of years and visit in the Windhoek gaol when he was in solitary confinement there in 1966.[24]

Meeting these men outside their formal legal consultations, at times at Goldblatt's home or at Kapuuo's home in the Old Location, was highly unusual in the colony. As Ruth First aptly phrased it:

> Whites and Africans meet, of course, but as administrator and headman, constable and convict, master and servant. In the Windhoek of 1962 there are three white men who from time to time meet Africans on a basis of equality to talk over the territory's problems. There is not a single political organization in South West Africa to which both Whites and Africans belong; there has never been a forum in the country for both White and non-White speakers (First, 1963, p. 14).

For obvious reasons, Ruth First did not provide any names of the three 'white' men, nor any names of their African counterparts. Israel Goldblatt was one of them. Their conversations often led to discussions about the situation in South West Africa, as is indicated by Goldblatt's notes. Another man who regularly met African leaders was Bishop Robert Mize, head of the Anglican Church in Namibia since 1960, who maintained closer relations with Kapuuo and other African politicians than is generally known. His involvement, which included support of resistance by the Old Location residents, led to his becoming a target of the Security Police, like Goldblatt himself. Not surprisingly, in August 1968, Mize was the first foreign clergyman to be deported by the South African government, with many others following in the early 1970s (Winter, 1977, p. 16, 23ff). The third person Ruth First might have been referring to was one of the journalists interested in African politics, Ferdinand Lempp, Dan Minnaar or Hannes Smith ('Smithie').

Goldblatt's encounters and meetings with African nationalists took place regularly in the early and mid-1960s, and with Clemens Kapuuo until at least the late 1960s. Elsewhere I have dealt extensively with the content of these meetings, as recorded by Israel Goldblatt in his notes (Henrichsen et al., 2010). Their conversations concerned not only legal issues, for example, with regard to the on-going struggles by the remaining

---

23 On the development of the urban African intelligentsia, see the detailed analysis Ngavirue p. 286ff.
24 All the nationalists mentioned here are introduced in detail in the book by and on Goldblatt (Henrichsen et al., 2010).

Old Location residents. They also included, at least in 1962, classes and lectures which Goldblatt, on the request of Kapuuo and other African nationalists, provided on issues of 'law and administration'. Inevitably, their conversations involved discussion of daily occurrences that pointedly exemplified the web of apartheid laws and other restrictions that Africans had to face on a daily basis and against which they fought in various ways. The classes also opened up room for discussion of broader topics of concern, not only by the Africans, but also by Goldblatt, touching on structural issues of the colonial society in which they all lived, albeit on different sides of the racial apartheid line. From Goldblatt's notes, one senses a genuine interest that accompanied such discussions, which otherwise rarely took place in the colony at the time. It should be noted that Goldblatt also visited entertainment events in the Old Location at the invitation of Kapuuo, being, as Rev. Karuaera remembered, the only 'white' to do so (Henrichsen et al., 2010, pp. 78-88).

Teaching issues of law and administration to the African nationalists touched on the very foundations of rule and power in the colony. Not surprisingly, they gave rise, as the next section will outline, to rumours circulating through the 'white' community that Goldblatt, amongst others, was engaged 'in a plot to overthrow the government'! Indeed, settler society was deeply suspicious of any deviant (political) activity, as was, of course, the security apparatus of the South African government.

Settler Society and the Security Police

The activities of Goldblatt and the Study Group, his regular meetings with African politicians and his 'lectures' to Kapuuo and others, quickly became the subject of rumours in white Windhoek. The attention of the Security Police was also drawn to his involvement with Africans. In response to all this, sometime in 1963, Israel Goldblatt felt compelled to put things into perspective and wrote an essay entitled 'Growth of a Rumour'.[25] In it, Goldblatt sketches the background to the formation of the Study Group and his increasing involvement with African politicians. He summarised events and meetings with them and briefly recorded other responses. The essay provides a good overview of his contacts and meetings with the African nationalists up to 1963 and ends as follows:

> As a result of all this the public has formed the impression
> (1) That I have composed the telegrams that Kapuo [sic] etc. have sent to U.N.O.
> (2) That I made a lot of money coaching the Africans for their interviews with Carpio.
> (3) That I am engaged in a plot with the Africans for the overthrow of the Govt.
> The Security Police (Swanepoel) told me of the information supplied to them.[26]
> It was all fantastic.

---

25   Published in full in Henrichsen et al., (2010), pp. 69-72.
26   Piet Swanepoel, not to be confused with Major Theunis Swanepoel ('Rooi Rus'), also from the South African Security Police. Thanks to Kurt Dahlmann for pointing this out to me.

Goldblatt in fact never composed any UN related telegrams, nor did he, as he writes in his notes, ask fees from Kapuuo or the other men and women, whom he counselled or met in the 1960s. Nor did he engage 'in a plot with the Africans for the overthrow of the Govt'. He was, however, well aware of the limited opportunity for meetings between Europeans and Africans, and about the consequences of outwardly expressing controversial opinions, as he did in his publications on the role of the UN in the country's future. He knew perfectly well that his meetings and activities were unusual and of a politically sensitive nature. He was also cognisant of the role played by rumours that grow so rapidly on the dry Namibian soil.

By the 1960s, rumours of a plot against the Administration had been rife for some time. As far as is known, they all circulated among Europeans and they all concerned the anticipated actions of 'the natives' against colonial rule. They reflected the constant fears of a settler society, which had experienced what it called rebellions, uprisings or wars by Africans during both the German and the early South African period of rule. Rumours of a plot that concerned a member of the settler society in Namibia have so far not been recorded.[27]

The immediate question that arises is whether the rumours concerning Goldblatt did in fact exist? Had the Security Police, and specifically Lieutenant Piet Swanepoel, who had performed surveillance missions in Windhoek since late 1960, when he was transferred there from Durban, simply made them up as a warning to Goldblatt that his activities, given the growing tensions in the colony, were arousing concern within the South African Administration (Swanepoel, 2007, p. 18)?

There are indications that such rumours did exist outside the minds of the Security Police and were not wholly fabricated. The settler community could read Goldblatt's position on the crucial role of the UN with regard to SWA, or listen to one of his few public speeches on the topic. It does not come as a surprise to learn that he earned more criticism than support for his views and his clear plea for the intervention of the UN. In one of the public reactions to an address Goldblatt delivered in April 1962, he was accused of having provided a political 'After Dinner speech' on the UN's role in SWA and in it of having 'lost sight of the relation between truth and justice'![28] Another reaction accused him of having 'instilled fear'[29] in his audience. Settler society in general was not only anti-intellectual but, especially after 1960, under siege. Another reaction to his speech was a question from the audience: 'What shall we do to avert trouble?' As Bishop Mize recalled, Goldblatt and Kapuuo later 'chuckled together over the answer' which Goldblatt provided: 'Make an immediate study of repressed volcanoes'![30]

European journalists arriving in Windhoek in the early 1960s quickly picked up the local knowledge among Whites that 'Goldblatt was known for his good relations

---

27   The Anglican priest Michael Scott and the American activist Allard Lowenstein, mentioned in such rumours, were foreigners who stayed in the country only very briefly.
28   Readers letters by D. Bode (Menschliche Faktoren) and H. Meinberg ('Was ist wahr?'), in *Allgemeine Zeitung* 11 April 1962. Both referred to a speech which Goldblatt probably gave to the Rotary Club in Walvis Bay and which was then summarised in that newspaper as 'Die Uno und Südwestafrika', 9 May 1961.
29   In German: *das Gruseln beibringen*.
30   University of Kansas, Lawrence Kenneth Spencer Research Library, RH MS 1045, Bishop Robert Mize Collection: Manuscript 'On Chief Clements Kapuuo of Hereros. Martyr', p.2.

with the Herero'. Having interviewed him, some wrote that they believed, despite Goldblatt's 'quite emphatic denials', that he actually was the mind behind at least some of the 'Herero petitions to the UNO' (Henrichsen et al., 2010, pp. 73,77). Yet, by 1961, when Kapuuo and members of the Chiefs' Council consulted Goldblatt for the first time in his chambers, African politicians in Namibia had been petitioning the UN regularly for years. Chief Hosea Kutako, Kaptein Samuel Witbooi, Rev. Markus Kooper, but also many younger politicians like Kapuuo himself, as well as Toivo ya Toivo, Louis Nelegani and Hans Beukes, had sent petitions of complaint and protest to the UN since the late 1940s. These petitions often had to be smuggled out of the country, given the interception of mail by the Security Branch, as Goldblatt himself had to learn. The petitions were an effective strategy of international mobilisation for the SWA case. The petitions also very effectively filtered back into the country as local newspapers, notably the *Windhoek Advertiser* and the German daily, the *Allgemeine Zeitung*, not only received copies of petitions (often hand-delivered to the editors by the writers themselves)[31] but also regularly published them. There simply was no need for these African politicians to involve Goldblatt in their petition strategy in 1961. It is obvious, however, that European popular thinking needed to imagine such a role for a defiant member of its own community, illustrating the degree to which the settler society sought out scapegoats. Rumours by their very nature are about this and little else.

The Special Branch of the police obviously picked up on all this. Or, as Bishop Mize phrased it: 'In an apartheid nation, Whites who associate with Africans are under suspicion of the police.'[32] Crucial in this was Lieutenant Swanepoel, who in 1963 had been transferred from the local Security Branch to the local branch of the newly founded South African Republican Intelligence Service.[33] This security agency focused not only on African political parties but also, given the growing 'mania with internal security', on liberal 'whites' (Brewer, 2001, p. 252). It is thus not surprising that Swanepoel and Israel Goldblatt came into contact with one another. According to Swanepoel's memoir, Goldblatt was 'the only one acknowledged white liberal in the country' (2007, p. 20). When Swanepoel arrived in Windhoek in 1960, he had found a file on Goldblatt in the offices of the Security Branch and over the following years, he claims to have regularly written reports on his encounters with Goldblatt for his superiors in Johannesburg.[34] Goldblatt would also gain some personal experience of the activities of that branch of the police, though this was not at all comparable to what some of his clients and African visitors were to endure.

Goldblatt probably knew that the police were obliged 'immediately to pass on any information to the SB [Security Branch].'[35] Not surprisingly, Randolph Vigne, after meeting Goldblatt in 1961, stated that Goldblatt 'will do nothing positive to encourage

---

31 Pers. comm. by Kurt Dahlmann to Dag Henrichsen.
32 University of Kansas, Bishop Mize Collection: 'Manuscript on Clements Kapuuo'.
33 In order to cover Swanepoel's assignment to the RIS, he was made Head of the Firearms Squad. 'I cannot remember when, where or under what circumstances Adv. Goldblatt and I met, but by December 1964 we had come to know each other fairly well. He knew that I had been with the Security Branch...' Swanepoel to Dag Henrichsen, e-mail, 22 February 2008.
34 Swanepoel to Dag Henrichsen, e-mail, 22 February 2008. See also Brewer, 2001, p. 252; Swanepoel, 2007.
35 Ibid.

the security police to watch his movements, tap his telephone, etc., as they certainly would do if he should make any move in this direction.'[36] This was soon to change. When exactly Goldblatt, his home and his family were placed under regular surveillance by the Security Police remains unclear. Did it start when Ruth First visited Namibia in 1962 and socialised with Goldblatt and his family? While in Windhoek, First was under constant surveillance by the Security Police, among them Swanepoel.[37] It is quite possible that it was through Goldblatt that she met Kapuuo, Nganjone and other African politicians,[38] whom she interviewed for her critical investigations into the country's history, politics and conflicts.

As First was afterwards to write on her experiences in Windhoek:

> The police state in operation is not noisy or dramatic, except in time of emergency; it can be relaxed, even slovenly. The detectives on duty that first week-end wore shorts and rugby socks, and childish smiles on their faces as, in the prowling police car; they outdistanced me, the footslogger, on the way to an appointment. In the beginning there were two, later four, and even five and six on duty, working in pairs, padding along the pavement six paces behind me ... the trail to the dry-cleaner and the shoemaker, the skulking next to the telephone booth, both ends of the road and every exit of the hotel patrolled, detectives following me to the airport, to the post office to buy stamps, watching me at breakfast, interviewing people I had seen ... (First, 1963, p. 13).

Having escaped into exile after she was released from solitary confinement in Johannesburg in connection with the Rivonia Trial and the imprisonment of Nelson Mandela and other African National Congress and Communist Party activists, in 1964 First wrote from London to 'my dear Israel':

> Here above much else I think I enjoy the anonymity. You can't say the same in your town, but when I'm not around at least you're not tailed. Though you, of course, enjoyed that, as you enjoy everything.[39]

As his daughters Naomi Jacobson and Karen Marshall remember vividly, Israel Goldblatt was tailed regularly, though not, of course, in quite the intense and

---

36 Compare this with Swanepoel's (2007) remarks on phone tapping in Windhoek in the early 1960s, p. 19.
37 See First's remarks in her book (1963, p. 13f). For additional information see also Goldblatt (2010).
38 A list of Ruth First's possible contacts in Windhoek can be found in the Institute of Commonwealth Studies (ICS), London, Ruth First Archives, 1/7/1/3. The list has names and at times telephone numbers and addresses, and includes Israel Goldblatt, Ferdinand Lempp, Bishop Mize, Rev. J. Wing, Rev. F. Haithornethwaite, Rev. W. van der Syde, John Muundjua, Stadig Kambonde, Clemens Kapuuo, Levy Nganjone, Hosea Kutako, Rev. Karuaera, Gerson Veii and Werner Mamugwe. Some of these names have a tick next to them which could indicate that she met these men. Mize, in his reminiscences on Kapuuo, mentions that he first met Kapuuo and his council at his residency. See University of Kansas, Mize Collection, 'Manuscript on Clements Kapuuo', p. 3.
39 Ruth First to Israel Goldblatt, London, 5 June 1964. Letter held in private possession.

intimidating way they followed Ruth First. For Goldblatt the most noticeable sign over the years was the yellow VW beetle that regularly turned up in front of his home on Schwerinsburgweg. At times, so the family memory goes, he invited 'them' inside for tea. The issue of phone tapping, the daughters recall, was a constant concern, as were the intermittent telephone calls late at night, with only silence at the end of the line. Letters between him and Ruth First did go astray and he joked about it in those which did reach her in London.[40] Obviously, then, the Security Police had orders to at least scare off Goldblatt, while he himself seems to have regarded them more as an irritation than a threat. Yet, his house was not searched, as were those of Kapuuo, Nganjone and Rev. Karuaera,[41] nor, apparently, were his chambers touched. Karuaera in an interview in 2007 dismissed the question of Goldblatt's security with the laconic remark: 'He was too prominent'.[42]

In this 'undramatic' climate of the police state, fear was a crucial element instilled by the Special Branch into society, rumours being one of its (intended?) outcomes.[43] Goldblatt would not give in to this, nor would he abandon his principle of 'building bridges'. In this he displayed a different approach to, for example, Joachim Berker. When the latter apologised privately to the three African men who in 1960 were barred by Berker's 'Committee of the SWA Political Group' from attending a public lecture by Alan Paton in the Sam Cohen Hall in Windhoek, he, according to the *SW News*, added that he 'feared that he would be arrested'. 'You well know the situation in this country, said the Advocate'.[44] Goldblatt did not have such fears. Ruth First aptly summed up the situation in Windhoek at the time by remarking that 'this is a community where passers-by look askance at any conversation between a White and an African. Where flimsy cords of communication between the colours are spun, intimidation severs them instantly' (First, 1963, p. 14). Goldblatt continued, despite the signs of intimidation, to meet African politicians.

At one stage, the South African Administrator in Windhoek must have been informed about Goldblatt's activities as can be gleaned from a strongly worded letter of protest which Goldblatt wrote on 8 April 1963 to Wentzel ('Wennie') du Plessis.[45]

The letter was written after a confrontation between Goldblatt and du Plessis on Tuesday, 6 April, in the Administrator's office on the issue of, as Goldblatt put it in his letter, 'the Administration's refusal to permit Dr. [Kenneth] Abrahams of Cape Town to reside and practise in Rehoboth'. Kenneth Abrahams, a medical doctor from Cape Town, and his Namibian wife, Ottilie Schimming, who had grown up in the Old Location, had been active SWAPO members in Cape Town, and in January 1963 had settled in Rehoboth. The South African authorities regarded Abrahams as a 'prohibited immigrant', which prompted the Rehoboth Raad to declare Abrahams and his wife

---

40 See, for example, ICS, Ruth First Archives 1/3/9/3, Israel Goldblatt to Ruth First, n.d. (stamped: Windhoek 1966).
41 See, for example, Kapuuo's letter of 6 June 1961 to Randolph Vigne (in NAN, AACRLS 096) where he reports on the searches of his own home and those of the other two men.
42 In an interview with Dag Henrichsen.
43 This is also confirmed by Kurt Dahlmann's memories of the time in Windhoek. Pers. comm. to Dag Henrichsen.
44 *South West News*, 23 July 1960, No 6, p. 1
45 Letter kept in private possession.

citizens of Rehoboth with reference to the Raads Constitution and its special rights of self-rule in the Rehoboth Gebiet.[46] While Abrahams, together with other SWAPO members like Andreas Shipanga and Hermanus Beukes escaped to Bechuanaland,[47] the Raad continued to pursue the matter legally through Israel Goldblatt. The Raad, as Goldblatt explained in his letter, had sought an interview with the Administrator and 'I had been informed that the Raad wished me to represent them at the interview, that is as Counsel, and accordingly a consultation took place in my chambers last Monday.'

The interview with the Administrator took place the following day. Goldblatt's letter to the Administrator complained that, just as Goldblatt was about to speak:

> you stopped me, and said you wished the Raad to put its cases on these two points. … You ordered me to sit down! …
>
> No advocate, Your Honour, and certainly no advocate of standing, and I happen to be the most senior ranking advocate in the whole of the Republic and South West Africa — would submit to this discourteous, and in the circumstances insulting treatment. I accordingly, together with my attorney [of the firm Lorentz & Bone] immediately walked out of your office. …
>
> I wish, Sir, with respect, but strongly to protest against your conduct, and equally strongly against the fact that in the result you deprived my clients of the representation which they had asked you to permit and which you had agreed to.

After the incident, Goldblatt's letter ended, 'the Raad came to my chambers *'om hulle teleurstelling uit te druk'* [in order to express their disappointment]'.

The Administrator's treatment in preventing Goldblatt from properly representing his clients can be read as a calculated reaction to Goldblatt's history of acting as counsel, meeting and providing classes for African politicians.

Conclusion

What are we to make of a man, who, seemingly, was one of the very few Europeans in Namibia's settler society of the 1960s who regularly met and engaged, though in a very limited way, with a group of young African nationalists? Goldblatt's position was essentially that of a liberal outside of any political party framework who sympathised with independence in the context of his pro-UN position and who subscribed to a political system of universal franchise and, as such, a democratic, non-racial society. But he did not engage in any overt political campaigning for such causes and feared, like many

---

[46] On this affair, see Kenneth Abrahams (Leys and Brown, 2005, p. 145). Abraham's lawyer in Windhoek was Bryan O'Linn (Henrichsen et al., 2010, p. 150). See also Du Pisani (1986, p. 152).

[47] On the men's flight, and Abrahams' capture in Bechuanaland by the South African Security Police and his abduction to Cape Town, see Abrahams in Leys and Brown (2005), p. 148. Also *Allgemeine Zeitung*, 5 August 1963, p. 1.

South African liberals at the time, radical economic transformation. At the same time, he was castigated by not only rumours but also the 'white' press in Windhoek for his activities and his position, and was regularly under surveillance by the Security Police. As such, the limitations of dissenting political practices and thoughts in Namibia's settler society become quite apparent.

On the other hand, Israel Goldblatt was also heavily criticised by African nationalists more radical than, for example, Clemens Kapuuo or Rev. Karuaera. For SWANU's President Jariretundu Kozonguizi, Goldblatt was one of those 'liberal characters engaged in the anti-SWANU campaign. These are in the main political cowards in their own community.' In 1964 he referred to Goldblatt as:

> a leading Barrister whose contact with the Anti-SWANU elements in the Location is his own daughter [Karen Blum] ... We shall not be surprised if we were to learn that Kapuuo's cabinet as announced with the formation of the National Unity Democratic Organisation [NUDO, in 1964] is actually counselled, advised and assisted by a sort of White-anti-SWANU-Non-Nationalist-Broederbond-like background. By South African political standards this will be a Progressive rather than a Liberal group which means liberals in the old tradition ('nothing wrong to have a cup of tea with a native as long as he knows his place') and absolutely not progressive at all. ... The choice is between the White Nationalists on the one hand and the African Nationalists and Socialists on the other. No room for Liberals or liberals be they white, yellow or black.[48]

For Kozonguizi, 'Liberals/liberals' were, as he was to explain to Kurt Dahlmann, the editor of the German daily, the *Allgemeine Zeitung* when both met in London in late 1965, those, 'who in their own community had little or no influence and who have proven, that they are not successful in their (white) group.'[49] Kozonguizi's perspective, which I cannot analyse here (but see Henrichsen et al., 2010, pp. 89-93) was, of course, reflecting the increasing political radicalisation inside and outside of Namibia and was informed by intense political activism. Goldblatt was not an activist and his moderate position remained an isolated one.

Kozonguizi later modestly rephrased his judgement on Goldblatt and his daughter Karen Blum. In 1988 and then no longer in exile and no longer the President of SWANU (which he left in 1966),[50] and now a barrister and a member of NUDO himself as well as the Minister of Justice in the so-called interim government in Windhoek, he gave a lecture on the Namibian liberation struggle at a NUDO Youth League event. In his lecture, he categorically denied the historical role of 'the white man .. in the struggle for liberation'. However, according to the summary of his lecture in *The Namibian*,

---

48   In SWANU's magazine *Freedom*, 1964/65.
49   Kurt Dahlmann, 'Kozonguizi, die Liberalen und ich'. In *Allgemeine Zeitung*, 22 October 1965.
50   Ruth First Archives, ICS, 1/7/1/4: 'An open letter to the people of Namibia from Jariretundu Kozonguizi', ca 1972. According to this document he withdrew from politics in 1966 and in 1969 resigned from SWANU. He returned to Namibia in 1976, ironically as Legal Advisor to Kapuuo and as a Herero delegate to the Turnhalle Constitutional Conference. See his obituary, in *The Namibian*, 2 February 1995.

he 'apart from Michael Scott ... named Advocate Israel Goldblatt and his daughter Karen, and Hannes Smith of the *Windhoek Observer* as whites who were "prepared to ascertain the views of the black man".'[51] To 'ascertain the views of the black man' was, of course, different from actively supporting 'his' political struggle and it has to be acknowledged that it was Kapuuo who knocked at Goldblatt's door in the early 1960s, not Goldblatt knocking at the door of Kapuuo.

Goldblatt's social class and, perhaps, age (he was actively planning his retirement in Israel from the mid-1960s onwards) probably contributed to his restrained attitude, as did the general and intimidating climate in settler society. In comparison to some South African lawyers, for example Braam Fisher, a friend of Goldblatt, who in the 1960s because of his activist approaches, faced banishment and other police actions, Goldblatt was not 'a hotshot human rights lawyer' despite his numerous professional engagements.[52] He himself might have resolutely refuted such a label. As such, the limits of his endeavours for the cause of Namibian decolonisation and the establishment of a non-racial society become obvious.

Goldblatt's endeavours confirm that there existed hardly any political space for what Zed Ngavirue calls 'the possibility of an alliance across racial lines' in Namibia.[53] Whilst there were possibilities – Ngavirue cites the relationships between the SA Liberal Party and SWAPO in Cape Town in the early 1960s – there were no Europeans in Namibia who seem to have explored these possibilities at the time, not even Goldblatt, who believed in universal franchise, publicly emphasised the role of the United Nations and refuted South Africa's (legal) position in the dispute, who sympathised with national independence and provided council for people facing a repressive regime. Whilst a dissident figure in settler society, Goldblatt's actions, clearly reflect the limits of European political dissent in Namibia. It is not surprising to realise that traditions of non-racism in Namibia are actually located primarily in African politics. Namibia had a long tradition of anti-colonial resistance by African communities that was not simply presented as a racial struggle and, after World War II, the petitions to the UN by African political bodies, and the increasingly pronounced interventions by African clergymen, also presented a vision of a unified nation. The white community might also have read *South West News*, which defined itself as 'the only non-racial newspaper of the territory', and briefly appeared in the Old Location in 1960, produced by the first African publishing venture in the country. It is not known whether Israel Goldblatt read this newspaper.[54]

---

51   *The Namibian*, 9 December 1988, p. 9.
52   Thanks to Robert Gordon for this description. On Goldblatt's involvement with the case of SWAPO Vice-President Brendan Simbwaye, see Goldblatt (2010, p. 61).
53   When discussing the 'question of European membership' from the point of view of SWANU and SWAPO in the 1960s (Ngavirue, 1997, p. 241), it should be pointed out that social relations across the colour line were, of course, very frequent, but have not been researched at all for the period after World War I.
54   It is known that the teacher and amateur scientist Fritz Gaerdes (residing in Okahandja) read and collected this newspaper (Henrichsen, 1997. p. 5)

References

Allgemeine Zeitung, 11 April 1962, letters by D. Bode and H. Meinberg.

Allgemeine Zeitung, 5 August 1963.

Allgemeine Zeitung, 2 February 1995.

Brewer, J. (2001) *Black and Blue. Policing in South Africa.* Oxford: Clarendon Press.

Dahlmann, K. 'Kozonguizi, die Liberale und ich', *Allgemeine Zeitung,* 22 October 1965.

Du Pisani, A. (1986) *SWA/Namibia. The Politics of Continuity and Change.* Johannesburg: Jonathan Ball.

Dugard, J. (1973) *The South West Africa/Namibia Dispute: Documents and Scholarly Writings on the Controversy Between South Africa and The United Nations.* Berkeley: University of California Press.

Eberhardt, M. (2007) *Zwischen Nationalsozialismus und Apartheid. Die deutsche Bevölkerungsgruppe Südwestafrikas 1915-1965.* Berlin: Lit Verlag.

Emmett, T. (1999) *Popular resistance and the roots of nationalism in Namibia, 1915-1966.* Basel: Schlettwein Publishing.

First, R. (1963) *South West Africa.* Harmondsworth: Penguin.

Freedom (1964/65) SWANU magazine.

Gockel, K. (2010) *Mission und Apartheid. Heinrich Vedder and Hans Karl Diehl.* Cologne: Rüdiger Köppe Verlag.

Goldblatt, I. (1961) *The conflict between the United Nations and the Union of South Africa in regard to South West Africa.* Windhoek: Goldblatt.

Hancock, I. (1984) *White liberals, moderates and radicals in Rhodesia 1953-1980.* London: Croom Helm.

Henrichsen, D. (ed.) (1997) *A glance at our Africa. Facsimile reprint of South West News.* Basel: Basel Afrika Bibliographien.

Henrichsen, D., Jacobson, N. and Marshall, K. (eds) (2010) *Israel Goldblatt. Building Bridges. Namibian Nationalists Clemens Kapuuo, Hosea Kutako, Brendan Simbwaye, Samuel Witbooi.* Basel: Basel Afrika Bibliographien.

Leys, C. and Brown, S. (2005) *Histories of Namibia. Living through the liberation struggle. Live histories told to Colin Leys and Susan Brown.* London: Merlin Press.

Marks, S. (1995) *The tradition of non-racism in South Africa.* Liverpool: Liverpool University Press.

Ngavirue, Z. (1997) *Political parties and interest groups in South West Africa (Namibia): A study of a plural society.* Basel: P. Schlettwein Publishing.

Nujoma, S. (2001) *Where others wavered. The Autobiography of Sam Nujoma.* London: Panaf Books.

O'Linn, B. (2003) *Namibia: the sacred trust of civilization: idea and reality.* Windhoek: Gamsberg-Macmillan.

O'Linn, B. (2010) *Namibia: the sacred trust of civilization: ideal and reality, Revised edition Volume 1.* Windhoek: Gamsberg-Macmillan.

Rich, P. B. (1984) *White power and the liberal conscience. Racial segregation and South African liberalism, 1921-60.* Manchester: Manchester University Press.

South West News, 5 March 1960, Vol. 1. No.1.

South West News, 23 July 1963, No. 6.

Southwood, M. D. (1990) 'Fathers and their children on our Bench', *Consultus*, April 1990.

Swanepoel, P. (2007) *Really inside BOSS. A tale of South Africa's late intelligence service (and something about the CIA)*. Derdepoortpark.

The Namibian, 2 February 1995, Obituary for Jariretundu Kozonguizi.

The Namibian, 9 December, 1988.

Vigne, R. (1997) *Liberals against apartheid. A history of the Liberal Party of South Africa, 1953-1968*. Houndsmill: Macmillan.

Winter, C. (1977) *Namibia*. Michigan: Eerdmans.

Archival sources

Basler Afrika Bibliographien
PA.7 Israel Goldblatt - papers and notes
Secretary of the World Federation to Goldblatt, 5 February 1960
Fagan to Goldblatt, 9 June 1961

Institute of Commonwealth Studies, London
ICS117 Ruth First Archives
1/3/9/3 Israel Goldblatt to Ruth First, n.d.
1/7/1/4 'An open letter to the people of Namibia' from Jariretundu Kozonguizi

National Archives of Namibia
AARCLS 096 Randolph Vigne
Confidential Paper, 1961
Kapuuo's letter to Randolph Vigne 6 June 1961
Goldblatt's letter to Vigne 5 August 1961

Lawrence Kenneth Spencer Research Library, University of Kansas
RH MS 1045 Bishop Robert Mize Collection
Manuscript 'On Chief Clements Kapuuo of Hereros. Martyr'

8 The Caprivi African National Union (CANU) 1962–1964: Forms of Resistance[1]

Bennett Kangumu Kangumu

The history of the Caprivi African National Union (CANU) is barely covered in Namibian historiography dealing with the liberation struggle.[2] However, in this chapter I am not interested in presenting a historical narrative of the rise and fall of CANU, and thus to mistakenly assume a simple linearity of events regarding the history of the movement.[3] I will also not discuss the relationship between CANU and the South West Africa People's Organisation (SWAPO) in exile and the subsequent 'merger' of the two liberation movements.[4] The main focus will be to examine why the administration enforced a harsh clampdown on CANU activities and activists, forcing many into exile and preventing the movement from operating freely within Caprivi, beyond its official launch and its first meeting.

---

1 I acknowledge the assistance of Mr Alfred Ilukena, Permanent Secretary in the Ministry of Education, Republic of Namibia, who assisted me with conducting oral history interviews with CANU activists and family members of Brendan Simbwaye in April 2006. His family ties and the fact that he was a freedom fighter himself made it easier for me to secure appointments for interviews and get the confidence of the interviewees. I sincerely thank him. I would also like to thank Ellen Namhila for her persistent encouragement for research on Simbwaye to be undertaken, and Werner Hillebrecht and staff at the National Archives of Namibia for being very helpful and attentive during the many hours I spent in the archives.
2 Often it is presented as a minor and insignificant organisation, which is only an 'appendix' to the history of the South West Africa People's Organisation (SWAPO), with which it 'merged' in 1964 to fight for a common cause. References in the literature are usually to show how SWAPO was a broad based nationalistic organisation representative of the people of South West Africa, and not necessarily to write about the history of CANU (see among others, Mbuende, 1986; Katjavivi, 1988; Pütz, von Egidy and Caplan, 1989; Nujoma, 2001).
3 For a more detailed discussion of the history of CANU see Kangumu, (2008). 'Contestations over Caprivi Identities: From Pre-colonial times to the present', (PhD thesis, University of Cape Town). See Kangumu (2011), for the published version.
4 On 5 November 1964, CANU and SWAPO announced a 'merger' of the two movements in a joint press release signed by Albert Mishake Muyongo on behalf of CANU and Sam Nujoma on behalf of SWAPO. This agreement is a major source of contention in present day Namibian politics and lay at the core of secessionist tendencies by a group of people from the Caprivi region under Mishake Muyongo. The secessionists allege that SWAPO made an undertaking, in terms of the 'merger' agreement, that the Caprivi would be granted either special status or complete autonomy after Namibia's independence. Sam Nujoma of SWAPO strongly refutes this version of history and maintains that there was always an agreement for one nation (Flint, 2002, p. 421). The press release issued by the two parties does not support Muyongo's version. Michael Morris claims that the merger was first announced by SWAPO's Secretary-General, Jacob Kuhangua, in Dar es Salaam on 13 October, 1964 (Morris, 1971, p. 14).

Symptomatic of the suppression was the fact that Brendan Simbwaye, CANU's first president,[5] was arrested and banished from Caprivi altogether, and disappeared after several years whilst in the hands of the authorities. The chapter will, therefore, investigate CANU's political activities and strategies between 1962 and 1964, the period when it was accused of 'undermining' the administration. The Native Commissioner for the Eastern Caprivi Strip at the time criticised the activities of 'certain young men of CANU who, as you know, have been creating trouble here, doing and saying things to try and poison the minds of the people against the government.'[6] What was CANU 'doing and saying' that 'poisoned' people's minds? John Leif Fossé has described CANU's campaign as 'peaceful but successful' and argued that it proved difficult for the authorities to handle.[7]

The scope of the chapter will be limited to examining four aspects of the political activities in which CANU played a role to influence public opinion against the authorities:

1. participation in the Odendaal Commission's public hearings;
2. campaigning on the issue of cattle sales in Caprivi;
3. interventions in public debates on the education system; and
4. debating the functions of traditional authorities.

But before discussing these actions, a brief historical background of Caprivi will be provided to help put these issues into perspective.

The space that would become 'The Caprivi'[8] was inhabited by subsistence farming communities since time immemorial, who lived sparsely scattered under decentralised forms of governance or tribal administration. During the reign of Ngombala (1725-1775), the sixth ruler in the oral genealogy of the Lozi Kingdom, the Lozi established supremacy over these communities. This was followed, from 1838, by a period of occupation by the Makololo of Sibitwane and then, after 1864, the region fell under Lozi rule again. It was the Anglo–German Treaty of 1 July 1890 that created the Caprivi Strip (Zipfel), and made it part of German South West Africa. However, it took Germany about 18 years before they actually established an operational administration in the Caprivi Strip, and during this time it is alleged that the territory turned into a haven for criminals and poachers (Fisch, 1999 p.12).

In 1909 Germany established a post at a place they called Schuckmannsburg, from where they administered the territory.[9] This was short-lived for the outbreak of World War I intervened, and the Germans surrendered to the Allied Forces without firing a shot at the Allied Forces, making the capture of Caprivi one of the first victories of the Allied Forces in the war. Along with the rest of South West Africa, the Caprivi Strip

---

5   See chapter 9 in this volume for more details.
6   NAN LKM 3/3/3 File No. N1/15/2, Kruger, Magistrate Eastern Caprivi Zipfel, to Chief Moraliswani Maiba of the Masubiya, 8 September 1964.
7   John Leif Fossé (1996), 'Negotiating the Nation in Local Terms: Ethnicity and Nationalism in Eastern Caprivi, Namibia' (MA Thesis, University of Oslo) p. 155.
8   For the Masubiya, it formed part of their pre-colonial kingdom of Itenge, see Shamukuni, 1972. In 2013, the Caprivi Region was renamed 'Zambezi Region'. See Shamukuni (1972).
9   In 2013, Schuckmannsburg was renamed 'Luhonono'. See Shinovene Immanuel, 'Caprivi is no more', *The Namibian*, 9 August 2013.

was handed to South Africa at the Versailles Conference under the League of Nations Mandate. Between 1919 and 1989, the administration of the Caprivi was passed back and forth several times between various administrators in South Africa, South West Africa, and the neighbouring British colonies. The reason given for this constant transfer was the administrative difficulties caused by the geographical remoteness and isolation of Caprivi from Windhoek. The colonial administration also considered Caprivi as unsuitable for white settlement because it was malarial and generally of low economic potential. An official, Gibbons, inspecting the region for the British South African Company concluded that the Caprivi was: 'the poorest district that have [sic] come under my notice' (Fisch, 1999, p. 17). The territory was perceived as useless, for it did not have minerals such as diamonds and copper, nor, with its few inhabitants, was it a labour reservoir or even an outlet for products. The administration of the territory was based on dual tribal chieftainship under the supervision of one government officer, and the provision of education and health services was left in the hands of missionaries.

This perception of the region as a useless piece of land ensured that Caprivi remained a remote, sleepy, backwater for the most part, until the early 1960s, when the liberation struggle in southern Africa intensified with the launch of the armed struggle, and the strategic location of the Caprivi – in the heart of southern Africa – attracted a heavy South African military build-up there. It was at this crucial time, in 1964, that Northern Rhodesia gained its independence (becoming Zambia), and it became clear to apartheid South Africa that it would play a pivotal role in aiding and housing liberation movements in southern Africa. It was also at this time that CANU became very active as an underground movement, so its relationship with the United Independence Party (UNIP) of Zambia was closely monitored, and its activities were accompanied by political and security concerns. CANU had existed as an informal underground movement since the end of 1958,[10] although it only came to media attention in 1961[11] and was formally founded on 7 September 1962.[12] Among the resolutions passed on that day was that the creation of the organisation be kept secret for fear that the South African government would ban it before it could be publicly launched and publicised in Caprivi.[13]

---

10   Adrian Waluka Simubali, Bukalo, 16 April 2006. Simubali is a founder member of CANU and held the position of Treasurer.
11   See the *African Mail,* 17 October 1961, in Lusaka.
12   Albert Zacharia Ndopu, Katima Mulilo, 17 April, 2006. Albert Zacharia Ndopu was an executive committee member of CANU and served as its Secretary for Information and Publicity. Different writers provide different dates on which CANU was supposedly formed: Kaire Mbuende (1986, p. 154) says that it was formed in 1962; Peter Katjavivi provides two different dates – 1964 (1984, p. 575), and 1963 (1988, p. 51); Ernest Likando argues that it was formed in early 1963 (1989, p. 139) as do J. Pütz, H. von Egidy, and P. Caplan (1989, p. 90).
13   Shamukuni (1972).

The Odendaal Hearings

CANU began to engage the authorities even before it was publicly launched. One platform for action was provided by the Odendaal Commission's[14] public hearings that were held at Katima Mulilo over two days during February 1963. The Commissioners based their choice of respondents on a tribal formula and did not provide room for other organisations to make representations. They only interviewed the two tribal chiefs at the time, and their representatives, plus a native constable, Robert Nchindo; otherwise the others who provided statements were Europeans resident in the Caprivi (such as the medical officer, priests, the representative of the Witwatersrand Native Labour Association (WNLA), and William Finaughty, a store owner). Despite this attempt to block organisations and individuals outside the tribal authorities from making their voices heard, CANU managed to influence the tribal authorities and their representatives to unanimously call for the withdrawal of the South African government from Caprivi. Of the ten respondents who expressed their views, all save one, called for the removal of the South African government from Caprivi. They demanded that the Caprivi Strip be entrusted to the hands of another government, such as 'Russia, America, Rhodesia, Ghana, "UNO"[15], and the Queen's government.'[16] The more radical of the group believed that the people of Caprivi could govern themselves, for the 'government... had forgotten us.'[17] They accused the government of the day of being more interested in the preservation of wild animals than having the people's interests at heart.

When one compares the nature of the earlier grievances of the people in the 1940s and 1950s, and how they wanted them resolved, with what was being said at the public hearings in 1963, it noticeable that there had been a fundamental shift. Previously, demands had been made for the withdrawal of certain officials from the Caprivi Strip, and complainants had not directed their anger at the South African government itself. Demands had been practical and limited such as the need to open new stores and find a market for surplus cattle, or that the rounds of ammunition permitted to be bought by an individual annually should be increased. At the Commission's public

---

14 The Odendaal Commission of Inquiry into South West Africa Affairs was announced on 21 September 1962 through the Official Gazette Extra-Ordinary of South West Africa, No. 2430. Its terms of reference were phrased as follows in the notice: 'Having regard to what has already been planned and put into practice, to enquire thoroughly into further promoting the material and moral welfare and the social progress of the inhabitants of South West Africa, and more particularly its non-white inhabitants, and to submit a report with recommendations on a five-year plan for the accelerated development of the various non-white groups of South West Africa, inside as well as outside their own territories, and for the further development and building up of such native territories in South West Africa....' It can be noted that the Commission was asked to carry out its work within the context of 'what has already been planned and put into practice', which was the apartheid oriented socio-political structure. It is not surprising the Commissioners did not try to challenge the assumption on which apartheid thinking was based: the thesis that racial differences imply cultural and spiritual differences.
15 When one of the Commissioners told the Ngambela of the Masubiya, Kalundu Munihango, who proposed the UNO, that it is not a government but a grouping of different governments, he responded that 'it is even better because where there are many people with different opinions, they should be able to rule better' (quoted in Kangumu, 2008, p. 237).
16 Quoted from the Odendaal Commission public hearings transcript, copy held by the author.
17 Ibid.

hearings, speakers were vocal in their call for the total removal of the government, and they displayed awareness of the existence of the UN Trusteeship over South West Africa and knowledge of its significance. This, points in a sense, to the influence of an enlightened new generation of political activists. While the Commission went ahead and made recommendations contrary to the demands of the people, it became clear to the administration that political awareness was growing in the Caprivi Strip.

Cattle Sales

Finding a market for the disposal of surplus cattle had always been a major problem for the colonial administration in Caprivi Strip. This was due in part to the lack of veterinary controls in the territory after 1929 when the South West Africa Administration took over this responsibility from the Bechuanaland Protectorate Administration (which had provided periodic veterinary services to the area). By the time Pretoria took over direct control of the Eastern Caprivi Strip ten years later, in 1939, there was no outlet at all for the disposal of stock from the Caprivi Strip and an official inspection found the area to be 'overstocked'.[18] In this context, in 1963, the administration negotiated with the Northern Rhodesia Cold Storage Commission to buy cattle in bulk over two days at Katima Mulilo in April, and installed a weighbridge with the necessary kraals and races (narrow passages through which livestock were channelled) so that each transaction was one of a fixed rate determined by exact weight. It was agreed that the Commission would relate their offer to what they paid in Northern Rhodesia, but allowing for additional costs relating to the need to keep the cattle in quarantine and then drive them across to Livingstone through the island of Impalila.

Kruger, the Native Commissioner for Eastern Caprivi at the time, described the atmosphere during the cattle sale as 'oppressive' because of the way CANU agents 'were mingling with the crowd in a way that suggested they were up to no good.'[19] It is interesting to note that the administration, thus, acknowledged the existence of CANU at this stage, well before it was publicly launched. When the prices for the first cattle were announced, the sellers flatly rejected the price and refused to offer any other animals for sale. The administration investigated and found that people were not satisfied with the price offered, which they said was lower than that paid in Northern Rhodesia. Kruger confirmed this a few days later when someone brought a Northern Rhodesia newspaper to him in which prices paid by the Cold Storage Commission in Northern Rhodesia were published, and was astonished to find that indeed they were considerably higher than those that had been offered in Caprivi. He remarked:

> I don't believe the CANU agents, in their ignorance, knew the difference – if they did so much the worse. But their scheming had all the appearance of getting the better of the administration, leading the people generally, in their confused state, to a belief that I myself was not to be trusted.[20]

---

18   NAN 2267 A503/1-7. Louw, E.W., 'Inspection Report on the Eastern Caprivi Zipfel', 1939, p. 10.
19   NAN A.472. Kruger, C.E., 'History of the Caprivi, 1890-1984', p. 7.
20   Ibid.

CANU agents did not stop there, for subsequent events would prove that they were not ignorant and that they knew the difference. CANU decided to bypass the administration and to negotiate directly with the Cold Storage Commission on behalf of the cattle sellers. They sent two emissaries to Livingstone to negotiate with a representative of the Cold Storage Commission, who then sent a letter back to Kruger informing him about CANU's intentions.

Three things are clear from the above incident. Firstly, the fact that CANU was positioning itself as the rightful representative of the people demonstrated that they were able to take care of their interests, and were able to prevent even a single sale taking place on that day. It showed the limits of state power, however oppressive, over the actions of individuals. Secondly, one might be surprised that an ordinary cattle sale provided an opportunity for a contest between CANU and the administration.[21] It encourages historians to consider different ways in which resistance manifested itself in the history of liberation movements in southern Africa. Thirdly, given the lack of a market for the disposal of livestock, one would assume that the sellers were negotiating from a weak position and would offer their cattle for sale at any cost. With CANU influencing them, they chose resistance over individual needs, and offered CANU a victory over the administration.

Education

As an organisation that was formed by teachers, CANU was bound to poke its nose into matters related to education. In early 1964 when books and other materials were sent to a newly-established Bantu Community School at Kasheshe, about 30 kilometres west of Katima Mulilo, the community refused to accept them. Upon enquiry they reported that Brendan Simbwaye, the president of CANU, had told them not to accept the school books or Bantu Education.[22] This should be understood within the context of the transition in educational management that was taking place at the time in the Eastern Caprivi Strip. The provision of education in the Caprivi was left in the hands of the missionaries until the 1960s, but the government then started taking over the running of the schools, partly to institute the Bantu Education system. Political actors such as Brendan Simbwaye, who were products of missionary education, and were devout Christians themselves, did not take lightly to the fact that education was to be taken away from the church.

The incident concerning the refusal to accept textbooks at Kasheshe Bantu Community School was followed by a student strike at the Holy Family Mission School (Kizito

---

21 Evidence that there was opposition to cattle dipping in South Africa and cattle branding in southern Namibia highlights the need for further research into other forms of 'hidden' resistance to colonial rule in the early twentieth century. See Beinert and Bundy (1987) and Jeremy Silvester (1991), 'Black Pastoralists, White Farmers: The Dynamics of Land Dispossession and Labour Recruitment in Southern Namibia, 1915-1955' (PhD thesis, University of London).

22 The Bantu Education Act (No. 47 of 1953) was extended to Namibia and linked to the state taking over control of many schools that had previously been run by the different churches, although the Roman Catholics and Seventh Day Adventists retained control of many of their schools. For more details see Cynthia Cohen (1994).

College) at Katima Mulilo in March 1964, where Brendan Simbwaye and Zacharia Ndopu were teaching. According to the authorities, the strike, which they termed a 'night disturbance', was organised by two CANU members who were unhappy with the fact that a number of CANU office-bearers had been dismissed from teaching posts at schools run by the Roman Catholic Mission for their political involvement and questionable loyalty.[23] CANU activists and learners also recall that they were demanding better services at the hostel where, despite the fact that they paid hostel fees, learners were made to sleep on the floor or on traditional mats and had to bring food from home, which they cooked for themselves. When provided with food in the hostel, it was apparently of a very poor quality: rotten fish and cabbage; soft porridge without sugar (learners had to add salt and squeeze juice from lemons to add to the porridge to make it tastier); sugar was provided to the girls only in small quantities; and meat was served on Saturdays only. Some learners were forced to go fishing after school in the Zambezi otherwise they would have had nothing to eat.[24] The two CANU members who were arrested for being behind the strike, Adrian Waluka Simubali and Alfred Tongo Nalishuwa, were sentenced to imprisonment and the school boys who were picked up for questioning were subjected to a caning.

It was immediately after this strike that Brendan Simbwaye resigned from his teaching position at the Holy Family Mission to dedicate all his energies to CANU. Simbwaye argued that he could no longer tolerate the suffering of young learners who were being harassed by the police whilst the adults were silent for fear of losing their salaries.[25] It is interesting to note as well the collaboration that existed between the church and the state, that teachers could be dismissed from posts in a church school for their political beliefs. Perhaps this could be because the state subsidised the remaining church schools from their budget for the provision of education and health in Caprivi.

Traditional Authorities

The administration of the Eastern Caprivi Strip in the early 1960s was, officially, based on a dual chieftainship under the supervision of a government officer. The two tribal chiefs at the time were thus very important instruments of control and power dissemination during this period, especially given the fact that the territory was largely rural with the majority of households dependent on subsistence farming. CANU and the administration both vied for influence over these traditional institutions. The administration sought to use the traditional authorities to discredit CANU, claiming it was an organisation formed by young men without any credentials and who were disrespectful towards constituted authorities and the elders in traditional authorities. On the other hand, CANU knew all too well that in order to unseat the Pretoria government, the confidence and support of the two chiefs was crucial. Two incidents illustrate CANU's strategy.

---

23   J. Pütz, H. von Egidy and P. Caplan (1989), p. 44.
24   Interview by author with former learners at the school in 1964, among others: Konard Kaela Machinga, Bukalo, 16 April 2006; Fidelis Mayumbelo, Bukalo, 15April 2006.
25   Interview by author with Konard Kaela Machinga, Bukalo, 16 April 2006.

The first took place in early April 1964, when CANU influenced both traditional authorities to put in formal complaints against the administration with a long list of grievances, including the high price of maize, the failure to lift the restrictions on the sale of guns and ammunition, and the lack of stores and proper roads in the territory.[26] It appears CANU intended to cause mistrust in the administration and thus to position itself by developing a manifesto that would provide answers to all these concerns.

In the same year, Pretoria's representative to the United Nations provided the South African authorities with a copy of a petition, which had been addressed to the UN and signed by both chiefs in the Caprivi as well as representatives of their traditional authorities. In this petition the chiefs demanded that the South African government be replaced by the United Nations. Kruger investigated this matter (after expressing initial disbelief) and found that, indeed, the two chiefs had signed the petition. Kruger blamed CANU, arguing that since the chiefs could not read and write, CANU might have obtained their signatures through some dubious means. While efforts to locate a copy of this petition have yielded no result to date, the fact that it was sent is important. It adds another dimension or aspect to resistance in Caprivi – the use of petitions – which had hitherto only been reported to have been employed by the likes of Chief Hosea Kutako.

In some instances, CANU worked to make traditional institutions ungovernable for the administration, where it could not get its way, by working with certain individual members of a traditional authority. A classic example is what happened in May 1964 when the Ngambela[27] of the Mafwe[28] Traditional Authority was called to an irregular meeting at Mafulo, near Katima Mulilo, and then 'thrown out' of the office and ordered not to go near the Linyanti tribal headquarters. The administration blamed CANU for the eviction of the Ngambela from the meeting.

The police were ordered to immediately arrest two brothers singled out as ring leaders in this incident – Jackson Mazazi Lukonga and Alfred Siloiso Lukonga. The Bantu Affairs Commissioner described the two as of a critical turn of mind and having had some association with office bearers of CANU.[29] Indeed Jackson Mazazi Lukonga joined CANU and, later, served on the SWAPO Central Committee as a representative of CANU until he was expelled from the movement in 1980, together with Albert Mishake Muyongo. A clear reference to CANU's involvement in the dismissal of the Ngambela is found in a letter the Bantu Affairs Commissioner wrote to Induna (headman) Chunga of Linyanti, who was also suspected of involvement. He wrote:

> I hear…that you and others are supporting a letter written by CANU. Did you support your chief…or did you side with the rabble that threw out the Ngambela at Mafulo? Were you sitting on the important chair at Mafulo when the Ngambela was called

---

26 Kangumu (2008), p. 253.
27 Prime Minister or second-in-command. This is not a hereditary position but usually held by someone appointed from the ranks of the commoners, and he is the head of administration in the traditional setting.
28 The term is used here in its pre-independence format where it included non-Mafwe speakers such as Mayeyi, Mbukushu, Mbalangwe, Totela, and small pockets of Subiya and Barakwena who resided in the Mafwe areas.
29 NAN LKM 3/3/1, N1/2/1. Bantu Affairs Commissioner of Eastern Caprivi Strip, Katima Mulilo, to Secretary for Bantu Administration and Development, Pretoria, 29 March 1964.

by these men, through you, and did you respect him? You will answer these things, Chunga, you and the others with you. What is this nonsense I hear about the chief selling the country to the white men?[30]

The administration arranged for the case to be heard at the tribal *kuta* (court) at Linyanti. The Bantu Affairs Commissioner was surprised to see a three-ton lorry transporting scores of shouting and singing CANU supporters organised for the occasion. When all were gathered, the commissioner asked the *kuta* whether it was prepared to see justice done, by, firstly, upholding the position of the Ngambela and then proceeding to the trial of the two men. He reports that he was disappointed for 'not one of the *kuta* members present was prepared to agree, in the exception of the chief.'[31]

The two men were then released from custody and immediately surrounded by CANU supporters in a heroic manner. Kruger would conclude: 'another gain, if shallow, for the CANU upstarts.'[32]

The Core Role of CANU in the Liberation Movement

The preceding sections have shown that there was 'appreciable internal activity by [CANU] agents and their tentative converts, [with the aim of] supplanting of the South African government.'[33] This was adequate proof for the administration that CANU was intent on destabilising the Eastern Caprivi and it, thus, opted to adopt a 'shoot them before they grow' approach. However, one should also consider the influence of neighbouring territories on the political developments in the Eastern Caprivi, particularly the influence of the newly independent Republic of Zambia.[34]

Because of its geographical location and isolation at the time from the rest of South West Africa, the rise of CANU benefited from the close relationship of its leaders with those of the United Independence Party (UNIP). This fact is recognised by Sam Nujoma, who writes: 'the struggle in the then Northern Rhodesia led by UNIP inspired the Caprivians to form their own party since they had no contact with Windhoek.' (2001, p. 136). UNIP's Nalumino Mundia, who went on to become the Prime Minister in Kenneth Kaunda's government, was a former teacher in Eastern Caprivi and a colleague of Brendan Simbwaye at the Holy Family Mission School. From the administration's side, indeed, they were concerned that what was happening in Northern Rhodesia would spill over into the Eastern Caprivi Strip. Already in 1954, A. B. Collenbrander (Magistrate and Native Commissioner for the Eastern Caprivi Strip) expressed the fear that Eastern Caprivi Strip would become a 'hunting ground for political agitators from

---

30   NAN LKM 3/3/1, N1/2/1. Bantu Affairs Commissioner of Eastern Caprivi Strip, Katima Mulilo, to Induna Chunga, Linyanti, 15 August 1964.
31   NAN A.472. Kruger, C. E., 'History of the Caprivi, 1890-1984', p. 8.
32   Ibid., p. 9.
33   Kruger, quoted in Kangumu (2000). 'A Forgotten Corner of Namibia: Aspects of the history of the Caprivi Strip, c. 1939-1980', (MA thesis, University of Cape Town), p. 43.
34   For a more detailed discussion of the influence of Northern Rhodesia on Caprivi politics, see Kangumu (2008), pp. 239-242.

across the border'.³⁵ The same concern would be expressed by Kruger, ten years later in 1964. In a submission to have Brendan Simbwaye banished from the Eastern Caprivi Strip through a ministerial removal order, Kruger added: 'When one measures what is now being asked against the killing of well over 500 people in Northern Rhodesia in the last few weeks it hardly seems drastic.'³⁶

Whilst CANU has often been viewed as worthy of little more than a footnote in the history of Namibia's liberation struggle, I would argue that it played a central role for three main reasons:

1. The history of the CANU has not received attention in Namibian historiography, from academics, and within oral histories narrated by SWAPO, before and after independence.

2. Contrary to this anecdotal history to which the CANU has been relegated, the chapter showed that the movement was one of the core influences, among others, on the early Namibian nationalist movement, for the following reasons:
    i) The attention it received from SWAPO in the 'merger' which paved the way for the president of CANU to be made SWAPO Vice-President, albeit *in absentia*;
    ii) The subsequent role played by CANU activists who went into exile and were very influential in SWAPO especially in the ranks of PLAN, such as Greenwell Matongo and Richard Kapelwa Kabajani;
    iii) The adoption of 'hit and run' tactics by PLAN and laying of landmines as a military strategy employed in the Caprivi in the early 1970s, depended on the knowledge of the local terrain and languages which PLAN fighters from Caprivi possessed.

3. The relationship between SWAPO and UNIP of Zambia and subsequent setting up of SWAPO camps in Zambia were made easier by CANU for two reasons,
    i) The historical ties between the people of western Zambia and those of Caprivi;
    ii) The close ties between CANU and UNIP, which were sharing offices at Sesheke well before CANU was formally launched, and before CANU and SWAPO 'merged'. Prominent personalities in UNIP, such as Nalumino Mundia, who became Prime Minister in Kenneth Kaunda's government, were teachers in Caprivi Strip.

Because of the above facts, it defeats logic why CANU should be on the periphery of history, rather than being viewed as one of the core influences on the Namibian liberation movement.

---

35   NAN LKM 3/3/3 no. N1. Magistrate Eastern Caprivi, Katima Mulilo to Secretary for Native Affairs, 20 December 1954.
36   NAN BAD V5, Vol. II. Native Commissioner, Katima Mulilo to Minister Department Native Affairs, Pretoria, 15 August 1964, p. 2.

References

Beinert, W. and Bundy, C. (1987) *Hidden Struggles in Rural South Africa: Politics and Popular Movements in the Transkei and Eastern Cape, 1890-1931.* Berkeley: University of California.

Cohen, C. (1994) *Administering Education in Namibia: The Colonial Period to the Present.* Windhoek: Namibia Scientific Society.

Fisch, M. (1999) *The Caprivi Strip during the German colonial period 1890 to 1914.* Windhoek: Out of Africa.

Flint, L. (2002) 'State-Building in Central Southern Africa: Citizenship and subjectivity in Barotseland and Caprivi', *International Journal of African Historical Studies*, 36 (2).

Fossé, J. L. (1996) 'Negotiating the Nation in Local Terms: Ethnicity and Nationalism in Eastern Caprivi, Namibia', MA thesis, University of Oslo, Norway.

Henrichsen, D., Jacobson, N. and Marshall, K. (eds) (2010) *Israel Goldblatt. Building Bridges. Namibian nationalists Clemens Kapuuo, Hosea Kutako, Brendan Simbwaye, Samuel Witbooi.* Basel: Basel Afrika Bibliographien.

Kangumu, B. K. (2000) 'A Forgotten Corner of Namibia: Aspects of the history of the Caprivi Strip, c. 1939-1980', MA thesis, University of Cape Town, Cape Town.

Kangumu, B. K. (2008) 'Contestations over Caprivi Identities: From Pre-colonial times to the present', PhD thesis, University of Cape Town.

Kangumu, B. K. (2011) *Contesting Caprivi. A History of Colonial Isolation and Regional Nationalism in Namibia.* Basel: Basel Afrika Bibliographien.

Katjavivi, P. (1988) *A history of resistance in Namibia.* Paris: UNESCO.

Likando, E. (1989) 'The Caprivi: A historical perspective'. (Unpublished manuscript).

Mbuende, K. (1986) *Namibia, the Broken Shield: Anatomy of Imperialism and Revolution.* Lund: Liber.

Morris, M. (1971) *Terrorism.* Cape Town: Gothic Printing Co.

Nujoma, S. (2001) *Where Others Wavered, the autobiography of Sam Nujoma: My life in SWAPO and my participation in the liberation struggle of Namibia.* London: Panaf.

Pütz, J., von Egidy, H. and Caplan, P. (1989) *Namibia Handbook and Political Who's Who.* Windhoek: Magu.

Shamukuni, D. M. (1972) 'The Basubiya', *Botswana Notes and Records*, vol. 4, Gaborone: The Botswana Society.

Silvester, J. (1991) 'Black Pastoralists, White Farmers: The Dynamics of Land Dispossession and Labour Recruitment in Southern Namibia, 1915-1955', PhD thesis, University of London, London.

Archival sources

National Archives of Namibia (NAN)

A.472.

Kruger, C.E., 'History of the Caprivi, 1890-1984', p.7.

SWAA South West Africa Administration

[2267] A503/1-7, 1939, Louw, E.W., 'Inspection Report on the Eastern Caprivi Zipfel', p.10.

BAD Bantu Administration and Development

[23] V5, Vol. II, 15 August 1964. Native Commissioner, Katima Mulilo to Minister Department Native Affairs, Pretoria, p. 2.

LKM Magistrate Katima Mulilo

[3/3/3] no. N1, 20 December 1954. Magistrate Eastern Caprivi, Katima Mulilo to Secretary for Native Affairs.

[3/3/1] N1/2/1, 29 March 1964. Bantu Affairs Commissioner of Eastern Caprivi Strip, Katima Mulilo, to Secretary for Bantu Administration and Development, Pretoria.

[3/3/1] N1/2/1, 15 August 1964. Bantu Affairs Commissioner of Eastern Caprivi Strip, Katima Mulilo, to Induna Chunga, Linyanti.

[3/3/3] N1/15/2, 8 September 1964. Kruger, Magistrate Eastern Caprivi Zipfel, to Chief Moraliswani Maiba of the Masubiya.

9 Brendan Kangongolo Simbwaye: A Journey of 'Internal' Exile[1]

Bennett Kangumu Kangumu

Introduction

The Caprivi African National Union (CANU) was secretly founded on 7 September 1962[2] even though it had existed as an underground movement from late 1958. CANU did not survive within Caprivi beyond its very first public meeting, which took place in July 1964.[3] Brendan Kangongolo Simbwaye, founding President of CANU, and two others, Alfred Tongo Nalishuwa, and Vernet Maswahu, were arrested at that meeting and this marked the start of a life of perpetual detention, isolation, banishment and 'internal' exile or displacement for Maswahu and Simbwaye. After his arrest, CANU re-grouped in Zambia under Albert Mishake Muyongo and joined the South West Africa People's Organisation (SWAPO) in an alliance in 1964. Simbwaye was made SWAPO's Vice-President.

This chapter attempts to provide a historical timeline[4] of the life of Brendan Kangongolo Simbwaye between the period 1964, when he was arrested, and 1972

---

1. This chapter is part of a larger study, the research for which started in 2005 and was aimed at producing a short biography of Brendan Kangongolo Simbwaye. I wish to thank Ellen Namhila for her ongoing encouragement and belief that this was a story worth writing, and Werner Hillebrecht and his staff at the National Archives of Namibia for being very helpful in locating relevant files that contained information on Brendan Kangongolo Simbwaye. I wish to thank Mr Alfred Ilukena, Permanent Secretary in the Ministry of Education, Republic of Namibia, who assisted me with conducting oral interviews with former CANU activists and family members of Brendan Kangongolo Simbwaye. Lastly, I wish to thank all former CANU activists and the family of Simbwaye who shared their stories and memories of Simbwaye, and the 1960s period in Caprivi history.
2. Albert Zacharia Ndopu, Katima Mulilo, 17 April 2006. Albert Zacharia Ndopu was a founding Executive Committee member of CANU and served as the Secretary for Information and Publicity.
3. There is confusion regarding the actual date of this meeting. CANU activists interviewed separately maintain that it was in mid-July 1964 (Albert Zacharia Ndopu and Ignatius Matengu), with the latter even stating that Simbwaye was arrested on the morning of 15 July 1964, which would also be the date of the meeting. Ignatius Matengu, apart from being a CANU youth activist at the time, was staying in Brendan Simbwaye's house because he was Simbwaye's nephew. C. E. Kruger, the Native Commissioner for Eastern Caprivi Strip at the time, believes the meeting took place in the second half of August 1964. This is supported by Albert Mishake Muyongo, CANU's Vice President, in a short autobiography submitted to SWAPO and published in *Namibia News*, Vol. 3, No. 1-3, January/March 1970, pp. 9-12.
4. Following archival research and oral interviews I conducted on the life history of Brendan Kangongolo Simbwaye, I constructed a timeline of his life story that appeared in *New Era* in August 2006 to coincide with the celebration of Heroes Day, which was being celebrated for the first time at Katima Mulilo. The newspaper article was entitled: 'Heroism: A Glance at Brendan Kangongolo Simbwaye.'

when he is presumed to have 'disappeared' at the hands of the South African authorities in the east of the Caprivi Strip. The chapter will look at the available evidence about his arrest, his trial, the banishment order, his house arrest at Warmbad and Khorixas, his visit to Katima Mulilo in 1972, and his eventual disappearance.

Brendan Kangongolo Simbwaye was born in 1934 at Ndangamwa (Lukozi village) near Malindi in the eastern floodplain of the Caprivi Region. He started his schooling at Schuckmansburg Primary School and proceeded to the Holy Family Mission at Katima Mulilo where he completed his Standard Six Upper in May 1955.[5] He went for further education at Lukulu Teacher Training College in Northern Rhodesia (Zambia) where he completed a two-year primary education course in May 1957. He started at the Holy Family Mission in August 1957 teaching the Standard Four class, working as a boarding master at the school and also taking responsibility for football and athletics. Simbwaye was a Catholic and deeply religious; he was married to a trained nurse. He resigned from his teaching position in 1963 to devote his entire energy to CANU, with the purpose of terminating South Africa's occupation of the Eastern Caprivi Strip.

The authorities started to closely monitor Simbwaye's activities at the end of 1963 when he left for Lusaka (Zambia), to seek support from the United Nations which was then involved in Zambia's transition to independence;[6] and to cement ties with the United Independence Party (UNIP), among other things. It is reported that UNIP assisted with printing the first CANU membership cards, and drafting its first constitution.[7] It was on this trip that Simbwaye met members of the SWAPO leadership in Lusaka to pave the way for a 'merger' between CANU and SWAPO. He returned from Lusaka in March 1964 but was advised not to cross into the Eastern Caprivi Strip because the authorities were looking for him as he had left the territory illegally and was accused of fermenting political unrest in the Caprivi. He stayed on at Sesheke (Zambia) until May 1964, when CANU members in Caprivi had finished selling membership cards and recruited many to its cause, in order to prepare for CANU's first public meeting.

Public gatherings were prohibited in 'native areas' unless specially permitted by a tribal chief or the Native Commissioner, under Proclamation No. 198 of 1953. This was reinforced by a Minute issued by the Secretary for Native Affairs on 4 July 1958, with the agreement of the Secretary for Justice. The Minute, entitled 'Control of Meetings or Gatherings in Native Areas' was directed to all officials in the Department of Native Affairs:

> Because attempts are being made nowadays to undermine the authority of the chiefs and the government, often through the medium of unlawful gatherings and meetings,

---

5   Bennett Kangumu Kangumu (2006). 'Heroism: A Glance at Brendan Kangongolo Simbwaye', *New Era*, 25 August.
6   The United Nations' Special Committee of Twenty-Four that was dealing with issues of decolonisation heard petitioners (including Kenneth Kaunda) from Northern Rhodesia (as Zambia was known at the time) in 1962 and 1963 arguing the case for independence and the end of the Federation fo the Rhodesias and Nyasaland. See United Nations (1965), *The United Nations and Decolonisation: Summary of the Work of the Special Committe of Twenty-Four*; Vol. 3(4), pp. 43-44.
7   Bennett Kangumu Kangumu (2008), 'Contestations Over Caprivi Identities: From pre-colonial times to the present' (PhD thesis, University of Cape Town), p. 246.

it is imperative that the provisions of Proclamation No. 198 of 1953 should again be brought to the attention of all chiefs and headmen. The Department has reason to doubt whether the chiefs really understand the implications of, and the firm support given them by, this legal enactment.

CANU activists reportedly approached the authorities three times requesting permission to hold a public meeting but this was refused.[8] It was then that they decided to proceed to hold a public meeting to launch CANU at Mafulo near Katima Mulilo. It was at this public meeting that the police, headed by Sergeant Hartmann and his son-in-law, Sakkie Bosman, and accompanied by a score of black askaris (black policemen), arrested Brendan Kangongolo Simbwaye and Alfred Tongo Nalishuwa. Vernet Sibanda Maswahu would join them later in prison when he was arrested on his way to take a petition to the UN in Lusaka (the petition was also confiscated by the police).[9]

The Trial

The three accused were brought to court for trial at Katima Mulilo, which attracted a sizable crowd. They were accused of holding an illegal meeting under the provision of Proclamation 198 of 1953 (cited above) which prohibited meetings or public gatherings without permission from the authorities. Simbwaye was also charged with leaving the Eastern Caprivi Strip without permission. The charges were read and the accused called to plead but no answer was forthcoming and a 'not guilty' plea was entered. The accused were asked if they wished to put any questions or make statements. Simbwaye ignored the presiding officer and declared in a loud voice that he did not recognise the court, that they wanted to be tried internationally on an international level and he and his co-accused declared that they would only submit to the United Nations.'[10] For this, they were immediately sentenced to one month's imprisonment for contempt of court without the option of a fine. On the main charge they were fined £2.00 for holding an illegal meeting and Simbwaye was fined a further £2.00 for leaving the country without a permit.

Before the accused were sentenced, the Native Commissioner made an impromptu visit to Pretoria to report on what had taken place; to ask for banishment or removal orders to be served on Simbwaye and Maswahu; and to ask that the three (Simbwaye, Maswahu and Nalishuwa) serve their sentences elsewhere in South West Africa as the prison facilities at Katima Mulilo were inadequate. The three were then transferred in the dead of night and handed over to police from Rundu at the Manyeha crossing (now Kongola), to be taken to Grootfontein. Simbwaye reported to Israel Goldblatt that, at Grootfontein, the three prisoners were told that their sentences had been increased from one to three months. They served their prison sentence in the Windhoek Central

---

8	Interview by author with Adrian Waluka Simubali, Bukalo, 16 April 2006. The same is reported by advocate Israel Goldblatt in his notes of a conversation with Brendan Kangongolo Simbwaye on 2 October 1964.
9	Interview by author with Adrian Waluka Simubali, Bukalo, 16 April 2006.
10	NAN BAD, V5, vol. II: C. E. Kruger, in a Submission for Removal in terms of South West Africa Proclamation 15 of 1928 of Brendan Kangongolo Simbwaye and Vernet Sibanda Maswahu, 15 August 1964.

Prison. Upon their release, a banishment order was served on Brendan Simbwaye and Maswahu, while Nalishuwa was taken back to Katima Mulilo, from where he immediately crossed the border to join SWAPO in exile.

The Banishment or Removal Order

The following Order of Restriction was served on Simbwaye, and a similar one on Maswahu each signed by Hon. Michael Daniel Christian De Wet Nel, Minister of Bantu Administration and Development of the Union government:

> To Brendan Kangongolo Simbwaye, a Native of the Masubiya in the district of Eastern Caprivi Zipfel in the territory of South West Africa.
>
> WHEREAS I am satisfied that you are engaged in activities likely to undermine duly established authority and the maintenance of law and order in the district of Eastern Caprivi Zipfel in the territory of South West Africa, and to cause dissension, unrest, violence and lawlessness in the said district;
>
> AND WHEREAS your said activities have resulted in a request from the Masubiya tribal authority for your removal from the said district of Eastern Caprivi Zipfel;
>
> AND WHEREAS I am satisfied that your presence in, or at any place within easy access of the said district of Eastern Caprivi Strip in the territory of South West Africa, is inimical to the peace, order and good government of the Natives in the said district;
>
> AND WHEREAS I deem it expedient in the general public interest that you be removed from your present place of residence in the said district of Eastern Caprivi Zipfel;
>
> NOW, THEREFORE, under and by virtue of the powers vested in me by paragraph (d) of section one of the Native Administration Proclamation, 1928 (Proclamation No. 15 of 1928) (South West Africa) read with section three of Eastern Caprivi Administration Proclamation, 1939 (Proclamation No. 147 of 1939) (South West Africa), I do hereby order you, the said Brandon Kangongolo Simbwaye, that within two days of the service of this order on you, to remove yourself from your place of residence in the said district of Eastern Caprivi Zipfel to Ohopoho in the district of Kaokoveld in the territory of South West Africa, subject to the following terms, conditions, and arrangements:-
>
> At Ohopoho you shall reside at a place to be indicated to you by senior officials of the Department of Bantu Administration and Development of Ohopoho.
>
> Until such time as this order is withdrawn you may not return to the Eastern Caprivi Zipfel except with written permission of the Secretary for the Bantu Administration and Development.
>
> Given under my hand at Pretoria on the 24th day of September One Thousand Nine Hundred and Sixty Four.
>
> (signed) Minister of Bantu Administration and Development

With the above order, Simbwaye's fate was sealed and his journey of 'internal exile' commissioned. Four important points emerge from the wording of the restriction order. One is that the administration's perception of Simbwaye as a troublemaker and political agitator (likely to cause 'unrest') was more serious and a greater determining factor in his banishment than the crime he was charged with – leaving the country without a permit and holding a meeting without permission. The second point is the assertion that his restriction order was requested by the Masubiya tribal authority. There is no evidence to suggest that the said authority requested Simbwaye's removal. On the contrary, Kruger actually states the following in his submission to the Minister requesting for the restriction order to be issued: 'I have reason to think that the chiefs would favour their [Simbwaye and Maswahu] removal though they have not been directly asked.'[11] The Native Commissioner does not provide evidence of why he thought the chiefs would favour the removal of the two from the Eastern Caprivi Strip. What we know is that the two chiefs at the time actually cooperated with and supported CANU's activities and had co-signed a petition that was sent to the UN demanding the termination of South Africa's control over the Eastern Caprivi Strip.[12] Perhaps the authorities wanted to legitimise their political repression. The third point is that the two day's notice given in the removal order meant that the duo could not go back to Eastern Caprivi to bid farewell to their families. Finally, it is significant that they were clearly prohibited from returning to their home areas and the banning order was open ended with no set date for its termination.

Research has not yielded any evidence of the two men's stay at Ohopoho as directed in the restriction order. Available evidence [13] only starts with their arrival at Warmbad. However, it is clear the duo were indeed at Ohopoho as reflected in the notes of one of Simbwaye's conversations with advocate Israel Goldblatt on 2 October 1964. Their discussion centred around the legality of the restriction order and Simbwaye's intention to challenge it in a court of law. Advocate Goldblatt advised Simbwaye that it would be futile for him to mount a court challenge because, according to him, section 1(d) of Proclamation 15 of 1928 read with section 3 of Proclamation No. 147 of 1939 permitted such removals and empowered the Minister to make that order and therefore it was 'legal'.[14] Simbwaye made reference in their discussion to the fact that the authorities had given them (he and Maswahu) R5 each to buy blankets, and R4 per month while at Ohopoho.

---

11 NAN BAD, V5, vol. II: C. E. Kruger, in a Submission for Removal in terms of South West Africa Proclamation 15 of 1928 of Brendan Kangongolo Simbwaye and Vernet Sibanda Maswahu, 15 August 1964.
12 Bennett Kangumu Kangumu (2009), 'The Caprivi African National Union (CANU), 1962-1964: Forms of Resistance'. Paper presented at the *'Moments, Monuments and Memories: Tracing the Footprints to Independence'* Conference, Windhoek, December 2009. See chapter 8 of this volume.
13 See for example Bennett Kangumu Kangumu (2006), Archival Research Report: 'The Life History of Brendan Kangongolo Simbwaye: A Missing SWAPO Vice-President'. Submitted to the Steering Committee of the AACRLS Project, an initiative of the National Archives of Namibia, February 2006.
14 Advocate I. Goldblatt, Notes of 2 October 1964. A transcript of the notes was kindly given to me by Dag Henrichsen of the Basler Afrika Bibliographien (BAB) of Basel, Switzerland.

It is not known when and under what conditions Simbwaye and Maswahu were transferred from Ohopoho to Warmbad. We come across Simbwaye again through Goldblatt's notes on 27 May 1966 at 10h00 in the Windhoek Central Prison, whilst in solitary confinement for the second time. The officer in charge of the gaol, a certain Captain Slabbert, explained it was actually not 'solitary confinement' but that Simbwaye was just kept separate from the other prisoners as he was regarded as a political agitator. At this meeting Simbwaye told the story to Goldblatt of his stay at Warmbad in southern Namibia, mainly a tale of times spent in and out of jail.

Archival records show that on 14 October 1965[15] Simbwaye was sentenced in the Karasburg magistrate's court to a prison sentence for 'common assault and malicious damage to property' and given a jail term of seventy (70) days, which he served in the Keetmanshoop prison. The first four weeks were in solitary confinement with a 'spare diet'. As he would relate to Goldblatt, he was arrested for assaulting a 'woman, a sister (nun)' who tried to prevent him from sitting in the 'whites only' section of a church in Warmbad. He was discharged from the Keetmanshoop prison on 4 December 1965 and sent back to Warmbad. The same day he was reportedly seen with a group of local people seated around him at his hut. A white policeman came to demand an explanation, but nothing happened. Four months later, on 8 April 1966, Simbwaye was arrested again in Warmbad for 'fermenting racial strife' or contravening section 20 of Proclamation 15 of 1928, which prohibited the promotion of any feeling of hostility between Europeans and Non-Europeans. This was in reference to the incident of 4 December 1965 when the group of people had been seen sitting with him outside his hut. He explained to the court that the people came to him to find out about his jail experience and that he was complaining about the lack of food and poor living conditions. However, the constable who testified for the state at the trial, Mteka, accused Simbwaye of 'fighting the government' and uttering the following words to those present:

> ...julle is te sleg, julle is toe. Julle moet vergaderings hou en saamstaan. Julle moet veg teen die boere. Julle kan klippe en ysters vat om te veg. Julle moet die boere met klippe vrek gooi. Ons sal Windhoek brandsteek en sal al die boere vrek maak. Die wat oorbly, sal onder ons werk, en self vir ons kinders 'bass' sé. Julle moet teen die witmense veg, en ons sal julle wapens gee. Januarie, sal julle ander dinge sien. Julle en die Roomse Vader is mos toe. Bantoestans is dood, Angola, Sudwes-Afrika, Mossambiek en die Republiek sal in Januarie val.[16]

> You are very bad, you are blind. You should hold meetings and stand together. You should protest against the Boers. You can pick up stones and iron to fight. You must kill the Boers with stones. We will set fire to Windhoek so all the Boers will die. Those that remain, will work under us and call our children 'Boss'. You must protest against the whites and we will give you weapons. You will see changes in January. You

---

15 Goldblatt records the date as 6 October 1965. However, the date of sentence which appears on the court papers (docket) is 14 October 1965. Perhaps Simbwaye remembered the day on which the trial began and that is what he conveyed to Goldblatt. The docket papers are found in the NAN LKW 1/2/22, 1945-1969, 1566, 1/1/12.
16 NAN LKW 1/2/22, 1945-1969, 1566, 1/1/12. Translation into English by Limba Mupetami.

and the Catholic Father are blind. Bantustans are dead, Angola, South West Africa, Mozambique and the Republic will fall in January.

Simbwaye was sentenced to another six months imprisonment on 14 April 1966 at Karasburg magistrate's court, and was sent back to Keetmanshoop prison. He served only two months there and then was transferred to the Windhoek Central Prison, where we meet him through Goldbatt on 27 May 1966. At this meeting in the Windhoek Central Prison, Simbwaye explained to Goldbatt that he feared that he would be removed to some other place without a proper order being issued, and this is what Goldblatt had to say:

> If your removal [to Warmbad from Ohopoho] was effected without an order by the Minister it is in my opinion illegal, and if you will again be removed, as you fear, to some other place, again without a proper order, it will also be illegal.[17]

It follows from the above that the removal order and detention of Simbwaye and Maswahu were rendered illegal by their removal from Ohopoho (currently found in the Kunene Region of Namibia) which was the specified place of detention in the original restriction order. Simbwaye's fears about being removed to another place were correct. The duo shortly thereafter found themselves isolated on a remote farm (Halt Farm No. 379) near Welwitschia (now Khorixas) in the former Damaraland Homeland. Simbwaye's stay in Damaraland was not welcome. The Bantu Affairs Commissioner for Damaraland at the time, H. F. J. de Bruin, argued in several letters to the Chief Bantu Affairs Commissioner in Windhoek and to the Secretary for Bantu Administration and Development in Pretoria that Simbwaye should be removed from Damaraland. The commissioner reasoned that Simbwaye was politically active, judging from the correspondences that passed through his office to and from people such as Goldblatt and Herero Leader Clemens Kapuuo. The Commissioner argued that as Simbwaye was now fluent in Afrikaans and since Damaras spoke Afrikaans, he would soon influence them, especially the learners at the local high school with whom he mingled when he came to town.[18] The Damara Council also made two representations, the first in June 1968, and the second on 25 April 1972 asking for the removal of Simbwaye from Damaraland.

Despite all the representations for the removal of Simbwaye from Damaraland, the authorities in Windhoek and Pretoria were not convinced, especially of the suggestion from the Damaraland Bantu Affairs Commissioner to take Simbwaye back to Eastern Caprivi Strip, arguing:

> *Met die huidige situasie wat in die Oos Caprivi heers, is dit vanuit 'n veiligheidsoogpunt beskou, glad nie gewens dat hy daarheen verwyder word, en weer by sy mense geplaas*

---

17   NAN BAD, V5, vol. II. Advocate Israel Goldblatt to Simbwaye, 23 March 1968.
18   NAN BAD, V5, vol. II. Damaraland Bantu Affairs Commissioner to Chief Bantu Affairs Commissioner, Windhoek, 9 January 1972.

word nie. My hoofkantoor is daarmee eens dat Simbwaye in Damaraland moet aanbly soos aanbeveel, totdat die huidige politieke klimaat verbeter het.[19]

With the current situation happening in East Caprivi, it is better to look at the situation from a safe point of view as we are not at all convinced that he should be removed and taken back to his people. My office has stated that Simbwaye should remain in Damaraland as instructed until the current situation gets better.

One encounters numerous attempts by the authorities to persuade Simbwaye to denounce and renounce the struggle. However, he repeatedly turned down those overtures whenever they were presented to him. In one letter to Goldblatt he writes, in reaction to an offer of employment by the government at a monthly rate of R18 if he renounced the struggle: 'The administration ascertains that I should get employment, and who can employ a politician?'[20] For him, a politician could only be employed by the people through a popular vote. As a trained teacher, he could easily find employment in the reserve. The Damaraland Native Commissioner also tried to persuade him to work with the administration back home (Caprivi) in return for his freedom, and he relates:

Ek het Brandon persoonlik al gevra wat hy dink van die Tuisland ontwikkeling. Hy het erken dat wat hy sien wat te Welwitschia gedoen word 'n goeie ding is maar dat hy nooit met die Hoofmanne in die Caprivi sal kan saamwerk nie, omrede hulle die Blanke regering steun. Hy verklaar egter dat endien hy ooit teruggestuur word hy liewers na Zambia toe sal gaan waar hy baie vriende het.[21]

I personally asked Brandon what he thinks of the Homeland development. He admitted that what he saw being done in Welwitschia was a good thing, but that he will never work with the Headmen in the Caprivi because they support the White government. He is adamant that when he finally gets sent back he would rather go to Zambia where he has a lot of friends.

Simbwaye indicated to Goldblatt that should he be taken back to Caprivi, he would rather cross into Zambia where he could freely express his political convictions. This made the authorities uneasy for they knew that he would then have access to the international arena to direct 'subversive' activities against them. His request or desire to be allowed to cross into Zambia should also be seen in the context of family attachments, for his wife, a trained nurse, was working in Zambia at the time. Simbwaye was taken to the Pretoria Central Prison during the time of the Terrorism Treason Trial (1967-1968). But, because there was no evidence to show that his 'crimes' amounted to treason, he was released (from Pretoria) back to detention at Khorixas. Whilst in South

---

19   Ibid. J. G. Myburgh, South African Police to Chief Bantu Affairs Commissioner, Windhoek, 25 May 1972. Translation into English by Limba Mupetami.
20   NAN BAD, V5, vol. II. Simbwaye, Warmbad, to Advocate Israel Goldblatt, Windhoek, 18 July 1966.
21   Bantu Affairs Commissioner, Damaraland to Chief Bantu Affairs Commissioner, Windhoek, 12 February 1971. Translation into English by Limba Mupetami.

Africa, Simbwaye shared a prison cell with fellow political activists from the Eastern Caprivi Strip in the Pretoria Central Prison.[22]

Despite the security concerns raised against permitting Simbwaye to travel to the Eastern Caprivi Strip, a special permit was finally signed by the South African Minister for Bantu Administration and Development on 9 August 1972, to allow him to visit the Caprivi for six months. It is difficult to know why there was a change of heart on this issue from the administration's side. One can speculate that it could partly be because earlier in March 1972, the Caprivi Legislative Assembly had been inaugurated at Katima Mulilo, as recommended by the Odendaal Commission of Inquiry into South West Africa Affairs. The administration could have reasoned that perhaps if Simbwaye saw such 'developments' he might have a change of heart and renounce the struggle or even accept a post in the new political structure, even though he had already made his position very clear regarding this issue. Secondly, his visit to Caprivi might have been allowed in light of the pending visit by the United Nations Special Representative, Dr Alfred Fischer, who was scheduled to visit Namibia, and the Caprivi Strip, later in 1972. The authorities might have deemed it proper to have him in the Caprivi in case Dr Fischer enquired about him on his visit, although there is no evidence to show that Simbwaye was presented to Dr Fischer.

It was on this visit to the Eastern Caprivi Strip in 1972 that Simbwaye disappeared without trace. He was last seen when he was taken to visit his mother at Limbeza village in the Kabbe area. After the police picked him up from the village later in the evening, no one saw or heard from him ever again after that. Theories abound as to how he met his death,[23] the most popular one being that when the police picked him up from the village they did not travel to Katima Mulilo but instead headed to the Zambezi where they boarded a boat, put him in a sack, and drowned him. It is not known whether they killed him before drowning him or whether he was drowned alive. The other story is that he was killed near the Witwatersrand Native Labour Association (WNLA) border post, where the police made him dig his own grave and buried him in that pit. It has never been clearly established how he died or the location of his grave (if he was buried). As for his colleague, Vernet Sibanda Maswahu, he was transferred from Khorixas to the Windhoek mental hospital. He is still missing and research has yet to be conducted on whether he died in that hospital and, if so, where he was buried, or if he was ever discharged from hospital. He remains a silent figure in the historiography of the Namibian liberation struggle.

Conclusion

This chapter chronicled the journey of detention, displacement, imprisonment, incarceration, suffering, and disappearance of Brendan Kangongolo Simbwaye. He was arrested in 1964 when he was about to address the first CANU public meeting, tried and sentenced to one month's imprisonment which he served at Windhoek Central Prison. Upon release, he was served with a restriction order that confined him to Ohopoho in the

---

22　Interview by author with Lutokwa, Charles Sampati, Katima Mulilo, 30 July, 2006. He was arrested and taken to Pretoria Central Prison.
23　Group interview by author with Sylvester Matengu, Ignatius Matengu, Pastor George Matali, Kabbe, 16 June 2006. These are family members, and the second interviewee, Ignatius, is a CANU youth activist.

Kaokoveld, from where he was transferred to Warmbad, and then to Welwitschia (now Khorixas). While at Warmbad he served two prison terms at Keetmanshoop Prison, and the Windhoek Central Prison, where he was kept in solitary confinement and given a sparse diet, for he was branded a political agitator. In between, he was taken to the Pretoria Central Prison during the time of the 'Terrorism Trial' of 1967-68. Because there was no evidence to show that what he was accused of amounted to treason, he was released (from Pretoria) back to detention at Khorixas. In 1972 he was issued with a permit to visit his home town of Katima Mulilo and disappeared there without trace

References

Kangumu, B. K. (2006) 'The Life History of Brendan Kangongolo Simbwaye: A Missing SWAPO Vice-President'. Archival research report submitted to the Steering Committee of the AACRLS Project, an initiative of the National Archives of Namibia, February 2006.

Kangumu, B. K. (2006) 'Heroism: A Glance at Brendan Kangongolo Simbwaye', *New Era*, 25 August 2006.

Kangumu, B. K. (2008) 'Contestations Over Caprivi Identities: From pre-colonial times to the present', PhD thesis, University of Cape Town, Cape Town.

Kangumu, B. K. (2009) 'The Caprivi African National Union (CANU), 1962-1964: Forms of Resistance'. Paper presented at the '*Moments, Monuments and Memories: Tracing the Footprints to Independence' Conference, Windhoek, December 2009*.

Kangumu, B.K. (2011) *Contesting Caprivi. A History of Colonial Isolation and Regional Nationalism in Namibia*. Basel: Basel Afrika Bibliographien.

Namibia News (1970) vol. 3, Nos 1-3, January-March 1970.

United Nations (1965) *The United Nations and Decolonisation: Summary of the Work of the Special Committee of Twenty-Four*, Vol. 3 (4).

Archival Sources

National Archives of Namibia (NAN)

BAD Bantu Administration and Development

[23] V5, vol. II, 15 August 1964. C.E. Kruger, in a Submission for Removal in terms of South West Africa Proclamation 15 of 1928 of Brendan Kangongolo Simbwaye and Vernet Sibanda Maswahu.

[23] V5, vol. II, 18 July 1966. Simbwaye, Warmbad, to Advocate Israel Goldblatt, Windhoek.

[23] V5, vol. II, 23 March 1968. Advocate Israel Goldblatt to Simbwaye.

[23] V5, vol. II, 9 January, 1972. Damaraland Bantu Affairs Commissioner to Chief Bantu Affairs Commissioner, Windhoek.

LKW Magistrate Karasburg/Warmbad

1/2/22, 1945-1969, 1566, 1/1/12. Simbwaye Court papers 14 October 1965. Translation into English by Limba Mupetami. See also:

[1/1/12] Criminal cases. Case 15/1966, Appeal 1/1966. The State against Brendan Kongongola Simbwaye.

10 The Kavango Legislative Council

Aaron Nambadi

Introdution

The Bantustan policy, as implemented by the South African colonial government in South Africa and later in South West Africa (Namibia), served different social, political and economical purposes. After the victory of the National Party in 1948, the colonial government of South Africa embarked upon the strategy of separate development for the different 'native nations'. The Bantustan system fragmented the African majority population in South Africa and South West Africa into groupings along ethnic lines (the 'divide and rule' strategy). The strategy entailed the actual granting of home-rule and then self-determination and eventually independence to a few African ethnic states, the homelands. The introduction of homelands for the majority of the African people promoted controlled political and economic opportunities in the Bantustan peripheries, which would be sufficient to entice an emergent African beneficiary class into collaborating with South Africa in the control and suppression of the subordinated population, without simultaneously providing the class with sufficient muscle to become a significant competitor for power. It might be argued that the success of Namibia's liberation struggle was also dependent upon the failure of this alternative political framework. However, the existing historiography has largely ignored the internal political dynamics of the homelands, whilst the relevant literature that does exist has focused mainly on 'Ovamboland' (Tötemeyer, 1978; Kössler, 2005; Cooper, 2001)

This chapter is drawn from a more extensive thesis that was concerned with examining the Kavango Legislative Council, its constitution, its powers, the role of the traditional authorities within the body, and the legislation passed by the Council. It focuses on the period 1970 to 1979, covering the first and second Kavango Legislative Councils. It is concerned with answering two central questions: Firstly, who was recognised as the legitimate authority in the Kavango Region during this period? Secondly, what was the actual meaning and substance of the 'self-government' provided by the Legislative Council?

Initially, it is important to examine the composition of the Kavango Legislative Council and to provide a short overview of its history since such a history is lacking. Indeed, my research was motivated and driven by a desire to chart an unexplored political narrative and to seek answers to several unresolved questions. On the one hand, it is argued that the Kavango Legislative Council was simply a tool to facilitate colonial control and obtain the compliance of the population. On the other hand, South Africa claimed that it was a genuine initiative aimed at providing meaningful political development that would replace traditional authorities with a democratic system and self-governance for the Kavango. The chapter will consider these different arguments not only by providing a descriptive account of the proceedings of the Kavango Legislative Council, but also by focusing on five key issues that were discussed by the Council: the notion of Kavango independence, the attempt to construct a 'Kavango' identity, the contract labour system, the Kavango Education Act and the Turnhalle Conference. By selecting specific debates and motions, the chapter helps to look at the extent to which the South African government imposed its colonial administration on the people of Kavango through the council and how the Council dealt with these issues.

In order to deliberate effectively on the role of the Council, a number of more specific questions need to be considered: Did any members of the Kavango Legislative Council use the chamber as a means to challenge the South African colonial administration of South West Africa at that time? What was the actual substance of the powers allocated to the Kavango Legislative Council by the Republic of South Africa? Was the chamber a forum for debate that reflected conflicting opinions, or was it merely a space used to applaud South African interventions? What was SWAPO's public position on the legitimacy of the Legislative Councils and is there any evidence that the Kavango Legislative Council could claim any popular support? Only a detailed analysis of the Kavango Legislative Council and its work can provide nuanced answers to such questions. One final important issue needs to be highlighted: in what ways did the establishment of the Kavango Legislative Council impact on the roles and rights of the existing traditional authorities? How did the Kavango Legislative Council modify and relate to the established structures of the traditional authority?

Various political, social and economic factors led to the establishment of 'Homelands' in South Africa after the National Party's election victory in 1948. Although not at the same level, time or pace, these factors were similar in Namibia and ensured that the African population in the two countries was divided and ruled along ethnic lines. The government in South Africa and Namibia sustained a system that, as Harold Wolpe (1972) argued in his classic article, provided cheap African migrant labourers to sustain the economy. In both South Africa and Namibia, the homeland system was viewed as providing a solution to the political question by providing a strategy for preserving white domination. Africans could claim political rights, but only 'outside' South Africa in the different 'native' homelands or 'outside' the 'Police Zone' which embraced the commercial farming and urban areas of Namibia. The contract labour system in Namibia served to ensure the control and regulation of migrant labour from the different homelands. It was a system that was justified by the colonial administration as a means to supplement South Africa's financial contribution to the various homelands, particularly following the expansive development projects contained within the Report of the Odendaal Commission (1964).

My research examined one of the ten homelands established in Namibia. By critically engaging with the politics of power, as reflected in the composition, legislation and authority of the Kavango Legislative Council, this chapter focuses on the issue of the distribution of power and the way power was diffused between the Council, the traditional authorities and the colonial government of South Africa between 1970 and 1979. The study ends in 1979 because after 1979, the Legislative Councils in Namibia were included in a three-tier national alliance government under the leadership of Dirk Mudge and the Democratic Turnhalle Alliance (following their victory in a national election held on 4 – 8 December, 1978). The 1978 election that led to this government was the first in which Namibians were able to vote for locally-formed parties, rather than local versions of parties that had been formed in South Africa (Soggott, 1986, pp.250-268).

It is important to recognise that during the open hearings and meetings South African officials and the Bantu Affairs Commissioner held with Kavango residents in the 1960s, some local people raised reservations about the implementation of the homeland plan in Kavango and the general development of homelands in Namibia. These reservations were mainly based on their past experience with the colonial government in the Kavango. In the end, the government of South Africa ignored these reservations and passed the Development of Self-Government for Native Nations in South West Africa, Act No. 54 of 1968, which led to the establishment of the various homelands in Namibia. The first 'Legislative Council' was established in Ovamboland with the first session officially opening on 17 October 1968 (Dugard, 1973, p.135).

In October 1970, the Kavango homeland was given home-rule powers and individuals were nominated to serve on the first Kavango Legislative Council, based mainly on their status in society or position in the traditional leadership. The first Kavango Legislative Council had five departments, each headed by one member from the five recognised ethnic groups in Kavango (Gciriku, Kwangali, Mbunza, Mbukushu and Sambyu) and it held three sessions each year until 1972. In 1972, the Kavango Legislative Council, through the Executive Council, requested the South African government to grant it self-governing status. The request was granted and, as a self-governing homeland, the constitution of the second Kavango Legislative Council changed; some members were still nominated, but others were elected. The change reflected a discourse of development which claimed that the political system should be cautiously 'modernised' with the gradual introduction of democracy.

My earlier research outlines the systems of governance used by the traditional authorities before the Legislative Council of Kavango was established.[1] The point that I would like to emphasise here is that incorporating traditional authorities in the Kavango Legislative Council changed the image and political culture of traditional authorities. After 1970, the five traditional authorities were incorporated into a 'modernised' ethnic government that catered not only for their individual tribes, but for the entire people of Kavango – creating a new 'Kavango' identity. Five Ministers were elected from the individual traditional authorities to serve on the Executive Council of the Kavango Legislative Council. Collectively, as members of the Executive Council, they had to decide on plans and policies for the entire Kavango homeland as a unit, rather than five separate 'tribal' territories. The conversion of traditional authorities into paid government officials also changed the whole question of tradition, because traditionally these chiefs were never paid a salary. Before 1970, the chief's subjects worked in the chief's agricultural fields (*Mazanza*) as a matter of honour, social duty and respect. The chiefs also shared fines with the victims, who brought cases to him to resolve (Gibson et al., 1981, p. 69).

---

[1] Aaron Nambadi (2007), 'The Kavango Legislative Council, 1970-1979' (MA thesis, University of the Western Cape).

The granting of self-government by South Africa to Kavango did not mean total independence from the colonial government and, in fact, there was never a single homeland in the whole of Namibia that was ever really 'independent'. Kavango was only granted self-governing status and as a result, the Kavango Legislative Council received limited powers. All the resolutions and Acts passed in the Kavango Legislative Council were subject to approval by the South African State President. It is debatable whether the Kavango Legislative Council even requested such a status or whether it was just imposed by the colonial administration as it was clearly a strategy to establish South Africa's colonial 'divide and rule' policy in South West Africa. The minutes of Council debates reveal that the entire Council did not thoroughly discuss nor clearly understand the powers and the implications of 'self-governance'. Archival research has indicated that self-governing status was only requested by the small Kavango Executive Council, whilst some members of the Legislative Council believed that the Council had never requested the new status. The fact is that the Executive Council of Kavango first engaged in discussions with the South African administration before presenting it to the entire Legislative Council. Yet the Legislative Council was allegedly the highest decision-making organ, and as such, had the power to override the Executive Council.[2]

The constitution and the positions held by some individuals in the Kavango Legislative Council played an influential role in directing the work of the Council. Dr Romanus Kampungu, for example, played a very significant role in organising the work of the Legislative Council, both in his capacity as a person with impressive academic qualifications and as the chairperson of the Council. An influential elite, with prestige and status based on their religious titles and educational qualifications, would play a significant role in the Council and its activities. The status of Council members was enhanced by the significant financial rewards which enabled them to exercise patronage within their communities.

The material and financial benefits given to the Kavango Legislative were enormous, especially in comparison to the total revenue actually collected in Kavango. Chief Minister Alfons Majavero argued during the tabling of the Amendment Law on the Remuneration and Privileges of the Kavango Legislative Council of 1978:

> Mr Chairman, the Government of the Republic of South Africa has said repeatedly that the salaries of the Cabinet and members of the Legislative Council should be met from our own revenue. You will notice that the total estimated expenditure amounts to the sum of R112 404. The Kavango tax budgeted for 1978/79 is only R12 000, which means that the Government of the Republic of the Republic of South Africa must subsidise this Council with R100 404. Mr Chairman, this is not a healthy state of affairs and I feel that it is also unfair to the Republic of South Africa's inhabitants. Mr Chairman, I feel that it is my duty to give consideration to increasing our Labour export which will bring in more revenue and reduce much reliance on financial subsidy from the Republic.[3]

---

[2] See Proclamation R.115 of 1973 'Kavango Declaration of Self-governing Area and Constitution of Legislative Council'.

[3] NAN F002-AP 7/3/4, A motivational speech by the Chief Minister Alfons Mayavero, Kavango Legislative Proceedings of the Sixth Session of the Second Kavango Legislative Council, National Archives of Namibia, Windhoek, (21 April-3 May 1978), p. 142.

South Africa's huge financial contribution suggests that the Council was bound to support South Africa. How could the Council oppose the hand that fed it? At the same time, some interviewees argued that it was a matter of survival and obtaining a job. It was very possible that these financial benefits directed the Council's decisions and acts and its political role in the Kavango homeland, although these allegations remain a contentious issue today. While SWAPO made its total opposition to the homelands very clear, the evidence suggests that the Kavango Legislative Council functioned unopposed by the people inside Kavango, including the five traditional authorities of the different tribes. The composition of the Council, which included the five chiefs and other traditional leaders from the traditional authorities, might have contributed to the people's silence, as opposition to the Kavango Legislative Council might have been regarded as a direct challenge to the traditional authorities. The deployment of South African military forces inside South West Africa also had a direct impact on the lack of visible opposition to the Kavango Legislative Council, although there was certainly also a strong element of the 'politics of the belly'.

The implementation of the homeland system in Kavango came at a time when nationalism in South West Africa was growing. Almost every invited South African official who spoke at an official opening of the Council warned of SWAPO's threat to the unity of Kavango and, particularly, to the survival of Kavango as a self-governing state. The self-governing state of Kavango however, seemed undisturbed by external threats and went about its normal business, passing acts and submitting these to the South African State President for approval before implementation, without any mention of SWAPO. In fact, all the motions had to go through the Office of the Secretary of the Council, making it impossible to present a motion that was considered inappropriate by the secretary. As the person who had the final say before a motion was tabled, he was in a position to reject or accept any motion. The lack of education and qualifications by the local people, meant that nearly all administrative posts were held by white South African officials, making it almost (if not entirely) impossible for the Council or the individual Councillors to oppose South Africa.

It is important to put the question of Kavango 'citizenship' in perspective. Before the establishment of Kavango as a homeland for the sole occupation of 'Kavangos', Kavango people lived on both side of the Kavango River, but immediately after its declaration as a homeland, the Kavango was declared a land that was to be occupied solely by those Kavango people on the southern side of the Kavango River. Unfortunately those who found themselves on the Angolan side of the river were classified as 'foreigners'. Kavango had (and still has) a significant number of 'foreigners', especially Angolans, that fled the 1970s civil war in Angola. However, it is interesting to note that the traditional territories of the five communities that were officially included in Kavango all included land in Angola, north of the river.

The Kavango Nation Enactment Act was discussed and passed. Other homelands in South Africa, and specifically Owamboland (in South West Africa), had similar legislation and therefore the Executive Council stated that it was necessary to have such legislation for Kavango, and to distinguish 'the Kavango nation' from the others. Only Kavango 'citizens' were allowed to participate in the election for the constitution of the second Legislative Council, which basically dealt with the question of Kavango nationhood and political sovereignty. The Kavango people needed to be registered to allow the Kavango government to deal with the question of 'foreigners', especially when dealing with issues such as employment provision.

On Tuesday 11 May 1976, Councillor Gerhard Shakadya tabled the '*Motion on the Pledge by White Officials*'. In motivating the motion, Councillor Shakadya said:

> This motion is submitted with the object of requesting the Government of South Africa that white personnel who are sent to Kavango and who are prepared to work amicably with the inhabitants of Kavango, give a pledge that they will assist the Government of Kavango for at least three years. After expiration of the period of three years, and if the person concerned is prepared to work longer in Kavango, and provided the Kavango Government so desires, the period can be extended.
>
> The Legislative Council further requests the Government of the Republic of South Africa that if there are white officials who do not want to co-operate with the Government of Kavango, the Cabinet be permitted to confer with the Honourable Commissioner-General about such person with a view of having such person transferred from Kavango.[4]

The passing of this motion can be regarded as a milestone for the Kavango Legislative Council in its challenge against the Government of South Africa and, specifically, in dealing with white South African personnel who worked in Kavango. However, it should be noted that the 'Government of Kavango' could make 'a request', which implies that such 'a request' could be turned down by the Government of South Africa. The Government of South Africa was at liberty to accept or refuse any request from the homeland government and there was nothing that the Council could do about it. However after passing the motion, the Council did use it to transfer or remove white officials from Kavango, especially those who were suspected of contravening local laws, or their employment contracts, or job description. Lorenz Haupindi referred to two specific cases that involved a Doctor Kushke, a medical practitioner, and Mr Louis Burger, a Director of Education. The Kavango Legislative Council asked the two white South African officials to leave the Kavango after the Council discovered and concluded that they were not complying with the laws of the Kavango and that they mistreated the local people.[5]

The Kavango Legislative Council was never independent of the South Africa colonial administration. In fact, many of the acts passed were passed on condition that they were in line with the apartheid ideology. Conditions and legislation was put in place to control the work of the Council and establish boundaries to its authority. The colonial administration placed administrative staff in key positions to ensure that the Council made decisions and passed acts that were favourable to the colonial administration

---

4   NAN, F002-AP 7/3/4, Councilor Gerhard Shakadya motivating the motion on pledge by white officials, Kavango Legislative's Proceedings of the Fourth Session of the Second Kavango Legislative Council (23 April-13 May 1976), p. 115.
5   Interview by the author with Lorenz Haupindi, Rundu, 4 April 2007.

and anything beyond that was simply not allowed to be discussed, let alone brought to Council.

Following the establishment of the Kavango Legislative Council, nine schools were named after members of the Council: Max Makushe Secondary School, Linus Shashipapo Secondary School, Maria Mwengere Secondary School, Leevi Hakusembe Secondary School, Kandjimi Murangi Secondary School, Andreas Kandjimi Senior Primary School, Romanus Kamunoko Secondary School, Dr Romanus Kampungu Secondary School and Rudolf Ngondo Senior Primary School. The first five secondary schools were named before Namibia's national independence in 1990 and, specifically during the Kavango Legislative Council's era, after traditional leaders who served in the Council (the four chiefs and one queen of the five Kavango tribes);[6] the others, after ordinary Councillors who were members of the Kavango Legislative Council.

It is interesting to note that some schools were named after the country gained independence. The naming of schools before independence can mainly be attributed to the fact that all these schools were approved, built and run by the education department of the Kavango Legislative Council, and it only makes sense that, because these schools were built in the five tribal areas, they were named after the chiefs to honour them and to show respect to the chief. Having been a teacher myself at one of these schools (Kandjimi Murangi Secondary School), one gets a sense that there are no plans now, or in the near future, to change these names and my understanding is that the question of personal respect to the former chief's history and memory, and ethnic pride play a major role. The fact that the last four schools, i.e. Andreas Kandjimi Senior Primary School, Romanus Kamunoko Secondary School, Rudolf Ngondo Senior Primary School and Dr Romanus Kampungu Secondary School, were named after independence also brings to the fore the question of memory, and specifically, the ways in which communities remember the people who played a role in the history of the Kavango region.[7] In conclusion, the fact that these specific individuals are today recognised as having played an historical role whilst serving in the Kavango Legislative Council is important, as it might be expected that the 'memory work' of the state since independence would have excluded all the leaders who had played a role in the homeland governments from public memorialisation.

The fact that schools are still being named after individuals who were members of the Kavango Legislative Council should be understood in a regional and historical context. Many former Kavango Legislative Councillors were also tribal chiefs who led their individual tribes during the colonial era and this gave them a dual identity and made them eligible for recognition and respect. The fact that these schools still retain these names demonstrates some form of enduring respect for these individuals and for traditional institutions.

Lastly, in the 1990s, the Namibian government embarked upon a system of decentralisation and, as a result, Regional Councils were established in the thirteen regions of the country with the aim of ensuring regional development, decentralisation

---

6   Max Makushe, Linus Shashipapo, Maria Mwengere, Leevi Hakusembe and Kandjimi Murangi.
7   The Primary Schools were built after independence, whilst Dr Romanus Kampungu Secondary School was built during the 1980s and was formerly known as Rundu Junior Secondary school. It was only renamed Dr Romanus Kampungu after the country's independence.

and the preservation of regional identities. Apart from procedures, legislation, a democratically-elected government and the fact that executive authority in Namibia is vested in the different ministries at the national level and not in these Regional Councils, these Regional Councils do seem to have similar levels of power to the former Homeland Legislative Councils. Whilst the delimitation of regional boundaries after independence made a deliberate effort to avoid the old ethnic, homeland boundaries in some regions, such as the Caprivi and Kavango, it has proved difficult to make significant changes due to geographical constraints. A worthwhile topic for future research would be a comparative study to indicate the differences and similarities between the former Legislative Councils and the Regional Councils in an independent Namibia.

References

Cooper, A. (2001) *Ovambo Politics in the Twentieth Century.* Lanham, MD: University of America Press.

Dugard, J. (1973) *The South West Africa/Namibia Dispute: Documents and Scholarly Writings.* London: University of California Press.

Gibson, G., Larson, T. J. and McGurk, C. (1981) 'The Kavango Peoples, *Studien zur Kulturkunde*, 56. Wiesbaden: Franz Steiner.

Keulder, C. (1998) *The Traditional leaders and Local Government in Africa: Lessons for Africa.* Pretoria: HSRC.

Kössler, R. (2005) *In search of survival and dignity. Two traditional communities in southern Namibia under South African rule.* Windhoek: Gamsberg Macmillan.

Nambadi, A. (2007) 'The Kavango Legislative Council, 1970-1979', MA thesis, University of the Western Cape, Cape Town.

Proclamation R.115 of 1973 'Kavango Declaration of Self-governing Area and Constitution of Legislative Council'.

Soggot, D. (1986) *Namibia: The Violent Heritage.* London: Rex Collings.

South Africa, Republic of (1964) Report of the Commission of Enquiry into South West African Affairs, 1962-63. Pretoria: Government Printer (RP. No. 12).

Totemeyer, G. (1978) *Namibia Old and New: Traditional and Modern Leaders in Ovamboland.* London: C. Hurst and Co.

Wolpe, H. (1972) 'Capitalism and cheap labour-power in South Africa: From segregation to apartheid', *Economy & Society*, 1 (4).

Archival sources

National Archives of Namibia

AP Offical Publications

7/3/4, Kavango Legislative's proceedings of the fourth session of the Second Kavango Legislative Council, 23 April-13 May 1976. Councilor Gerhard Shakadya motivating the motion on pledge by white officials.

7/3/4, Kavango Legislative Proceedings of the Sixth Session of the Second Kavango Legislative Council, 21 April-3 May 1978. A motivational speech by the Chief Minister Alfons Mayavero.

11 The 1978 Election in Namibia

Timoteus Mashuna

Introduction

A generation of Namibians has participated in the democratic elections that have taken place in Namibia since 1989 to elect the President, National Assembly, Regional Councils and Local Authorities. However, it is often forgotten that the first national democratic election in Namibia took place in 1978. Up to this date some elections had taken place for political structures (such as the Legislative Assembly), but the electoral roll had been limited to whites only. A historical analysis is required to consider the reasons why a democratic, national election was held in 1978, and the continuing limitations of the electoral system that led SWAPO, the leading nationalist party, to boycott the election.

Sources covering debates of the United Nations (UN) during the 1960s indicate members of the UN were increasingly concerned that progress toward the complete emancipation of many countries and people under colonial status was too slow and should be accelerated. This concern led, for example, to the adoption of a declaration aimed at granting independence to colonial countries in September 1960. Growing international pressure prompted South Africa to rethink her colonial approach in Namibia and hence in 1963, South Africa commissioned the Odendaal Commission of Enquiry to investigate the affairs of Namibia and propose some sort of internal settlement that would prevent the emergence of nationalism so as to maintain South Africa's upper hand in running the affairs of Namibia (UNIN, 1986, p. 39).

However, despite these declarations and many other resolutions passed by the UN in an effort to end colonialism in Namibia and in many other countries of the world, the UN's intervention only became significant in the 1970s. In 1970, the United Nations Security Council (UNSC) referred the Namibian issue to the International Court of Justice (ICJ) in order to seek an 'advisory opinion' (Du Pisani, 1985, p. 186). This led to the termination of South Africa's mandate to administer Namibia in 1971. After this, the United Nations' General Assembly passed a number of resolutions demanding the transfer of power to the people of Namibia, and even went as far as threatening South Africa that failure to do so would prompt punitive measures (Mushi, 1988 p. 682).

South Africa responded by proposing talks with representatives of several population groups of Namibia in order to reach an 'internal settlement'. This new strategy eventually resulted in the Turnhalle Conference in September 1975 (Du Pisani, 1985, p. 293). The conference proposed a democratic transfer of power through national elections that were set for December 1978. The elections were held, but in a highly volatile political environment with no clear electoral procedures to ensure the free and fair conduct of the elections.

Election Preparations

The final draft proposal of the Turnhalle Conference, issued on 18 August 1976, stated that Namibia would become 'independent' on 31 December 1978 (Du Pisani, 1985, p. 405). The envisaged independence was to come after holding a national election to elect an interim government which would then draft an interim constitution for the country and prepare the territory for internationally supervised elections (O'Linn, 2003, p. 119). South Africa, having accepted the final draft proposal of the Turnhalle Conference, appointed Louis Pienaar as Administrator-General (AG) for Namibia in order to oversee the implementation of the election process (O'Linn, 2003, p. 119). The Administrator-General explained his job description when he assumed his post:

> As you all know, one of my tasks is to create conditions for a free and unhampered expression of the true will of the inhabitants of the Territory with reference to their political and constitutional future through a countrywide election. That supposes that all political parties and organisations taking part in such an elections be granted a just and equal opportunity thereto (Du Pisani, 1985, p. 377)

Obviously, the Administrator-General had a hard task ahead of him, because the political situation inside the country was far from being conducive to the conduct of free elections and it was unlikely that elections would go ahead unhampered as envisaged by the AG. The war between South Africa's Defence Force (SADF) and the Peoples' Liberation Army of Namibia (PLAN), the armed wing for SWAPO, was still going on. Discriminatory and restrictive laws, which could inhibit the conduct of free elections, if not amended, were still constitutional in Namibia (South West Africa Administration, 1978). Thus, for the AG to ensure that conditions were conducive to free elections and that elections could go ahead unhampered, it was urgent to bring an end to the military hostilities between SADF and PLAN. Moreover, the AG needed to amend the existing legislation and promulgate new legislation in order to set modalities for the electoral processes.

Pursuant to these aims, the AG, upon accession to office on 1 September 1977, invited all political parties, including SWAPO, to participate in the Turnhalle election. He also issued an invitation to Namibians in exile to return home freely, and urged SWAPO to lay down its arms and fight at the polls (Soggot, 1986, p. 209). SWAPO rejected the AG's call to participate in the Turnhalle election and vowed to intensify its military attacks (SWAPO, 1981, pp. 222-227). Towards the end of 1977 and in early 1978, SWAPO's military wing (PLAN) was involved in over 100 military clashes with the SADF and assassinated a number of South African 'collaborators'.[1] The most prominent incidents included the assassinations of Toivo Shiyagaya, the Owambo Minister of Health, in

---

[1] Local people who were targeted by SWAPO's PLAN fighters were those who were considered to be collaborators with the South African government. However, it seems possible that not all local people who were attacked by SWAPO were collaborators. At some point, local people made use of the PLAN fighters in order to get rid of their personal enemies, simply by implicating them as supporters of the South African government and *vice versa*. I am thus using the word 'collaborators' although I am aware that not everyone who was attacked by PLAN was a collaborator.

February 1978 and Clemens Kapuuo, the Herero leader on 27 March 1978 (O'Linn, 2003, pp. 131,132; Gewald, 2003). The escalating level of violence obviously put at risk the safe conduct of the elections and to ensure that nothing could hamper holding these elections, the South African government responded by increasing its military presence in the north.

David Soggot, who visited the north in 1978, described the presence of the South African military:

> From the moment of touchdown at Ondangwa Airport – enlarged to accommodate military transport planes – we were struck by the changed face of Ovamboland. We saw hundreds of riflemen; movement in and out of the sprawling military encampment. There were military patrols everywhere; it was a country at war without – for the moment – visible death and destruction (1986, p. 219).

Soggot gives a sense of the escalating militarisation of the north and the context within which the 1978 election would take place. The months leading up to the election of December, 1978 would also see two significant milestones in Namibian history. On 4 May 1978 an airborne South African force attacked and destroyed SWAPO's camp at Cassinga (as well as a number of others), and on 29 September 1978 Resolution 435 was adopted by the UN's Security Council. Resolution 435 set out a UN approved template and plan for the transition to independence in Namibia and UN-supervised elections – and an implicit rejection of the internal, South African approved elections planned for December 1978. The international context within which the electoral process for 1978 was crafted and the widespread belief that Namibian independence could actually be achieved in 1978 requires a detailed analysis that still needs to be written. The complex triangular relationship between the armed struggle, internal political developments and the crafting of Resolution 435 during the period 1977-1978 needs detailed research and analysis. However, my more limited objective in this chapter will be to focus on the electoral process within Namibia itself during 1978.

Apart from increasing the scale of the security operation, the AG also repealed a number of pieces of legislation to enable political parties to prepare for the envisaged elections. The most important was the repeal of Proclamation 17 of 1972 (Authority, 1978). This proclamation had, since 1972, prohibited the holding of public meetings unless these meetings were in the interest of the government or had to do with sporting events. However, following the repeal of this proclamation, all public gatherings, including political gatherings, were permitted. In addition after this repeal, the government was no longer allowed to prevent certain individuals from attending public meetings (Authority, 1978, p. 60).

The legalisation of political meetings alone could not guarantee that political meetings could to be held freely without people being subjected to political violence. The AG, therefore, introduced a new proclamation (Proclamation 26 of 1978)[2] in order to enable the detention of persons who, it was believed, might commit political violence. In

---

2 Detention for the Prevention of Political Violence and Intimidation Proclamation (AG 26 of 1978) was introduced on 18 April, 1978 (Herbstein & Evenson, 1989, p. 77).

the statements preceding this proclamation, the AG argued that the proclamation was aimed at ensuring 'public safety' in order to enable the people of Namibia to engage in the elections in a democratic and peaceful manner (South West Africa Administration, 1978, pp. 1, 2).

A month before the registration of voters started, the Administrator General issued yet another proclamation, referred to as the 'Registration of Voters Constituent Assembly Proclamation of 1978' (Landis, 1982, p. 17). The purpose of this proclamation was to provide a regulatory framework within which the registration of voters was to be conducted. For instance, the proclamation defined who qualified and who did not qualify to register for the 1978 elections. It also stipulated penalties and offences so, for example, any person who encouraged, instigated or incited any other person not to register would be fined R300 or subjected to a three year term of imprisonment (South West Africa Administration, 1978, p. 5).

However, this proclamation did not stipulate any penalties or offences for those who might use force or intimidate others to register in order to break the election boycott that SWAPO was campaigning for. Another crucial aspect omitted from this proclamation was the question of who would be responsible for ensuring that all voters had registered. The proclamation only stipulated the conditions for the appointment of the chief registrar and registration officers.

Participant Political Parties and their Programmes

Five political parties participated in the 1978 elections. These were: *The Aksienfront Vir Die Beihoud Van Die Turnhalle-Beginsels* (AKTUR), the Democratic Turnhalle Alliance (DTA), Herstigte Nationale Party (HP), Liberation Front (LF) and the Namibia Christelike Demokratiese Party (NCDP). It is significant that the names of the five parties all implied that they sought votes from a national (rather than ethnically targeted) constituency (Africa Institute of South Africa, 1980, p. 30.) A brief overview of the origins and the political objectives of these parties follows.

The Democratic Turnhalle Alliance (DTA)

DTA was formed in November 1977, immediately after a bitter leadership contest between Abrahim Du Plessis and Dirk Mudge, both having campaigned to become the leader of the National Party in Namibia. The presidential contest resulted in the splitting of the National Party into two political factions, one for Mudge and the other one for du Plessis (O'Linn, 2003, p. 121). This culminated in a major political realignment after Mudge and his faction left the National Party and formed the Republican Party (RP) in 1977. Mudge then entered into an alliance with a number of ethnically defined political parties that had participated in the Turnhalle Constitutional Conference (O'Linn, 2003, pp. 121, 122).

This alliance was thus named the Democratic Turnhalle Alliance, in short the DTA. The parties and tribal groups that formed this alliance were: the Republican Party (RP); the National Unity Democratic Organisation (NUDO), a political arm of the

Herero Chiefs' Council; the National Unity Party (NDP); the Labour Party (LP); the Rehoboth Baster Association (RBA); South West Africa People's Democratic United Front (SWAPDUF); and four other independent groups drawn from the Homeland Councils of Kavangoland, Caprivi, Bushmanland and Tswanaland.[3] Given the nature of this alliance, the DTA was able to draw support from almost all ethnic groups in Namibia. This widened its support base such that in 1978, a year after its inception, observers frequently referred to DTA as the major threat to SWAPO's claim to be the sole representative of the Namibian people (De Villiers, 1978, p. 4).

During the 1978 election, the DTA advocated a government based on a three-tier administration system. On the first tier, was the central government, which would deal with issues of national importance. On the second tier were the representative authorities who dealt with the affairs of each ethnic group separately, and on the third tier were the local authorities of all the municipalities (Du Pisani, 1985, p. 377). Unlike some of the parties that participated in the 1978 election, the DTA demanded that Namibia should be treated as a sovereign state (rather than a South African colony) and that most of the state's power should be vested in the central government, rather than divided between the 'Bantustans'. In terms of its constitution, DTA campaigned for a bill of fundamental human rights, which, it demanded, should be binding on government and all its agencies and should be enforced by the Court (DTA, 1978). However, critics claimed that most of the funding for the DTA during the 1978 elections came from the South African government (Christian Centre, 1978, p. 1).

Action for the Retention of the Turnhalle Principles (AKTUR)

AKTUR was formed from the faction of the National Party that remained after Mudge and his followers had left the National Party and merged with other non-white representatives from the Turnhalle Conference (Du Pisani, 1985, p. 376). The remaining faction of the National Party (the 'Du Plessis faction') then formed AKTUR as an election front after they were excluded from the alliance formed by Mudge and the black Turnhalle representatives. The leader of AKTUR was Abrahim Du Plessis, who at the same time was the President of the National Party, after he had defeated Mudge during the 1978 National Party's presidential contest (Africa Institute of South Africa, 1978, p. 21).

AKTUR drew most of its support from conservative white Namibians in the 'whites-only' National Party and from a handful of coloured individuals. AKTUR supported the three-tier administration system as advocated in the final constitutional proposal of the Turnhalle, but it disagreed with the DTA in terms of how power was to be allocated between the first and second tiers of administration. The final constitutional proposal of the Turnhalle emphasised that more power should be granted to the central government or the 'first tier' administration, a proposal that was strongly supported by DTA. However AKTUR wanted more power vested in the second-tier 'homeland' authorities (Du Pisani, 1985, pp. 377, 413).

---

3 Basler Afrika Bibliographien (BAB), PA 48. Emmett, T. (1978) *Clemens Mutuurunge Kapuuo 1923-1978* (a short report compiled by the DTA Secretariat in co-operation with the Herero Chiefs' Council, 1978), p. 2.

In principle AKTUR supported ethnic segregation and was seeking to maintain white exclusivity. It was completely against the desegregation of residential suburbs, schools, hospitals and other public institutions as advocated by DTA (Africa Institute of South Africa, 1978, p. 13). AKTUR supported the Turnhalle Conference's call to end racial discrimination but not the desegregation of public institutions.

Herstigte National Party (HNP)

The Herstigte National Party (HNP) was part of South Africa's Herstigte National Party, a party formed in 1968 as a response to the perceived easing of Apartheid by the National Party government towards the end of the 1960s (Africa Institute of South Africa, 1978, p. 21). It began participating in the political affairs of Namibia in the early 1970s, after it became clear that the National Party government had abandoned its plan to incorporate Namibia into the Union of South Africa and was negotiating with the UN over a possible transfer of power to Blacks in Namibia. This, according to HNP, was unlawful because Namibia constituted an integral part of South Africa and no government, including the National Party government, had any right to give Namibia away (Du Pisani, 1985, pp. 32-77).

In Namibia, the HNP never existed as an independent political party, separate from the HNP in South Africa. Instead, HNP only had an executive committee, under the leadership of Sarel Becker, who worked as the party's 'Regional Secretary' in Namibia. However, in 1978, HNP participated in the 1978 elections, as a political party for South West Africa. Like its counterpart in South Africa, the HNP in Namibia was supported by extreme right-wing Afrikaners who favoured the balkanisation of Namibia's territory into ethnic homelands. The party supported separate development as advocated in the Odendaal Commission of Enquiry. It argued that separate development was ideal for the survival of minority races. Unlike any of the other parties that participated in the 1978 elections, the HNP opposed the treatment of Namibia as an independent sovereign state. Namibia, they argued, should be incorporated into the Republic of South Africa as a fifth province and 'South West Africa' should never be referred to as Namibia.[4]

The Namibia People's Liberation Front (LF)

The Liberation Front was a coalition between the Damara Executive Committee,[5] and the Voice of the People's Party.[6] The two moderate political parties had been part of the Namibia National Front (NNF): an alliance of anti-Turnhalle parties, which had been formed in April 1977 (Du Pisani, 1985, p. 299). In 1978 the Voice of the People's Party was expelled from the NNF and this resulted in the Damara Executive Committee also breaking away from the NNF during the same year (Africa Institute of South Africa,

---

4   Gwen Lister, 'Oom Sarel-a worthy opponent'. *The Namibian,* 9 November 2006, p.1.
5   The Damara Executive Committee was a political party in Namibia that targeted the Damara community. It was formed by a group of people based in the Damara Tribal Executive Committee (DTEC), which was not a political party. Also see BAB, PA, 48, Tony Emmett Papers: *South West Africa, a summary on political parties in Namibia,* by Mburumba Kerina; p. 3.
6   The Voice of the People's Party was a political party in Namibia, led by Kephas Conradie.

1978, p. 20). In that year, 1978, the two groups (Damara Executive Committee and the Voice of the People's Party) merged and formed the Namibia People's Liberation Front (NPLF) under the leadership of Kephas Conradie. The NPLF had most of its support among the Damaras in Windhoek and a few Bondelswarts led by Chief Anna Christians.[7] In 1979 NPLF's support base was further enlarged after the Damara Christian Democratic Party (DCDP) joined it, but this was only for a short time until it withdrew from the NPLF in 1986. The NPLF's policy was to unite the Nama and Damara people, hence its support was confined to the Namas and Damaras people to whom it appealed (Africa Institute of South Africa, 1978, p. 20).

Namibia Christelike Democratiese Party (NCDP)

The NCDP was founded in 1978 under the leadership of Ben Pillay. It advocated a bill of individual rights, entrenched in the constitution, which could not under any circumstances be amended. It supported capitalism as the moral order and opposed the formation of big governments. The NCDP envisaged a democratic form of government build upon Christian principles. It further stressed that Christian beliefs should provide the primary ideological principles for the people of Namibia.[8] Its support base was very small and the members were mainly regarded as individualists or eccentrics (Africa Institute of South Africa, 1978, p. 20).

Voters' Registration

Towards the end of June 1978, the wheels of the election process were set in motion. The Voters Registration Proclamation, which served as a guide for the registration of voters, was established (South West Africa Administration, 1978, p. 15) By mid-June 1978, a registration apparatus staffed by 400 registration officers, together with staff, interpreters and vehicles, at a cost of R1,500 000, was already on standby (Soggot, 1986, p. 250). Other legislation necessary for the conduct of free and unhampered elections, according to the AG, was already in place. By 1978, perpetrators of political violence and intimidation could be prosecuted, and political parties could hold public rallies because the notorious Riotous Assembly Proclamation had been amended (Authority, 1978, p. 15).

During the third week of June 1978, the AG announced that voters' registration would start from the fourth week of June 1978 and would continue until September (Soggot, 1986, p. 250). In order to register, voters had to fill in a registration form in which they stated their name and address. In addition to that, voters had to indicate on the registration form that they were 18 years of age or older and had been born within the territory (excluding Walvis Bay) or had been a resident in it for a continuous period of four years (Du Pisani, 1985, p. 415). To ensure that people from all corners of the country were informed about the registration process, Radio South Africa, tribal

---

[7] BAB, PA 48, Tony Emmett Papers. *South West Africa, a short description of political parties in Namibia*; by Mburumba Kerina, p. 4.

[8] BAB, PA of 48 Tony Emmett Papers. *NCDP party programme* (Windhoek, 1979).

vigilantes, chiefs, headmen, SADF soldiers and some of the political party agents, began spreading the news, informing voters on every possible occasion, even during funeral and church services (Christian Centre, 1978, p. 9).

The AG's announcement for the registration of voters coincided with the announcement by the National Party Government in South Africa, that it wanted the UN Secretary-General to despatch an emissary to Namibia for the UN to familiarise itself with the preparations for the elections (Soggot, 1986, p. 250). This, according to Justin Ellis, created a great deal of ambiguity among voters, who became confused as to whether the registration process was for a UN supervised and internationally recognised election (as planned in Resolution 435, which had been adopted by the United Nations earlier in the year) or for a South African-supervised election. Ellis (1978, p. 39) claimed that most voters registered under the impression that they were registering for the UN-supervised elections

However, one should be cautious to arguing that it was only due to the ambiguity surrounding the election that a large number of voters registered. A number of contextual factors that might have accounted for the high number of registered voters need to be taken into consideration. One must consider what had taken place during previous ethnic elections. In 1973, a one-day election was held in Owamboland to endorse the establishment of the Owamboland Bantustan Authority, the first election in Owamboland in which individuals were permitted to vote. During these elections, less than 3 per cent of the eligible voters in Owamboland registered. In 1975, similar elections were held in different homeland areas and on this occasion there was a much greater turnout in Owamboland. In homeland areas where there was a high concentration of South African soldiers, 75 per cent of the electorate voted, whereas amongst Oshiwambo-speakers in the remainder of the country only 4 per cent voted (Ellis, 1978, pp. 21, 39).

The reluctance of the Owambo people to participate in the first election in Owamboland led to the public flogging of many civilians in Owamboland. The Committee on South African War Resistance noted that after the Owamboland election in 1973, political opponents of the Ovamboland Bantustan Authority were flogged by the security personnel of the Ovamboland traditional authority (Katjavivi, 1986, p. 221). The terror inflicted on civilians after these elections might have contributed to the high voter registration during the 1978 elections. During the campaigning for the 1978 election, voters in Owamboland were subjected to immense intimidation. It was alleged that they were told that if they did not vote they would not be permitted to plough or obtain employment and would be refused medical services, and that those who were employed would lose their jobs (Ellis, 1978, p. 35). Taking these factors into account, the high turnout of the eligible voters who registered and voted in the 1978 election, should be seen as a result of positive publicity and negative violent coercion and political intimidation.

Election Campaigns

The campaigns for the 1978 elections started towards the end of 1977 and ended shortly before the commencement of the actual voting process, on 8 December 1978. Of all the parties that took part in the elections, the DTA was the first party to embark upon what Soggot calls a 'massive political campaign'. From 1977, the DTA started holding rallies in different parts of the country and, sometimes, organising free food and drinks at barbecues for their supporters. The DTA also purchased an estimated 132 vehicles, opened 36 local offices and trained and deployed about 425 field workers. The main task of the field workers was to 'educate' and mobilise the public, whereas the purchase of vehicles was largely aimed at ensuring that voters could reach the polling stations during the registration and election campaigns. Other political parties participating in these elections (AKTUR, HNP, NCDP and LF) had fewer resources at their disposal, and this limited their campaign coverage (Soggot, 1986, pp. 254-255). In addition to that, the last two parties (NCDP and LF) had only been formed a few months before the elections and therefore did not have enough time to organise large-scale political campaigns (Africa Institute of South Africa, 1978, p. 20).

Radical political parties (e.g. SWAPO and NNF), who opposed the 1978 elections, also held a number of protest rallies. SWAPO, in fact, had been holding rallies in various parts of the country since 1977 (Soggot, 1986, p. 255). The political campaigns organised by SWAPO and the NNF were aimed at informing their supporters about the reasons why they were not participating in the elections. For instance, in a large two-page advertisement published in the *Windhoek Observer*, the NNF wrote: 'the Namibia National Front is not participating in the unilateral elections proclaimed for the week commencing on 4 December 1978, their reasons, inter-alia, being the following.' These were then followed by a number of reasons, such as the fact that the NNF did not consider the elections to be 'free and fair', that the NNF supported an initiative made by five Western states to implement Resolution 435, and the NNF rejected the impartiality of Radio South Africa, etc.[9]

Similarly, in a number of press releases and during protest rallies, SWAPO emphasised the reasons why it was not willing to participate in the elections. SWAPO stressed that it was unwilling to participate in the elections because South Africa had refused to allow the United Nation to supervise and control the elections. Other reasons were that many SWAPO activists imprisoned under the so-called Terrorism Act were still in prison and that the Walvis Bay issue was still not resolved.[10]

For DTA and AKTUR, the two main contenders for power in this election, the focus during the election campaigns was on getting enough supporters to the polling booths and ensuring that local people had acquired the legal documentation that would enable them to vote. This meant that they had registered for the elections and had at least pre-confirmed their loyalty to the party of 'their choice' before the elections. This is illustrated by one episode, cited in the post-election report issued by the Christian Centre for Namibia. DTA and AKTUR election organisers came to Mbeyo, a village 60 km south of Rundu, and went from house to house requesting to see the DTA membership cards and registration cards of all the people in the village. They continued, thereafter, to issue AKTUR membership cards before handing all the other cards back (Christian Centre, 1978, p. 9).

---

9   *Windhoek Observer*, 4. November 1978, pp. 15-16.
10 BAB, PA48, Tony Emmett Papers. 'No Elections under South African Control' (Press release), SWAPO, Department of Information, 28 June 1977, p. 1.

The enforced issuing of party membership cards, particularly with regard to the DTA, was widespread and a common practice during the elections campaigns. Evidence contained in the report of the Christian Centre suggests that it was not only DTA electoral officers who demanded DTA membership cards from the local people. Even members of the SADF, chiefs and tribal vigilantes, kept demanding DTA membership cards during the election campaigns. For example, on 24 May 1978, black and white soldiers of the SADF visited a village, called Onamgolo in the Ondonga area and then searched for DTA party membership cards from one house to the other. Namido Kauluma, a resident of Onamgolo village, was reportedly beaten by SADF soldiers during this incident for not possessing a DTA membership card (Christian Centre, 1978, p. 5). Namido's case was just the tip of the iceberg; more and more cases in which DTA membership cards were forced on civilians feature in the report, with the allegation that homeland ministers, chiefs, and tribal vigilantes had all played a substantial role in intimidating the electorate.[11]

The Voting Process

The actual voting process started on 8 December 1978 and ended on 12 December, five days later (Soggot, 1986, p. 254). Over a thousand polling stations were established all over the country. To cope with the distance in a country as vast as Namibia, the South African administration established mobile polling stations in order to reach remote areas and those who, for whatever reason, were unable to reach the fixed polling stations. The DTA and several other employers provided transport to communities living miles away from the polling stations. The DTA was noted to have hired around a hundred vehicles that it used to pick up people from their houses and drive them to the polling stations. Numerous employers were also reportedly seen bringing their workers to the polling stations (Ellis, 1979, pp. 28, 42).

The political situation was still tense and there was no actual cessation of the war. South Africa had to ensure that the voting process could not be hampered by any possible military attack. Therefore, a convoy of military detachments, armed with anti-land mine armoured personnel carrier military vehicles, was deployed to accompany the mobile polling stations. SADF soldiers were also deployed at each polling station to provide security and, to make matters worse, the South African authorities erected barbed wire fences surrounded by military sand bags at the fixed polling stations (Soggot, 1986, pp. 254-255).

The general atmosphere during the voting process was not different from that during the registration of voters and election campaigns. Though there were no cases of murder reported during the voting process (unlike the election campaign), the situation remained fearful and tense. South Africa feared that SWAPO would disrupt the voting process with a surprise military attack. Hence, South Africa decided to increase military patrols during the voting process, particularly in Owamboland (Soggot, 1986, p. 255). Some

---

11 Judging from the evidence contained in the report of the Christian Centre (1978, pp. 6-8), it is clear that even if DTA electoral officers and the South African military played a crucial role in forcing civilians to register for the DTA party membership cards, tribal vigilantes, chiefs, and homeland ministers also played a big role in forcing local people to have DTA membership cards.

political parties were also worried about the safety of the people at the polling stations. DTA, for example, had to arm some of its members to protect people during the voting process. *The Financial Mail* of 8 December 1978 described the voting atmosphere in these few lines, 'there was constant movement of troops and military vehicles in the territory, while some places were beehives of military activity. Helicopters were hovering overhead, while Mirage fighter planes took off constantly' (Ellis, 1979, p. 41).

During the voting process, substantial electoral irregularities were exposed, as had been the case during the registration of voters and election campaigns. Members of the SADF, who manned each polling station and toured most parts of the country, persuading voters to go and vote, often showed DTA signs. Reports published by several church groups indicated that vehicles that carried workers and local people to the polling stations were either owned by the DTA or by individuals who were DTA supporters. Civic educators were, also, often political party agents, who did not conceal their political affiliations at the time they were conducting voter education (Soggot, 1986, pp. 42, 254). Photographs in Justin Ellis's report show that some electoral agents were wearing DTA T-shirts whilst explaining to the voters the voting procedures. In addition, the voting process was characterised by a high degree of political manipulation. In an episode recorded in the western area of the so-called 'Bushmanland', a DTA election organiser was reported to have gone ahead of the mobile polling station, handing out sweets and DTA T-shirts to the voters.[12]

Just as with other phases of these elections, the voting process was heavily criticised. Critics of the 1978 elections claimed that voters feared to lose their jobs and other related services, should they refuse to vote. They argued that votes cast were not secret. In addition, it was claimed that chiefs, tribal vigilantes, SADF soldiers and radio journalists warned people not to abstain from voting.[13] Chief Josea Taapopi of Uukwaludhi, Radio Oshiwambo and Radio Kavango were reported to have threatened prospective voters that should they fail to vote, punitive steps would be taken against them (Christian Centre, 1978, p. 7).

Election Outcomes

Of the 412,351 eligible voters who, it was claimed, had registered for the elections, 331, 055 voted. In other words, 81 per cent of registered voters' cast their vote with only 4, 791 per cent or 1, 5 per cent of the cast votes, declared as spoiled ballots. Most of the seats were taken by the DTA, which scooped 41 of the 50 seats (Christian Centre, 1978, p. 7). This left a total of nine seats for the other political parties to share. Of these seats, six were taken by AKTUR and the other parties (HNP, LF and NCDP) got one seat each (Soggot, 1986, p. 256).

The election results were highly praised by the South African administration as well as by political leaders of the DTA. In an interview conducted by the *Afrikaans Duitse Kultuuruinie,* Dirk Mudge, Chairman of DTA, noted that he was satisfied with the outcome of the elections, most importantly due to what he termed 'a festival mood' in

---

12   *Suidwester*, 8 December 1978.
13   Ibid.

which these elections took place. Moreover, the AG, in a similar interview, commented that he was not only satisfied with the election results, but he was also extremely grateful. To him the entire electoral process was a great achievement. The AG based his satisfaction on the large number of voters who turned up at the polls and argued that the fact that more people voted indicated that the people of South West Africa wanted to express their true will. Making similar comments, J. W. F. Pretorius, a member of the party management of AKTUR, expressed similar satisfaction, with minor reservations. He argued that, even though he was satisfied with the outcome of the elections, AKTUR could have got more votes, but the financial support which was made available to the party was minimal and that had limited AKTUR's political campaign. Another aspect that Pretorius thought might have shaped the election's outcome was the political awareness of the Namibian people. Pretorius claimed that the people of Namibia were still 'not politically developed' to an extent that they could distinguish philosophical differences between AKTUR and the other political parties. As a result, most of the voters voted for DTA as that was the party that they associated with their traditional authorities (*Afrikaans Duitse Kultuuruinie,* 1978, pp. 5-6).

Conclusion

The preparations for the 1978 elections led to the promulgation of several pieces of legislation in order to guide the conduct of the electoral process. Some of the proclamations were promulgated as a response to political events that were observed in the country prior to the elections; others were simply put in place to ensure that prospective voters completed all the necessary steps to ensure that they could participate in the election.

The electoral proclamations were ambiguously and inadequately formulated to ensure the conduct of credible elections. For instance the voters, by virtue of the voters' registration proclamation, were forced to register, regardless of whether they wanted to register or not. At times, force and all sorts of coercive mechanisms were used to ensure that every prospective voter had registered and voted in the elections. The electoral proclamations for the 1978 election were also silent regarding measures that might be taken in response to the use of force or threats to prevent people from participating in the election and there was no legislation that could guide the electoral agents to stop them from being partial when they were conducting voter education.

As such, instead of being impartial as is the general norm for credible voter education, the electoral agents were simply forcing people to vote for political parties to which they were affiliated. Nonetheless, it was not possible to dispute the credibility of the elections on the basis of the few reported incidents. The point was that there were no legal instruments put in place that could have shown up violations and hence prove electoral irregularities. South Africa simply bulldozed through the 1978 elections in an attempt to reach an internal settlement for Namibia, regardless of whether there were adequate legal instruments in place to ensure a credible election and to respect the Namibian people's right to choose whether to vote or not.

References

Africa Institute of South Africa. (1980) *Africa Insight.* Vols 10–13.

Afrikaans-Duitse Kultuurunie (1978) *Results of the first general one-man-one-vote-election in South West Africa: 4–8 December 1978.* Windhoek: Afrikaans-Duitse Kultuurunie.

Episcopal Churchmen for South Africa. *Report on the Registration and Election Campaigns in Namibia 1978.* New York: Episcopal Churchmen for South Africa.

Democratic Turnhalle Alliance (1978) *Draft Constitution of the Democratic Turnhalle Alliance.* Windhoek: DTA.

De Villiers, B. W. and Cowley, C. (1978) 'The Namibian Drama', *Africa Institute Bulletin*, Vol. 16.

Du Pisani, A. (1985) *SWA/Namibia: The Politics of Continuity and Change.* Johannesburg: Jonathan Ball Publishers.

Ellis, J. (1978) *Elections in Namibia.* London: British Council of Churches and Catholic Institute for International Relations.

Ellis, J. (1979) *Namibia-negotiation and "elections".* Stockholm: SIDA.

Gewald, J-B. (2003) 'Who killed Clemens Kapuuo?' *Journal of Southern African Studies*, 30 (3).

Herbstein, D & Evenson, J. (1989) *The Devils are Among Us: The War for Namibia.* London: Zed Books.

Katjavivi, P. H. (1986) 'The Rise of Nationalism in Namibia and its International Dimensions'. DPhil. thesis, St Anthony's College, Oxford.

Landis, E. (1982) 'Namibian Law: Self-determination, law and politics'. Bloomington: Episcopal Churchmen for Southern Africa.

Lister, G. 'Oom Sarel - a worthy opponent'. *The Namibian,* 9 November 2006.

Mushi, S. S. (1988) 'Namibia: South African Strategy and independent Africa'. In Wood, B. (ed.) *Namibia 1884–1984: Readings on Namibia's history and society.* London: Namibia Support Committee and the United Nations Institute for Namibia.

O'Linn, B. (2003) *Namibia The Sacred Trust of Civilization: Ideal and Reality.* Windhoek: Gamsberg Macmillan.

Soggot, D. (1986) *Namibia: The Violent Heritage.* London: Rex Collins.

South West Africa Administration. (1978) *The Laws of South West Africa.* Vol. 62. Windhoek: South West Publishers.

Suidwester, 8 December 1978.

SWAPO (1981) *To Be Born A Nation: The Liberation Struggle for Namibia.* London: Zed Press.

United Nations (1978) *Objective Justice* 9 (1).

United Nations Institute for Namibia (1986) *Namibia: Perspectives for National Reconstruction and Development.* Lusaka: United Nations Institute for Namibia.

Windhoek Observer, 4 November 1978. Two page advertisement for the NNF.

Archival sources

Basler Afrika Bibliographien (BAB)
PA 48, Tony Emmett Papers

Mburumba Kerina n.d. *South West Africa, a short description of political parties in Namibia.*

Press release 28 June 1977, 'No Elections under South African Control', SWAPO, Department of Information.

Clemens Mutuurunge Kapuuo 1923-1978, a short report compiled by the DTA Secretariat in co-operation with the Herero Chiefs' Council, 1978.

NCDP party programme (Windhoek, 1979).

12 Waking the Dead: Civilian Casualties in the Namibian Liberation Struggle

Jeremy Silvester and Martha Akawa

Prelude

One day in early January 1984, an old Ford truck set out from Ruacana. Twenty-five workers stood crowded in the back. After travelling just five kilometres from the small town the truck drove over a double landmine. The explosion left a huge crater in the ground and immediately killed ten of the people in the truck, whilst another six were severely injured, losing hands, arms and legs. None of the names of those who had died were provided in the press coverage of the incident.[1]

On 23 January 1988, four young people were driving a Toyota Hilux van near their home when a unit of the Koevoet paramilitary police unit opened fire on their vehicle riddling it with bullets and totally destroying it. Cornelius Nghipukuula, aged 27, was killed immediately and two of the other occupants were wounded. The three survivors were told to report to the police station the next day to pay a R100 fine as an 'admission of guilt' for driving during a curfew.[2]

These were just two incidents amongst many that occurred during the Namibian war of independence in which the casualties were not soldiers, but civilians. Yet the absence of the names of those killed in one of the largest landmine explosions that took place during the war seems symptomatic of the way in which civilian victims of the war remain unrecognised in accounts of the liberation struggle.

Introduction: War Monuments and Peace Memorials

It is generally argued that there is a simple difference between monuments and memorials: monuments celebrate victory, whilst memorials are more concerned with reflection and remembrance and are, therefore, more likely to encourage reconciliation. However, war memorials tend to focus on remembering the sacrifice of soldiers, rather than the other victims of war, civilians – the 'collateral damage' as it is termed in the language of the twenty-first century that dehumanises and falsely sanitises the horror of war.

Throughout the world the focus of the heritage that commemorates war is on the military. However, Michael Rowlands has argued that 'one of the features of nationalist

---

1   'Landmine Blast That Killed Ten', *Windhoek Observer,* 14 January 1984, p. 7.
2   Chris Shipanga, 'Curfew Claims More Lives in the Far North', *The Namibian,* 29 January 1988, p. 5.

war memorials has been their capacity to turn traumatic individual deaths into acts of national celebration and heroic assertions of collective values' (Rowlands, 1999, p. 129) In Namibia, a massive heritage project, for a small country, has been the construction of Heroes Acre (essentially a memorial graveyard containing the virtual graves of early leaders of anti-colonial resistance and the actual graves of selected leaders who have passed away since Heroes Acre was opened in 2002). The dominant figure at the site is a huge statue of a soldier, carrying an AK-47 and throwing a hand grenade. Funerals provide an opportunity to celebrate the lives of individuals and use the eulogies on their lives to assert collective values and a national identity. Heroes Acre not only contains military leaders, but also civilians who are considered to have contributed to the struggle for independence.

Critics have contrasted the focus at Heroes Acre on a few individuals with the 'democracy of death' planned in the South African equivalent, Freedom Park, in Pretoria which will attempt to name and remember, as far as possible, all those who have been killed as a result of past conflicts in the country. It can be argued that a monument such as Heroes Acre located, as it is, in Windhoek, far from the regions where much of the fighting took place does not provide an adequate site of remembrance for the thousands of people who lived in the war zone in Namibia and were killed during the conflict.

In defence of Heroes Acre, it might be argued that this is not its intended purpose, but that in the pursuit of nation-building there is a conscious effort to forget the suffering of the past and to celebrate the triumph of the liberation movement. Michael Rowlands has argued that 'Triumphalism . . . achieves this through the assertion of collective omnipotence and by banishing from memory those acts of humiliation when the nation failed to protect its own young' (1999, p. 131). Memories of the feared knock on the door at midnight, the horrific images of cars and bodies randomly ripped apart by landmine explosions, the cries of the children caught in the crossfire of war. These are the memories that most people would probably want to banish from their minds, but they are also the reality of a war which has left profound physical and mental scars on Namibia and Namibians. Indeed the absence of a detailed account of the impact of the war on the civilian population of Namibia may result in a version of the war that downplays the terrible impact of the conflict inside Namibia.

At present it is not even known how many civilians died during the war. Efforts have been made to document the names of those who suffered in the struggle but, to date, it has only been the names of the soldiers on both sides that have been remembered and memorialised. SWAPO published a book in 1996 entitled *Their Blood Waters Our Freedom,* which contains the names (or combat names) of 7,792 members of PLAN (the People's Liberation Army of Namibia) who died during the liberation struggle. The memorial list not only includes those who died in combat, but also those who died in car crashes and other accidents.

On the other side in the liberation war, the South Africans were able to more publicly acknowledge their military dead during the war itself. A monument was erected in Tsumeb in July 1981, with the following inscription in Afrikaans 'Tsumeb commemorates its fallen whites who died as a result of terrorism'.[3] White SADF soldiers

---

3   Engel Nawatiseb, 'Shrine Causes Stir in Tsumeb', *New Era,* 27 January 2006.

were often flown to South Africa for burial, but the deaths of black soldiers fighting in SWATF and Koevoet were not so publicly commemorated or buried. Indeed there were reports that in some instances Koevoet and PLAN fighters were anonymously buried together in mass graves.[4] Today the South Africa War Graves Project has created a web site that lists the names of each and every South African soldier who died during what is dubbed the 'South West Africa Border War' – a total of 2,365 names. It is interesting to note that the figure contrasts significantly with the 715 members of the security forces that Willem Steenkamp claims were killed during the 'Border War' in a book published towards the end of the war (1989, p. 185). Furthermore it seems that whilst this list includes those who died in the South African army from all races (and clearly includes those from 32 'Buffalo Battalion), it may not include the considerable number of people who served in the South West Africa Territorial Force (SWATF), the notorious counter-insurgency police unit (*Koevoet*) or those who served in various paramilitary organisations such as the Ovamboland Home Guard or as bodyguards.[5]

In contrast to these military lists no list has yet been compiled bearing the names of civilians who died during the war. Indeed the only figure that has been suggested can be found in Steenkamp's book where he claims that 1,087 civilians died between 1981 and 1988. His book was published in 1989 and so does not include figures from the final months of the war and he claims that the statistics for the period 1966-1980 were not available. Steenkamp also claims that his, unreferenced, statistics demonstrate that the majority of civilian deaths were '. . . killed by mines PLAN had laid' (1989, p. 235). It is in this context that the 'Civilian Casualties Project' has been conceived and initiated.

An Overview of the Civilian Casualty Project

The Civilian Casualties project had very limited objectives, mainly because it had very limited resources. The South African Truth and Reconciliation Commission spent three years gathering information and had dozens of researchers. In our project two researchers, Dr Jeremy Silvester of the Museums Association of Namibia and Dr Martha Akawa of the History Department at the University of Namibia, spent just 18 working days. We also benefitted from the hard work of two student assistants, Ms Romie Nghiulikwa and Ms Helena Showa.

Most of the time was spent conducting an initial survey of newspaper coverage of the war, although we were also able to consult some official inquest files. We have been able to cover the period 10 December 1959 to 30 April 1989. The newspaper coverage and inquests have enabled us to identify 1,278 individual war-related civilian deaths to date. The project has produced two products. Firstly, we have compiled five files listing, in alphabetical order, individual cases. Each case consists of an information cover

---

4   Oswald Shivute, '11 More Graves Found', *The Namibian*, 25 November 2005.
5   One of the few remaining traces of those who died fighting on the South African side during the war that remains in Namibia is the derelict graveyard at the old 'Buffalo' base of the 32nd Battalion in the Kavango East Region, which contains a large number of unnamed graves. Isaaskar Haikaere, Kletus Likuwa, Shampapi Shiremo and Jeremy Silvester, *Heritage Hunt Report for the Kavango Region*, 3rd Edition (unpublished report), Windhoek: Museums Association of Namibia and National Heritage Council, 2010, pp. 122-126.

sheet containing information and any references to an individual case (this provides a framework which could be expanded upon if the project was extended) and also a typed version of any newspaper article referring to each case. The computer file containing all the typed newspaper articles is searchable. Secondly, a searchable database has been established containing all the key information using Microsoft Access software.

At present the database lists 328 cases where it has not yet been possible to identify the name of the victim, which means that 26 per cent of the civilians listed as killed during the liberation struggle remain unidentified to date. Of those killed at least 424 were killed by landmines or unexploded ordinances, and at least 316 were killed by assassination squads that took them from their homes, usually during the night, and executed them. In 92 cases the cause of death is not yet clear owing to insufficient information, whilst the remaining 446 were killed in a variety of other ways. At times the researchers had to make decisions as to whether or not deaths should be considered war-related or not. For example, cases involving car accidents in which the victims collided with military vehicles that were in northern Namibia as a result of the militarisation of the region, or the 34 individuals who were killed during violent clashes (officially described as 'riots') in Katutura during March 1978, fall into this category.

The information collected on each individual includes their full name, age and gender, the date and site of their death, the cause of death and the sources from which information has been obtained. Of course, the information obtained from the newspapers is often vague and incomplete, but it does already enable us to provide the initial basis for some interesting statistical analysis. For example, we were able to identify the gender of the victims in 746 cases and in those cases the figures revealed that 29 per cent of the victims were women. When the database is more comprehensive in its coverage, we will also be able to provide both a more detailed analysis of the regional distribution of violent incidents and a summary of annual and seasonal differences, which will provide alternative ways of mapping the impact of the war inside Namibia.

The chapter will continue by considering three major challenges that face us in our research (locating source material, defining the spatial and temporal boundaries of the project and debating the concept of a civilian), and also consider three important issues that may be raised by the presentation and circulation of this research in the public domain in Namibia.

Challenging the Anonymity of Death: The Search for Sources

The biggest challenge facing the project was to identify the most time-efficient way in which to locate the required information. It is for this reason that we started with a newspaper survey and worked back from the date of independence. The initial survey consulted one of three newspaper sources for each month covered. The newspaper *The Namibian* was used to cover the period 1985-1989. *The Namibian* had a staff permanently based in the north and, therefore, tended to provide the most detailed coverage of events in the war zone. The *Windhoek Observer* was launched in May 1978, and provided extensive coverage of inquests. The *Windhoek Observer* was, therefore, consulted for the period 1978-1985. The *Windhoek Advertiser*, another English-language paper, was used for the period 1959-1978. The *Windhoek Advertiser* seems to have relied exclusively on South African Army Press Conferences as its source of information on the war and, therefore, its accounts contain far less detail than was normally found in the other two papers. However, newspapers as a source have severe limitations and we realised that newspaper coverage of civilian casualties was far from comprehensive – over a quarter of the victims mentioned in the newspaper articles we looked at remained unnamed and oral histories suggest that many deaths were not reported to the authorities, and so not picked up by journalists.

Time constraints meant that the project could not be very ambitious in terms of the scope of the distribution of the draft database for verification or the range of sources consulted. We believe that we have created a useful research tool, but that a far larger research project is needed in order to create as comprehensive and inclusive a database of civilian casualties as possible. Ideally, a six-point strategy should be developed to expand on the list and to obtain public feedback.

1. **Media Coverage.** An interim list of the names appeared in *The Namibian* newspaper in August 2007 and we received fifteen telephone calls and letters that provided us with additional information as well as requests for information about people who had disappeared during the struggle. Unfortunately we did not have the resources to make site visits or to conduct follow up interviews. Ideally, if the resources were available, we would recommend that a national media campaign should be launched so that members of the public could make corrections and verify the information on our initial database, or provide additional names and details to enable the database to be expanded.

2. **Circulation through the Church Network.** When the project was initiated a meeting was also held with the Council of Churches, which expressed its willingness to assist with the circulation of the list. However, this proposal has not yet been implemented.

3. **Cross-referencing of Newspapers.** As the initial survey has provided a list of dates of incidents, cross-referencing should be made with the Afrikaans press, such as the *Suidwestafrica* and also the contemporary South African press and the different accounts should be added to the files. This is particularly important given the dubious spellings of some of the names of places and people found in the newspaper articles consulted to date.

4. **An Oral History Project.** The interviews carried out by Martha Akawa into the assassination of her own uncle and aunt during the war demonstrate the considerable extra details that can be obtained from this source. Oral history research will be particularly important in order to identify cases where individuals were killed, but the incident was never covered in the newspapers. Unless this element of the project can be carried out the list will certainly remain inaccurate and incomplete.

5 **Consult documents in the SWAPO and SADF archives.** It seems likely that both archives would contain information about incidents involving civilians. An initial survey of *The Combatant*, the newsletter of SWAPO's guerrilla forces, reveals that in the early years of publication (during 1980 and 1981) it would list assassinations carried out by SWAPO's armed forces. A total of 11 assassinations carried out by SWAPO were acknowledged in 1980 and 1981, but it seems that no further cases were described after this date. However, of the eleven cases listed only two were reported in contemporary newspapers inside Namibia. A further list that would be interesting to consider is the infamous death list referred to in a church newspaper, *Omukwetu*, which claimed that 50 prominent businessmen in northern Namibia had been listed for assassination by a South African hit squad. The completion of the database and case files would enable comparative analysis of such information. The archives of the SADF have also, largely, not been investigated, but are available at the archives of the South African Department of Defence. It seems likely that the relevant material, if it still exists, could be accessed through South Africa's Freedom of Information legislation if it has not yet been de-accessioned.

6 **Inquests.** Legally, an inquest was meant to be held into the death of each individual at a Magistrate's Court. Initial investigations suggest that the majority of cases involving war-related deaths were heard at the Magistrates offices at Oshakati or Tsumeb. Ideally these cases should also be examined and the information that they contain included with the case files to create a more complete thematic archive. An initial sample survey suggests that the inquest records, which are in Afrikaans, can help to identify many of those who were killed whose names were not listed in the newspaper coverage, although there were also examples, for example, involving landmine explosions where it had not been possible to establish the names of the victims even several months after the explosion. It would be desirable to transcribe and translate inquest records to make the information and statements that they contain more accessible.

Mapping the Chronological and Spatial Boundaries of the 'Namibian Liberation Struggle'

The first major challenge facing the project working has been placing spatial and chronological boundaries for the liberation struggle on our database, since these could be contested in a number of ways. Our initial research covered the period 1979-1989, which includes most of the period when the guerrilla war had its most serious impact inside Namibia. Whilst there were some high-profile incidents in the earlier years of the war, such as the assassination of the Ndonga King, Fillemon Elifas on 16 August 1975, it is generally argued that the war in northern Namibia became far more intense after the withdrawal of the SADF from Angola at the end of March 1976, and the consolidation of SWAPO's military bases in Angola close to the Namibian border (Brown, 1995; Namakalu, 2004). Our initial intention was to cover the period from 26 August 1966, when the battle of Omugulugwoombashe is generally taken as marking the launch of the armed struggle in Namibia, and end on 1 April 1989, with the implementation of UN Resolution 435, which marked the start of the transition to independence in 1990.

In South Africa the memorial concept behind the *Sikhumbuto* section of the new Freedom Park has been far more expansive. An effort is being made to name and remember everyone who '...laid down their lives in the struggle for humanity and freedom cutting across eight conflict areas: These are Pre-Colonial, Genocide, Slavery, Wars of Resistance, South African War (Anglo-Boer War), First World War, Second World War and the Liberation Struggle.' Initially a register of names suggested by members of the public was developed on the internet. A wall was then constructed that has space for 120,000 names and which has been inscribed with 75,000 of the names that have been suggested and approved to date. Indeed, the Archives of Anti-Colonial Resistance and the Liberation Struggle also takes a broader view and preferences a long historical perspective that collates 'anti-colonial resistance' with the start of formal colonialism in Namibia in 1878 (with the annexation of Walvis Bay by Britain).[6]

However, as resources were limited, it was decided that our database would start with the highly prominent deaths of thirteen civilian victims who were killed by police during a demonstration against the forced removal of the Old Location in Windhoek on 10 December 1959, and does not, for example, attempt to identify the names of civilians who died in early conflicts – for example, those who died in the prison camp on Shark Island in 1905-1906. The end of the conflict for civilians is also more difficult to fix than it might at first appear. For example, in September, 1989, six months after Resolution 435 came into effect, a high-profile white member of SWAPO, Anton Lubowski, was assassinated in Windhoek. The impact of landmines on the civilian population also did not magically end with the declaration of independence. The 2006 edition of the International Landmine Monitor notes that in Namibia 'Since 1999, landmines and UXO have killed more than 138 civilians and injured at least 450.'[7] At this point we have not attempted to include the names of those civilians in our database, but they are, surely, also innocent victims of the war.

A further issue has been a spatial one. At one level we had to consider the geographical scope of our study. A great deal of the fighting between South African forces and PLAN combatants took place in southern Angola. During this fighting, hundreds of Angolan civilians were also killed. Should these be identified and added to the toll of civilian casualties in the Namibian Liberation Struggle? If many of the casualties that were inflicted by the South Africans during the attack on Cassinga were civilian casualties, shouldn't they also be listed on the database, even though they died beyond the border? At present, owing to limited resources, we have only focused on casualties on Namibian soil.

A further problem has been presented by a number of cases in which we, as researchers, have to decide whether or not a civilian who had been reported missing should be listed as having died in Namibia. Perhaps the most prominent example of such a case would be that of the SWAPO Vice-President, Brendan Simbwaye (see chapter 9 in this volume). But another, more typical, example would be the case where the mother of Hishiinawa

---

6 See <http://www.freedompark.co.za> {Accessed on 1 February, 2011}.
7 *Landmine Monitor, Annual Report*, 2006. < http//www.icbl.org/lm/2006/namibia>{Accessed 3 March, 2011}.

Haludilu, stated in September 1987 that her son had been taken to the SADF's Sector 10 base on 8 August that year, but that he had subsequently disappeared and had not been seen for six weeks. In such cases it is difficult to know whether Haludilu returned at a later date, might have been released and left the country, or might have been killed.[8] Due to the uncertainty surrounding such cases and the fate of the 'disappeared' we did not include such cases in our database, even though the International Red Cross concluded in its 1989 report that there were at least 34 cases where the South African security forces had failed to account for people, like Brendan Simbwaye, who had been arrested and then disappeared. The further investigation of such cases would require access to the military archives in South Africa containing records of arrests and the co-operation of former military personnel.

Defining 'Civilian' Status and the Implication of Guilt or Innocence

The second major challenge facing the project has been the haziness surrounding the definition of a 'civilian' (a challenge that has also faced historians writing about the attack on Cassinga). The fact that civilians should be protected during wartime has been a moral principle that has been at the heart of efforts to create international rules of warfare. Article 51(1) of Protocol I of the Geneva Convention relating to the Protection of Victims of International Armed Conflicts (an amendment to the original Geneva Convention of 1949) adopted in 1977 clearly states that: 'The civilian population and individual civilians shall enjoy general protection against dangers arising from military operations.'[9] One of the central features of international law regarding the rules of war in recent decades has been an effort to make the distinction between 'the combatant' and 'the civilian'. The fact that 'South West Africa' was given international status and not accepted as a part ('a fifth province') of South Africa, meant that the Geneva Convention's guidelines on the treatment of civilians should have been legally binding on both sides of the conflict from the date of the General Assembly resolution in 1970 at the latest (Kwakwa, 1992, p. 74). The division has rested on the basis of the idealised presumption that war should consist of a simple conflict between two armed forces that avoids as far as possible death or destruction to the 'innocent' civilian population on both sides.

However, writing this paper against the backdrop of the ongoing conflicts in Afghanistan and Iraq has highlighted the complexity of guerrilla warfare. In both the Namibian case and these current conflicts, a question has been raised about the definition of a civilian in the context of a guerrilla war being waged against what is perceived as an illegal occupation. As armies become increasingly technologically advanced and difficult to confront on the open battlefield, to what extent are the logistical support systems (such as the railway lines and trucks carrying fuel, food and ammunition) legitimate targets? If such operations are run by civilians does this make them legitimate targets?

---

8 'Undersiege by Soldiers', *The Namibian*, 18 September 1987, pp. 6-7.
9 <http://www.icrc.org/ihl.nsf/full/470?opendocument>. {Accessed 1 December 2009}.

The Geneva Convention attempts to define the role of the 'non-combatant' as a category that is somewhat different to that of a civilian, but in recent conflicts the grey areas seem to grow ever larger and ever greyer. A further layer of complexity comes when a liberation movement views an illegal occupation as being buttressed by the establishment of a supportive local administration consisting, as in Vichy France during World War II, of officials who were perceived by the resistance forces as 'collaborators' and 'puppets'. In northern Namibia, in particular, the homeland government in the form of the Ovamboland Legislative Assembly in its various forms was considered the most provocative example of a South African engineered ethnic alternative to SWAPO's vision of 'One Namibia, One Nation'. Did the participation of individuals in this administrative system make them legitimate targets?

Protocol 1 of the Geneva Convention deals particularly with the status of civilians during armed conflict and clearly states that for an organisation to be recognised as a 'combatant' it should 'enforce compliance with the rules of international law applicable in armed conflict' (Ricou, 2005, p. 94). Failure to comply with the rules of war is one of the criteria which leads an organisation to be branded as a 'terrorist' organisation. However, the distinction between 'combatants' and 'civilians' is not as simple as it might first appear since, even according to the Geneva Convention, an individual or group might be attacked and viewed as a 'combatant' in cases where they are involved in 'activities closely associated with the direct infliction of violence'. Activities such as gathering intelligence to enable particular targets to be attacked or servicing a weapons system (for example, providing ammunition for a weapon) might, therefore, be considered 'direct participation' in hostilities (Ricou, 2005, p. 156).

Heaton Ricou argues that a broader interpretation of this seemingly clear phrase would mean that activities such as supplying information that provides an advantage to one side in a conflict (such as 'spying' or 'informing') might also fall within this category, as it could be directly linked to the infliction of violence by one side on the other, whilst the simple supply of food and water to combatants would be 'considered sufficiently removed from the infliction of violence that civilians providing such services to combatants are unlikely to be considered to have taken a direct part in hostilities' (2005, p. 157). However, it is clear that this 'grey' area provides a space in which it is possible to debate whether an individual has been involved in activities that enable them to be treated as a 'combatant' and, therefore, a 'legitimate' target, rather than a 'civilian'. The Civilian Casualties Project has, therefore, not attempted to engage in such subjective judgements, but has worked on the definition of a combatant that is provided in the extensive definition provided in Article 4A of the Third Geneva Convention of 1949 relative to the Treatment of Prisoners of War.[10]

In cases where it has already been possible to cross-reference sources, it is clear that there were often conflicting accounts about the circumstances surrounding the death of an individual. For example, the *Windhoek Observer* of 3 July 1982 contained a brief report on an inquest into the death of Ruben Mbwalala. His young wife was reported to have simply explained that he was 'fetched one evening by five unidentified and unknown black men' and told to 'drive them to Angola' in his Toyota truck. The next day Mbwalala's body was found near his home with a single bullet through his head.

---

10 <http://www.icrc.org/ihl.nsf/full/470?opendocument> {Accessed 1 December 2009}.

The report did not give the date of the incident or the age or occupation of Mbwalala. However, the issue of *The Combatant* dated April 1981 provided more details and an alternative interpretation of the incident. It stated that on 5 April 1981: 'An enemy collaborator, Ruben Mbwalala, was eliminated at Etilyaan, about 60 km south west of Oshakati. His vehicle, a Toyota and a .303 Mauzzer [sic] rifle were captured' (SWAPO, 1981, p. 9). The fact that the report in *The Combatant* alleges that Mbwalala was armed might support the allegation that he played a role in the local administration and was perceived by the guerrillas as a legitimate target.

In South Africa, the Truth and Reconciliation Commission did not work with the concepts of civilians and combatants, but rather considered the abuse of human rights. The advantage of this approach was that it enabled them to also consider the cases of the abuse of captured guerrillas and to consider the morality of the way in which people were treated according to international standards that, for example, condemn torture or the execution of people without trial. This enabled the TRC to consider not only cases such as the torture and killing of captured ANC guerrillas, but also cases where people in the townships were 'necklaced' (killed by a burning tyre). We decided that the Civilian Casualties Project does not have the resources, mandate or sufficient information to judge whether the death of a particular individual might or might not be justified in military terms. We have, therefore, listed all individuals as civilians who were not, as far as we were aware, members of one of the organised armed units taking part in the war. Thus, for example, the armed bodyguards organised and employed to protect politicians have been viewed as combatants, whilst politicians (who might have had their own personal weapons) have been treated as civilians.

Playing with Pandora's Box, Research and Reconciliation

The third and final challenge that has faced our research has been our consideration of the consequences of putting our research into the public domain and addressing an audience of relatives, rather than researchers. An article in the December 2006 edition of *Insight* magazine discussed the consequences of the discovery of a number of mass graves near former South African military bases in northern Namibia. The article was entitled 'Opening Pandora's Box' and made the point that once Namibians started asking questions about the identity and cause of death of the bodies that had been found, the Government might face further demands to research and remember the many other combatants and civilians who died or disappeared during the liberation struggle at known grave sites (such as at Cassinga in Angola) or in lesser known incidents such as those being documented by the Civilian Casualties Project.[11]

However, as researchers we should also be aware, despite our efforts to be as objective as possible and not to ascribe blame to one side or the other for individual deaths, that the release of the information that we compile may raise a number of other difficult issues. The most obvious of these will be, firstly, the political reception that such research

---

11   'Opening Pandora's Box', *Insight*, 3 December 2006.

might receive given the commitment to national reconciliation[12] that has been made by the Namibian government and the form that this has taken (namely, an amnesty for any perpetrators of violent acts on either side of the conflict that took place during the liberation struggle). The second issue that had to be considered is the possibility that the publication of such research might encourage claims for compensation and linked to this, thirdly, the likelihood that such research might encourage questions about responsibility and accountability for individual deaths that have been documented and highlighted in the public domain for the first time. The production of history is always an intervention in the present and as historians we know that we should not be naive about the consequences of our actions.

Reconciliation

South Africa chose to establish a Truth and Reconciliation Commission that could provide amnesty to individuals on the condition that they provided full disclosure about their involvement in past human rights abuses during the apartheid era. In contrast, in Namibia, a blanket amnesty was announced with the public being encouraged to forget about the past, not to open old wounds, and to move forward as a new unified nation. Critics argued that 'The problem with this approach is that it does not leave any room for accountability. In this way, perpetrators were absolved of responsibility and victims were effectively told that the government will not entertain any complaints' (Amoah & Greenbaum, 2005).

However, as stated previously, substantial publicity was given to the unearthing by builders of mass graves near a number of former SADF military bases in northern Namibia in November, 2005. This resulted in the Government making a public commitment to try to identify the victims. An investigation resulted in a report that included in its recommendations the view that archival research and oral history should be used to obtain information to help the authorities identify those buried in the mass graves.[13] On 6 December 2005, a Ministerial Committee chaired by the Minister of Justice, Pendukeni Ithana, was appointed to take forward the recommendations of the report.[14]

It seems highly unlikely that the Government would want to prosecute on the basis of these investigations, but it does suggest a new openness to acknowledge, document and identify the victims of the war and perhaps to deal with the psychological legacy of the war and its impact. A 2005 survey of five Southern African countries and their 'victim support service' specifically criticised Namibia on the basis that 'there is no official government support for victims' (Amoah & Greenbaum, 2005). The South African-based Transitional Justice Programme urged the introduction of psychological counselling for the direct and indirect victims of wartime violence, but no formal Government programme to provide

---

12 Despite constant references during political debates to the 'Policy of National Reconciliation', no written policy document on this subject has yet been made public. See for example the report on President Hifikepunye Pohamba's speech at Cassinga Day in 2012: Poolman, J. 'Pohamba Warns Against Tribalism', *The Namibian*, 7 May 2012, p. 1.
13 'Namibia', *Annual Report 2006*, Equipo Argentino de Antropologia Forense, EEAF, p. 83.
14 'Opening Pandora's Box', *The Namibian*, 3 December 2006.

counselling for those affected by the war inside Namibia has been introduced in Namibia. Questions remain as to ways in which unresolved and difficult memories linked to the violence of the past might be linked to contemporary social problems amongst survivors such as alcoholism and domestic violence.

Compensation

It seems possible that the recent publicity on the mass graves and our own research into civilian casualties might encourage claims for direct financial compensation for the families of the victims. On 15 April 2003, President Thabo Mbeki of South Africa announced that people who had been identified as 'victims' of the apartheid regime by the Truth and Reconciliation Commission would receive a one-off symbolic payment of R30, 000 as compensation for their suffering (Doxtader & Villa-Vicencio, 2004, p. 15). The issue of compensation for those who suffered during the liberation struggle has been a re-occurring one in Namibia and remains politically sensitive. The demands for compensation to date have come primarily from ex-combatants and those who were children in exile. In November 1995, a special Ex-combatant Trust Fund was established, but during 1998 ex-combatants, were involved in a number of high profile protests. In 2006 there were renewed calls for monetary compensation by an organised group of ex-combatants, which led President Pohamba to announce the establishment of a new Ministry for Veterans' Affairs and the allocation of N$5.8 million for the building of new homes for veterans, with a further N$2 million to be budgeted in a five-year plan. In 2009 the Government moved 540 Struggle Children to Berg Aukas and suggested that they might receive preference in the allocation of Government jobs.[15]

However, whilst it should be relatively easy to provide conclusive evidence that a person was or was not an active member of PLAN, it becomes more difficult to determine compensation for civilian victims of the war. One of the main reasons for this would be that there is considerable uncertainty about the actual identity of those who carried out many of the killings during the war and, therefore, issues of 'accountability' would be problematic as they would involve, in some cases, claims for reparations from a neighbouring power, South Africa.

Accountability

The issue of 'accountability' would prove highly problematic in the Namibian context, given the absence of disclosure or autobiographical statements by those responsible for particular deaths. Indeed the prevalence of allegation and counter-allegation and the use of subterfuge by the South African forces would make it difficult to determine with certainty which side was responsible for many of the killings, with both sides often denying responsibility – particularly for assassinations.

As early as January 1979, SWAPO announced that the South Africans had established a special assassination squad consisting of '40 whites and 50 blacks'. Over the next few months a large number of violent incidents were attributed to an organisation

---

15   'Struggle Kids at Berg Aukas', *The Namibian*, 10 November 2009.

that was known as 'Koevoet' or 'One Way' (or to local people as the *Omakakunya* – bone suckers).[16] SWAPO claimed that these assassinations were then being blamed on their guerrilla forces. In June 1980 a church newspaper, *Omukwetu*, announced that it had obtained a copy of a death list containing the names of 50 prominent leaders and businessmen in northern Namibia. It was alleged that the list had been found on the body of a car crash victim, Leevi Naftali Amadhila (also known as 'Kamwonga'), who SWAPO described as the commander of the 'false guerrillas'.[17] The South African Administrator-General Viljoen, responded by initially denying the existence of any 'Koevoet' unit.[18] Today it is well documented that Koevoet was established by a small group of men, including Eugene de Koch, who was later implicated in the activities of 'Death Squads' in South Africa.

Koevoet was, technically, a police unit, but there is evidence that such deception tactics were also used by army units following the development of 'Operation Barnacle' after April 1979 (Potgieter, 2007, p, 5). Two SADF soldiers from the 'Recce' unit, for example, were actually prosecuted for killing a watchman on 6 September 1981, dressed in SWAPO uniforms with SWAPO issue boots and weapons that were readily available at their base,[19] and the following year there were further reports of soldiers pretending to be guerrillas in the Kavango Region.[20] Peter Stiff has also acknowledged in his work based on interviews with many former South African soldiers that it was not uncommon for soldiers to disguise themselves as SWAPO guerrillas and that they justified this as a tactic that assisted them to obtain information about guerrilla movements (Stiff, 2004, pp. 45, 207). Towards the end of 1981, the SADF announced that it had captured three diaries from SWAPO guerrilla leaders, one of which also contained a death list which 'mostly contain the names of those who have been labelled as 'informers'.[21] However, whilst it is difficult to substantiate all these claims and counter-claims over responsibility (without more concrete evidence from those directly involved in these operations), the confusion would make it very difficult for the Namibian government to facilitate individual claims for compensation.

Conclusion

The Civilian Casualties Project seeks to provide greater insight into an important aspect of the Namibian Independence Struggle. It is not an attempt to create a Namibian Truth and Reconciliation Commission, but it might be viewed as having the potential to contribute to a different kind of memorial to the war, which could further national reconciliation and assist in promoting collective national values. For example, we have already documented that landmines were one of the major causes of death of innocent civilians. The landmines that caused these deaths were certainly planted by both sides,

---

16 '90 SA Assassins in SWA', *Windhoek Advertiser,* 29 January 1979, p. 3.
17 'Alarming Whispers about Death Squad Code-Named Koevoet', *Windhoek Observer*, 7 June 1980, p. 20; 'A black-listed editor flees', *The Combatant*, Vol 2 (1), August 1980, p. 5.
18 'Viljoen Statement' *Windhoek Observer*, 14 June 1980, p. 9
19 'Murder Whispered/Smart Police Work Leads to Multitude of Clues – and then Arrests/Held for a Day in a Bomb Shelter and then Machinegunned', *Windhoek Observer*, 5 February 1983, pp. 5-9.
20 'SWAPO or Soldier', *Windhoek Observer*, 19 June 1982.
21 'War Diaries of Insurgents Captured', *Windhoek Observer*, 28 November 1981, p. 14.

as both sides openly admitted that they deployed landmines as a weapon of war and, once under the earth, landmines explode when trodden on, whether the victim is a soldier, a cow, or a small child. Since independence the Namibian Government has taken a strong and principled position on the issue of landmines. It has signed the Ottawa Convention of December 1997 'prohibiting the stockpiling, production and transfer of anti-personnel mines', and the Namibian army destroyed its own stockpile of 50 tons of landmines in a large controlled explosion on 24 July 1998.[22] One way in which this strong stand might be publicised in Namibia could be a memorial to all those Namibians who have been landmine victims. This, we would suggest, might be just one way in which Namibia might use a memorial to civilian casualties to reflect on its painful past in order to promote national values that enable the building of a better future.

References

Amoah, J. and Greenbaum, B. (2005) 'Has Everything Been Done? The Nature of Assistance to Victims of Past Political Atrocities in Southern Africa'. Cape Town: Centre for the Study of Violence and Reconciliation.

Brown, S. (1995) 'Diplomacy by Other Means. Swapo's Liberation War'. In Leys, C. and Saul, J. *Namibia's Liberation Struggle. The Two-Edged Sword.* London: James Currey.

Chesterman, S. (ed.). (2001) *Civilians in War.* Boulder: Lynne Rienner.

Doxtader, E. & Villa-Vicencio, C. (2004) *To Repair the Irreparable: Reparation and Reconstruction in South Africa.* Claremont: New Africa Books.

Equipo Argentino de Antropologia Forense, EEAF (2006) 'Namibia', *Annual Report*.

Freedom Park Trust (2005) *Freedom Park: A Heritage Site for Reconciliation, Humanity and Freedom in South Africa.* Pretoria: Freedom Park Trust.

Insight, 'Opening Pandora's Box', 3 December 2006.

Kwakwa, E. (1992) *The international law of armed conflict: Personal and Material Fields of Application.* Dordrecht/Boston/London: Kluwer Academic Publications.

Landmine Monitor (2006) *Annual Report*.

Lamb, G. (2001) 'Putting Belligerents in Context: The Case of Namibia and Angola'. In Chesterman, Simon (ed.) *Civilians in War.* Boulder: Lynne Rienner.

Museums Assocation of Namibia and National Heritage Council. *Heritage Hunt Report for the Kavango Region.* Unpublished report, 3rd revision, Windhoek.

Moyo, T. 'Nam edges closer to being proclaimed landmine-free', *The Namibian,* 31 August 1998.

Nabulsi, K. (2001) 'Evolving Conceptions of Civilians and Belligerents: One Hundred years After the Hague Peace Conference'. In Chesterman, S. (ed.) *Civilians in War.* Boulder: Lynne Rienner.

Namakalu, O. (2004) *Armed Liberation Struggle: Some Accounts of PLAN's Combat Operations.* Windhoek: Gamsberg-Macmillan.

Nawatiseb, E. 'Shrine Causes Stir in Tsumeb', *New Era,* 27 January 2006.

---

22 Tobby Moyo, 'Nam edges closer to being proclaimed landmine-free', *The Namibian,* 31 August 1998.

Potgieter, D. (2007) *Total onslaught: Apartheid's dirty tricks exposed.* Paarl: Zebra Press.

Ricou, H. (2005) 'Civilians at war: reexamining the status of civilians accompanying the armed forces', *Air Force Law Review*, Winter.

Rowlands, M. (1999) 'Remembering to Forget: Sublimation as Sacrifice in War Memorials'. In Forty, E. and Kochler, S. (eds) *The Art of Forgetting.* Oxford/New York: Blackwell.

Shivute, O. '11 More Graves Found', *The Namibian*, 25 November 2005.

SWAPO (1981) 'Combat Reports', *The Combatant*, Vol. 2. No. 9 (April).

Steenkamp, W. (1989) *South Africa's Border War, 1966-1989.* Gibraltar: Ashanti Publishing.

Stiff, P. (2004) *The Covert War: Koevoet Operations, Namibia, 1979-1989.* Alberton: Galago.

The Combatant, 'A black-listed editor flees', Vol 2 (1), August 1980.

The Namibian, 'Struggle Kids at Berg Aukas', 10 November 2009.

The Namibian, 'Opening Pandora's Box', 3 December 2006.

The Namibian, 'Pohamba Warns Against Tribalism', 7 May 2012.

The Namibian, 'Under siege by Soldiers', 18 September 1987.

Windhoek Advertiser, '90 SA Assassins in SWA', 29 January 1979.

Windhoek Observer, 'Murder Whispered/Smart Police Work Leads to Multitude of Clues – and then Arrests/Held for a Day in a Bomb Shelter and then Machinegunned', 5 February 1983.

Windhoek Observer, 'SWAPO or Soldier', 19 June 1982.

Windhoek Observer, 'War Diaries of Insurgents Captured', 28 November 1981.

Windhoek Observer, 'Alarming Whispers about Death Squad Code-Named Koevoet', 7 June 1980.

Windhoek Observer, 'Viljoen Statement', 14 June 1980.

13 Okongo: Case Study of the Impact of the Liberation Struggle in the Ohangwena Region

Lovisa Tegelela Nampala

Introduction

This chapter will present the history of Okongo (although the South African military base at the town was known as 'Nkongo') and the ways in which the residents' daily lives came to be completely changed during the liberation struggle.[1] Traumatic memories include cases of interrogation, harassment, violence, deaths, and the climate of fear created by the conflict between South African forces and the Peoples' Liberation Army of Namibia and the presence of armed combatants from both sides in the community.

Okongo is a village situated in Ohangwena, one of the 14 political regions in Namibia. The chapter will give background on how Okongo village was established and how it became a politically active centre where many acts of violence such as executions, landmine explosions, harassment and detentions took place during the liberation struggle (1966-1989). The limited availability of literature on the impact of the war on communities in northern Namibia during the liberation struggle, especially in Ohangwena Region, motivated me to carry out research on this topic. The information to be presented will be largely based on a set of seven interviews that I conducted with local residents and their personal accounts of the events that took place in the area where they lived.

In this chapter witnesses share their wartime experiences through oral interviews and so are based on human memories of events that took place many years ago. Oral sources present the challenge that the information provided may sometimes not be reliable since memories fade, depending on the length of time that has passed since an event. When a story is told the sequence of events can also become confused and oral narratives are seldom in chronological order, with the exact date that an event took place often being only vaguely remembered. However, as more than two decades have already passed since the end of the war, this history will be forgotten unless the new generation of Namibian historians take action. Today we tend to use sweeping statements to talk about the liberation struggle and lose sight of the thousands of individual incidents and personal tragedies that combine to create the 'collective memory' of northern Namibia. The casualties of the war remain largely anonymous.

---

[1] See <http://www.wikimapia.org/25376381/Nkongo-Okongo>. {Accessed on 20 February 2011}.

The aim of the chapter is to focus on the impact of the war on one village, Okongo, in order to convey a real sense of the impact of the war on the communities living in the war zone. The memories and experiences of people who witnessed the liberation struggle reveal the changes the war brought to their everyday lives (such as the dusk-to-dawn curfew), their attempts to give safety to their loved ones during the attacks of the Peoples' Liberation Army of Namibia (PLAN) and the South African Defence Force (SADF) and their locally recruited allies in the South West African Territorial Force (SWATF) and the para-military police unit (Koevoet).

Research identified sites where some of the most violent incidents in the war took place in the area around Okongo and the graves of some of those who lost their lives when they were shot for 'breaking' the curfew, killed by landmine blasts or executed in the middle of the night. The war changed the community's social life and some cultural activities had to stop being practised, such as the tradition of children dancing under the moon light (*okudanauka oshihamwedi*) or helping with weeding and threshing (*oikukula noikungungu*). Old men hardly came together as was normal, in peacetime, for a cup of traditional beer (*omalodu oilya*) or marula juice (*omaongo*) and to discuss the news of the day. Informal education that normally took place at the main seating area after supper was suspended for as long as the war was in the area. People rarely travelled to visit their distant relatives as they feared they would end up being arrested and interrogated if they were suspected of being PLAN fighters. As in other parts of northern Namibia, the display of the bodies of dead PLAN fighters on the mudguards of Casspirs (armoured military vehicles) that were driven through Okongo was another practice that had a traumatic impact on the community (Kamonga, 2011, p. 130).

Figure 13.1 (From left to right) Ms Nampala, Mr Ndadi and Hon. Mwahanyekange at a steel drum that was used to hold prisoners at the Okongo Military Base. Hon. Mwahanyekange shows the 'breathing holes' provided to give air to prisoners in the drum. On the top of the drum one can see the hatch which prisoners had to climb through to enter the drum
(Jeremy Silvester)

Many people abandoned the area that was a 'hot spot' in the conflict, and travelled to the west to the relative safety of towns such as Ondangwa and Oshakati, whilst some were either forced or volunteered to join either the PLAN fighters in Angola or the South African security forces. One concern about going into exile was that it risked the lives of those who remained behind, because South African soldiers and PLAN fighters harassed the relatives of those who had left the country and interrogated them about the whereabouts of absent family members.

The relationship between the South African military bases and the community was difficult as people's lives were in danger, especially during conflicts between the two groups. Civilians were sometimes detained in a large, uncomfortable metal drum that was used as a kind of prison in the military base at Okongo. One could imagine that prisoners hardly had enough oxygen as the holes that were made in a pipe at the top of the drum, to supply air, were very small.[2]

One Sunday, whilst the community was in a church service, the South African Defence Force came and dumped a mass of corpses at the church entrance and requested people to come and witness how they had killed SWAPO. Sometimes they also flew corpses tied to a helicopter above the town to warn those who might like to join SWAPO what would happen to them if they were caught while crossing the border. The South African Defence Force tried to intimidate the civilians in as many ways as possible. The local residents took the responsibility to make sure that dogs did not feed on the corpses, but were only able to bury them once they received an order from the SADF camp. Graves provide one of the most visible reminders on the landscape of the painful memories of the war. The community under the leadership of their headman, Moses Kakoto, decided to bury the corpses in mass graves and as a result there are today two mass graves in Okongo settlement where two groups of PLAN fighters were buried just a few metres from the military base.[3] Research has yet to be conducted to cross-reference the community's accounts of these atrocities with archival sources. Memorial tombstones have been erected at both grave sites stating 'A Namibian Hero SWAPO/PLAN Combatant Lies Here', but giving no information about the number of guerrillas buried at each site, nor giving the date of their deaths.

Residents' lives were in danger when PLAN fighters and the SADF fought, as the shooting was indiscriminate. In that way, several houses caught fire or were destroyed, and some livestock were reported killed. The landmines planted by both PLAN fighters and the South Africa Defence Force were everywhere, and the community used to be vulnerable and many people and animals lost their lives by being blown up by landmines. In Okongo there are several graves that provide evidence of the large number of landmine victims and some of the people who were killed in the area were buried elsewhere (for example Cornelius Ndjoba and one of his bodyguards are buried in Ongwediva in Oshana Region after his assassination on 25 November 1982).[4] The graves of the victims of all these incidents provide a visible reminder of the war to this day.

---

2   Jeremy Silvester, Lovisa Nampala and Erica Ndalikokule (2010), *Heritage Hunt Report for Ohangwena Region* Third Edition, Windhoek, pp. 76-80.
3   Ibid, pp. 61-69.
4   'At the Noon Hour they Passed safely, but Three Hours later the Road Roared', *Windhoek Observer*, 19 March 1983, p. 6.

The Origins of Okongo

Okongo was an area with plenty of wild animals that was initially the home of members of the San Community or *Ovakwanghala / Aakwankala* as they were commonly known by the Ovawambo communities. The *Ovakwanghala* name was given to the San communities by the Ovawambo because of their habit of not leaving food for tomorrow and their belief that 'God will provide for tomorrow'. Oral traditions indicate that the Kwanyama people moved from Eenhana and Omundaungilo in search of mahangu fields as well as grazing for their livestock, and found the San people still practising the hunting-gathering system as their ancestors had done when moving into Namibia and the rest of Southern Africa.[5] It seems likely that this expansion westwards was a consequence of the forced migration of thousands of people from the northern parts of Oukwanyama (on the Angolan side of the border) following a major battle with Portuguese forces at Omongwa in 1915.[6]

In the 1950s, when the Evangelical Lutheran Ovambo-Kavango Church (ELOC) came into the area, it still found the San people living and surviving through hunting and gathering. The reason the missionaries settled among the San community was to convert them to Christianity, a challenging task since the San people did not stay in one place. They were always on the move searching for wild fruit and animals and were never united as one group. In the 1950s, missionaries erected a clinic and a church in Okongo. OshiKwanyama-speaking pastors such as: Loth Kaishungu, Paulus Kapulwa, Tomas Kalunduka, Hanyango and Sakeus Shikongo, took over from the missionaries and began to work with the San communities in the four settlements that Erkki Heinnen (a Finnish missionary) had established. The settlements were established at Ekoka, Onamatadiva, Oshana and Eendobe. The centres came to be known as *omapyatumo gaayelele yokOkongo* – 'Mission centres for the San people in Okongo'.[7]

The inhabitants who initially settled in the Okongo area were very few and scattered. In the 1960s and 1970s the number of residents began to increase, and that forced the South African Administration to build schools in and around Okongo. Parents sent their children to Okongo to continue Standard 3 (equivalent to Grade 5 today) as most of the schools were only up to Standard 2.[8]

SWAPO was aware of a new military base being built at Okongo in 1975 (SWAPO, 1975, p. 44). The South African Defence Force (SADF) had taken over responsibility from the South African Police (SAP) for border security on 1 April 1974. In 1979 the 'operational area' was divided into three sectors with 'Ovamboland' designated as Sector 10. Sector 10 was covered by 4 'modular battalions' – 51 Battalion's headquarters was at Ruacana, 52 Battalion's headquarters was at Oshakati and 53 Battalion's headquarters was at Ondangwa (Heitman, 1991, p. 14). The headquarters of 54 Battalion was at

---

5   Interview by the author with Paulus Mwahanyekange, 10 October 2009, Okongo, Ohangwena Region.
6   P. Hayes, (1992) 'A History of the Ovambo of Namibia, c. 1885-1935'(PhD thesis, University of Cambridge, Cambridge), p. 91.
7   Interview by the author with Paulus Mwahanyekange, 10 October 2009, Okongo, Ohangwena Region.
8   Interview by the author with Asser Mukumangeni, 10 October 2009, Okongo, Ohangwena Region.

Eenhana, with satellite bases at Okongo, Elundu and Okankolo (Fowler, 1995, p. 143). The base was also used at various times as a 'tactical headquarters' by 32 Battalion (also known as 'Buffalo Battalion') which had been formed out of former guerrilla fighters from the Angolan FNLA movement (Bothma, 2008, p. 125).

The Armed Struggle

People in Namibia were divided on the issue of how to bring pressure to bear on South Africa. Having failed through political means to gain independence, SWAPO decided, at a special secret congress in 1961, to start preparations to take up arms against South Africa (Brown, 1995, p. 20). In 1966 the International Court of Justice failed to declare South Africa's rule in South West Africa illegal. That was a huge disappointment to the SWAPO movement, as it wanted South Africa to put Namibia under the Trusteeship of the United Nations, who in turn would prepare Namibia for independence (Dugard, 1973, pp. 242-263).

According to Nehason Hangula life in the former 'Ovamboland' changed significantly after the battle of Omugulugwoombashe on 26 August 1966, and the wave of arrests that followed. Hangula argues that the social impact of the militarisation of northern Namibia has been understated in the historiography, and that the regions next to the Angolan border (namely Ohangwena and Omusati Regions in independent Namibia) suffered the most from the conflict.[9] After the International Court of Justice finally declared South Africa's occupation of Namibia 'illegal' in 1971, the South African regime increased its efforts to develop an 'internal solution' on the basis of the 'Homelands' system suggested in the 'Odendaal Plan' (South Africa, 1964).

After the first major clash between SWAPO's guerrilla fighters and the South African Defence Force (SADF) in 1966, and the capture and imprisonment of most of the members of the first SWAPO military units to infiltrate Namibia, there was a period of calm, before a series of military attacks on South African forces took place in the Caprivi Region during the early 1970s. However, the war came to have a far greater impact in the north of Namibia, following the mass mobilisation and politicisation of workers and students that was linked to the contract workers strike of 1971-1972 and the forced deportation of hundreds of workers to 'Ovamboland'. Large numbers of young people started to cross the border into exile and these numbers grew rapidly when some of the traditional authorities became involved in the persecution of political activists. Thousands of people crossed the border into Angola after the collapse of Portuguese colonial rule in 1975, and some of the people living near the border played an important role as guides.[10] The proximity to the border meant that Ohangwena was one of the regions from which it was relatively 'easy' to cross the border into Angola.

After Angolan independence in 1975, South African forces invaded Angola to try and prevent the MPLA from forming a government as it was perceived as Marxist. However, after the invading forces withdrew from Angola (in March 1976), SWAPO

---

9   N. Hangula, 'The impact of the Liberation Struggle on Ohangwena region'. Paper presented at the 'Public History, Forgotten History' Conference, Windhoek, 2000.
10 Interview by author with Paulus Mwahanyekange, 10 October 2009, Okongo, Ohangwena Region.

was able to establish a number of camps and forward bases in southern Angola, from which operations could be mounted across the border into Namibia.

The militarisation of northern Namibia escalated. Two large military bases were established in Okongo. The first base at Omufimba was established in 1973 and one of my interviewees was, initially, the only black soldier at the base after he completed his training as a translator. Festus proudly claimed that he was the very first black person in Ovamboland to be recruited into the South African Defence Force on 15 May 1973, and that he was trained at Ondangwa Airport (the first South African military base to be established in Ovamboland). In the same year, the South African army vacated the Omufimba military camp (which was later made available to UNITA) and moved to Omauni, closer to Okongo. Shortly afterwards, the South African Defence Force came to construct a more permanent military base at Okongo, in Jerobiam Haiyaka's *mahangu* field. The base would be used by the SADF's 54 Battalion that had its headquarters at Eenhana.[11]

Haiyaka described how a South African military officer ordered his soldiers to erect temporary tents on his mahangu field in 1976 and later approached his wife (Lovisa Taukuheke Haiyaka) for permission to settle permanently. The family was then compensated with R2000 and moved to the northern side of Okongo village. The amount was offered with a tight deadline so that Mrs Haiyaka had no time to consult her husband about it. An air strip was constructed alongside the camp for planes to deliver weapons and medical supplies as well as to fly patients to Oshakati State Hospital.[12]

A second military base containing some Koevoet units was located in Epangwe village (20 km from Okongo settlement). After the attack, the camp was then moved closer to the community in the hope that PLAN would not attack them as they would try to spare the lives of people in the community. Koevoet's military base was then erected where Okongo Police Station is currently situated.[13] An account by Sisingi Kamongo, a Koevoet tracker, indicates that by 1985 the 'Security Police' had a base, known as 2-1 Echo, at Okongo, and from 1987 as 'Zulu Oscar', from which the Koevoet unit Zulu 4 operated (Kamongo 2011, pp. 96-97, 143).

The Okongo Community and the Curfew

A dusk-to-dawn curfew was introduced in northern Namibia as early as 1979 and covered 'Ovamboland' and much of the Kavango region. Those found breaking the curfew could be shot with impunity.[14] Mukumangeni clearly remembers the curfew, which was widely known in Oshiwambo as *okangendjo koufiku* (literally meaning 'the bell for the night'), as the harshest of the South African laws passed and imposed on the Namibian people. It was a prohibition on people's movement throughout Ovamboland from 18.00 until 06.00 the following morning. He recalls an incident that happened around 1987 or 1988, when South African soldiers from Okongo military base came

---

11   Interview by author with Helao Festus, 10 October 2009, Okongo, Ohangwena Region.
12   Interview by author with Mr Haiyaka, 10 October 2009, Okongo, Ohangwena Region.
13   Interview by author with Helao Festus, 10 October 2009, Okongo, Ohangwena Region.
14   Nehason Hangula, 'The impact of Liberation Struggle on Ohangwena region'. Paper presented at the 'Public History, Forgotten History' Conference, Windhoek, 2000, p. 7.

to his house around 20.00 accusing him of breaking the curfew. He told them that he had been out that day but that he had returned home around 17.00. They demanded that his car bonnet be opened (to check whether his car engine was hot or not). Even though the engine was cold, they forced him to agree that the engine was still hot and instructed him to follow their military vehicle and drive to the military base for further questioning. At the base's entrance he was ordered out of the car and blindfolded before being taken inside. All civilians that entered the military base had to be blindfolded as South African soldiers did not like the idea of civilians obtaining knowledge about the defensive structures surrounding the base, as they feared that they would spy for the 'SWAPO terrorists' and make it easier for them to attack.

Mukumangeni was accommodated in the sick bay where he slept on the floor and was guarded by an armed white soldier to make sure he did not escape, but was released the next day.[15]

Neshingo, in another interview, recalled a further incident involving the curfew where his car was shot at around 16.00 while entering Okongo from Ondangwa. Edwig Sheuyange's wife was wounded and Jonas Nghinaunye was shot in the stomach so badly that his intestines were exposed (the incident also left Nghinaunye permanently disabled in his right hand). South African soldiers picked them up and brought them to the military base to receive initial first aid, and they were then flown to Oshakati State Hospital for medical treatment.[16]

Kakoto recalled another incident involving a young man, Hannu Andreas Kapulwa, who was shot whilst walking with a PLAN fighter as he was returning from a Christian youth meeting (*Oxungi*) held at Onheleiwa. Kakoto said that he still carries the painful memory of the deceased's family arguing with the South African soldiers, who refused to provide the corpse so that the family could give it a decent burial. The South Africa soldiers claimed that they had shot a 'terrorist' and decided to burn the corpse and reduce it to ashes, as this was the way they dealt with 'terrorist' corpses at the base.[17]

Festus argued that while South Africa's military presence at Okongo posed a risk to the Okongo community living nearby, it also brought some benefits. One of the most important was the fact that patients from Okongo received medical services free of charge, whilst those who were in a critical condition were cared for by South African medical doctors when flown to Oshakati State Hospital. They were also returned by plane when discharged.[18] An example of the medical benefits that residents received was provided by Haiyaka. He told me that he remembered very well a time when he was returning home from Walvis Bay in 1981 and his car set off a landmine at Omupembe village (whilst he was on his way back from a political mission). His colleagues, Aili Kapulwa and Hafeni Shangheta, died on the spot. His son Joram survived and was not injured, but one of his ears was blown off (it was eventually found on the vehicle's ceiling) and he inhaled toxic fumes from the explosion. He explained that he was admitted to hospital for some time to have his ear stitched back on and a special fluid drip was attached to him to clean out the explosive powder that he had inhaled.[19]

---

15   Interview by author with Asser Mukumangeni, 10 October 2009, Okongo, Ohangwena Region.
16   Interview by author with Moses Neshingo, 9 October 2009, Ekoka, Ohangwena Region.
17   Interview by author with Moses Kakoto, 16 June 2009, Okongo, Ohangwena Region.
18   Interview by author with Helao Festus, 10 October 2009, Okongo, Ohangwena Region.
19   Interview by author with Jerobiam Haiyaka, 10 October 2009, Okongo.

Kapia and Haiyaka confirmed that civilians wounded in landmine explosions were often collected by South African soldiers and taken to their military base for medical attention. There were no medicals doctors at the local Okongo hospital and the ones that attended to patients in emergencies were, therefore, the South African doctors attached to the military base. Kapia further stated that patients with minor ailments who were admitted to the military hospital at the base were supplied with food from the soldiers' kitchen during their stay.[20]

Safety During the Attacks

Kakoto described the times when PLAN attacked the base at Okongo as very dangerous. Attacks were sometimes launched to coincide with significant anniversaries. For example, the *Windhoek Observer* of 9 May 1981 reported that mortar bombs had been fired at the base on 4 May to mark the third anniversary of the Cassinga Massacre (Cawthra, 1986, p. 185). Kakoto remembered that several attacks were actually launched from the *ominghudi* tree in his mahangu field. Fortunately, the logs that the homestead was constructed with protected them by blocking the bullets and preventing them from going right through the homestead. Shootings normally occurred whilst people were asleep, and the safest place at such moments was to hide under your bed. When the shooting started the elders would call family members to a gathering place that was considered to be safe. Everyone would be told to lie flat on their stomach next to the biggest logs in the homestead, as it was believed that if the bullet hit the log before it reached you it would be better than if a bullet hit you directly.

Kakoto remembered one particular attack when a grenade landed in his kraal and killed 6 cattle.[21] Mukumangeni also stated that to avoid being shot during a battle one had to throw oneself to the ground wherever one found oneself. The number of attacks on the Okongo base forced Mukumangeni to relocate his house, which was close to the military base, and move it 5 km to the east.[22]

The presence of the base, and the proliferation of firearms, meant that there was a constant danger of weapons being discharged and injuring the community living near the base. One South African soldier who was stationed at the base in the 1980s reported that: 'Every night there were accidental discharges of various weapons, including a M-79 grenade launcher' (Greeth, 2001, p. 78). Festus and the other black soldiers based at Okongo were actually never accommodated in the base. Instead they had their own houses in the settlement close to the military base. Festus remembered the time when a rocket fired grenade landed in the kitchen in his house, nearly killing his pregnant wife. He took the grenade with him to work the next morning and complained to the commander of the base. Festus clearly recalled that, as a result, the base commander ordered his soldiers not to fire in the direction where the translator for the base lived, as this would put them at risk of injury. The commander stated that reliable translators, like Festus, would be hard to replace should something happen to

---

20 Interview by author with Kapia, 16 June 2009, Okongo, Ohangwena Region. Interview by author with Jerobiam Haiyaka, 10 October 2009, Okongo, Ohangwena Region.
21 Interview by author with Moses Kakoto, 16 June 2009, Okongo, Ohangwena Region.
22 Interview by author with Asser Mukumangeni, 10 October 2009, Okongo, Ohangwena Region.

them. However, Festus also complained that they were never treated as the equals of their white counterparts.[23]

The commander of the Okongo base himself reportedly made statements such as: *'Kyk daar almal mense is fuck en SWAPO daai'* – meaning 'look all those people are SWAPO', referring to local civilians. The reason he said this was that the white South African soldiers were frustrated when they could not distinguish the PLAN fighters from the local civilians. Mukumangeni remembered one PLAN fighter who deliberately made friends with black South African soldiers, who introduced him to the layout of the base. A month later the man disappeared and the Okongo military base was then attacked by PLAN.[24]

Did the Curfew Restrict Terrorist Movements?

The curfew did not prevent attacks by PLAN fighters on the Okongo military base and attacks generally took place at night, during the curfew. One of the largest scale attacks on a South African base inside Namibia took place on 13 February 1979, when an estimated 250 PLAN fighters attacked the Nkongo base, and it was acknowledged that seven South Africa soldiers were wounded (Steenkamp, 1989, p. 86). Mukumangeni stated that the South African troops would sometimes lay an ambush along the path at the entrance of the village to trap the civilians and PLAN fighters that moved during the curfew at night. The fighters were reluctant to walk on less popular paths as their boots would leave visible tracks and these paths were generally covered with dried leaves and sticks that made it noisy, and therefore risky, to use them, especially on a bright moonlit night. The South African tactic of laying ambushes was one that led to a lot of deaths, but the PLAN fighters also developed tactics to help them avoid sustaining high casualties. The PLAN fighters would move in a stretched-out line following one another at some considerable distance, so that if shooting broke out it was easier to scatter or to retreat. Sometimes PLAN fighters also came into the area during the day wearing civilian clothes, which made it difficult for them to be distinguished from civilians. They would stay in local houses and then be close to the base and ready to attack it in the early hours of the morning.[25]

The South African strategy was to try and restrict the mobility of the PLAN fighters. As the South Africans believed that PLAN fighters sneaked into villages during the night in order to attack the South African military base, after a battle the South African soldiers would go to nearby houses to harass civilians and search for PLAN fighters. They usually demanded identity documents, and if people failed to provide these they would be arrested. Young males or other suspects were often detained and taken to the military base for questioning, and were sometimes transferred to Ondangwa and Oshakati for further interrogation. Mukumangeni explained that the war forced many young men to become members of the military as they either crossed the border to join PLAN or joined the South West African Territorial Force.[26]

---

23   Interview by author with Helao Festus, 10 October 2009, Okongo, Ohangwena Region.
24   Interview by author with Asser Mukumangeni, 10 October 2009, Okongo, Ohangwena Region.
25   Ibid.
26   Ibid.

Neshingo stated that one disturbing tactic that was used during the war was that South African soldiers would come at night pretending to be PLAN fighters and then take a person away, telling the family that he had been taken away because he was a 'puppet'. Another version of this tactic was that soldiers would pretend to be PLAN fighters needing help, but if they received help, other members of the security forces would arrive the very next morning and interrogate the family about the help that they had provided to the 'terrorists' the night before. However, civilians started to detect these tricks and understand who was really responsible for the atrocities that took place in the area. The tactics meant that civilians became very suspicious and cautious of strangers.[27]

Nehason Hangula argues that the visible impact of war changed the demographic balance between the town and countryside in northern Namibia, when as many as 250,000 people living in northern Namibia were displaced from their homes and settled in the area around Ondangwa and Oshakati.[28] One might suggest that it might also have influenced the number of men who sought to be recruited as contract workers as a way of avoiding the harassment that took place, especially in the areas near the Angolan border. Many families were destroyed by the war. Young people who left to join PLAN or the South African army were missed by their parents, who wished the war would end so that they could be reunited with their children.

Lives Lost Through Landmines or Explosive Devices

The B8 road that passes through Okongo claimed a lot of lives during the liberation struggle (both of people and of animals) as a result of explosive devices. Most of these devices were landmines planted either under the roads used by all (pedestrians, animals and vehicles) or on the paths leading to buildings. Landmines would be planted outside a sleeping shack or in a cuca shop. SWAPO planted landmines on roads that they suspected would be used by military vehicles from the base, and claimed some success in destroying military targets in this way. SWAPO claimed that on 2 January 1978 they had already blown up an 'enemy troop carrier' killing five soldiers (SWAPO, 1978, p. 13). Whilst the casualties claimed by SWAPO and acknowledged by the South African security forces always dramatically differed, it was recognised that *'Oom Willie se Pad'* (Uncle Willie's road), as it was known to South African soldiers, was the most dangerous road in the operational area (Kamongo, 2011, p. 140). Colonel Jan Breytenbach described '...burnt-out wrecks of Hippo mine-protecting vehicles every few kilometres between Nkongo and Eenhana' (2003, p. 193). SWAPO repeatedly reported that it had inflicted landmine casualties on the roads around the Nkongo base. On 18 September 1984, it reported that a double landmine completely blew up and destroyed an enemy truck at Oidiva, 15 km southeast of Nkongo (SWAPO, 1984, p. 19). A couple of years later it was also claimed that four soldiers were injured when 'an enemy vehicle' was blown up by a landmine on 2 February 1986, near Nkongo base (SWAPO, 1986, p. 50).

Explosive devices were of different weight and sizes. Some were manufactured to target vehicles, whilst others were 'anti-personnel mines' aimed particularly at

---

27   Interview by author with Moses Neshingo, 9 October 2009, Ekoka, Ohangwena Region.
28   N. Hangula, 'The Impact of the Liberation Struggle on Ohangwena Region'. Paper presented at the 'Public History, Forgotten History' Conference, Windhoek, 2000, p. 6.

pedestrians. If a human being stepped on the one intended for vehicles it would not explode, whilst if a vehicle drove over a mine intended for pedestrians it would not cause very much damage. Once strange items were detected by community members, a message would be sent out to warn others. The device would either be surrounded with branches from nearby bushes or a cluster of stones to warn people about the presence of a landmine. Such visual warnings were taken very seriously and these simple measures taken by members of the local community saved many lives. The South African army was always notified to remove the device and responded quickly.[29] However, the South African security forces also planted a substantial number of mines around the town. For example, the SADF planted a 56,000 square metre landmine field around their camps in Okongo (Vines, 1997, p. 116).

The most famous person to lose his life on the Okongo road was Pastor Cornelius Tuhafeni Ndjoba. Pastor Ndjoba was a former teacher, a preacher and a headman from Eenhana. He was appointed as the Chief Minister of the Ovambo Administration (widely known in Oshiwambo as *Epangelo Owambo*) on 26 August 1978, and was also the President of the newly formed Democratic Turnhalle Alliance (DTA) Party following the assassination of the previous DTA leader, Clemens Kapuuo on 27 March 1978 (Gewald, 2004). Ndjoba was killed by a landmine explosion on Thursday, 25 November 1982, with newspaper reports indicating that five of his six bodyguards were also killed in the explosion, although only four names were provided.

Pastor Ndjoba was an important person in Ovamboland and for this reason his death attracted more media attention than that of the many 'ordinary' people who were killed during the war in Ohangwena Region. There were two different accounts of Ndjoba's death published in the English-language press at the time.[30] The relevant newspapers were the *Windhoek Advertiser* and the *Windhoek Observer* (as *The Namibian* was only launched in 1985, three years after Ndjoba's death). The *Windhoek Advertiser* merely announced Ndjoba's death, whilst the *Windhoek Observer* revealed a greater commitment to investigative journalism and tried to visit the area and speak to both soldiers and local residents. The *Windhoek Observer* reported that local residents believed that Ndjoba and his men had tried to attack some PLAN fighters that he had noticed under a tree whilst he was on his way to buy some goats. However, the oral sources that I consulted stated that Ndjoba's vehicle was blown up by a landmine on the way from Oshalumbu village (situated 40 km to the east of Okongo). Only one person survived and escaped as he was offered a lift away from the place by a local resident whilst PLAN fighters were still tracking him down. According to local residents, Ndjoba, his six bodyguards and Timoteus Muunda were returning from a party organised by Stefanus Weyulu (Muunda's nephew), the headman for Oshalumbu. Ndjoba then decided to buy goats from that area as they were cheaper than those in his own area.

There is a difference between the contemporary newspaper accounts and current oral history regarding Ndjoba's case. I believe the newspapers involved also gathered information from contemporary 'eye witness' oral sources and had it printed, and even though it cannot be 100 per cent relied upon, at least the story then was still fresh in

---

29 Interview by author with Jerobiam Haiyaka, 10 October 2009, Okongo, Ohangwena Region.
30 'Ndjoba – earmarked for death', *Windhoek Advertiser*, 29 November 1982. p. 1. 'How Ndjoba Died', *Windhoek Observer*, 19 February 1983, p. 3.

people's memories. Since oral history is drawn from human memories, the current oral history can also be relied upon, even though not as much as the account in the newspapers. A story told after 27 years may be remembered with difficulty and those who tell it might never have actually witnessed the event. The other factor that must be taken into consideration is that the way in which the event is remembered will have changed because of the totally different political context today. Witnesses might have been hesitant to provide details at the time when providing information (to either side), as this could have had deadly consequences. Likewise, today the story will be told differently now that the speaker is aware that those listening are living in an independent Namibia under a SWAPO government.

Because of the strong communication network between the local community and PLAN fighters, local people believe that the landmine that blew up Ndjoba's vehicle was deliberately planted by PLAN to target the Chief Minister and his bodyguards, on the basis of information about Njoba's plans that were provided to a PLAN unit. Owing to the limited time available I have not been able to contact the single reported survivor of the attack. When I took my school's History Club to Okongo on 16 June 2009, to conduct research on the lives lost on the Okongo–Ondangwa road during the liberation struggle (as part of a school competition funded by the AACRLS project and organised by the Museums Association of Namibia), I managed to visit some of the places where landmine explosions had taken place, and at many of these sites the mangled wreckage of the vehicles still remain. For example, it was still possible to locate the remains of Njoba's car, the remains of an ambulance that was blown up in another explosion and the remains of a minibus that was destroyed in the most deadly landmine explosion of the entire liberation struggle. The scars of the war can still be found on the landscape of Ogongo.

Figure 13.2 The mass grave situated in the ELCIN Graveyard at Okongo contains sixteen victims killed in a landmine explosion on 15 October 1978. It was, allegedly, the single deadliest landmine explosion that took place during the liberation struggle

(Jeremy Silvester)

Conclusion

Okongo history is so significant that it needs to be recorded for the outside world, as well as future generations, to learn the impact that the liberation struggle had on this community and region. It would be seen that people lived in fear and intimidation, were interrogated on a daily basis, and imprisoned for no good reason (especially those suspected of having assisted PLAN fighters).

What interested me about the Okongo community is the level of reconciliation between former South African collaborators and those who had assisted PLAN fighters that could be felt. Everybody had buried the past and held no feelings of revenge regarding who had supported who during the liberation struggle. It is unclear, however, what platform was used to create that local community spirit of reconciliation spirit to reach this point. According to my observations, Okongo is a place with many potential heritage sites and, if developed carefully, such sites could be turned into a heritage trail telling the story of the local impact of the liberation struggle on the region.

The sites deserve to be preserved and the former military base could be turned into a memorial museum for landmine victims and the remains of all the vehicles blown up by landmines in the area could be preserved for history. The threat to this proposal comes from Raubex (a South African company) that is currently busy constructing the road between Nkurenkuru and Eenhana and that may remove the remains. Another problem is that the community needs to understand the significance of heritage sites. There is no evidence that heritage has yet been integrated into the regional development plan, particularly given the growing importance of Okongo, with the projected increase in local and international visitors to the town owing to the construction of the new tarred road. I would argue that, at least, a museum or a shrine about the liberation struggle should be built or erected in Okongo to pay tribute to the fallen heroes as well as providing a space where the community could recall their memories and experiences of the war.

References

Bothma, L. J. (2008) *Buffalo Battalion: South Africa's 32 Battalion – A Tale of Sacrifice.* Johannesburg: Piet Nortje Publications.

Breytenbach, J. (2003) *The Buffalo Soldiers: The story of South Africa's 32 Battalion, 1975-1991.* Johannesburg: Galago.

Brown, S. (1995) 'Diplomacy by Other Means: SWAPO's Liberation War'. In Leys, C., Saul, J. and Brown, S. (eds) *Namibia's Liberation Struggle: The Two-edged Sword.* Oxford: James Currey.

Cawthra, G. (1986) *Brutal Force: The Apartheid War Machine.* London: IDAF.

Dugard, J. (1973) *The South West Africa/Namibia Dispute: Documents and Scholarly Writings on the Controversy between South Africa and the United Nations.* London: University of California Press.

Fowler, B. (1995) *Pro Patria.* Johannesburg: Sentinel Projects.

Gewald, J-B. (2004) 'Who Killed Clemens Kapuuo?' *Journal of Southern African Studies*, Vol. 30 (3).

Greeff, J. (2001). *A Greater Share of Honour: The Memoirs of a Recce Officer*. Ntomeni Publications.

Hangula, N. 'The impact of the Liberation Struggle on Ohangwena region'. Paper presented at the 'Public History, Forgotten History' Conference, Windhoek, 2000.

Hayes, P. (1992) 'A History of the Ovambo of Namibia, c. 1885-1935', PhD thesis, University of Cambridge, Cambridge.

Heitman, Helmoed-Römer (1991) *Modern African Wars: South West Africa*. Oxford: Osprey Publishing.

Kamongo, S. and Bezuidenhout, L. (2001) *Shadows in the Sand: A Koevoet Tracker's Story of an Insurgency War*. Durban: 30° South Publishers.

Leys, C., Saul, J. and Brown, S. (eds) (1995) *Namibia's Liberation Struggle: The Two-edged Sword*. Oxford: James Currey.

South Africa, Republic of (1964) *Report of the Commission of Enquiry into South West Africa Affairs, 1963-1964 (Odendaal Report)*. Republic of South Africa, Pretoria.

Steenkamp, W. (1989) *South Africa's Border War, 1966-1989*. Johannesburg: Ashanti Publishers.

Silvester, J., Nampala, L. and Ndalikokule, E. (2010) *Heritage Hunt Report for Ohangwena Region*, unpublished report, 3rd revision, Windhoek: Museums Association of Namibia, June 2010.

SWAPO (1975) *Namibia News*. Vol. 8. Lusaka: Department of Information and Publicity.

SWAPO (1978) *Namibia Today*. Vol. 2, No. 1. Lusaka: Department of Information and Publicity.

SWAPO (1984) *The Combatant*. Vol. 6. Luanda: Department of Information and Publicity.

SWAPO (1986) *SWAPO Information Bulletin*. Luanda: Department of Information and Publicity.

Windhoek Advertiser, 'Ndjoba – earmarked for death', 29 November 1982.

Windhoek Observer, 'How Ndjoba Died – Observer visits who know', 19 February 1983.

Windhoek Observer, 'At the Noon Hour they Passed safely, but Three Hours later the Road Roared', 19 March 1983.

Vines, A. (1997) *Still Killing: Landmines in Southern Africa*. New York, Washington, London, Brussels: Human Rights Watch.

14 The Liberation Struggle Inside Namibia 1966-1989: A Regional Perspective from the Kavango Regions

Herbert Kandjimi Karapo

Introduction

The armed nationalist struggle for independence in Namibia lasted over 20 years, leaving Namibians with a broad awareness of prominent historical landmarks and battles associated with the war, which are marked by national monuments or commemorative events. It is in this way that states manage memory. However, this chapter seeks to provide an alternative perspective by focusing on the changing impact of the conflict over time on one geographically defined community. The Kavango regions are located in the northeastern part of Namibia, but this chapter will focus particularly on the traditional territory of uKwangali, situated in the Kavango West Region in the Mpungu and Nkurenkuru constituencies.

The emphasis on the western part of the Kavango regions is because the district shares a regional border with the former 'Homeland' of 'Ovamboland' in the west of the district, which was the main theatre of war during the period under discussion.[1] It is argued here that the Kavango was another important area of conflict, but that the events that took place there are less well known to the Namibian public. Documenting and collecting the living memories of the inhabitants of the Kavango regions fills a gap in the national historiography of Namibia, so as to include the previously unexplored micro-politics, experiences and contributions of the people of this area during the Namibian armed struggle for independence.

The military archives of both sides that might document the conflict in the region are inaccessible, so this paper will draw heavily on oral history provided by informants who live in the region and in the area of study in particular. The chapter explores the political interaction between SWAPO and civilians, the effects of the militarisation of the Kavango and the impact that South African militarisation had in uKwangali. The complexity of the Namibian armed liberation struggle is twofold in the sense that the struggle was fought in two ways. The first was the military action of those individuals who left the country for exile and later came back as guerilla fighters. The second involved those people who did not leave, but fought the struggle inside the country by supporting the PLAN fighters and employing various forms of passive resistance.

---

1   J. B. Diescho (1983) 'A critical evaluation of the Odendaal commission of enquiry into South West Africa affairs 1962-63' (MA dissertation, University of Fort Hare), p. 12.

Political Dimensions of the Struggle in the uKwangali District of the Kavango, 1966-1989

Nestor Mufenda, a long-serving SWAPO activist in the region, has recalled that the activities of the South West African People's Organisation (SWAPO) in Kavango started in the 1960s. During this period, many of the people who left the country to join the armed liberation struggle travelled on foot from Ovamboland to exile via Kavango.[2] This route was long and dangerous. Local homesteads provided vital help with food and water and temporary accommodation. At the time, contract labourers were recruited at Nkurenkuru in the uKwangali area to go and work as migrant labourers in mines in South Africa.[3] When Portuguese rule collapsed in Angola in 1974, Cuangar, the Portuguese town opposite Nkurenkuru, was occupied by UNITA which was co-operating with SWAPO at the time. So, for example, when Voitto Jasson, known by his combat name *Kondjereni* (you have to fight for your rights), went into exile on 26 December 1974, the UNITA commander at Cuangar helped him reach a SWAPO camp.[4] This was a route which most of those leaving for exile used. In some instances it used to take a month before they went through the Nkurenkuru labour recruitment centre. Mufenda noted that the late Dr Alpo Mauno Mbamba was one of many people who left for exile using this route. Mbamba travelled with Nangolo Mbumba, and Nahas Angula, who were among a group who had travelled all the way from Oshigambo High School in Ovamboland. From Rundu, this group travelled with transport intended for migrant workers to Francistown in Botswana, but instead of going to work as migrant workers, they went into exile in neighbouring Zambia and Tanzania.[5]

Helao Shityuwete's autobiography (1990) reveals that the first SWAPO guerrillas were actually captured in the Kavango region several months before the battle at Omugulugwoombashe on 26 August 1966. The group of ten guerrillas, led by Lazarus 'Chinaman' Sakaria, with Helao Shityuwete as his Deputy-Commander, crossed the Kavango River into Namibia on 23 March 1966, but three of the group were arrested by the traditional authorities and handed over to the security forces on 27 March 1966. Eventually, nine of the ten members were captured (Namakalu, 2004, p. 12). The lack of political awareness of SWAPO activities among civilians and certain traditional headman in Kavango led to the arrest of the group who were later all sentenced to lengthy prison sentences on Robben Island – with the exception of Leonard Phillemon 'Castro' Nangolo Shuuya, who was recruited by the South Africans to work as a spy within SWAPO (Shityuwete, 1990, pp. 119-127).

Many years passed before another guerilla operation could take place in the region. However, in the late 1960s a local business man, David Ausiku, nicknamed *Lyangurungunda*, started a political party called *Muzogumwe* meaning 'One Way

---

2 Interview by author with Nestor Mufenda, Rundu, Kavango Regional Council, 28 December 2007.
3 Ibid. For more on the contract labour system in Kavango see K. Likuwa, (2012) 'Voices from the Kavango: A study of the contract labour system in Namibia, 1925-1972' (PhD thesis, University of the Western Cape) and chapter 15 of this volume.
4 Milk, H. 'Kavango during the Namibia war of liberation'. http://www.kavango.info/Voito.htm. {Accessed on 26 April, 2013}.
5 Interview by author with Nestor Mufenda, Rundu, Kavango Regional Council, 28 December 2007.

Forward', and started mobilising SWAPO in the Kavango.⁶ However, nationalist political mobilisation was difficult in the Kavango regions during this period. The pass laws and the development of ethnic 'Homelands' after the publication of the Odendaal Commission's report of 1964 meant it was difficult to travel and to connect with people in other regions of Namibia. South African propaganda about the social consequences of communism also contributed to community mistrust of SWAPO. South African propaganda presented SWAPO as an ethnic, 'Ovambo' movement that had no relevance to other ethnic groups. The most effective strategy used by the South African regime to spread its propaganda to the local people was by circulating leaflets and cartoons at schools that claimed that SWAPO was militarily weak (Nujoma, 2001, pp. 301-303). A former South West African Territorial Force (SWATF) soldier, Karangane Florry, explained that the distribution of anti-SWAPO leaflets was a measure taken by the South African forces and its intelligence services to influence civilians against SWAPO.⁷ For example, he recalled leaflets showing SWAPO leaders in exile struggling to get help and war materials from the international community, particularly Cuba. However, despite these challenges, the collapse of Portuguese colonial rule in Angola in 1975 created an opportunity for SWAPO to revive its military operations in the Kavango regions.

Selima Kadiva, a teacher at Gava, vividly recalled that, initially, people thought that SWAPO's armed wing, PLAN, cadres were FNLA forces from Southern Angola who had infiltrated into Namibia because of the civil war in Angola that broke out in 1975.⁸ When the Portuguese government was toppled by a coup in Lisbon, Portugal and the Portuguese deserted Fort Cuangar in southern Angola, opposite Nkurenkuru in uKwangali, FNLA forces arrived on the northern banks of the Kavango River, (IDAF, 1982, p. 64). PLAN combatants entered the uKwangali district in an unprecedented number in 1978 on a reconnaissance mission. The second group that entered the district the same year came to provide political education for civilians.⁹ SWAPO was regarded as a communist movement and some local people were influenced by the South African propaganda about the negative impact of communism as an 'anti-Christian' ideology. Robert Karapo, who has lived at Muparara village since 1973, explained:

> The first PLAN cadres who came in uKwangali arrived in February 1978. When they arrived, he [Karapo] was in his field with his family and community members who came to help him cultivate his crops. Upon hearing from Leena Katumbu Mpasi (who deserted her house because of fear of the unknown soldiers) Karapo, with one Bushman called Kahenge, left all the people at the field and went back to his

---

6   J. B. Diescho (1983), 'A critical Evaluation of the Odendaal Commission of Enquiry into South West African Affairs' 1962-1963'. (MA dissertation, University of Fort Hare, Eastern Cape), p. 48.
7   Interview by author with Karangane Florry, a former member of the South West Africa Territory Force (SWATF), Force No. 87879900, Otjomuise, Windhoek, 25 January 2008. Florry's military identification number was 8781900.
8   Interview with Selima Wayera Kadiva, Gava village, uKwangali district, 24 July 2007: 'The Chipenda faction of the FNLA was reported to have a base just north of Calai by July, 1975.' Piet Nortje (2012), *The Terrible ones: A complete History of 32 Battalion*, p. 60.
9   Interview by Nambadi, A. with Kalomoh Ndeulitufa, the former PLAN commander designated to operate in Kavango, Tutungeni, Rundu, 13 May 2005.

homestead to see who the soldiers were.¹⁰ Upon arriving at his homestead, they found a group of 80 unknown armed men who were scattered around the water point near his homestead. The armed man welcomed him with a question, asking him whether he knew them. Karapo told them that he thought they were SWAPO's armed forces. One of them asked him whether people believed that they had tails, and asked 'Can you see it?' Out of fear he did not respond to the question.

After talking, they asked him to give them something to eat; he gave them *Sikundu* [a traditional soft drink].

Among them was a tall man who claimed that when they used to come to the village with the church youth activities, the structure of the dam was still incomplete. While they were busy chatting, they heard a SADF soldier coming on a motorbike, and the PLAN cadres hid in the nearby bushes.

When the PLAN cadres left the scene, Karapo also left to inform the people whom he had left at the field to come back home. When they arrived, the whole area near his homestead was occupied by the SADF armed forces and this left him with no choice but to present himself for identification. This saved their lives, otherwise the soldiers would have shot them all.¹¹

The account by Karapo indicates that the arrival of PLAN cadres in uKwangali started as early as 1978 and this marked the beginning of PLAN's new infiltration.

However, Oswin Namakalu relates that there were earlier efforts to infiltrate the Kavango Region which was designated by SWAPO as the 'Eastern Front'. In May 1973, a platoon led by Commander Mandume 'Kayala' Iyambo and Commissar Hanganee Kavezeri Katjipuka penetrated into the Mbukushu area of the region. Katjipuka subsequently became the Field Commander for the 'Kavango Front' in September 1975, a position he held until his death in Zambia on 22 February 1977 (Namakalu, 2004, pp. 36-37, 57-58; SWAPO, 1996, p. 105). Ndeulitufa Kalomoh, a PLAN commander who operated in the Kavango region, explained that the inhabitants of uKwangali district showed a positive attitude towards SWAPO as a movement and contributed to the struggle for independence in many ways.¹² The political education which they conducted amongst the local people helped them to get support from members of the communities, as well as civil servants, for example, teachers, nurses and church leaders, especially from the Evangelical Lutheran Church in Namibia (ELCIN), which had three main church stations in uKwangali (at Rupara, Nkurenkuru and Mpungu).

The strong relationship that developed between SWAPO cadres and the inhabitants of the uKwangali area during the 1980s led the South African security forces to introduce a curfew as a measure to control people's movements. The curfew restricted people from moving about in public and required them to remain indoors between specific hours, at

---

10 Interview by Aaron Nambadi with Robert Karapo, Muparara village, uKwangali district, 21 May 2003.
11 Ibid.
12 Interview by Aaron Nambadi with Kalomoh Ndeulitufa, former PLAN commander designated to operate in Kavango, Rundu, Tutungeni, 13 May 2005.

night. The curfew system had serious social and political implications because everyone who was caught travelling after 6 p.m. could be shot. If a car was caught travelling after this time, everybody in the vehicle would be searched and would not be allowed to travel until the next day. Even when someone was sick, people were not allowed to travel after 6 p.m. People who owned vehicles, which were scarce at that time, were suspected of transporting and supplying the needs of PLAN combatants. Teachers who lived in the interior of uKwangali and owned vehicles were accused of supplying PLAN combatants with batteries to enable them to communicate with their military bases in southern Angola. People living on the banks of the Kavango River were ordered to remove their canoes from the river that marked the border with Angola.[13]

The Social and Political Impact of the Armed Liberation Struggle on Civilians

The most traumatic memories of the struggle for civilians were of the atrocities and brutalities committed by the South Africa Defence Force (SADF) and Koevoet members who operated in the Kavango. The first Koevoet unit in the Kavango regions was established by Captain Willem Fouche in 1981 with 75 men based at a camp in Rundu that became known as *Arendsnes* ('The Eagle's Nest'), in reference to the fish eagle emblem of the unit. It was given the call sign 'Zulu Four' (Stiff, 2004, pp. 147-148). The death of Jonas Hamukwaya, a teacher at Namutuntu in uKwangali district in Kavango West, who was interrogated by the Koevoet forces unit members for hosting and collaborating with PLAN cadres, was one of the worst incidents that is still remembered locally (Herbstein and Evenson, 1989, p.92). Hamukwaya and Kaduma Katanga (from Kakoro village) were allegedly beaten to death by Koevoet members on 18 November 1982.[14]

Naingwendje Isack, an 80-year-old man who lives at Simanya in western Kavango, vividly recalled the trauma experienced by civilians:

> PLAN combatants used to visit our homestead during the night to avoid being seen by their enemies (the SADF and Koevoet forces). They used to tell us (civilians) that they had come to liberate the country and we must not tell their enemies their whereabouts. This resulted in us having dual ways of dealing with these forces. For example, whoever came, civilians were expected to co-operate, and we always pretended to be non-supporters of either force.[15]

Individuals in the region still live with their traumatic memories. Civilians who collaborated with SWAPO cadres and provided assistance to PLAN cadres were under strict surveillance and experienced threats and harassment, creating a climate

---

13 Interview by author with Kandjimi Willem, Gava village, uKwangali district, 26 December 2007.
14 'Kavango detainees savagely beaten, eye-witnesses relate', *Windhoek Advertiser*, 30 November 1982. p. 1.
15 Interview by author with Naingwendje Isack, Simanya, uKwangali district, 25 June 2007.

of fear. Individuals caught by PLAN for collaborating with South African forces were assassinated. Whilst the actions of the PLAN cadres can be justified as an act of self-defence, their brutal actions had a profound impact on some families. Koevoet, too, were feared and were associated with physical abuse, as every Koevoet unit that operated in Kavango had a skilled interrogator; people believed Koevoet executed those who refused to reveal the whereabouts of PLAN fighters (Herbstein and Evenson, 1989, p. 73). The reality was that if civilians supported SWAPO against Koevoet, they got into trouble with Koevoet; if they supported Koevoet against SWAPO, they got into trouble with PLAN. Civilians found themselves between a rock and a hard place. The testimonies of the civilians in uKwangali give us a sense of the micro-politics of the time and add breadth and depth to the broader national narratives of the Namibian armed liberation struggle.

During Koevoet operations, units used to drive their military vehicles through the fields, crushing crops and causing the loss of agricultural production. Generally a Casspir was occupied by white officers and one indigenous soldier who would help with translation (Hinz and Gevers, 1989, p. 50).

Johanna Hausiku who lived at Zigizi and whose daughter left the country to flee into exile explained that all those suspected of collaborating with SWAPO were arrested, blindfolded and kept in a Casspir. The victim was then driven around and disorientated, beaten with a rifle butt and threatened with death if they did not co-operate. Once the blindfold was removed, they would be roughly interrogated by an unknown officer. She also recalls that one day she was visited by the South West African Police (SWAPOL) and told that her daughter had died in a military contact, although this was not true. The Koevoet and army units regularly patrolled villages with their armoured vehicles and conducted searches and raids (Hinz and Gevers, 1989, p. 42). One can describe the military presence in the region as one that 'normalised' everyday violence. Mrs Hausiku personally recalled: 'One day I was, myself, slapped by a Koevoet member who looked drunk. On this day my parents were not around. When Koevoet arrived I ran to hide at the San huts near our homestead, but I was singled out in the hut by one Koevoet member and taken back home where I was given some slaps before they departed.'[16] Koevoet liked to give 'performances' of their power.

The most degrading and traumatic form of violence was that of exhibiting dead corpses. Bodies of PLAN insurgents killed during operations were tied to the spare wheels or at the back of a Casspir and people were invited to 'see their SWAPOs' (Hinz and Gevers, 1989, pp. 45-46). I, too, experienced the lasting trauma of this brutal display. In 1983, one PLAN fighter was killed at Ngururasi, 10 km east of Muparara village, and when the Koevoet members arrived at Muparara, everybody in the homestead of Robert Karapo was ordered out of their huts to view the corpse. It was my home and it was the first time I had seen a dead person. I was only 11 years old. The photographs of Koevoet armoured vehicles and the dead corpses of PLAN combatants tied onto a Casspir still revived a sense of fear amongst interviewees many years later (Stiff, 1999, pp. 38, 357). Brison maintains that trauma generates frequent 'flashbacks' to events of extreme violence and that we should not underestimate the lasting impact of violent encounters (1999, p. 39).

---

16   Interview by author with Johanna Hausiku, Zigizi village, uKwangali district, 25 July 2007.

One of the most important forms of assistance needed by the PLAN cadres was logistical support. Ndeulitufa Kalomoh used individuals who owned vehicles to charge his radio batteries to communicate with SWAPO HQ in Luanda. Robert Karapo was arrested in September 1983, accused of giving such assistance.[17] Luckily the battery that was taken from Karapo's homestead by the SADF proved too weak to power a radio and this probably saved his life as he was released from detention.[18]

The South African forces had informers who provided them with reliable information. Sometimes PLAN cadres who were captured by the SADF or Koevoet, after severe interrogation revealed the names of civilians who had supported them. Whilst civilians faced the danger of being accused of providing information to one side or the other, they also faced dangers when attempting to travel around the region doing their normal business.

Gabriel Munguya, a nurse at Nepara clinic, explains that from 1980 onwards the inland road from Nepara up to Muparara was not safe to travel because of landmines, although the road was used by both civilians and the South African military. Landmines were planted by both PLAN combatants and the SADF, leading to incidents where landmines planted in the road were detonated by civilians.[19] For example, the main road from Nepara village to Muparara village suffered four landmine explosions. Munguya believes that South African forces would plant a landmine in the road deliberately, and once detonated by civilians, the South Africans would accuse PLAN combatants of planting landmines and killing innocent civilians.

Gabriel Munguya argues that a landmine that exploded near Nepara clinic was planted by the SADF in the main road, and was meant for the *Hompa* (Chief) of uKwangali who was regarded as an influential SWAPO collaborator. Fortunately on the day of the incident, the *Hompa* did not travel to his village but those who travelled in his car on that day were two of his brother's sons, Moses Kandjimi and Pius Kandjimi. The two men drove over the landmine, detonating it. The explosion seriously injured Pius Kandjimi and led to the amputation of his leg.[20] During the 1980s, the Nepara-Muparara road became very unsafe, especially for those whose children were at secondary schools across the region.

SWAPO activists were subjected to frequent arrest, detention, beating and torture. Section 30 of the 1957 South African Defence Act granted absolute immunity to the members of its security forces to murder, assault and commit other criminal acts for the purposes of the 'prevention and suppression of terrorism' in any operational area (Herbstein and Evenson, 1989, p. 80). This Act had a huge impact on the inhabitants of the Kavango region, and on uKwangali district in particular. In all the declared war zones, the security forces used the Administrator General's proclamation AG 9 Act of 1977, which allowed detention without trial and for prisoners to be held incommunicado for 30 days. (Hinz and Gevers, 1989, p. 52). AG 9 allowed South African officers to arrest people without any warrant and interrogate them without them having committed

---

17 Interview byAaron Nambadi with Robert Karapo, Muparara village, uKwangali district, 21 May 2003.
18 Ibid.
19 Interview by author with Gabriel Munguya, Nepara village, uKwangali district, 27 July 2007.
20 Ibid.

any offence. The proclamation (Detention for the Prevention of Political Violence and Intimidation) was used by the security police to remove SWAPO activists for an indefinite period (Herbstein and Evenson, 1989, p. 77). These Acts used by the South African forces affected civilians both socially and politically.

Schools were also affected by the armed struggle. Thadeus Nekaro, a former learner at Kandjimi Murangi Secondary School, explained that the struggle had a tremendous social impact on schools across the region. He recalled that in 1983 the SADF military base, which was located close to Kandjimi Murangi Secondary School in uKwangali, was attacked by PLAN and, as a result, the base was moved into the school premises where the soldiers acted as vigilantes to protect the lives of the learners and teachers (which included some white South African soldiers).[21] In the same year, a white teacher living on the school premises was killed by PLAN combatants who threw a hand grenade into his bedroom. The house of the principal, W. Johnson, was also attacked on the same night, but he sustained only minor injuries. Nekaro recalled that, during that week, no teaching took place and the situation in the school was chaotic. The entire school was under strict military control and learners were not allowed to leave the premises. Josef Kandjimi, the first black principal at the Kandjimi Murangi Secondary School, also remembers that the situation was complicated in the sense that control in the schools was both military and academic.[22] During 1983, the secondary school was guarded by South African soldiers who stayed in the school day and night.

The soldiers used to shoot wildly throughout the night.[23] The motive behind the shooting was that South Africans had, allegedly, learned through their informers that PLAN combatants were planning to abduct all the learners from the school and take them to Angola. A truck from the Department of Water Affairs that was en route to Rundu was attacked by PLAN at Rupara. Two South African soldiers (white teachers) were seriously injured and one girl from Kandjimi Murangi Secondary School, Hermine Sadwere, died in the ambush.[24] Immanuel Shikukumwa, the first black Inspector of Education in the Kavango region, explained that the presence of the Koevoet units and its operations disrupted school activities in the region because the Koevoet members accused the children of clearing away the footprints of the PLAN combatants in the morning on their way to school. The retired inspector explained that, though he was the Inspector of Education, his power was not respected at all.[25] He vividly recalled how Koevoet disrupted the teaching process, as learners were taken out of classes for questioning and their teachers were accused of teaching their learners communist ideology. Wellem Kandjimi, a retired principal, agreed that teaching was disrupted. Koevoet normally visited schools in the early hours of the day and would spend an hour questioning learners and teachers. During the mid-1980s, some inland schools even closed down, for example the schools at Gava, Sikarosompo, Ncungu, Ncancana and Kamupupu.[26] Learners sometimes deserted their homesteads with their parents to

---

21 Interview by author with Thaddeus Nekaro, Tutungeni, Rundu, 10 December 2007.
22 Interview by author with Josef Kandjimi, Tutungeni, Rundu, 11 December 2007.
23 Ibid.
24 Interview by author with Thaddeus Nekaro, Tutungeni, Rundu, 10 December 2007.
25 Interview by author with Immanuel Shikukumwa, retired Inspector of Education, Cassava village, uKwangali district, 13 December 2006.
26 Interview by author with Wellem Kandjimi, Gava, uKwangali district, 26 December 2007.

settle along the Kavango River, while some crossed into Angola. Sometimes this was the end of their school career.

The *Hompa* of uKwangali district, Daniel Sitentu Mpasi, explained that the struggle had serious social and political impacts on the inhabitants of his territory. Mpasi claimed that the South African regime suspected that the majority of PLAN combatants were originally from Ovamboland but infiltrated through the uKwangali district. The position of the chiefs in Kavango was sensitive; all the chiefs were members of the Kavango Legislative Council and received some military protection. The chief noted that when the civilians in his district were ill-treated, he tried to intervene and urged the South African forces to stop mistreating innocent people. The same sentiment was echoed by Kasoma Paulus, a former Koevoet member who stated that the Chief of uKwangali and his people were affected by the armed liberation struggle.[27]

Kasoma reported that on several occasions the *Hompa* convened meetings with the senior South African military personnel in the region at the Kahenge tribal office to complain about assaults and the destruction of mahangu fields and grain stores.[28] Muzimba, a Nyemba who emigrated from Angola to escape war, settled at Ngururasi, a village in uKwangali in 1983. He and his wife and children were assaulted by Koevoet members who accused them of providing SWAPO cadres with food.[29] His *mahangu* (pearl millet) grain stores were set on fire as he watched. This led Muzimba and his family to return to Angola. The Chief of uKwangali also pointed out that his palace was attacked several times by the South African forces. In one incident six mortar bombs were fired at his homestead, but fortunately none of the shells hit his palace or injured people in the house. The attack followed his visit to meet SWAPO leaders abroad in the 1980s.

The main reason for the strict control over the Chief's palace, according to Kasoma, was that he was accused of allowing PLAN combatants to infiltrate and operate in his tribal territory.[30] The chief invited journalists from England, Switzerland and France to come to Mayara village to witness what was taking place in his territory. His actions were not supported by the South African regime and the chief was accused of exposing internal matters to the international community. The invitation to foreign journalists prompted a South African senior military officer (based in Rundu) also to visit his palace. The military officer from Rundu, whose task was to investigate, stayed a full week at the Chief's palace to investigate all the accusations made against the SADF.[31] The findings of the military officer were similar to those of the foreign journalists and this saved the chief from being accused of spreading misinformation. The chief's life was at risk during this period. Every day at curfew time he had to enter his bedroom and lock himself in, and he always used to sleep with his pistol next to him. The chief's

---

27 Interview by author with Kasoma Paulus, a former Koevoet member, Rundu, Donkerhoek Location, 24 July 2007.
28 Ibid.
29 Personal communication regarding assaults and destruction of people's property conducted by the Koevoet forces on civilians, 1983-1989.
30 Interview by author with Kasoma Paulus, a former Koevoet member, Rundu, Donkerhoek Location, 24 July 2007.
31 Interview by author with Daniel Sitentu Mpasi, the chief of uKwangali district, Mayara village, 25 July 2007.

principal guards were the very fierce dogs he owned, which intimidated everyone who came to his palace. These memories still give Chief Sitentu Mpasi nightmares.[32]

Paulus 'Njege' Kasoma, a former Koevoet soldier, remembered that the increased infiltration of PLAN combatants into uKwangali district in the early 1980s resulted in concentrated Koevoet operations in the area. Kasoma recalled that there were only a few individuals who could be bribed with goods to provide them with information. The basic strategy used for interrogations was violence, for example, using radio batteries to give electric shocks to captives. Once the terminals of the battery wires were clipped on to the victim's ears, and the handle turned (as with the telephones at that time) the battery produced an electric current that shocked.[33] Wellem Kandjimi, who was detained at Nepara base, claimed that every detainee arrested was tied and locked up in a room where a generator that provided power (electricity) to the base was kept.[34]

Many prominent figures in the Kavango region were arrested and beaten. Among them were Severinus Siteketa, a prominent businessmen, the late Jaakko Kangayi, the principal of Nkurenkuru combined school, Jonas Hamukwaya, a teacher at Namutuntu who died after being interrogated and tortured by Koevoet forces, and a number of civilians who owned vehicles.[35] Kangayi, the Principal of Nkurenkuru Secondary School, described his interrogation in early 1982 to a French journalist:

> I was blindfolded. They started beating me. I fell down. They sat me in a chair and put electrodes in my ears. Before each discharge, someone asked me a question, but no one was listening to my answer. They seemed to be enjoying themselves. They forced me to open my mouth to put electrodes in it, and the shocks started up again under the tongue, then on the nape of my neck. This lasted three long days. On New Year's Eve, others came to torture me. They were slightly drunk. They spat the scraps from their meals in my face. They laughed like madmen. They then carried me into a cell where I found, lying shoulder to shoulder, four other prisoners who were in bad condition. The cell consisted of a metal structure two metres long and one metre high. It was impossible to stand up, especially since the ceiling, which had a circular arch, was lined with barbed wire. They allowed us a daily 15-minute 'walk' in the courtyard. We had to trot in a circle and, depending on the day and the guard's whim, imitate the cries of pigs, cows or chickens. This was effective; finally, I no longer felt the least bit human.[36]

The physical conditions in which political detainees were kept were inhumane. In most cases, suspects were detained and questioned at military bases, with those arrested in uKwangali normally being detained at Nepara military base. In terms of AG 9, suspects were arrested and detained for 30 days without any trial. An extension of an extra 30

---

32   Ibid.
33   Interview by author with Kasoma Paulus, a former Koevoet member, Rundu, Donkerhoek Location, 24 July 2007.
34   Interview by author with Wellem Kandjimi, Gava, uKwangali district, 26 December 2007.
35   Interview by author with Nestor Mufenda, Rundu, Tutungeni location, 28 December 2007.
36   P. Claude (1982) 'On the Angolan Border—The South African Army Has Lost the "Battle for Hearts!"' *Le Monde,* 26 March, p. 7. Translation in Foreign Broadcasts Information Service, *Sub-Saharan Africa Report,* No. 2642, 18 June 1982.

days could be requested after the first 30 days lapsed. The most prominent activists in uKwangali who were victims of AG 9 were the late Jaakko Kangayi, Severinus Siteketa, Remigius Siyave, Nimrod Muremi, Silas and Mufenda Nestor.[37] Mufenda recalled that many of those who were arrested were taken to Osire. Inside Namibia, civilians were the only channels through which PLAN combatants could obtain what they needed in terms of food, money, information and clothing, so PLAN combatants frequently went to the homesteads of these prominent activists, which placed a strain on the resources of these homesteads and made it difficult to maintain security

Safety and Security of the Inhabitants of uKwangali in Kavango West during the Armed Liberation Struggle

During the 1980s, the disappearance of civilians from uKwangali became common. For example, in December 1987, SWAPO alleged that Jonathan Liu and Jonathan Shushe, both elderly men from Kakuwa village in uKwangali, in the western part of Kavango region, had been abducted by the security forces, and they were never seen again. SWAPO highlighted their concern that 'the police were under no obligation to release information on detainees held under AG 9' (SWAPO, 1987, p. 17). AG 9 was a tool that gave huge powers to the South African security forces.

The South African regime's strategy of using 'Recce' (Reconnaissance) units dressed in the same uniforms as PLAN combatants, walking barefoot, speaking Oshiwambo and carrying AK-47 automatic rifles, made matters confusing for local residents (Stiff, 1999, p. 219).

Growing up in uKwangali, my experience of the 'Recce' units was that they used to visit people's homesteads during the night under the pretext of being PLAN combatants, while they were in fact units of the SADF. Community members provided food and other assistance, and then the next morning the same forces would come and harass and assault people in the homestead because they had been hosting 'PLAN cadres' and provided them with food. Civilians were filled with doubt and mistrust as to who was really PLAN.[38] The 'Recce' units used AK-47 rifles and uniforms similar to that of SWAPO's military wing PLAN (SWAPO, 1987, p. 18). However, PLAN adapted to the South African strategy of disguising themselves as PLAN fighters by using combat names that made it easier for villagers to distinguish between the real PLAN fighters and fake ones. Selma Kadiva, a resident at Gava, confirmed that civilians lived in an environment of distrust.[39] Marital and family relationships were destroyed simply because those who were labelled as collaborators left their families for the security of towns such as Rundu or farms in the areas of Grootfontein, Otavi and Tsumeb.

---

37 Interview by author with Nestor Mufenda, Rundu, Kavango Regional Council, 28 December 2007.
38 Interview by author with Gabriel Munguya, Nepara village, uKwangali district, 27 July 2007.
39 Interview by author with Selma Kadiva, uKwangali district, Gava village, 25 July 2007.

Political Interaction Between SWAPO, Traditional Authorities and the Civilians of uKwangali District

As the struggle for independence gained momentum in the early 1980s, the uKwangali district became one of the areas most heavily infiltrated by the People's Liberation Army of Namibia (PLAN). During the first half of the 1980s, there was a period of intense military activity in the Kavango and PLAN, SADF or Koevoet units made frequent visits to homesteads. Ndeulitufa Kalomoh, the PLAN commander who was deployed with his men to operate in the uKwangali district, explained that his unit entered uKwangali district for the first time in 1980 via Wiwi, a village in Mpungu constituency. From Wiwi district they proceeded to Katope Komugoro, where they split up into smaller units of four to five men. He remembers the fear that made many people flee their homesteads and cluster near the river because they had been told that PLAN cadres were terrorists.

The PLAN combatants responded to the fearful reaction that they initially encountered. Kalomoh scheduled a meeting with the senior headman Muranda and *Hompa* Sitentu Mpasi in 1983 at Namungundo. Reportedly, *Hompa* Mpasi had been a DTA supporter up to early 1982, but had been angered by attempted South African intimidation.[40] At the 1983 meeting, Kalomoh told the two traditional leaders to tell the people that they must not live in fear and should return to their fields and livestock. He emphasised that they did not come to kill innocent civilians, but to fight the oppressors (whites).[41]

The fact that a former member of the Kavango Legislative Council attended the meeting convened by Kalomoh gives a clear indication that, though some traditional leaders were members of the Legislative Council, they also worked with SWAPO. Rudolf Ngondo, a member of the Kavango Legislative Assembly, was allegedly, on the mysterious Koevoet 'death list' that surfaced in early 1980.[42] However, in April 1981, a unit of bodyguards for members of the Kavango Legislative Assembly was established and it was these men who formed the basis for the first Koevoet unit that was established in the Kavango regions in 1982 (Stiff, 2004, pp. 147-148).

The message conveyed at the meeting with the Kwangali Traditional Authority was similar to that which had been found on a captured SWAPO leaflet signed by the 'Chief in Commander, Namibia Liberation Army, Dar-es-Salaam', which read:

> Freedom fighters must not attack missionaries or burn churches in particular given areas unless they act in self-defence. Freedom fighters are strictly forbidden to attack women, children and elderly people and civilians, unless the situation constitutes danger and the freedom fighters have to act in self-defence (Stiff, 2004, p. 21).

---

40   P. Claude (1982) 'On the Angolan Border—The South African Army Has Lost the "Battle for Hearts!"' *Le Monde,* 26 March, p. 7. Translation in Foreign Broadcasts Information Service, *Sub-Saharan Africa Report*, No. 2642, 18 June 1982.
41   Interview by Aaron Nambadi with Ndeulitufa Kalomoh, a former PLAN commander designated to operate in Kavango, Tutungeni, Rundu, 13 May 2005.
42   'Alarming Whispers about Death Squad Code-Named Koevoet', *Windhoek Observer*, 7 June 1980,. p. 20.

The outcome of the meeting was that the people of uKwangali returned to their villages and started to co-operate with PLAN cadres, and the uKwangali Traditional Authority led by Chief Daniel Sitentu Mpasi urged the local people to give logistical support to PLAN fighters. The PLAN commander, Kalomoh, known by his combat name 'Hakushida', acknowledged that if the Chief of uKwangali had not encouraged his people to provide support, it would have been difficult for PLAN to carry out their activities in uKwangali. However, Hilka Leevi, a survivor of the Cassinga massacre, argued that from the early 1960s to the late 1980s most of the chiefs in Kavango would not associate themselves with political activities. She noted that it was not easy for the traditional leaders to be involved in political affairs because they were used by the South African colonial administration to serve as councillors. Cecil Thornberry, a senior official in UNTAG (the UN force that monitored the transition to independence in Namibia in 1989-1990) expressed a similar opinion; when they met with the traditional leaders in Kavango on 25 June 1989, the leaders said, 'Until today we saw the exiles as enemies, but now we can accept them as our children' (Thornberry, 2004, p. 256)

Paulus Kasoma (known by his combat name 'Njege') explained the South African military strategy of using secret informants as 'spies' or 'informers', who received allowances from their employers, and who created tension, mistrust and misunderstanding between PLAN cadres, the civilians and the traditional leaders. In most cases those identified as spies were discouraged by the PLAN cadres from engaging in such practices and those who did not co-operate were assassinated. For example, Olavi Munango, who worked for the Kavango Radio that used to broadcast anti-SWAPO propaganda, was assassinated by PLAN in 1984 at Mpungu village.[43]

Paulus Kasoma maintained that the relationship between the traditional leaders of uKwangali and PLAN combatants who operated in uKwangali was good.[44] He claimed that the influence of the traditional leaders of uKwangali over the civilians enabled PLAN cadres to operate in the area until the late 1980s. During the ten years Kasoma served in Koevoet, most of their military contacts took place in uKwangali. The reported journey of Chief Daniel Sitentu Mpasi to visit the President of SWAPO, Sam Nujoma, abroad in 1986 contributed to an increased South African military presence in uKwangali. The increased infiltration of PLAN combatants in uKwangali in the early 1980s also led to the establishment of more temporary and mobile military bases, apart from the two major bases at Musese and Nepara. The resignation of Reverend Nathanael Sirongo from the Legislative Council (he was the Vice-Chairperson in 1973) gives further evidence that the position of the members of the Council was complicated, as many youths went into exile from the Mpungu, Simanya and Nkurenkuru areas of uKwangali.

---

43 Milk, H. 2003, 'Kavango during the Namibian war of liberation', <http://kavango.info/Voito.htm.>. {Accessed 9 March 2008}.
44 Interview by the author with Kasoma Paulus, a former Koevoet member, Rundu, Donkerhoek Location, 24 July 2007.

South African Militarisation of the uKwangali District, 1975-1989

The collapse of Portuguese rule in Angola in 1974 led to a massive militarisation of northern Namibia, with major bases being quickly constructed to provide support to 'Operation Savannah', the South African operation to try and prevent the establishment of an MPLA Government in Angola. The declaration of Ovamboland, Kavango and Caprivi in the 1970s as 'security districts' under the control of the South African Defence Force (SADF) military rule resulted in the clearance of a 1 000 metre wide 'no man's land' intended to prevent SWAPO infiltration from Angola into Namibia. The development of South African military rule in uKwangali led to the establishment of major military bases at Musese (905 Battalion), Nepara (55 Battalion), Nkurenkuru and Mauni (Battalion 906) on the western side of Kavango. In June 1975 new military battalions were formed in Namibia; the 35 Battalion was recruited in Ovamboland and the 34 Battalion in Kavango (SWAPO 1981, p. 247). The two battalions were re-designated 101 (Ovambo) and 202 (Kavango) Battalions within the South West Africa Territorial Force (SWATF) in 1984 (IDAF, 1982, pp. 5, 30).

Proclamation R89 of 1976 extended the power of detention without trial to the Kavango and Caprivi (Amnesty International, 1982, p. 3). As the conflict intensified the legislation became increasingly draconian. In May 1979, martial law under AG 9 was applied to the northern 'homelands' of Ovamboland and quickly extended to the other recently created ethnic homelands of Kavangoland and Caprivi (IDAF, 1982, p. 9). The operational area was divided into three military sectors namely, Sector 10 (Kaokoland and Ovamboland), Sector 20 (Kavangoland, West Caprivi, Bushmanland) and Sector 70 (East Caprivi). The military headquarters of the three sectors were at Oshakati in Ovamboland, Rundu in Kavangoland and Katima Mulilo in Caprivi (IDAF, 1982, p. 14). On the eastern side of the Kavango, two military bases were located at Mashare and Bagani, 60 km and 200 km respectively along the Kavango River east of Rundu. In February 1983, Musese military base was established, 90 km west of Rundu in uKwangali.[45] The base had a checkpoint, a fuel filling station, and a military watch tower, which was occupied all the time by soldiers with binoculars, to regularly monitor the movement of people coming to the base from Angola and Namibia.

Alloys Gende, a former Captain in the SADF from Kavango, remembered that the first military bases in uKwangali were at Nkurenkuru, Simanya, Mpungu, Nepara and Musese.[46] He acknowledged that although there were two military bases in Rundu, the biggest base in Kavango was at Nepara in uKwangali district, because of its strategic location, as the base had a borehole for water, a filling station supplying diesel fuel for helicopters and armoured military vehicles, e.g. Casspirs and Buffels. Nepara base also had an airfield strip and a radio, which facilitated communications for SADF military operations. However, Rundu, the administrative capital of Kavango, was gradually transformed into one of the most heavily militarised towns in Namibia. In 1986, extensive reconstruction to extend the runways at Rundu airfield increased the logistical capacity to allow larger helicopters, which carried up to 20 soldiers, to land and take off. The helicopters flew from Rundu to conduct military operations within

---

45 Interview by author with Alloys Gende, Sambyu district, Kayengona, 27 December 2007.
46 Ibid.

the region and in Angola. Whenever the Koevoet forces were tracking a PLAN guerilla fighter in the region, a South African Air Force (SAAF) Alouette helicopter gunship and a spotter plane provided support. Mirage jets were also stationed at Rundu airfield on standby, awaiting orders. By mid-1986, the SADF had installed huge radar controlled anti-aircraft guns around the whole perimeter of the Rundu military airfield.

The South African military build-up around Rundu was further reinforced with an array of Casspirs, Buffels and other types of armoured vehicles (SWAPO, 1987, p. 1). In September 1986, over 1,000 military trucks arrived at Rundu carrying military equipment, hardware and other logistical supplies. Nepara was a strategic base where SADF military units assembled before being dispatched to smaller bases further west, like Mauni and Kongo. To ensure successful military operations, a new road was constructed in 1987 to link Nkurenkuru, Nepara and Mpungu.

To prevent PLAN infiltration, Musese base operated a road block where every vehicle and passenger was searched. The identification demanded at the checkpoint was an identity card, and those who were not in a position to produce identity cards were suspected of being PLAN combatants. The checkpoint at Musese base was also used to screen SWAPO supporters buying fuel and agricultural products like maize meal. For intelligence purposes, SADF informers (spies) used to report PLAN combatants' related activities and operations at Musese military base. Informers would also come to the base with the ostensible purpose of buying agricultural products and fuel but actually to provide information.[47]

The increasing presence of the PLAN cadres in uKwangali also led to the establishment of temporary military bases and military personnel at South African administrative institutions such as schools, tribal offices, and agricultural extension offices. Allegedly, this was a measure taken to protect state property and the white staff members who worked at these institutions.[48] Thus, temporary military bases and personnel were established at Kandjimi Murangi Secondary School and the Kahenge tribal office in uKwangali district in Kavango West.[49] Militarily, the eastern part of the Kavango was not as heavily infiltrated by PLAN combatants as the western part, especially during the 1980s. Hilka Leevi argues that this was because of military developments in Angola, with the eastern part of Angola being occupied by UNITA with its military headquarters at Jamba and Kakuchi, while the western part of Angola was occupied by the MPLA, SWAPO's allies.[50]

Impact of the South African Security Forces in uKwangali District

The presence of the two military forces created divisions in the community as some individuals whose relatives had left the country to join the armed struggle collaborated with PLAN combatants, while those whose relatives were recruited into the South

---

47 Interview by author with Kasoma Paulus, a former Koevoet member, Rundu, Donkerhoek Location, 24 July 2007.
48 Interview by author with Alloys Gende, Sambyu district, Kayengona village, 27 December 2007.
49 Interview by author with Kasoma Paulus, a former Koevoet member, Rundu, Donkerhoek Location, 24 July 2007.
50 Ibid.

African forces supported the SADF. The establishment of the South West Africa Territorial Force in August 1980 led to increased recruitment of young men of 25 or younger at every Tribal Office. A former SADF instructor, Alloys Gende, noted that as early as 1976-77 a total of 50 able-bodied boys from each of the five recognised ethnic groups in the region had been recruited into the SADF from uKwangali.[51]

The South African Defence Force used the differences that emerged between the people as a strategy to segregate them politically and militarily in order to detect SWAPO collaborators. On this basis, civilians with personal motives used to report each other. Veronika Shillinge, who has lived at Mukekete village in Mpungu constituency since the 1970s, recalled a case in 1978 when PLAN combatants took a truck from the workers of the Department of Water Affairs who were fixing a water pump at Mukekete. At night the SADF visited the villagers to ask how the truck was stolen and accused them of having knowledge of the incident. The theft of the truck led directly to the establishment of an SADF military base at Mpungu. The insecure situation in Mukekete led to some families deserting the village in 1983. In the same year, Joseph Haindongo and his wife, Hillia Haindongo, were assassinated by an armed man with an AK-47 who, his daughter said, had questioned Haindongo about his possession of a rifle. This incident forced more villagers to desert Mukekete, leaving their livestock and property behind for better security and safety.[52] Shillinge suspected that these atrocities were committed by SADF members simply because the son of Josef and Hillia Haindongo had left the country to join the liberation struggle in exile. Shillinge also believed that the armed men who killed the couple were SADF members, although they were wearing PLAN uniforms.[53] The geographical location of the village, which is close to the former Ovamboland border, made it a strategic place.

Fillip Kanguma, a senior member of the same family, was also killed by an unidentified gunman at Mukekete. Shillinge, the daughter of the late Kanguma, explained that the death of Kanguma had a serious psychological effect on the entire family. The incident took place at night. They just heard dogs barking and later the sound of a gunshot – the shot from an armed man that killed him. The entire family left Mukekete and settled at Mpungu village in November 1983. When Veronika left Mukekete and relocated with her entire family at Mpungu, she stopped teaching. The school at Mukekete then closed down as other teachers left the area; people lived in fear. The school at Mpoto, a village near Mukekete, also closed down completely from 1983 for a whole year.[54]

Paulus Kasoma believes that 'The inhabitants of uKwangali district experienced many problems during the late 1970s and early 1980s up to 1989 and during the first general election campaign'.[55] In 1983 a terrible incident took place at Gava, when the SADF infantry unit ambushed a house where people were suspected of harbouring PLAN combatants. Heavy gunfire injured most of the people in the house and five

---

51 Interview by author with Alloys Gende, Sambyu district, Kayengona, 27 December 2007.
52 Interview by author with Veronika Shillinge, Ncancana, uKwangali district, 14 December 2007. For a contemporary newspaper account of the murders, see '13 Spent Cases at Scene of Double Slaying', *Windhoek Observer*, 15 October 1983, p. 30.
53 Interview by author with Veronika Shillinge, Ncancana, uKwangali district, 14 December 2007.
54 Ibid. For more details see: 'Man , 83, Shot', *Windhoek Observer*, 10 December 1983, p. 37.
55 Interview by author with Kasoma Paulus, a former Koevoet member, Rundu, Donkerhoek Location, 24 July 2007.

died on the spot.[56] The presence of South African forces in the district put the lives of civilians at risk.

Cattle herders were also accused of deliberately destroying the footprints of PLAN cadres, and so villagers were not allowed to release their livestock for grazing into the fields before 9 a.m. Mahangu (millet) crops and fences were also destroyed by Koevoet on the pretext that PLAN combatants were hiding in those fields.[57] Wellem Kandjimi, who lived at Gava in 1983, explained that one day PLAN cadres requested him to charge their battery as usual. When the PLAN cadres came to collect their battery, a 'Recce' unit, pretending to be PLAN cadres, arrived at his house at the same time. A serious military contact took place and one boy, 'David', who ran out of the house for safety, was shot dead.[58]

The insecurity created by the South African forces resulted in many people leaving their villages to live permanently in Angola. PLAN combatants regarded individuals who deserted their villages as South African collaborators, while the SADF and Koevoet regarded them as SWAPO collaborators. If one person in the family left the village, this created a problem where the entire family or village would be held accountable for the absence.[59] The situation was unbearable because people were caught in the middle.

A large number of detentions took place during the period in the early 1980s, when PLAN operations in the Kavango Region were at their height. In December 1983, a group of more than 20 detainees were released, including Gideon Nestor, Rev. Heikki Hausiku and Nestor Mufenda from uKwangali. In June 1984, Severinus Siteketa, a political activist in uKwangali, was arrested at Mukekete and taken to Mururani control post along the Rundu – Grootfontein tarred road. At Mururani, the Special Forces used the police station with its four cells to keep detainees in solitary confinement, torture them with electric shocks, deny them food, or give them bad food. This treatment nearly killed Severinus Siteketa. After six months of such treatment he was released with others, including Mpasi Hausiku and his brother.[60]

The second arrest of Severinus Siteketa was in terms of the notorious AG 27. Under this proclamation, the Administrator-General, all commissioned and non-commissioned members of the South African security force, the military and the police, were empowered to detain any person uncharged and incommunicado for up to 30 days for interrogation, and the detainees had no right to know the reason for their arrest. This time Siteketa was arrested while he was shopping at the ENOK shop in Rundu, and he was taken to Osire, 600 km away. At Osire, Siteketa was detained for four months before the security forces transferred him to Bethanie in the south of Namibia. During this time he was with 40 other detainees from Kavango, including the late Jaakko Kangayi, Kaoko Nairenge, and Gideon Mpasi.

---

56   Ibid.
57   Ibid.
58   Interview by author with Wellem Kandjimi, Gava, uKwangali district, 26 December 2007.
59   Interview by author with Kasoma Paulus, a former Koevoet member, Rundu, Donkerhoek Location, 24 July 2007.
60   H. Milk (2003) 'Kavango during the Namibian war of liberation,' <http://kavango.info/Voito.htm.> {Accessed on 2 March 2008}.

At Bethanie, Siteketa was kept with 12-15 other political detainees in a cell. Two weeks after his release in January 1986, Koevoet took him to a notorious camp called *'Bitter Soet'* (now the Elizabeth Nepemba Rehabilitation Centre). This camp was hidden in thick forest about 2 km east of the tarred road to Grootfontein, 30 km south of Rundu. Even the military believed it was a police training camp, sometimes referred to as 'Malan's Camp'. In reality it was a detention camp equipped with torture facilities used by Koevoet, far away from inhabited areas. Kept in extremely harsh conditions, Siteketa suffered the incredible heat of the day and the cold of the night in a small cell made completely of corrugated iron. Every detainee arrested in the region went through *Bitter Soet* for interrogation and torture and some are likely to have been broken by their treatment. Torture and mistreatment was part of the daily routine of the Koevoet soldiers, who kept themselves unidentifiable. When they opened the cell door to push in his food, Siteketa had to turn away and face the corrugated iron sheet wall. After another six months, he was set free. After this systematic mistreatment, the then 43-year old Siteketa looked like an old, broken man, unrecognisable even to his family.[61]

Looting people's goods was a common practice of the South African forces, and when they wanted meat, people's livestock in the field or on the roadside were shot. Sometimes cattle were severely injured, which forced the owners to kill them. Haindongo Risto from Mbandja in Southern Angola, who had migrated to Mpungu and lived there since 1959, complained that his goats were killed by the South African forces without his consent. Haindongo complained that the security forces entered the homesteads of villagers at any time they wished, day or night.[62] This affected the social economy of the villagers, since most depended on subsistence farming where livestock are important assets in terms of family resources.

Conclusion

The geographical location of the Kavango Regions and South African strategy combined to initially isolate the residents of the regions from the liberation struggle. However, Angolan independence in 1975 led to PLAN increasingly infiltrating the region from 1978, and the early 1980s saw a period of particularly heavy military activity in the region. The increased presence of PLAN cadres in Kavango during the 1980s complicated the political atmosphere for the inhabitants of uKwangali. The armed liberation struggle in uKwangali had diverse social and economic impacts on its inhabitants. The presence of the South African military forces in uKwangali has left memories of brutality, and mental scars that still haunt many residents. However, another legacy of the liberation struggle is the many individual stories that should be recorded and documented by young Namibian historians. Recording the experiences of different people from that time will ensure that future generations have a clear understanding of the many ways in which the conflict has shaped their community, and build a mosaic that will provide a more complete representation of Namibia's history.

---

61 Ibid.
62 Interview by author with Haindongo Risto, Mukekete village, uKwangali district, 26 June 2007.

References

Amnesty International (1982) *Human Rights Violations in Namibia.* Amnesty International, USA.

Brison, J. S. (1999) *Trauma narratives and the remaking of the self, acts of memory cultural recall in the present.* Hanover and London: Dartmouth College Press.

Claude, P. (1982) 'On the Angolan Border—The South African Army Has Lost the "Battle for Hearts!"' Newspaper article in *Le Monde,* 26 March. Translation in Foreign Broadcasts Information Service, *Sub-Saharan Africa Report*, No. 2642, 18 June 1982.

Diescho, J. B. (1983) 'A critical evaluation of the Odendaal commission of enquiry into South West Africa affairs 1962-63'. MA dissertation, University of Fort Hare.

Herbstein, D. and Evenson, J. (1989) *The devils are among us: The war for Namibia.* London: Zed Books.

Hinz, M. and Gevers, N. (1989) *Koevoet versus the people in Namibia*. Utrecht: Working Group Kairos.

International Defence and Aid Fund (1982) *Apartheid's Army in Namibia: South Africa illegal military occupation.* London: IDAF.

Likuwa, K. (2012) 'Voices from the Kavango: A study of the contract labour system in Namibia, 1925-1972', PhD thesis, University of the Western Cape, Cape Town.

Milk, H. (2003) 'Kavango during the Namibian war of liberation,' <http://kavango.info/Voito.htm.>. {Accessed on 2 March 2008}.

Namakalu, O. (2004) *Armed Liberation Struggle: Some Accounts of PLAN's Combat Operations.* Windhoek: Gamsberg Macmillan.

Nortje, P. (2012) *The Terrible Ones: A Complete History of 32 Battalion*, Vol 1. Cape Town: Zebra Press.

Nujoma, S. (2001) *Where others wavered: The Autobiography of Sam Nujoma*. London: Panaf Books.

Shityuwete, H. (1990) *Never follow the wolf: the autobiography of a Namibian freedom fighter.* London: Kliptown Books.

Stiff, P. (1999) *Silent War: South African Recce Operations, 1969-1994.* Alberton: Galago.

Stiff, P. (2004) *The Covert War, Koevoet Operations Namibia, 1979-1989.* Alberton: Galago.

SWAPO Information Department (1981) *To Be Born a Nation: The liberation struggle for Namibia.* London: Zed Press.

SWAPO (1987) *SWAPO Information Bulletin.* Luanda: SWAPO Department of Information and Publicity, December.

SWAPO (1996) *Their Blood Waters Our Freedom.* Windhoek: SWAPO Party.

Thornberry, C. (2004) *A Nation is Born: The Inside Story of Namibia's Independence.* Windhoek: Gamsberg Macmillan.

Windhoek Advertiser, 'Kavango detainees savagely beaten, eye-witnesses relate', 30 November 1982.

Windhoek Observer, 'Alarming Whispers about Death Squad Code-Named Koevoet', 7 June 1980.

Windhoek Observer, '13 Spent Cases at Scene of Double Slaying', 15 October 1983.

Windhoek Observer, 'Man, 83, Shot', 10 December 1983.

15 The Gendered Politics of the SWAPO Camps during the Namibian Liberation Struggle

Martha Akawa

Introduction

This chapter looks at the sexual politics of the SWAPO camps (civilian and military) in Angola and Zambia.[1] Its purpose is to explore issues around allegations of sexual abuse and unwelcome sexual advances, and issues of sexuality, against the backdrop of SWAPO's policy on gender equality. Did these allegations undermine the goals and objectives of the leadership, particularly the women's leadership that had gender equality and women's emancipation as one of its main goals? The chapter will also seek to question whether a rhetorical commitment to equality was translated into practical equality in terms of the political structures and socio-economic power relationships in the camps.

SWAPO made a clear and a firm ideological commitment in publications and speeches that, in the liberation struggle, women were equal to men and that equality between men and women was a central principle of the party. Iina Soiri has argued that the rhetoric of sexual emancipation became more pronounced from the mid-1970s because of a combination of factors. The United Nations announced that the International Decade for Women would take place between 1975 and 1985 and, in 1976, SWAPO adopted a more radical 'Political Programme' based on the principles of 'scientific socialism' (Soiri, 1996, pp. 67, 85). However, the depiction and representation of women in the liberation movement as being fully liberated from gender oppression does not seem to reflect the actual experience of women in the camps. Allegations of sexual abuse and excessive party control over female sexuality were levelled against those in power and this suggests that, despite the firm pronouncements on gender equality, men and women in exile were not equal after all. In the war, people found themselves in situations that they were unaccustomed to and this might have had an impact on the socially constructed notions of gender, gender power relations, and gender identities. As men and women got drawn into the war, gender meanings and relations between them were altered and shifted.

---

[1] This chapter is a revised version of one in my doctoral thesis. See Martha Akawa (2010) 'The sexual politics of the Namibian liberation struggle' (Institute of History, University of Basel), published in 2014 as *The Gender Politics of the Namibian Liberation Struggle*.

Shifting Sexuality Patterns in Namibia

Namibians who found themselves in SWAPO's camps in exile came out of a society that had its own ideas, beliefs, and understanding of issues around sex and sexuality. Patterns of sexuality have changed over time and this has shaped how sexuality is perceived. Before the arrival of missionaries, different societies in Namibia had different rituals that were regarded as rites of passage, which informed what was right or wrong in terms of sexuality. *Efundula*[2] was one of the most significant in northern Namibia. There were a lot of traditional myths and taboos around the issue of sex and sexuality. It was believed that sex outside marriage could cause an illness and that an unfaithful married woman, if she became pregnant, would die of cramps when delivering (*oshaatu, oshiwato, oshihi*), or the baby would die of cramps. A husband's extra-marital affairs (*oshithitikila*) might cause death to the woman or problems during delivery. If a breastfeeding mother had sexual intercourse with someone else, rather than the father of her child, the child would get diarrhoea, mental illness or a disability. If people had sex during the day, some of the cattle might die. A pregnant woman had to wake up early in the morning every day and get out of her sleeping hut, before anyone who had slept elsewhere returned to the house (it could be someone from the same house or neighbours (*okulyatelela*)), or else she would have difficulties during delivery. (Mufune, 2003, pp. 425-428).

Mufune argues that these taboos were used to explain the unfortunate consequences when the accepted principles around sex and sexuality were not followed; as a result, taboos increased a sense of social responsibility and provided a moral framework for sexual behaviour. However, nowadays, with advanced medical technology and access to health facilities, maternal deaths and child mortality have been reduced, hence popular belief in the taboos has been eroded. Consequently, people ignore these taboos and they are no longer relevant in restraining immoral sexual behaviours and they are no longer used to explain the misfortunes that might happen to people (Mufune, 2003, p. 435).

With the coming of missionaries and the introduction of Christianity in northern Namibia, the practices of *efundula, ewilo* and polygamy were pronounced 'heathen'. The men who had more than one wife were asked to relinquish all their wives but one. *Ewilo, efundula* and polygamy were strongly discouraged and eventually ceased to exist (although *Efundula* has been revived in some places since independence).[3] People were encouraged to marry before engaging in sexual activities (Becker, 2004, p. 47). A sense that it was sinful to have sex before marriage was inculcated in young people. The missionaries monitored sexual behaviour by encouraging confessions, and threatening expulsion from the church of women who had sex outside of a Christian marriage. A woman who fell pregnant before marriage was regarded as having transgressed the sixth commandment; 'Thou shall not commit adultery.' Both the woman and the man

---

2   *Efundula* is an initiation ceremony that girls were supposed to go through and pass before they could have sexual intercourse. However, *ewilo* was practised. *Ewilo* entailed a man placing his head on the chest of his partner or girlfriend who had not gone through *efundula*. Full sexual intercourse did not take place.
3   Helvy Shaanika, 'Olufuko festival attracts thousands', *New Era*, 24 August 2012.

had to go through *oskola ye kuthilo* ('lessons of repentance') initiated by the church, and confess their sins. If they did not confess, then they would be excommunicated from the church. Falling pregnant before marriage is regarded as shameful and sinful and the obligation to verbally confess to such sins is still practised today.[4]

The missionaries set new concepts as to what should entail accepted sexuality, which was for the woman to maintain her virginity until she had a Christian marriage and then to remain faithful within a monogamous marriage. It is interesting to note that if a person steals for instance, s/he is not required to confess their sins and ask the congregation members to forgive him/her, although 'Thou shalt not steal' is the seventh commandment! However, some people continued practising polygamy and some shifted from being open to being closet polygamists. Ellen Namhila, in her autobiography, remembers that her grandfather in northern Namibia had four wives. After being converted to Christianity, he was forced to separate from all but one. Although the three were no longer his legal wives, he extended his homestead, built each of them a house, and gave them land to farm. The wife who remained had to look after all the children and grandchildren of the wives who left. The children could visit their mothers whenever they wished as they all lived around the grandfather's house. What the church did was only to change him from an open polygamist to a hidden one (Namhila, 1997, p.15).[5]

The other influence that altered sexuality in Namibia was the colonial state. The state, together with the local elite (who were mainly men), conspired to control the sexuality, labour and mobility of women (Becker, 2004, p. 43). Women from the north were excluded from the contract labour system and so were unable to work on the mines, farms or in the fishing and manufacturing industries. As the 'border controls' to the Police Zone,[6] were tightened it became very difficult for women to travel to the south. Even women in the Police Zone who wanted to live in an urban area had to report their presence to the municipal offices at a town and were required to carry passes.[7] This was probably done to make sure that women were left in the homelands to maintain the households, which their husbands would return to, since men were only allowed to stay in towns when working on a fixed-term contract. They would also have to return to the north if they were injured or sick, or simply when their labour was no longer needed.

Polygamy and the Colonial State

The colonial state had a big influence on the control of polygamy. Customary law never enjoyed legal recognition prior to independence, and in particular customary

---

4 Personal communication.
5 This must have been around 1969, because in the story Namhila indicated that she was about five years of age at the time. She left Namibia for exile in 1976 when she was twelve. This was not a special and isolated case; it was a familiar experience.
6 The 'Police Zone' was established during the German colonial period and reinforced during the South African colonial period. It covered the huge area of central and southern Namibia that included the commercial farms obtained by white settlers. The majority of the black population, lived to the north and north-east of this area on communal land, whilst black residents of the Police Zone were left only with remnants of their former territories that were reduced to small 'reserves'.
7 SWAPO, *Namibia News* (September/October) 1972.

law marriages, because of their polygamous nature. The Native Administration Proclamation of 1928 (Proclamation no. 15 of 1928) did not recognise marriage under customary law. As a result, a person married under customary law, while so married, could conclude a subsequent marriage under common law and such a person would not be guilty of bigamy. However, the Marriage Act no. 81 of 1963, and regulations under it, prohibited a person married under common law, whilst married, to conclude a subsequent marriage under the common law. Bigamy was, in other words, a common law offence. The second marriage would be void and would not have the normal legal consequences of marriage (Law Reform and Development Commission, 2003).

The migrant labour system did not allow men to move with their families to their new places of work. Loneliness, and inaccessibility to their family, forced some men to resort to 'second house' relationships. Most of the second house relationships were publicly known, sometimes even by the man's legal wife. Children were born from these unions and they grew up seeing what their parents were doing, namely that their fathers had multiple partners and that women tolerated what their husbands were doing. There were no laws to regulate second house relationships and informal cohabitations. In Namibia, adultery is not a crime, but can be the grounds for divorce (Hubbard, 2003). However, at a traditional level, adultery is viewed as taking place only when a man (married or not) cheats with a married woman, but not when a man (married or not) cheats with an unmarried woman. 'A man who has a sexual relationship with a married woman would be asked to pay damages for stealing from the other man [the husband of the woman with whom he had a relationship]' (Mufune, 2003).

Definition of Rape and Sexual Abuse

The notion of rape and sexual abuse has been understood differently over time, hence its definitions vary. After independence, Namibia changed the rape law, and The Combating of Rape Act (2000) was enacted, which triggered a heated debate, especially regarding the clause that rape could occur between husband and wife within marriage when the husband forced an unwilling wife to have sexual intercourse. In exile, SWAPO was guided by the following definition of rape; 'whoever acquires a carnal knowledge (has sexual intercourse) of a woman not living in matrimonial union with him and does so by violence or by threatening with a direct attack on life or limb shall have committed a felony' (SWAPO, 1977). The earlier SWAPO definition, therefore, indicated that rape could not occur within marriage. The main question to be considered in this chapter, however, is whether or not there were cases of sexual abuse of women whilst they were in exile and, if so, under what circumstances these might have occurred.

The Journey to Exile

When people left the country, they might have left as a group of friends, they might have been abducted, or they might have co-ordinated their journey with soldiers who were operating inside the country. One of the main aims of guerrillas operating inside Namibia was to help people cross the border of Namibia into Angola, Zambia or Botswana, using the route that was safest at the time. The dependence of young women going into exile on the males who guided them was likely to have created a gendered power relationship. A former male PLAN combatant put it in this way:

> Mhhh...for instance young girls coming from home, 16, 17 years or so on. They find the soldiers; the soldiers take them, those who are responsible for taking them to the nearest camp. Sometimes they spent time, up to weeks with these girls because of the situation of the war and that is when the soldiers might help themselves to these girls. At the end of the journey, when they drop them, and in the situation of the war, they (the soldiers) are not supposed to tell them when they are going back. After a month, the girl might find out that she is pregnant and when asked who was responsible, she would say it is Bazooka or Pepesha [combat names], When asked; which one? She would say; the one we came with, and there were so many Bazookas and Pepeshas. Wherever there are people, things will not always go as you want, it happened, especially in the military situation.[8]

In situations like these, it is not very clear how things happened.[9] Whether the acts were consensual or coerced, one cannot rule out the impact a presence of a gun and uniformed men would have had on these young people. Keshi Nathanael also describes his disappointment as a SWAPO Youth League activist when senior PLAN combatants imposed themselves on young girls who had recently arrived in exile, and broke the dating protocols traditionally observed in northern Namibia (2002, pp. 64, 66)

'Ondjolo': Goodies for Sex

Ondjolo literally means 'bait'. When the going was getting tough, some women used their bodies to get the things that they did not have, simply by exchanging sexual favours for basic goods, favours or opportunities, with the men who were in a position to provide them. A former male PLAN commander comments:

> There are so many things that attract women to men. Wealth, beauty, intelligence, fame etc. If somebody goes for training in the USSR or wherever, when you come back, you might come back with a few things, sweets, soaps, underwear...this was to target the vulnerable or the material girls out there. You could do anything with a packet of sweets... You know..., '*Oha ka kwatwa naashi ha ka li.*[10]' It is still happening here, it is natural.[11]

---

8   Interview, 8 July 2008. Owing to the sensitive nature of the topics discussed I have not revealed the names of many of my informants. The interviews referred to in this chapter have been deposited at the National Archives of Namibia but are not currently accessible.
9   Of all the people that I have interviewed, no one has admitted to being either a victim or a perpetrator of sexual abuse in the SWAPO camps. Apart from the narration of Keshi Nathanael, most accounts of the liberation struggle are written within a nationalist discourse and so do not touch on the issues that might be regarded as unpatriotic. A highly critical account of the abuse of power is given in Nathanael (2002), although his account was published after he had left SWAPO and been branded a dissident.
10 This can be translated as 'it is trapped with what it eats'.
11 Interview, 12 August 2008.

Another ex-combatant elaborated further:

> Women did not want us, the ordinary soldiers. We had nothing to offer them, an ordinary soldier can stay at the front even up to five years without having gone anywhere, maybe you can go on a mission, inside the country to fight, but not to foreign countries where you can bring nice things. In addition, in the situation when there was not enough food, commanders could have better food, like meat. Ordinary soldiers would only eat *omahola,* [boiled pearl millet]. If a girl is going out with a commander, then she gets to eat those nice food...You know... you girls... [laughs sarcastically]. However, it was not all commanders who did that, only some individuals who took advantage of that and abused their positions. [12]

Everyday survival, but also longer-term benefits (such as opportunities to study) lured women into having affairs with commanders, as a commander of the camp mainly did the preliminary selections.

'No Comrade Says "No" to Another Comrade'

Some commanders and various men who were in positions of power used the 'no comrade says no to another comrade unless you are an agent' line to get to sleep with women. With the security complex that was common to many guerrilla movements (and that led in Namibia's case to incidents such as the Lubango dungeons or the 'spy drama' of the 1980s),[13] no one wanted to be labelled a spy; so many of the women would just give in. This would mainly happen to the new arrivals who were not yet familiar with how things worked in the camps. The commanders liked these new arrivals. A former occupant of a camp commented that:

> People preferred the new arrivals as they were still fresh. When they are just coming from the country/home so they still had roll-ons and nice lotions, unlike those who have been in the camps for long, they did not have roll-ons and their armpits smelled and would smell of *ekandanga*.[14]

Rumours even circulated that some women were sent as South African agents with the mission to go into exile. Security officials allegedly believed that these women had had razor blades inserted in their vaginas and had instructions to go and have sex with specific top male leaders of SWAPO. This apparently meant that, if that

---

12 Interview, 6 August 2008.
13 This was a group of people who were suspected of being South African agents and were accused of spying on the activities and programmes of SWAPO in exile and reporting back to the South African Administration. They were detained and kept in the dungeons. The ex-detainees allege that this was a gross violation of human rights on the side of SWAPO. They alleged that prisoners were mistreated, starved, interrogated and even executed. A large amount of critical literature on the subject already exists. See, for example, Basson and Motinga, 1989.
14 Interview 8 July 2008 . *Ekandanga* was a type of soap that was renowned for its particular smell.

specific commander were to sleep with such a woman (with a razor blade), he would be assassinated as he would bleed to death.[15] However, despite the rumours, no such assassinations were ever reported in SWAPO publications.

Although there were other wings present in the camps (the SWAPO Women's Council, SWAPO Youth League and SWAPO Elders' Council), life operated on military grounds. The arrivals were made to understand that in the army 'discipline and obedience are supreme, a non-negotiable item, if I told you to jump, you cannot ask why, maybe you can ask how high...'[16] A former female soldier adds that:

> What I noticed is that we were disciplined. Maybe even in some instances, if we were abused, we would not have noticed, because the discipline that we had was so good. I compare SWAPO with a church service, even if you do not understand; you would not stand up and question the pastor that, I do not understand this or that.[17]

Resisting an order issued by a superior was one of the offences against military and political discipline in SWAPO, according to the official rules. What is an order is loosely defined and this ambivalence can be misinterpreted by anyone who is dubious. The reference to an 'order' does not indicate that it should be related to the activities of the movement, however when it is left vague, it can be misinterpreted and used the wrong way. It would be interesting to know whether all people knew about and had access to the Laws Governing the Namibian Peoples' Revolution (SWAPO 1977a).

'Rape? I do not Know What you are Talking About'

The question of rape in the camps was the most provocative question that I asked during my interviews. One can understand this because in Namibia a lot of secrecy and taboos surround issues concerning sex and sexuality. After a couple of interviews, I decided to avoid the word 'rape' and replace it with 'unwanted sexual advances' but still there were some people who dismissed it and answered in such a manner that I could not ask any more questions about it. Two female participants who were in exile responded:

> That allegation I do not know. Maybe it was happening at the camps that I was not staying, but I stayed in Nyango, but I have not experienced it.[18]

> Rape? I do not know what you are talking about. I do not want to talk about things that I do not have basis to stand for. It could be allegations or propaganda. If there is any one that can justify that, they can, but in my view, I have not experienced that, what I can call sexual abuse.[19]

---

15 Personal communication, November 2008. The claim was made to the international arena in statements made at the Second Session of the International Commission of Inquiry into the Crimes of the Racist and Apartheid Regime in Southern Africa, Luanda, 30 January-3 February 1981.
16 Interview, 8 July 2008.
17 Interview, 16 July 2008.
18 Interview, 18 June 2008.
19 Interview, 7 May 2008.

Allegations of rape were generally made by women who had been detained and imprisoned by SWAPO. For example, at a press conference given by ex-detainees shortly after their return from Angola, one woman held a baby who, she told journalists, had been born after she was raped by a prison guard.[20]

Controlling Female Sexuality: 'No Foreign Men'

The SWAPO Family Act indicates that 'Namibians may establish matrimonial and family relations with foreigners under different conditions spelled in this Act' (SWAPO, 1977b). However, it became apparent that Namibian women were strongly discouraged or even not allowed to marry men who were foreign nationals.

> Women were not allowed to marry foreign nationals, that is true, because if they were allowed to marry foreigners, they might give away important information about the liberation struggle; maybe the man you are marrying is sent by the enemy. [21]

Women in this case are stereotyped as the weak and fickle ones, who risk revealing important information about the liberation struggle. There were other reasons as to why women were restricted from marrying foreigners. A former male commander explained that:

> But if we allowed them [women to marry foreign nationals], we could have lost about fifty per cent of them today, there is no question about that.[22]

A woman who was in exile agrees that:

> Who would want to live in a camp if you can get married to a Zambian and live in a house? Or eat *omahola* [boiled pearl millet] in a camp if you can get married, eat meat and live in a house?[23]

However, when it came to men marrying foreigners, the whole thing was seen differently. Apparently, even though men were not really allowed to marry foreigners, in most cases it was acceptable, for various reasons. Other interviewees felt that it was understandable and tolerable for Namibian men to be allowed to marry women of other nationals because they could then bring them to the camps and eventually to an independent Namibia.[24] Other respondents feel that it was mainly the early male exiles that married foreign women because of the lack of Namibian women at the time. It was believed, by several interviewees, that after 1974 (when there was great exodus into

---

20   Christian Williams (2011), 'Exile History: An Ethnography of the SWAPO Camps and the Namibian Nation', (PhD thesis, University of the Western Cape, Cape Town), p. 191.
21   Interview, 6 August 2008.
22   Interview, 12 August 2008 (b).
23   Interview, 12 August 2008 (a).
24   The most common example given was that of a Namibian doctor who married a Zambian woman and she came to live in the SWAPO camp and eventually moved to Namibia at independence.

exile) those men often divorced their foreign women and then married Namibians.[25] This cannot, however, be applied universally as not all men who married foreign women divorced them after 1974, or even after independence, and some Namibian men married foreign women in the 1980s. The accountability of SWAPO to its people and the need to make sure that they contributed to the liberation struggle is understandable. However, allowing only men to marry foreign nationals and not allowing women to do the same thing amounted to double standards and a male attempt to have total control over female sexuality.

Not all relationships that were formed in exile were forced. The majority were genuine and formed out of mutual agreement and real love. Some people married while in exile and still kept their partners when they returned to Namibia. It is also significant that whilst SWAPO publications and speeches used Marxist rhetoric, the party also employed pastors in the camps who conducted weddings (Dobell, 2000, pp. 57-59).

Position of SWAPO Regarding Rape and Sexual Abuse

Every person spoken to, without any doubt or hesitation, agrees that SWAPO, as a movement, was very serious when it came to issues of sexual abuse and rape. By 1977, SWAPO had in place a document entitled 'Laws Governing the Namibian People's Revolution' that formalised the rules that were to be enforced in SWAPO's camps. The liberation struggle of the Namibian people was opposed to any form of felony or dishonesty, and that is why it regarded acts such as rape, murder and theft as indirect attacks against the objectives and accomplishments of the movement, which is why they were included as the gravest among the non-political crimes. The laws were adopted by the Central Committee of SWAPO in 1977, and signed by the SWAPO President Sam Nujoma (SWAPO, 1977a). This shows the total commitment of the movement at the highest level to ensure the maintenance of discipline and order among the people.

Disciplinary Measures and Structures

As indicated earlier, SWAPO as a mother body had different wings and organs to execute various duties and functions, but operations and camp activities were carried out in a military fashion. The channels that the occupants of the camps had to go through, if they had any complaints, were those of the hierarchy of the military ranks. The residents of each camp were organised into military units. People were organised into a section, which was composed of 11-15 people; then three sections formed a platoon; three platoons formed a detachment and three detachments formed a company. The camp commander would be the highest commander. For someone who had to lodge a problem, first they had to go to the section commander. If it could not be settled there, then it would be passed to the platoon commander and then the detachment, commander, until it reached the camp commander if it could not be solved by the lower structures.[26] In most cases, the top military ranks were occupied by men,[27] which could

---

25   Interview, 25 July 2008; Interview 12 August 2008 (b).
26   Interview, 8 July 2008.
27   Of all the respondents that I have spoken to, no one can recall having a woman camp commander.

prove to be an impediment, when investigating a case of rape or sexual abuse. The victim might be too ashamed to report this to a man or worse, the person to report to might even be the perpetrator, the case might get held up at a certain level and might not be taken further for action to be taken. After all, many respondents had the view, neatly summarised by one interviewee that: 'The main aim was to fight for independence, other things were secondary'.[28]

The SWAPO Women's Council (SWC), as the wing dealing with women's issues, appeared critical of the system. During a workshop deliberating on issues relating to family planning and sexual abuse, the women were worried that:

> the existing system of passing complaints should be streamlined and changed. Currently when complaints of forced pregnancy are made to the SWAPO Women's Council in the camp, this is usually referred to the executive for decision. There is no feedback downwards to the SWC, because the executive is overloaded with work and does not deal with such issues as fast as it is hoped.

In the same workshop, women proposed that the SWC 'should set up mechanisms to enforce disciplinary measures agreed upon [having women in the executive, dealing with problems swiftly, etc.] by the central committee as part of its policy implementation.' It was during the same workshop that women made additional proposals for short-term controls such as 'to make it compulsory for men not to have more than one girlfriend, limit polygamous tendencies and to force men to marry the impregnated girls'.[29] This demand apparently yielded no fruitful outcome because a former commander and now a high-ranking official stated that:

> I have many children. It is not a secret. I did not marry; I married when I came back. You see... I spent 16 years at the front. The women... those girls...they fell pregnant, whether they wanted to have babies with the chief or they wanted to fall pregnant and go to the rear, one might not know. But other men have many kids as well; some of us are singled out because we are in the limelight.[30]

The insignificant representation of women in the leadership structure may have meant the problems of women were not given the serious attention they deserved, even though it must be understood that not only women can solve women's problems.

Although the 'Laws Governing the Namibian People's Revolution' were adopted by the Central Committee of SWAPO in 1977 and signed by the SWAPO President, by 1980, there were still only 3 women in the Central Committee out of 72 members.[31] Respondents recall that Ndaiponofi Nehova and Aira Shikwambi were the only women to be members of the military council, the highest decision-making body of PLAN (the military wing of SWAPO). During a workshop looking at the issues relating to family planning and sexual abuse in 1980, the women suggested, 'there should be representation of female members within the executive to ensure that such

---

28 Interviews: 15 July 2008; 6 August 2009; 16 August 2008.
29 UNAM Archives, Peter Katjavivi Collection. Sex Education, SWC, n.d. (1980?).
30 Interview, 22 July 2008.
31 *Namibia Today*, No 7/8, 1980.

complaints [forced pregnancies] are handled as swiftly as possible.'[32] Lack of women's representation in the decision-making structures raises doubts as to how much SWAPO was committed to uplifting women's emancipation and gender equality. This can even raise questions as to how many women, if any, were part of the drafting and passing of these laws. For instance Article 11 of the 'Laws Governing the Namibian People's Revolution' under the heading 'Apartheid' recognises only racial discrimination as a crime, but there is no similar law to cover gender discrimination (SWAPO, 1977a).

Momeya iha mu Inyenge Mwaana Okapuka[33]

Although interviewees made many comments such as 'it is natural', 'that was part of life', 'these are isolated cases', 'it could be allegations or propaganda', 'look at things in perspective', 'what was happening in the camps was not really rape in a direct way as such', the number of possible incidents of rape and sexual abuse should not be underplayed.[34] Although some allegations were made by the 'dissidents', some issues of concern were backed up by people who still hold the SWAPO party in high regard. During the liberation struggle these issues were, at times, tabled and discussed at the level of the military council.[35]

The manner in which this issue (of sexual politics in the camps) developed through the duration of the liberation struggle, and the failure to achieve social and political gender equality in the camps, raises questions about SWAPO's level of commitment to gender equality and the emancipation of women – despite the statements and pronouncements made time and time again by the SWAPO movement's leadership (of both sexes) whilst in exile.

The first question should be: How autonomous was the SWC in executing its duties and activities, not forgetting that it was a wing of a mother body, but that, its main duty was, to concentrate on women's issues? At the time, SWC was launched and it must have developed strategies and systematic methods and been influenced by its continental and international co-operations and contacts during its existence. The second question to ask would be: Did the SWC have an agenda outlining how and when things had to be done – an agenda from before independence, with tangible, attainable and time-bound objectives? Were there any reflections and assessments on the side of the SWC to provide a vision and a plan of how things could be done differently and better?

There is no doubt that women entered the male domain during the liberation struggle; whether it was a breakthrough for women's rights or because the situation demanded it, women became soldiers and commanders and even sat in the military council. Regrettably, this did not fully guarantee them the equality and emancipation that some of them were advocating. The camps in exile could have provided the best chance for the male comrades to prove and reinforce their commitment to the emancipation of

---

32 UNAM Archives, Katjavivi Collection. Sex Education, nd. (1980?).
33 An Oshiwambo proverb that literally means 'the water will not move unless there is an insect in the water'. It carries the same meaning as 'there is no smoke without fire'.
34 Interviews: 7 May 2008; 20 June 2008; 8 July 2008; 16 July 2008; 12 August 2008. See also Shikola (1998), pp. 140-141.
35 Interview, 22 July 2008.

women and to walk the talk, not just talk the talk. In practice, the evidence suggests that all comrades were equal, but that some comrades were more equal than others.

References

Akawa, M. (2010) 'The sexual politics of the Namibian liberation struggle', PhD thesis, Institute of History, University of Basel.

Akawa, M. (2014) *The Gender Politics of the Namibian Liberation Struggle*. Basel: Basel Afrika Bibliographien.

Basson, N. and Motinga, B. (1989) *Call them Spies*. Windhoek: Africa Communication Projects.

Becker, H. (2004) 'Efundula: Women's initiation, gender and sexual identities in colonial and post-colonial Northern Namibia'. In Arnfred, S. (ed.) *Re-thinking sexualities in Africa*. Uppsala: Nordiska Afrikainstitutet.

Dobell, L. (2000) *Swapo's struggle for Namibia, 1960-1991: War by other means*. Basel: P. Schlettwein Publishing.

Hubbard, D. (2003) *Faithfulness, adultery and the law*. Windhoek: LAC. Available from: http://www. Lac.org.na/projects/grap. {Accessed 8 April 2009}.

Law Reform and Development Commission (LRDC) (2004) *Law Reform and Development Commission on Customary law marriages*. Windhoek: LRDC (12), October. Available from: http://www.lawreform.gov.na. {Accessed 7 April 2009}.

Mufune, P. (2003) 'Changing patterns of sexuality in Northern Namibia: Implication for the transmission of HIV/AIDS', *Culture, Health and Sexuality*, 5 (5).

Namibia Today, No 7/8 1980.

Namhila, E. N. (1997) *The Price of Freedom*. Windhoek: New Namibia Books.

Nathanael, K. (2002) *A journey to exile. The story of a Namibian freedom fighter*. Aberystwyth: Sosiumi Press.

Shaanika, H. 'Olufuko festival attracts thousands', *New Era*, 24 August 2012.

Shikola, T. (1998) 'We left our shoes behind'. In Turshen, M. et al. (eds) *What women do during the war*. London: Zed.

Soiri, I. (1996) *The Radical Motherhood: Namibian Women's Independence Struggle*. Uppsala: Nordiska Afrikainstitutet.

SWAPO, *Namibia News*, September/October 1972.

SWAPO Department of Legal Affairs (1977a) SWAPO documentation: 'Laws governing the Namibian people's Revolution'. Luanda: SWAPO Department of Information and Publicity.

SWAPO (1977b). 'SWAPO Family Act'. Luanda: SWAPO Department of Legal Affairs (promulgated 1 December, 1977).

Williams, C. (2011) 'Exile History: An Ethnography of the SWAPO Camps and the Namibian Nation, PhD thesis, University of the Western Cape, Cape Town.

Archival sources

University of Namibia (UNAM) Archives
Peter Katjavivi Collection
Sex Education, n.d. (1980?).

16 Solidarity with Liberation in Namibia: An Analytical Eyewitness Account from a West German Perspective

Reinhart Kössler

When asked for an eyewitness account, one's own personal experience takes centre stage. In addition to drawing on that experience, I have carried out scholarly studies on the solidarity movement, particularly in relation to Southern Africa.[1] It is a different task to reflect on my own involvement. I had been active in the student movement, in the movement against the war in Vietnam, and similar work for some years, before Southern Africa became the focus of my attention. I remember being part of a campaign in Heidelberg in 1968, aimed at alerting people to the colonial wars in what were then the Portuguese colonies of Angola, Mozambique and Guinea-Bissau. That was my first stint of solidarity work with national liberation movements in Southern Africa.

In 1979, after completing my PhD, I got my first job as Executive Secretary of the *Informationsstelle Südliches Afrika* (Information Service Southern Africa) in Bonn, popularly known as ISSA.[2] That catapulted me into intense work in 'counter-information', writing articles for a monthly magazine and publishing solidarity literature, all efforts devoted to making the West German public aware of the reality of apartheid and colonialism, to propagating the aims of the national liberation struggles and the overwhelming case for majority rule, and to helping activists in the local chapters of a whole range of organisations to strengthen their hand when they had to argue their case during public events, as well as in everyday life. The move turned out to be much more decisive than I had thought when I started the job. Even though I took

---

1 R. Kössler and H. Melber (2002) *Globale Solidarität? Eine Streitschrift*. Frankfurt am Main: Brandes and Apsel. R. Kössler and H. Melber, 'The West German solidarity movement with the liberation struggle in Southern Africa. A (self-) critical retrospective', in Engel, U. and Kappel, R. (eds) *Germany's Africa Policy Revisited. Interests, images and incrementalism*. I also profited from perusing under the auspices of AACRLS, the archives of the German Anti-Apartheid Movement (Anti-Apartheid Bewegung, henceforth, AAB), now housed at Archiv für Alternatives Schrifttum (AFAS) in Duisburg. My task was to identify materials of potential relevance to the National Archives of Namibia. I could not carry out complete archival research, but this work has strengthened my insight immensely. Thanks to Jürgen Bacia at AFAS for his willing assistance and cooperation. After this text had been written, Hans-Georg Schleicher and I interviewed people who had been involved in solidarity work with the Namibian liberation struggle. These interviews were conducted in late 2010 and early 2011 under the auspices of AACRLS and are available at the National Archives of Namibia, file AACRLS.304.
2 ISSA website: <www.issa-bonn.org>; see also the journal website <http://www.afrika-sued.org/home/> {last accessed 6 May 2013}.

on a university appointment after barely a year, as a board member, I have remained close to ISSA ever since. In the capacity of a researcher and writer of scholarly as well as more journalistic contributions, I have followed developments in the region during the last three decades. In this way, my professional life has been closely enmeshed with my commitment to solidarity, and has remained so to this day. It is from this perspective that I would like to offer the following recollections and reflections.

When approaching the West German solidarity movement, one has to take note of a situation that today is hardly imaginable. In the divided Germany, official attitudes towards the anti-colonial struggles and national liberation differed starkly. The same was true of the presence of members and representatives of liberation movements. While in East Germany (GDR), support for liberation struggles was state sponsored and advertised as meritorious and a contribution to the future development of socialism and world peace, in the West it meant confronting your own government about collaborating with the perpetrators of apartheid and the last stalwarts of colonialism, and to be engaged in an uphill campaign for a reversal of those official attitudes (for more on the GDR see Winrow, 1990). As my experience is limited to the latter situation, my account is pointedly from a West German perspective. It leaves out what happened in East Germany, although the presence of the German Democratic Republic was an important reality that conditioned aspects of solidarity work in the West, not least amongst them recurrent insinuations that activists in West Germany were being paid or sponsored by the GDR. Of course, this was nothing new to those who had gone through the exciting years of the student rebellion of the late 1960s (Thomas, 2003). The student movement and left wing mobilisation in general were often accused of being traitors, or at least of inadvertently pursuing the aims of the enemy, epitomised in the routine quip encountered in street discussions, 'Why don't you go over there,' that is, to the GDR.

In this way, the solidarity movement that formed during the early 1970s, with respect to Southern Africa, profited on the one hand, from a social and political mobilisation that was unprecedented in post-World War II Western Germany, and on the other hand, had to operate in a difficult and, at times, even hostile environment. This was due in large measure to divided public opinion about Apartheid. There were certainly plenty of opponents of apartheid in West Germany, but there was not the level of public outcry that was found, for instance, in Sweden. For all its unquestionable impact, the broad anti-apartheid movement remained largely restricted to small committed circles and organisations of a few hundred members at best. A clear distance between activists and official West German politics always existed. In some situations, there was open confrontation. On several occasions, SWAPO accused the West German Government of being directly involved in efforts to destabilise the movement (Kössler and Melber 2002, p. 310).

Who were the people that came together and worked for solidarity with liberation struggles in Southern Africa? The membership of the broad anti-apartheid movement was drawn from roughly three main social groups. First, there were existing political activists. People who had been involved in the student movement of the late 1960s and during the early 1970s started to move into professional life, many of them becoming teachers, who tried to make an impact on the educational system and the outlook of the younger generation. At the same time, a considerable number were drawn into newly founded organisations that donned the mantle of the Communist Party, but who, regardless of their quite sectarian politics, also developed a fair degree of activity in the broad field of Third World solidarity. Yet another strand of solidarity with the struggles in South(ern) Africa was represented by the West German African Studies Association, which on various occasions intervened in public debate (VAD, 1986).

A second important contingent of people who got involved in the solidarity movement came from the churches. To some extent, church organisations were involved in fund raising and also in development projects, but to this must be added a serious re-orientation of missionary societies. With reference to Namibia in particular, the Rhenish Mission (now United Evangelical Mission) had, by the early 1960s, started to revise their paternalist (and even racist) positions and began to come out clearly as opponents of apartheid at the side of their Namibian counterparts. Pastor Siegfried Groth, for example, worked in SWAPO's camps in Zambia and was the Secretary for Human Rights at the United Evangelical Mission in Wuppertal (Torreguitar, 2009, p. 264). A third group were returning development workers who had first-hand experience of what was going on, particularly in the frontline states of the day, Zambia and Tanzania. Of course, there was considerable overlap between all three of these groups.

Organised forms of solidarity with Southern Africa first took the shape of local committees, while on the national scale, a group worked in particular on Mozambique, Angola and Guinea-Bissau. One of the earlier formations was the church-based group, Mainzer Arbeitskreis Südliches Afrika (Mainz Working-Group on Southern Africa, MAKSA), which was instrumental in founding the Anti-Apartheid Bewegung (AAB) – the Anti-Apartheid Movement – in 1974. In the context of the Cold War, even activism against the apartheid and racist polities of South Africa was labelled subversive, with one publication claiming: 'The Anti-Apartheid Movement (AAB) with headquarters in Bonn, is also a recently founded communist-inspired front organization' (Drachkovitch and Gann, 1979, p. 149).

Some years earlier, returning development workers had founded the Information Centre on Southern Africa (ISSA), which published a journal and books; sustained efforts to work with interested journalists in the media, and aimed at providing 'counter-information' to confront the highly biased mainstream media coverage. The body still exists and continues to publish a bi-monthly magazine on the region. A further grouping was aligned to various sub-organisations of the Maoist groups that had issued from the student movement. By the 1980s, these had largely disappeared, but there were a number of local groups with a Southern Africa concern who specifically objected to the line taken by the AAB, which focused on the ANC and SWAPO, disregarding, they argued, other movements and in particular, the Black Consciousness Movement. However, by and large a mainstream had been established by the late 1970s.

Third World solidarity in Western Germany has, with some foundation, often been criticised for its volatility. The real mass movement was the protest against the Vietnam war (Klimke, 2009). In other contexts, people committed their energy to changing places and regions and transferred their commitment when the open struggle was over, or when the prospects for a socialist transformation of society that was seen as the central aim of liberation movements, visibly floundered. Good examples are Vietnam itself, Chile, Grenada and, to some extent, Nicaragua. Southern Africa was unique because of the tenacity of apartheid and the long-term perspective this required of those who saw a need for solidarity action with those fighting the racist regime. In Western Germany, this and other factors, contributed towards the formation of a movement rather numerically limited, but which in part at least, developed a high level of quasi-professional expertise, in particular in uncovering clandestine cooperation between the West German government and the Apartheid Regime. Along with the great dedication of members when it came to taking public action, this meant that regardless of the comparatively low numbers, the movement could make an impact. However, at no time could the broad German anti-apartheid movement muster the mass support that swept 15 000 people into Trafalgar Square in London on the occasion of the Sharpeville Massacre in 1960, or the crowds that could continue to be roused at important turning points of the struggle (Lodge, 2011, p. 237). Neither could it count on a government strongly supportive of the liberation struggle, as in the Nordic countries and above all, in Sweden (Sellström, 2002). However, the movement made its impact, not least by painstaking research into the murkier dimensions of West German–South African relations.

Solidarity movements in Western Germany had routinely found themselves at loggerheads with the powers that be, for instance, accusing the government of collaborating within NATO structures with the Portuguese dictatorship in its war against liberation movements in Mozambique, Angola and Guinea-Bissau in the 1960s and early 1970s (Madureira, 2011, p. 284). There was a trajectory leading from this to a closer look at how the Cultural Agreement between Bonn and Pretoria worked (Anti-Apartheid Bewegung, 1984).

The Agreement served as a conduit for scientific knowledge and know-how, and so the first and arguably most incisive and remarkable campaign stemming from this constellation was that against military-nuclear collaboration between the two governments. This was not merely a public campaign with meetings, billboards and the occasional demonstration. Uncovering what both governments desperately wished to keep within the closet called for a campaign to uncover and make public the secret agreements that had been made between West Germany and the Apartheid Regime. This took a lot of hard work and study as well as ingenuity, carried out mainly under the auspices of the AAB. A few people started to be called to international conferences, in particular those staged by the UN, to testify, but they also ran a good chance of being roughly handled by deeply unsympathetic police when they took the issue onto the streets. A big international congress staged in Bonn late in 1978 helped to publicise the issue and forced the hand of the then social-liberal government to the point that they tried to disprove the allegation by publishing a glossy brochure. Today there can be little doubt that the government was covering up the extent of what amounted to economic and also military support for South Africa, while accusing its critics of lies and fabrications.

During the 1980s, the West German banks became the focus of AAB activity, since even in the face of widespread disinvestment by other actors in the international banking system, large West German banks continued to finance the Apartheid Regime (Kössler and Melber, 2006, p. 122). This support was instrumental in giving the regime another lease of life to continue its war in northern Namibia and southern Angola, as well as in the townships across the country. Activists investigated and publicised these loans, and formed human carpets, lying down on the pavement in front of the banking buildings, so that their fellow citizens would literally stumble over the facts that were meant to remain concealed from them. Another campaign advocated against buying the 'fruits of apartheid', calling for a consumer boycott against South African grapes, oranges, apples, etc. Carried out in a large measure by church women, it certainly had a significant impact on people's awareness of how they were complicit in supporting apartheid in their daily lives, even though the campaign might not have hurt very much economically.

When one sits back today and recalls those rather shabby offices, crammed full of papers and files, where people on sometimes quite symbolic salaries were running their small organisation, preparing for action, organising seminars, networking within the country and with representatives of liberation movements or like-minded organisations abroad, researching and writing articles and sometimes books and also publishing them along with journals, lobbying potentially sympathetic deputies and doing a number of other things as well, it may be said that what was achieved, most of the time on a shoestring and constantly under financial duress, attests to the energy and dedication of those involved.

Most of the groups specifically focusing on Southern Africa had their head offices in Bonn, then the seat of government, and AAB, the largest organisation, had a fair number of chapters across the country, as well as in West Berlin. ISSA on the other hand, functioned as a service organisation, providing information and materials for the broader movement and trying to cater for the needs of various groups, even if these had arguments over policy matters among themselves. There were other organisations coordinating local groups that dissented from the AAB; local church and trade union bodies committed to solidarity work, as well as some NGOs such as Terre des Hommes or Amnesty International who, within their framework, had specialised groups. During the 1980s there were trade union activities too, most notably by the national federation (DGB) and the metal workers' union (IG Metall), in support of the burgeoning trade union movement in South Africa. In the late 1980s, the teachers' union, GEW, established a special secretariat 'Education against Apartheid' as a means to channel relevant teaching materials on a national scale (Helbig and Melber, 1988). The activities of church academies and virtually continuous reporting by the Protestant churches Evangelical Press Service (epd) also deserve mention.

All this said, one might ask: 'But what about Namibia in all this activity?' Certainly, South Africa as the occupying power was likely to be the main target of protest, and the illegal occupation of its colonised neighbour could be seen as just one more item on the long list of apartheid's crimes and transgressions. In the final analysis, the enemy was apartheid, and the primary objective of the solidarity movement had to be to assist as much as possible in eradicating it. However, this reasoning required that Namibia should by no means be subsumed under South Africa and, within the solidarity movement, this certainly never happened. On account of the very limited personal and material resources of the movement and its organisations, however, the focus on South Africa as the strategic core of the regional problem appeared quite natural.

A number of activities were organised that specifically addressed Namibia. From the mid-1970s onwards, a 'Namibia week' took place annually, involving information, maybe some cultural events and round trips by the representatives of SWAPO. Up until the early 1980s, West Germany was covered by the SWAPO representative in Stockholm, and it was only in the early 1980s that a SWAPO office was established in Bonn (Sellström, 2002, p. 259). This made liaison a lot easier and to some extent enabled people in the solidarity movement to cooperate more closely. At the same time, a number of German-speaking SWAPO members who lived in West Germany cooperated with the office or were employed there. This forged a particular relationship in connecting solidarity work with a small, but active, minority of German-speakers in Namibia who either sided with the liberation movement outright or who advocated speedy, internationally legitimate independence, in stark contrast to South African-sponsored attempts at unilateral solutions.

In terms of official politics, the specific relationship between Namibia and West Germany was reflected very differently. The official position was based on a number of issues to do with the presence of a German-speaking settler community in Namibia. West Germany maintained a consulate in Windhoek on the basis that, as it argued in 1980, there were as many as 20 000 West German passport holders living in Namibia (Legum, 1980, p. 93). As had been the case from 1920 under its predecessors, the West German government continued to provide support for the German school system in Namibia (Melber, 1981; Helbig, 1990). An important element consisted in sending teachers and annually dispatching a small commission to administer the certified West German secondary school diploma (*Abitur*), which would enable graduates to study at West German universities. Members of the solidarity movement pointed out that such a practice violated the proclaimed cultural boycott which was meant to put pressure on the Apartheid Regime, and which, of course, was also meant to apply to occupied Namibia. The West German consulate in Windhoek was eventually closed down in 1977 after much clamouring and protest, but the support for the schools continued and indeed has continued in a revised form after Namibian independence.[3] These were probably the most important ways in which official West Germany conveyed to German speakers in Namibia a sense that they were considered 'part of the fold', an appeal that they eagerly responded to.

Quite different activities in the cultural field also deserve mention here. The Namibia Project, based at Bremen University, cooperated closely with the United Nations Institute for Namibia (UNIN), then based in Lusaka, which at the time was thought to provide the core of a future university in independent Namibia and formed cadres and experts under the purview of SWAPO. The Namibia Project cooperated closely with the SWAPO office in Bonn as well as with AAB, and in a few publication ventures with ISSA. In a remarkable single-handed initiative, Werner Hillebrecht, who later became the Director of the National Archives of Namibia, toured around Western Europe to glean from library catalogues publications relevant to Namibia, which formed the

---

3   G. Wellmer, 'Background Paper on Relations between the Federal Republic of Germany and Namibia as occupied by the armed forces of South Africa' *International Seminar on The Role of Transnational Corporations in Namibia,* Washington, DC 29 November-2 December, 1982.

beginnings of a national bibliography and developed into what is now the Namlit Data Base.[4]

It is remarkable that in the solidarity work with Namibia, the country's past under German colonial rule did not figure very prominently. One important way in which this was taken up concerned local campaigns to try and change the names of streets in some cities that were named after colonial leaders such as Lüderitz, Leutwein and von Trotha, although many streets were only renamed after Namibia achieved its independence in 1990. For example von-Trotha-strasse (the author of the 'extermination order' against the Herero in 1904) in Munich was renamed Hererostrasse in 2006.[5] Although at the time these initiatives did not have much tangible success, they created good opportunities to sensitise the public not only to the colonial past but also to the acute problems and challenges of the present. Similarly in one case, a local group in Münster took exception to a war memorial that memorialised members of a regiment, some of whom had been killed in the genocidal wars in Namibia during the period 1903-1908. At the time, their attempt to add a plaque to the memorial recalling the genocide was rebuffed by the city authorities (Zeller, 2010, p. 72).

One important issue concerned the exploitation of Namibia's natural resources while the country was still illegally occupied by South Africa. Such exploitation had been made illegal in terms of international law by Decree No 1 of the UN Council for Namibia. Solidarity groups demanded time and again that West Germany adhere to this provision, but there was constant concern over violations. The issue became especially serious when the Rössing uranium mine opened because a West German company, Uranit, was one of the three international companies involved in purchasing 'yellowcake' from the mine.[6] The solidarity movement then attempted to link the continued denial of independence to Namibia with the burgeoning movement in West Germany that opposed the building and operation of nuclear power plants. The reasoning was that, on top of installing an extremely hazardous technology, the nuclear power industry in Germany was also abetting the prolongation of colonialism by clearly illegal means.

Even if this line of argument had limited effect, it was connected to changes in West German public debate and in the political landscape that also had an impact on solidarity work with Namibia. When the Green party first entered the Bundestag in 1983, the party at large projected a clearly anti-colonial, anti-apartheid stance. Some of the Green deputies showed intense interest in Third World problems and in Southern Africa in particular. It was therefore not an accident that one of the most important events during the 1980s 'where solidarity with the Namibian liberation struggle was proclaimed' took the form of a public hearing held in 1985 on the initiative of the Greens (ISSA, 1987). This occasion brought representatives of groups working inside Namibia, such as Namibia Peace Plan 435, to Bonn. In particular, however, it castigated the collusion of the West German government in abetting the foot dragging around the issue of Namibian independence, which meant that UN Security Council Resolution 435 eventually took

---

4   Starting points had been provided by Toré Linne Eriksen (1984) and the library and archival collection established with passion by Carl Schlettwein at the Basler Afrika Bibliographien.

5   Afrika-Hamburg *'Renaming colonial street names First overview of initiatives and activists' groups'* 26 January, 2010. Afrika-Hamburg.de <http://www.afrika-hamburg.de/rename.html.> {Accessed on 4th May, 2013}.

6   'Action on Namibia'. 1985. London: *Bulletin of Namibia Support Committee*, p. 48.

more than 11 years to be implemented. The West German government was deeply implicated in this process as one of the five countries in the 'Western Contact Group', which was supposed to implement the resolution (Vergau, 2010). It would have been hard for participants at the conference to imagine that today, the then West German foreign minister, Hans Dietrich Genscher, is honoured in independent Namibia by a long street along the outskirts of Khomasdal and Katutura.

At the time, most participants in the solidarity movement saw little use in cooperating with their government on issues related to Southern Africa. This was also reflected in strong opposition to any development cooperation before Namibia had achieved independence. The only partial exception was funds channelled through the Council of Churches in Namibia. It can therefore be considered symbolic that two members of the Green party, one of them an MP, and both of whom later emerged as quite prominent politicians, topped their visit to the country in 1986 by joining in a pro-independence demonstration in Windhoek, where they were promptly arrested by the South African Police.[7]

From the mid-1980s onwards, people committed to Namibia's solidarity started to be confronted with an issue that has remained a haunting one. At first, reports about the plight of detainees kept by SWAPO in the dungeons at Lubango could be shrugged off easily, since they were publicised in Germany by the International League of Human Rights, a notoriously CIA-sponsored player in the Cold War. I remember this attitude vividly from meetings of the ISSA board, on which I have served since 1980. One may well say that, in hindsight, this was an excuse for not further investigating a problem that, for some at least, shook to the core their commitment to liberation struggles in Southern Africa and beyond. Such an approach of blind loyalty to SWAPO was no longer sustainable when on 'Africa Day' (25 May) 1989, after their repatriation, survivors of the dungeons spoke out publicly in Windhoek and provided incontrovertible proof of the grave human rights violations that had been perpetrated against them (Williams, 2010). The response within the West German solidarity movement was divided. An early and clear call for open and critical debate had come from Helga and Ludwig Helbig, authors of one of the pioneering popular books in support of the Namibian liberation struggle that busted the 'myth of German Südwest' (Helbig & Helbig, 1983). An outright confrontation rocked the ISSA board. Henning Melber, who had stood out for his SWAPO activism and joined the board in the early 1980s, had gone public about the detainee issue on national TV. At its next meeting, the board was split, both on the proposal to support the publication of a brochure on the detainee issue with other, broadly like-minded NGOs, and on the issue of providing at least symbolical support to Melber, who was about to return to Namibia, after having been banned from the country for 15 years and who now faced uncertain prospects, even though eventually the concerns raised proved unfounded.

The detainee issue sparked one of the few intensive political debates that occurred within the solidarity movement with Southern Africa after the demise of the Maoist groups in the late 1970s. In a way it focused a wider and simmering controversy about the agenda of those involved in international solidarity. The controversy found

---

7   'International Newsbriefing on Namibia', 1986. *Bulletin of Namibia Support Committee*, No. 41, p.73.

expression in repeated joint meetings of the boards of AAB and ISSA about the nature of their cooperation, and particularly the focus and positions to be taken by the jointly published journal. Here, the issue boiled down to whether to give priority to the stances of SWAPO and ANC as the primary liberation organisations in Namibia and South Africa, as advocated by more directly action-oriented AAB members, or to provide more critical and possibly, also distanced analyses, including problems and contradictions that were deemed in the end also to be more credible to an interested public. This longrunning tension had never reached breaking point, but the ex-detainee issue provided a much sharper edge. The basic issue was who to side with, and for what reasons.

One argument was that loyalty to an organisation and indeed, to its leadership took precedence, in this case, to SWAPO in exile. Activists felt they should, as Pastor Groth put it, maintain a 'wall of silence' to protect the movement (1995). In the event, such loyalty prevented the solidarity movement taking action that seemed appropriate from the other stance: to address the severe violations of human rights as a departure from the very principles that had formed the basis for activists' commitment to the liberation struggle and the vision of justice, freedom and human rights that it stood for. To this distress was added deep consternation about what appeared as obduracy in long-time, trusted, and valued colleagues and comrades. ISSA's next annual general meeting was the best attended ever and featured intense debate. The decision to address painful issues openly, like that of the ex-detainees, and to follow the trajectory of liberation organisations turning into ruling parties from a critical position, not giving up solidarity but insisting on the fundamental principles that had defined the notion of 'liberation' in the first place, prevailed. It has guided the NGO's work ever since. In a way, one might see a parallel in a Namibian context with the path taken on a much grander scale with many more risks by *The Namibian* newspaper, founded in the mid-1980s as a means of providing counter-information against South Africa and to 'speak to power', without succumbing to the allure of simply becoming uncritical of those in power once the aim of independence had been achieved. SWAPO imposed a ten-year ban on Government advertising in the newspaper because of its critical reporting, a ban that was only lifted in 2011.[8]

To be sure, the AAB board also addressed questions about the detainee issue to the SWAPO leadership. There was genuine concern, but the dilemma and tensions within the solidarity movement were resolved by trying to keep the discussion within the inner circles and not attempting to start a more far-reaching and public debate. When Namibia's independence was achieved at last, conditions for solidarity work in Germany also changed. Of course, in Germany unification between East and West (or the absorption of the East by the West on voluntary grounds) was by now an obvious course of events, consummated later in 1990. Still, differences persisted, certainly in the background of experience and personal contacts that would form the basis of continued solidarity work under changed circumstances and the institutional settings as some parastatal structures from the GDR transformed into private societies.

In the West, the attempt to set up an umbrella body for cooperation with Namibia, as had been done before in the cases of Mozambique and Zimbabwe, as well as in limited ways of Angola, proved rather short-lived. 'Koordination Namibia' lasted only a few

---

8   'Cabinet ends boycott', *The Namibian*, 28 August 2011.

months. This does not preclude the acknowledgement that various local initiatives have been created, frequently in the form of school partnerships and also partnerships between church congregations. Clearly, these are different forms of relating to Namibia in the post-colonial period than simply support for the former liberation movement.

At the time of Namibian independence, AAB membership was at a high plateau of well over 1 000, but this began to drop drastically shortly after people started to believe that apartheid had been overcome. This was quite contrary to the view, repeated many times during the years of support for the liberation struggle, that independence or the attainment of majority rule would imply a solution for the problems and contradictions created by racism and colonialism, but rather at best, the beginning of such a solution. Because of this, the argument continued, it would be all the more necessary to persist in a commitment to further beneficial development in the interests of the disadvantaged victims of colonial and minority rule. From this premise, the reasoning branched off in two different, but not mutually exclusive, directions.

True to its commitment prioritising practical action, AAB now shifted its focus to support specific development projects in Southern Africa by campaigning for targeted donations and, in the process, informing the German public about the practical and social issues involved. This shift of emphasis went along with a change of name. While preserving its acronym, the organisation was now styled as the Southern Africa Coalition for Action (*Afrika süd Aktionsbündnis*). In the ISSA tradition it was felt that continued commitment should include critical monitoring of social and political developments in the region. This has remained one of the main tasks ISSA continues to pursue, chiefly through a journal now published on a bi-monthly basis. While AAB was dissolved in 2001, a coordinating body continues to exist, bringing together small local groups as well as individuals that set themselves the task of providing information as well as support for civic groups or community projects, as far as their limited means allow.

It would be a misconception, however, to see a once lively and strenuous solidarity movement sustained over some two decades merely petering out. There are also new initiatives. Since the late 1990s, a number of cities have become interested in investigating and publicising the specific links that exist between such places and German colonialism. These include particular localities such as street names, memorials, graves of more or less prominent colonial soldiers or administrators, centres of missionary societies or locales of important events, to name just a few. In some cases, this has resulted in public initiatives to re-name von Trotha-Strasse or Lüderitzstrasse or to change the message conveyed by memorials, which was most notably effected in 1996 when the German Colonial Memorial in Bremen, a huge elephant made from brick, was officially re-dedicated, in the presence of President Sam Nujoma, as an Anti-Colonial memorial (Maischak, 2013, p. 160).

These initiatives, which generally style themselves as 'post-colonial', such as *Hamburg postkolonial* or *Freiburg postkolonial*, received a considerable boost in 2004, on the occasion of the centennial of the colonial genocide in Namibia. To the surprise of some, what may well be termed public amnesia regarding Germany's past as a colonial power is now at least perforated by a range of commemorative activities throughout the year and beyond. This heightened awareness, if not on a mass scale or by the public at large, certainly took place in interested circles. In this situation, postcolonial initiatives served to make people aware that colonialism was not just something that had happened a hundred years ago, but that its legacy surrounds them still. Namibia has now become a special focus of such activities. One reason may well have been that the country stands out among the former colonies by virtue of the fact that some groups very energetically raise and voice their claims for appropriate recognition of past crimes as well as for legitimate reparation for injustice perpetrated in the name and under the authority of the German state (Sarkin, 2008). This has raised awareness among German organisations and institutions who also contribute their local knowledge to concerns such as the repatriation of documents in the context of AACRLS, or tracing and repatriating human remains that have been brought to Germany from all over the world, including Namibia, to serve as objects for the studies that eventually contributed towards a racist ideology parading as science. Ultimately, the success or failure of restoration initiatives will depend on negotiations between the two governments. Nevertheless, civil society bodies on both sides are even now demonstrating that they can provide indispensable support. Such common concern and the cooperation it entails can, for all the difficulties or organisational hiccups, help to establish new ties between Namibians and Germans sharing the same broad concerns, if from different perspectives.

All this points to a continuation of what has been an uphill struggle all along. This was underlined when, in late September 2011, a large delegation from Namibia arrived in Berlin to receive the first contingent of 20 skulls that had been deported to Germany in colonial times. Contrary to expectations, the German government refused to hand over the skulls officially to the Namibian Minister who headed the delegation. German officialdom slighted the delegation in other ways; at the memorial service, held at a church in central Berlin by Bishop Zephania Kameeta, all the seats reserved for German officials remained empty. Namibian delegates later acknowledged the support they received from various civil society bodies in Berlin, including Afro-German initiatives and post-colonial groups. However, at the handing-over ceremony, the Deputy Foreign Minister failed to find words of apology and acknowledgement for the colonial genocide in 1904-08, provoking angry protests by German activists. The result was the biggest media coverage for an issue related to Namibia for many years, but also an *impasse* in a constructive approach towards restitution issues that continues to today.[9]

The provocative attitude taken by the German government concerning the extremely sensitive issue of human remains must be linked to the incontrovertible fact that Namibia remains and will remain much less important to Germany than Germany is to Namibia. To some extent, this reproduces the colonial relationship and current global power differentials. At the same time, there is also the huge difference of population size that contributes to this situation. For those in Germany who feel they need to continue their commitment of solidarity with Namibia, or even start to get involved,

---

9   More extensively, M. Biwa (2012), *'Weaving the Past with Threads of Memory.' Narratives and Commemorations of the colonial war in southern Namibia* (PhD thesis, University of the Western Cape, 2012); R. Kössler (2012), 'Facing Postcolonial Entanglement and the Challenge of Responsibility: Actor Constellation between Namibia and Germany' in *Reconciliation, Civil Society, and the Politics of Memory. Transnational Initiatives in the 20th and 21st Century*, ed. by B. Schwelling (Bielefeld: transcript, 2012) pp. 303-309; 'Germany and genocide in Namibia' *Pamabzuka News*, Special Issue, Nr. 577, March 2012). Available from <http://www.pambazuka.org/en/issue/577> {Accessed 6 May 2013}.

this means a continuing struggle to try and alert their compatriots to issues that – rightly or wrongly – appear to them as marginal to their experience. Postcolonial initiatives can contribute to change just this. Such work however must also challenge a perception of Namibia that is likely to gain ground in Germany: the image of the country as a prime tourist destination with breath-taking landscapes and exotic animals, while humans feature in marginal roles or as exotic exhibits, such as Ovahimba or San (Papen, 2005). Such images are conveyed increasingly in popular culture in Germany as on TV soap operas or in cheap sentimental films set on Namibian farms and centering on the lives of German-speakers. While they may contribute towards attracting tourists on the look-out for just that, they are of little help in furthering mutual understanding or even reconciliation. Those aims remain an objective for committed, hard work and that struggle is far from over.

References

Anti-Apartheid Bewegung (1984) *Cancel the Cultural Agreement with South Africa!* Bonn: AAB.

Biwa, M. (2012) *'Weaving the Past with Threads of Memory.' Narratives and Commemorations of the colonial war in southern Namibia*, PhD thesis, University of the Western Cape, Cape Town.

Bulletin of Namibia Support Committee (1985) 'Action on Namibia'. London.

Bulletin of Namibia Support Committee (1986) 'International Newsbriefing on Namibia', No. 41.

Drachkovitch, M. M. and Gann, L. H. (1979) *Yearbook on International Communist Affairs.* Stanford: Hoover Institution on War, Revolution and Peace, Stanford University.

Eriksen, T. L. with Moorsom, R. (1985) *The Political Economy of Namibia: An Annotated Critical Bibliography*. Uppsala: Scandinavian Institute of African Studies.

Groth, S. (1995) *Namibia - the Wall of Silence: the Dark Days of the Liberation Struggle.* Translated from German by Hugh Beyer. Wuppertal: Peter Hammer.

Helbig, L. (1990). *Report on the German Schools in Namibia.* Bremen: Centre for African Studies.

Helbig, L. and Helbig, H. (1983) *Mythos Deutsch-Südwest. Namibia und die Deutschen.* Weinheim: Beltz.

Helbig, L. and Melber, H. (1988) *Erziehung gegen Apartheid. Südafrika und Namibia im Unterricht. Eine kommentierte Materialübersicht*. Frankfurt/Main: Gewerkschaft Erziehung und Wissenschaft.

ISSA (1987) *Im Brennpunkt: Namibia und die Bundesrepublik Deutschland. Eine Dokumentation der Öffentlichen Anhörung der Fraktion die grünen im bundestag in Zusammenarbeit mit der Informationsstelle Südliches Afrika (ISSA), 16./17. September 1985*. Bonn: ISSA.

Klimke, M. (2009) *The Other Alliance: Student Protest in West Germany and the United States in the Global Sixties*. Princeton: Princeton University Press.

Kössler, R. (2012) 'Germany and genocide in Namibia', *Pamabzuka News,* Special Issue, Nr. 577, March. Available from http://www.pambazuka.org/en/issue/577 {Accessed 6 May 2013}.

Kössler, R. (2012) 'Facing Postcolonial Entanglement and the Challenge of Responsibility: Actor Constellation between Namibia and Germany'. In Schwelling, B. (ed.) *Reconciliation, Civil Society, and the Politics of Memory. Transnational Initiatives in the 20th and 21st Century*. Bielefeld: transcript.

Kössler, R. and Melber, H. (2002) *Globale Solidarität? Eine Streitschrift*. Frankfurt am Main: Brandes and Apsel.

Kössler, R. and Melber, H. (2002) 'The West German solidarity movement with the liberation struggle in Southern Africa. A (self-) critical retrospective'. In Engel, U. and Kappel, R. (eds) *Germany's Africa Policy Revisited. Interests, images and incrementalism*. 2nd edition Berlin: Lit. Verlag.

Legum, C. (1980) *African Contemporary Record: Annual Survey and Documents*, (11). London: Africana Publishing Company.

Lodge, T. (2011) *Sharpeville: An Apartheid Massacre and its Consequences*. Oxford: Oxford University Press.

Maduereira, L. (2011) 'Kalashnikovs, not Coca-Cola, Bringing Self-determination to Angola: The Two Germanys, Lusophone Africa and the Rhetoric of Colonial Difference'. In Volker, M. L. and Salama, M. (eds) *German Colonialism: Race, the Holocaust and Post-war Germany*. New York: Columbia University Press.

Maischak, L. (2013) *German Merchants in the Nineteenth Century Atlantic*. Cambridge: Cambridge University Press.

Melber, H. (1981) 'Deutsche Privatschulen in Namibia und deren Bedeutung für gesellschaftlichen Wandel', *Die Deutsche Schule*, 73 (7/8).

Papen, U. (2005) 'Exclusive, Ethno and Eco: Representations of Culture and Nature in Tourism Discourses in Namibia'. In: Jaworsky, A. and Pritchard, A. (eds) *Discourse, Communication and Tourism*. Clevedon: Channel View Publications.

Sarkin, J. (2008) *Colonial Genocide and Reparations Claims in the 21st Century: The Socio-legal Context of Claims under International Law by the Herero against Germany for Genocide in Namibia, 1904-1908*. Westport: Greenport Publishing.

Sellström, T. (2002) *Sweden and National Liberation in Southern Africa. Vol. 2*. Uppsala: Nordic Africa Institute.

The Namibian, 'Cabinet ends boycott', 28 August 2011.

Thomas, N. (2003) *Protest Movements in 1960s West Germany: A Social History of Dissent and Democracy*. Oxford and New York: Berg.

Torreguitar, E. (2009). *National Liberation Movement in Office: Forging Democracy with African Adjectives in Namibia*. European University Studies (567), Peter Lang.

VAD (Vereinigung von Afrikanisten in Deutschland) (1986) *Südafrika zum Frieden zwingen. Eine Denkschrift der Vereinigung von Afrikanisten in Deutschland e.V.* Bremen: VAD.

Vergau, H.-J. (2010) *Negotiating the Freedom of Namibia: The Diplomatic Achievement of the Western Contact Group*. Basel: Basel Afrika Bibliographien.

Wellmer, G. (1982) 'Background Paper on Relations between the Federal Republic of Germany and Namibia as occupied by the armed forces of South Africa'. *International Seminar on The Role of Transnational Corporations in Namibia*, Washington, DC 29 November-2 December, 1982.

Williams, C. (2010) 'Remember Cassinga? An Exhibition of Photographs and Histories', *Kronos* 36 (1).

Winrow, G. (1990) *The Foreign Policy of the GDR in Africa.* Cambridge: Cambridge University Press.

Zeller, J. (2010) 'Decolonisation of the Public Space? (Post) Colonial Remembrance in Germany'. In Lindner, U. (ed.) *Hybrid Cultures: Nervous States. Britain and Germany in a (Post) Colonial World.* Amsterdam: Rodopi.

Archival sources

National Archives of Namibia (NAN)

AACRLS Archives of Anti-Colonial Resistance and Liberation Struggle

AACRLS.304. Interviews by Hans-Georg Schleicher and Reinhart Kössler with people who had been involved in solidarity work with the Namibian liberation struggle, conducted in late 2010 and early 2011 under the auspices of AACRLS.

17 Finnish Solidarity with the Liberation Struggle of Namibia: A Documentation Project[1]

Pekka Peltola

Freedom is Seldom a Gift

Namibia's independence was won primarily by the efforts of Namibians themselves. Acknowledging this, it is also important to remember that the liberation struggle of Namibians took place outside its borders as well: it started in Cape Town, spread to the United Nations in New York, established itself in Tanzania, then in Zambia and Angola. The diplomatic, political and armed struggle led by SWAPO could be fought only with the material, political, and other support given by many governments and non-governmental organisations. Thousands of people dedicated themselves to supporting the fight against apartheid and for a free and independent Namibia.

In order to write a comprehensive history of the struggle, a rich database documenting the mainly selfless efforts rendered by solidarity activists in other countries is necessary. For this reason Finland has contributed by collecting documentary evidence of the work done in Finland or by Finns for the struggle and, therefore, the initiative of the Archives of Anti-Colonial Resistance and the Liberation Struggle (AACRLS) project was welcomed in Finland, where a committee was formally established for that purpose in 2004 as a part of the Namibian effort to save this history.

Finnish Motives

Finland is far away from Southern Africa both in kilometres and in cultural terms and, therefore, a brief description and analysis of Finnish motives for helping the liberation struggle is necessary.

It is a well-known fact that Finnish evangelical Lutheran missionaries arrived in Owamboland in northern Namibia in 1870. A large number of church members back

---

[1] In this chapter, an overview of the work of AACRLS-Finland is described in some technical detail in order to help other, similar, projects when they contemplate solutions to some essential and costly issues. Discussion of relevant ethics, privacy, copyright, and some other politically laden issues are discussed in my paper Peltola (2009) 'Picking up the international pieces of struggle: Finnish support to the liberation struggle in Namibia and Mozambique', presented at the Nordic Documentation Project Concluding Workshop, Pretoria, South Africa, 26-27 November, 2009. All the members and project workers of AACRLS-Finland also contributed to both papers.

in Finland supported their work, support that has continued to this day. The long-term interest created through this missionary work, and through the family networks, spread information about this part of Africa to several generations of Finns. Missionaries visited schools and told their stories about 'Ambomaa' to many schoolchildren. They learned to speak Oshiwambo, and Finnish missionaries actually produced the first textbooks on the language and its different dialects and their grammar, and translated books (especially the Bible) into Oshiwambo (Buys and Nambala, 2003). They collected folklore, genealogies, songs, and proverbs in Oshiwambo, as well as artefacts, and they took photographs. The Emil Liljeblad collection from 1930 to 1931 covering this area is a dormant treasure, consisting of 5 000 pages of Owambo history, which otherwise might have been forgotten (Simola, 2001, p. 196).

Interest in the affairs of then South West Africa did not exist outside the activities of the church before the 1960s, when leftist ideas gathered momentum in the universities. Some students became aware of the evils of apartheid, started to spread information about it, and to organise a campaign against it. The first organisation against apartheid was the South Africa Committee, founded in 1965 with support from students and some trade unions. Activities included writing articles to the student press, helping travelling SWAPO emissaries, like Emil Appolus and Andreas Shipanga, to get publicity, and organising solidarity meetings. One very important and significant contribution of the student organisations was financing the studies in Finland of an exiled Namibian student, Nicky Iyambo, who graduated in both political science and medicine. He arrived in Finland in late 1964 and represented SWAPO for many years both in Finland and Scandinavia (Soiri and Peltola, 1999, p.120).

At the time, the Finnish government was not interested in anything relating to Southern Africa, other than the commercial interests of the Finnish paper industry in South Africa. The missionaries also had mixed feelings towards the new nationalist movement, SWAPO. Some were against, and some in favour of the liberation struggle. Then a new leader of the Missionary Society came onto the scene: Professor, later Archbishop Mikko Juva, who had visited Owamboland in 1961 and some years later personally financed Sam Nujoma's visit to Finland. By the end of the 1960s, Mikko Juva's firm guidance had shifted the position of the Missionary Society in favour of the liberation struggle waged by SWAPO. He had to use all his authority, but was supported by other strong personalities like Aarne Hartikainen and Rev. Mikko Ihamäki (Soiri and Peltola, 1999, pp. 59-63).

International influence and student pressure brought about a policy change in Finnish foreign politics. Having received, among others, Amilcar Cabral, the leader of PAIGC from Guinea-Bissau and Cape Verde, the President of Finland, Urho Kekkonen, began directly supporting a number of liberation struggles, including that of SWAPO, in 1973 (Soiri and Peltola, 1999, p. 19).

The Finnish government had its own reasons, too, for acting against apartheid. Its main concern was to keep its distance from its powerful neighbour, the Soviet Union, without offending her, so the Finnish Government wanted to be active in the United Nations and to participate in activities together with other Nordic countries: Sweden, Norway, Iceland, and Denmark. Sweden was the leading nation in this group and therefore Sweden's early initiatives to support opposition against apartheid carried weight. Other factors solidified Finnish public support: the horrific images that circulated after the Cassinga massacre of 5 May 1978, South African policies that flouted UN Security Council Resolution 435 of September 1978, and the unilaterally organised election in South West Africa in December 1978. It became increasingly clear that the South African occupation was in contravention of international law. The nomination of Martti Ahtisaari as the UN High Commissioner for Namibia in 1976 meant that Finland became directly concerned in opposing these negative developments in Namibia (Odugu, 2012, p. 213).

Going Strong

It was in this atmosphere during the early 1970s that many non-governmental organisations took up projects in support of SWAPO. The Finnish Namibian Society, Africa Committee of Finland, Espoo Namibia Project, National Union of Students, and individual student associations were prominent. Scholarships were granted; for instance, Leake Hangala, Elia and Maria Kaakunga, Raimo Kankondi, Kayele M. Kambombo, Joe Nakatana, Kaapanda Shaanika and many others studied and graduated from Finnish universities (Koponen and Heinonen, 2002, p. 21).

Towards the end of the 1970s, trade unions joined the solidarity movement by providing direct, practical, support to SWAPO. The first trade union training workshop was held in 1979 in the SWAPO transit camp in Viana, Angola. In the course of the next year, 22 students came to Finland for a course at the Kiljava Trade Union Institute, where it was decided to increase Finnish support by building the workers training camp in Kwanza Sul settlement; it was later named the Nduuvu Nangolo Trade Union Centre. The school opened in 1983, with the very first school day interrupted by fighting as the battle of Calulo took place nearby (Peltola, 1995, p. 144). Finnish trade union support to the National Union of Namibian Workers (NUNW) continued until independence and long afterwards. Trade unions benefitted from the experience of the missionaries in the training, and a good and effective cooperation was formed between these two large organisations. Almost all Finns belong to either the Lutheran church or a trade union, or to both. Little by little, every political party in Finland announced its support for the liberation struggle. It can be unequivocally stated that the Finnish people strongly supported the struggle for an independent Namibia.

In the light of this, it is only natural that during the 1980s a large number of NGOs actively worked in support of the Namibian liberation struggle. The Workers' Educational Association (WEA) of Finland built a successful brick factory at Kwanza Sul which produced enough fired bricks to construct several hundred small houses (Soiri and Peltola, 1999, p. 120). Doctors like Liisa Taskinen, Merja Saarinen and Birgitta Lång were sent to develop SWAPO's health services in the camps (Lång and Taskinen, 1986). Markku Vesikko started to work for the ANC and, intermittently, for SWAPO, too, whilst Väinö Myllymäki, ('Pumppu-Väiski') drilled water wells for SWAPO in Angola to help ensure that the residents of SWAPO camps had a reliable supply of fresh water (Soiri and Peltola, 1999, p. 140).

The Beginnings of AACRLS

Having heard of the existence of photographs taken by Finnish solidarity workers in Angola during the struggle, the then director of the National Archives of Namibia, Brigitte Lau, made contact and explained that she wanted to add these important historical records to the collection of the National Archives of Namibia. By the latter half of the 1990s it was already clear that the pictures should be provided in a digital form, which would add enormously to their accessibility and safekeeping. Although there was an understanding of initial support from the Finnish Embassy, the initiative remained on hold because of the ongoing construction of new premises for the Archives in Namibia, and other priorities that drained financial resources. However, the preliminary documenting of the Finnish material was completed with the support of the Nordic Africa Institute.

In 2000, the government of Namibia launched a project called 'Archives of the Anti-Colonial Resistance and the Liberation Struggle'. The purpose was to locate and arrange all kinds of documents concerning the liberation struggle of Namibia. In 2004, the AACRLS country committee of Finland was established with membership representing a wide variety of expertise: the Chairman of the Finnish-Namibian Society, who was a former Finnish Evangelical Lutheran Mission (FELM) co-worker in Namibia, Mr. Seppo Kalliokoski, was the chairman. The vice-chairman was a former trade unionist activist, Dr Pekka Peltola, and the secretary was the Director of the Mission Museum of the FELM, Ms Liisa Hovila-Helminen. Other members were Dr Harri Siiskonen, Professor of History at the University of Joensuu, Ms Tuula Haavisto, Information Specialist (2005–2006), Ms Päivikki Karhula, Chief Information Specialist of the Library of Parliament, Dr Ulla-Maija Peltonen, Director of Literary Archives of the Finnish Literature Society, Mr Jukka Pääkkönen, the communication director of the Trade Union Solidarity Centre, SASK, and Dr Minna Saarelma, Director of Publications of FELM. Mr Mikko Helminen, Mr Tommi Lehtonen, Ms Sisko Mattila and Ms Marja Olli served as project workers at various times (Lehtonen and Olli, 2007).

The project was formally located at the Mission Museum, but was an independent unit with the responsibility of organising and financing its own activities. After the establishment of the Country Committee, the Nordic Africa Institute (NAI) was approached for funds to execute the project. The application was accepted, and in October 2005, the Finnish AACRLS Country Committee hired two project workers, Ms Marja Olli and Mr Tommi Lehtonen, to start collecting and digitising relevant material concerning the liberation struggle of Namibia and Finland's role in it.

Activities

Cultural Cooperation Finland–Africa

From 10 to 28 October 2005, the Finnish AACRLS Country Committee organised a seminar in Finland on archival principles, practices and solutions. The purpose of the 90-hour seminar was to give a broad understanding about archival processes in

Finland. The African participants at the seminar were Mr Jade McClune from the National Archives of Namibia, Dr Shekutaamba Väinö Nambala, Director of Finance and Development of the Evangelical Lutheran Church in Namibia, and Dr Ezekiel Alembi from Kenyatta University, Kenya. Mr McClune was the project coordinator of the AACRLS in Namibia and Dr Nambala was a member of the Namibian AACRLS research committee. The director of the seminar was Dr Ulla-Maija Peltonen.

Financed by the Finnish Ministry of Education and the Finnish Literature Society, the seminar was appreciated by the participants, who found it very useful. All the participants agreed that it was necessary to continue cooperation on an international level in the field of various archival issues.[2]

Planning the Work and Organising the Material

After thorough research, the project workers drew up a working plan that they believed would provide a good basis for a long-term digitising project. Because the material that was going to be digitised was quite extensive, creating a good cataloguing system was a vital prerequisite for managing the project successfully, so the initial emphasis was on planning the proper structure for cataloguing.

The Excel-sheet proved to be a useful tool for cataloguing. For describing the material, project workers researched metadata standards like Dublin Core. It was necessary to use international and widely accepted standards for describing because, it was argued, the database would be more accessible and flexible for future users. Using international standards would also allow easier transfer from Excel to a different database.

The first decision was that the default data format should be a TIFF-format for photos and a PDF-format for documents. For photographs there were also separate JPG-files for viewing. PDF-files were scanned in a format that would make it possible to search information from them. The Committee decided to begin the work on the Finnish Evangelical Lutheran Mission Archives, after which the project workers planned to continue digitalisation work on the next archive, based on agreed priority principles.

Scanners and another laptop were delivered in January 2006. The project also acquired one film scanner (Nikon Coolscan V) and one flatbed scanner with an automatic document feeder (HP Scanjet 7650). During a three-month period, project workers scanned about 2 000 pages and 300 slides and photos. Photographs were scanned as TIFF-format with 300 dpi resolution and documents in a PDF-format with 300 dpi resolution. PDFs were scanned as 'searchable' using the scanner's own software so that readers would be able to search the document for key words such as the names of places or people.

The next archival objective was the papers of the Africa Committee of the Finnish Peace Committee. These were not organised at all. Therefore, before selecting the relevant material for describing and scanning, it was necessary to organise the Africa Committee's material according to the People's Archives Classification Scheme. The

---

[2] AACRLS Report on the Nordic-Namibian AACRLS Seminar in Helsinki 7-8 June 2006.

initial organising work took about two months, after which the scanning took a further five weeks.

Next, two personal photograph archives were scanned during the spring of 2006: the archives belonging to the missionaries Mr Matti Seppälä and Ms Helena Kekkonen who had both been actively involved in the Peace Education Institute's project – the 'Namibian Freedom Bus' and other projects.

Nordic-Namibian AACRLS Seminar in Helsinki 2006

The Finnish AACRLS Country Committee, together with the Nordic Africa Institute (NAI), organised a two-day seminar in Helsinki on 7-8 June 2006. The focus of the seminar was sharing experiences with other digitising projects and discussing different technical solutions for digitising documents.

During the seminar different phases of the scanning process were discussed. Dr Bill Minter, in particular, introduced relevant subjects and technical details into the discussion. Together with further discussions with Mr Werner Hillebrecht, the Director of the National Archives of Namibia, this formed the basis on which the project workers re-evaluated our methods, coming to the conclusion that PDFs were not a secure enough format for archival preservation. So the decision was made to create TIFF-files from documents with 300 dpi resolution (using greyscale) as well. Now the scanning and OCR (optical character recognition) was done separately. PDF-files were made from these TIFF-files by using the Readiris Pro 9-program that makes the text searchable. Another change was that the resolution for the scanning of photographs was increased from 300 dpi to 600 dpi.

In July 2006, the project workers acquired the slide and photograph collections of Mr Jukka Pääkkönen and Dr Pekka Peltola, and Mr Raimo Holopainen's photos, all of which were copied from a Kodak photograph CD as well. Work was also carried out in the Finnish Labour Archives where the Espoo-Namibia Committee's archives were catalogued and scanned, as well as the Namibia-related section of the Workers' Education Association's archive, and a large part of the International Solidarity Foundation's archive. The work took two months.

Microfilming and Agreements

At the AACRLS Country Committee's meeting on 6 November 2006, Prof. Harri Siiskonen suggested that a large amount of archival material should be microfilmed, because it is a lot faster than scanning. He reminded the Committee that a similar microfilming project of the Finnish Evangelical Lutheran Mission (FELM) Namibia related collection (documents made before 1938) had been done in the 1980s. Drafts of the agreements for transferring digitalised documents and photographs were made in cooperation with the FELM lawyer, in Finnish. These agreements aimed to protect individuals whose personal data might be in transferred documents.

To learn more about microfilming, project workers visited a microfilming service producing company, Monikko Oy, and the microfilming department of the National

Archives of Finland. These visits convinced us of the merits of the microfilming process compared with digital copies for archiving material that requires long-term preservation. The resources required are also considerably less. This issue was discussed with the director of the National Archives of Finland, Jussi Nuorteva, and it was clear that microfilming the material was the better choice.

Researching the Archives

Some kind of estimate of the material to be microfilmed was needed, and this required research in the archives of SAK (Central Organization of the Finnish Trade Union), SYL (the National Union of University Students in Finland) and the Ministry for Foreign Affairs. The Archives of the Ministry for Foreign Affairs Development Agency (FINNIDA) were not thoroughly researched, but some points can be made. The level of documentation varied widely. There were only brief summaries of the projects in which FINNIDA was merely one of the financing parties in their archives, but those projects in which FINNIDA was more directly involved in planning were documented more thoroughly. A preliminary listing was made, but because the archives of the 1980s were catalogued in an old database system, there was no proper catalogue. One must, therefore, always consult the Ministry's archivist to get access to FINNIDA's 1980s collection.

Archives on SAK's work are at the SAK Archives, also called the Union Archives. The best material seems to be the minutes of the Peace Committee's meetings, but most of them are in Finnish. In these files, the correspondence was alphabetically organised, but it is possible that some of the Namibian-related material is organised under A as Angola, because most of SAK's work took place in the Kwanza Sul and Viana refugee camps in Angola.

The archives concerning the development cooperation of the Union of Finnish Students (SYL) from 1921 to 1961 have been organised and can be found in the National Archives of Finland, as is also the case with the archives of the YKA´s activities. However, SYL's archives after 1961 are in very bad shape. Only the minutes of the board of SYL are in order; activities concerning scholarships and development cooperation are not in order, so it has not been possible to catalogue them.

Private Photograph Collections

During the spring of 2007 some private photograph collections were scanned. An MD recorder was used for recording the description of the photographs: the person doing the cataloguing tape-recorded a description of the picture as she or he looked at it. This technique was used in describing the collections of Mr Olle Eriksson, Mr Vesa Komonen and Ms Sinikka Savola. Photograph collections from Dr Merja Saarinen and Ms Taina Schingler were also scanned.

Interviews

Interviews have been an important source of information throughout the project. Without oral testimonies, a substantial part of the historical data would be lost. Unlike written documents or official reports, oral history often carries expressions of opinion, attitudes and emotions. Eyewitness testimonies may not have been documented elsewhere. The languages used in the interviews were either Finnish or English, with the interviews in Finnish also being translated into English.

The interviewees represent different organisations and professions and their involvement in the liberation of Namibia has varied accordingly. Ideology and religious commitment are factors that have influenced the ways and methods of involvement and these themes are often present in the interviews, either explicitly or implicitly. There is a range of time scales also. Finnish co-workers of ELOC (or ELCIN) Church, for example, were sometimes present in Namibia for decades and saw the political situation and local conditions change over the years. Others spent shorter terms in the country and they focus on a certain period in the interview. Nevertheless, even a single experience is often descriptive of the era and overall atmosphere in which it is situated.

People who were working in organisations directly in cooperation with SWAPO, in Kwanza Sul for instance, inevitably present a different point of view of the struggle. At least it can be said that the goal of liberating the country could be openly expressed here, whilst on the other side of the border, Finnish Church co-workers had to be cautious. Their situation, as is often expressed in the interviews, was delicate; they had to balance their position between the oppressive state power and their community, that is, the people and the Church. Open expressions of solidarity could lead to the denial of a visa. Some co-workers were expelled from the country for those reasons. A third element in the interviews, when it comes to Finnish solidarity work, is the campaigning, education and other kind of work that was done in Finland. Again, solidarity is expressed in various contexts and in terms of different ideologies, but one can note that at least to some extent, there was cooperation for a common goal across these dividing lines.

It is worth noting that interviews distort time and ideas. Interviewees, when they revisit their past, not only bring their past to the present, but also project their present ideas or ideology back in time when they reflect on past events. The place where interviews are carried out is often important, too: when people open up their life history, they often prefer to sit at home, in their armchair, on their own ground, surrounded by objects and photographs that symbolise and visualise their unique experiences (Sommer and Quinlan, 2009, p. 52).

The Oral History Interviews

One part of the project was to collect oral histories from the Finnish people who supported the liberation struggle of Namibia in various ways, or who otherwise followed closely the Namibian situation through their work. Interviewees represent different professional fields: missionaries, teachers, doctors, diplomats and NGO activists. The interviews were conducted by Mr Tommi Lehtonen and Ms Marja Olli.

The first oral history interview was made with Mr Olle Eriksson. The language used during the interview was English and the contents list was also drawn up in English. In December there was a further interview with Mr Eriksson and an interview with Ms Lahja Lehtonen. The project also produced summaries rather than transcripts of the interviews. An exact transcription was found too laborious, considering the possible benefits of the transcription and the time that would be spent doing it. However, some kind of summary was necessary, though the level of accuracy of the summaries may vary. The project interviewed the following people: Ms Marja Väisälä, Mr Ilkka Ristimäki, Ms Sinikka Savola, Ms Maria Rutenberg, Ms Tuija Stenbäck, Mr Tauno Kääriä, Dr Marja-Liisa Swanz, Mr Börje Mattsson and Mr Alpo Hukka.

The interviewing method was a semi-structured interview, with the structure of the interview usually following a lifespan. Interviewees spoke about their background, the development of their interest in Namibia, their work, their experiences and memories from that time. In many cases we were also able to copy parts of extensive photo collections and/or document collections belonging to the interviewees.

Interviews were recorded using a Sony NET MD Walkman MZ-N710 Minidisk recorder, after which the interviews were recorded as WAV-files and saved to the external hard drive Lacie 250 Kb. The minidisk copy has been archived in the archives of the Finnish Evangelical Lutheran Mission, and the WAV-files have been given to the National Archives of Namibia.

Project on Hold 2008

Because finance from the NAI came to an end, the project was on hold for most of 2008. Towards the end of that year, the Embassy of Finland in Windhoek granted enough funds to AACRLS-Finland to continue and to finish the work.

The Delivered Material

From 7 to 9 December 2009, the AACRLS conference, *Moments, Monuments and Memories: Tracing the footprints to independence,* organised by the Ministry of Education, took place in Windhoek. At the conference, the results of AACRLS-Finland were presented and the material delivered by the Chargé d'Affaires of the Finnish Embassy, Mr Asko Luukkainen, to the National Archives of Namibia in the form of a hard disk and a microfilm.

The Finnish AACRLS archive consists of digitised text documents, photographs, interviews and microfilmed material, collected between 2004 and 2009. The material describes the activities of key organisations, campaigns and individuals during the period 1960 to 1990. AACRLS-Finland has produced about 1 500 digital copies of photographs, most of which were taken by non-professionals. They illustrate the activities of solidarity projects, key persons, important events, and also, for instance, living conditions in camps, everyday life and so on. Over 3 000 written documents of organisations involved in solidarity projects have also been scanned and saved. Documents, chosen according to relevance, describe the key activities of each project.

Microfilmed material comprises approximately 2 000 documents from the archives of the Finnish Ministry of Foreign Affairs, as well as the field diaries of Dr Pekka Peltola. These files have been microfilmed and scanned as TIFF images. The collection itself summarises several co-operation and solidarity projects between Finnish institutions and SWAPO.

The Work Goes On

The delivery of the material formally closed the AACRLS-Finland project. However, in reality, the documentation work never ceases and, given the good relations and cooperation between Finnish researchers, activists, NGOs and the National Archives of Namibia, individual people and interested organisations will continue to work collaboratively as always.

References

AACLRS (2006) *Report on the Nordic-Namibian AACRLS Seminar in Helsinki 7–8 June 2006.*

Buys, G. L. and Nambala, S. V. V. (2003) *History of the Church in Namibia 1805–1990, an Introduction.* Windhoek: Gamsberg Macmillan.

Koponen, J. and Heinonen, H. (2002) 'Africa in Finnish Policy – Deepening Involvement'. In Wohlgemuth, L. (ed.) *The Nordic Countries and Africa: Old and New Relations.* Uppsala: Nordic Africa Institute.

Lång, B. and Taskinen, L. (eds) (1986) *Namibia: Tuska ya Toivo.* Helsinki: Suomen Rauhapuolustajat.

Lehtonen, T. and Olli, M. (2007) *Report of the Finnish AACRLS Project, 2005–2007.* AACRLS/Finnish Archives.

Odugu, I. (2012) *Liberating Namibia: The Long Diplomatic Struggle between the United Nations and South Africa.* Jefferson: McFarland.

Peltola, P. (1995) *The Lost May Day: Namibian Workers Struggle for Independence.* Uppsala: Finnish Anthropological Society, in association with the Nordic Africa Institute.

Peltola, P. (2009) 'Picking up the international pieces of struggle: Finnish support to the liberation struggle in Namibia and Mozambique', paper presented at the Nordic Documentation Project Concluding Workshop, Pretoria, South Africa, 26-27 November 2009.

Simola, R. (2001) 'Encounter Images in the Meetings between Finland and South West Africa/Namibia'. In Palmberg, M. (ed.) *Encounter Images in the Meetings between Africa and Europe.* Uppsala: Nordic Africa Institute.

Soiri, I. and Peltola, P. (1999) *Finland and National Liberation in Southern Africa.* Uppsala: Nordic Africa Institute.

Sommer, B. and Quinlan, M. K. (2009) *The Oral History Manual.* Rowman Lanham: Altamira.

18 Colonial Monuments in a Post-Colonial Era: A Case Study of the Equestrian Monument

Helvi Inotila Elago

Introduction

Colonial monuments litter the Namibian landscape, but a shallow reading of their significance fails to recognise the layers of meaning that have attached to these landmarks over the passage of time. The issue that we need to explore is what happens to the monuments, memorials, museums and other sites representing the previous regime's core values and memories when a new regime, based on very different values, comes to power? When the ruling government changes, the state is faced with basic decisions concerning the past and what to do with the inherited 'public history' such as the monuments, memorials, museums and other symbols of power of the previous regime. In some African countries, like Angola, Kenya, Malawi and Angola, heritage sites and objects from the past regime were removed and destroyed as a way of breaking away from the past (Kriger, 1995, p. 141; Marschall, 2008, p. 350; Salvador and Rodrigues, 2012, p. 423). But is this the right way of dealing with a painful past?

In Namibia and South Africa there has been little removal or destruction of colonial heritage. Instead, as an alternative for changing the symbolic inherited landscape, the governments have created new sites commemorating previously ignored events and heroes in the struggle to end apartheid, e.g. Heroes Acre in Windhoek, Namibia, and Freedom Park in Pretoria, South Africa. In fact, the Equestrian monument that used to stand next to the Alte Feste located in Windhoek, which was moved in 2009 and 'removed' in 2013 is the only colonial monument to date to have been changed since independence. The new Namibian regime has emphasised the importance of teaching the new generation about history and seems to have recognised the value of having tangible commemorative sites such as monuments and memorials.

This chapter concentrates on the Equestrian monument, which during the German colonial period was known as the 'Country War Memorial' *'Landeskriegerdenkmal'*. German speakers today often refer to it as the *'Reiterdenkmal'* (the soldier's monument), whilst English speakers call it 'The Rider'. The monument was erected in 1911 and inaugurated in 1912, in commemoration of the Germany military and civilian causalities who died in the colonial wars against the Ovaherero and Nama in Namibia (Vogt, 2004, p. 103). The relocation of the monument on 19 August 2009 and again on 25 December

2013,[1] provides an opportunity to engage with a wider debate about the ways in which the colonial legacy (in terms of the heritage landscape) should be dealt with in a post-colonial independent African nation.

The chapter provides a brief, contextual, overview of the ways in which Southern African countries have dealt with the 'dissonant heritage' that is, partly, represented by colonial monuments (Tunbridge and Ashworth, 1996). I will argue that the Equestrian monument has several complex layers of meanings – as a German memorial, as a symbol of the significance of the 1904 war in the visual historiography, and as an icon used by commercial companies and the tourism industry to highlight the unique Germanic cultural dimension to Namibian identity. I will argue that a clearer understanding of the significance of the monument to different audiences would assist in ensuring that the monument is not only physically moved, but that the way in which it is viewed is also changed, so it is not only re-positioned, but also re-viewed by those who visit it.

The chapter will explore, briefly, how other neighbouring countries in Southern Africa have challenged or preserved their colonial legacy in the post-colonial era; survey the heritage landscape in Windhoek; and focus, in particular, on the Equestrian monument and the reasons why it was moved, and then removed.

The Colonial Heritage

All over the world, monuments were created as a way of marking certain events people wanted to remember. However, in Africa, monuments from the colonial period were built to honour colonial soldiers and leaders for the role they played in conquering a territory. The monuments ignored the African perspective of history, which viewed those same figures as oppressors, rather than heroes. Still, throughout the region, there are complex issues connected to the challenge of re-imagining heritage institutions and re-presenting colonial heritage in post-colonial independent African states, and this heritage review includes monuments.[2]

One response has been to dismantle statues that are perceived as celebrating colonial rule. For instance in South Africa, the statue of Hendrick Verwoerd, known as one of the architects of apartheid, was removed from public display in Bloemfontein in 1994 and the statute of Cecil Rhodes was also swiftly removed from the centre of Harare, Zimbabwe, when the country became independent in 1980 (Saunders, 2007, p. 183). After Zimbabwean independence came a moment of celebration, triumphal and monumental.

> Crowning this triumphalism a national monument, Heroes Acre was build west of the capital Harare. The Heroes Acre was created with an expression for Zimbabweans to

---

[1] *The Equestian Monument (Reiterdenkmal), 1912-2014: A chronological documentation of reports, newspaper clippings and photos/illustrations*, 2014.
[2] For a more detailed analysis and recommendations on the ways in which the education system in Namibia could engage with heritage issues, see Jeremy Silvester and Helvi Elago (2011), *Heritage into Education, Education into Heritage*, Windhoek: Museums Association of Namibia/MDG Achievement Fund, March, 2011.

be the makers of their own history and to be their own liberator by participating in the protracted, arduous and bitter struggle for self-determination. It has aroused national consciousness, forges national unity and identity (Werbner, 1998, p. 77).

In Germany, the European country that had colonised Namibia, political changes meant that there were different approaches to the colonial commemorative remnants. In East Germany (GDR), colonialism was criticised and monuments were dismantled, but in West Germany, 'only those colonial signs were removed that stemmed from the Nazi period, and a few new monuments glorifying German colonialism were actually installed' (Hell and Steinmetz, 2006; Ladd, 2008, p. 192). The contrast between the iconoclasm of the GDR and the colonial nostalgia of the West reflected different ideological perspectives that since re-unification in 1990 have been channelled into debates about the notion of a unified German identity based on shared values. In Namibia at independence, also in 1990, the new government inherited a monumental landscape that was created during the German and South African colonial periods and, as part of the project of 'creating Namibians', had to decide what to do with monuments that are perceived as celebrating colonialism and imperialism. Ironically, both coloniser and colonised had to engage with the process of 'nation-building' at the same historical moment, and one of the most visible ways in which this engagement has taken place has been the re-shaping of the monumental landscape.

For the purpose of this chapter, 'heritage' will be considered as something that is created and influenced by the specific needs and desires of the social group who will utilise and embrace that heritage. Tunbridge and Ashworth argue that heritage comes into existence as a result of a 'process by which occurrences, artifacts and personalities of the past are deliberately transformed into a product intended for the satisfaction of contemporary consumption demands' (1996, p. 6). The language used here suggests that heritage is 'the commercialisation of history'; the past becomes a 'product' for consumers to buy. In contrast, Saunders provides a more neutral definition stating that 'heritage' is simply that which is created in the present to remember the past by, such as the names given to places and street names, or monuments. However, his argument also makes the point that monuments and memorials (as the name suggests) should be linked to a discussion of community, or, rather, 'community memory' and arguments about the ways in which particular stakeholders want to remember the past. Since most heritage sites are constructed or marked to commemorate a specific event or personality, the selection or creation of heritage sites is always a political statement (Tunbridge & Ashworth, 1996, p. 6).

One of the issues of 'transitional justice' that is associated with a change to a democratic society is the need to confront monuments and memorials that embody values that are not shared by the majority of citizens in a country. In South Africa some of the colonial monuments are simply referred to as 'Disgraced Monuments' (Coombes, 2003, p. 19). According to Henry Bredekamp in South Africa 'the country's cultural heritage was, until recently, Eurocentric. It focused primarily on an appreciation of the aesthetic value of colonial-inspired architecture and respect for Cape Dutch and British settler culture, i.e. on a colonial heritage that took roots on African soil after

1652.'³ Furthermore, South African heritage was regarded as biased in representation: 'after the change of political governance in 1994 the African National Congress (ANC) dominated Government's Department of Arts and Culture has been trying to redress imbalance in heritage and promote a more egalitarian culture as part of the general process of transformation' and this include monuments (Saunders, 2007, p. 185).

One focal point of debate has been the Voortrekker monument in Pretoria. When it became abundantly clear in the early 1990s that the black ANC government was set to take over the reins of power, alarm bells went off in some Afrikaner cultural circles. Of particular concern was the future of the Voortrekker monument with its brazen display of apartheid ideology. It was feared that the new government would not tolerate a monument that could be interpreted as extremely offensive to the new political rulers (Grundlingh, 2009, pp. 157-177). As a result, a Voortrekker Monument Company was established to preserve Afrikaner cultural identity. A variety of views were expressed, but it was argued that the monument should be kept, rather than destroyed, so that the monument could serve as a reminder of the oppression that black people had to overcome and a tribute to the black labour that assisted in building the monument. In order to learn lessons from the past, an alternative monument was created opposite the Voortrekker Monument as a kind of symbolic riposte and the monument was left as it was. Freedom Park, which is regarded as far more inclusive, was built on the hills opposite the Voortrekker Monument. Freedom Park honours those killed in the liberation struggle; the two world wars; the Boer war (or South African War as the designers like to remember it for the sake of inclusivity); the colonial wars; the victims of slavery; and the victims of the attempted genocide against the Khoisan.

The Voortrekker monument was built in 1938, in commemoration of the Battle of Blood River in 1838 – the Boer victory against the Zulus – and in honour of the Voortrekkers or 'Pioneers', who left the Cape during the period 1835 to 1854, to cut through the interior of the country in what became known as the Great Trek. The monument was a focal point for annual commemorative events for the Afrikaner community. However, after the ANC government was formed, 'in the debate over the future of monuments in South Africa there was criticism about the amount of government funding being apportioned to monuments dedicated to aspects of Afrikaaner culture' (Coombes, 2003, p. 22). Critics felt that too much money was spent on preserving colonial heritage, rather than on new monuments and heritage institutions that were created to mark events of significance to the 'New South Africa'.

Critics also complained about the biased narrative of history at the Voortrekker monument, which did not include the history of other ethnic groups in South Africa. According to Albert Grundlingh, various people have different interpretations or perceptions of the monument, 'for a politically aware black person to even approach the thing requires some profound self-examination'. For others, they are not quite aware or concerned about the precise meaning and symbolism of the building, it is 'just a monument' as the black tour guide at the monument argued 'to me the monument tells

---

3   H. C. (Jatti) Bredekamp (2007), 'The Cultural Heritage of a Democratic South Africa: An Overview'. In Theo Bothma, Peter Underwood and Patrick Ngulube (eds), *Libraries for the Future: Progress and Development in South African Libraries*, Pretoria: Library and Information Association of South Africa, pp. 1-12.

the history of the Voortrekkers and how they got the land in the interior, nothing else' (Grundlingh, 2009, p. 168). In terms of tourism, the monument attracts a lot of foreign visitors, and this has led to printed guide books in German, French, Italian, Portuguese, Spanish and Chinese, in addition to those in Afrikaans and English.

Namibia inherited a long list of 'National Monuments' at independence. However, these are predominantly 'colonial' in nature and many lack any relevance to the indigenous cultures of the peoples of Namibia themselves. However, according to Jeremy Silvester, such arguments are necessary but not sufficient to provide an adequate academic analysis of these monuments: 'By submerging all heritage production within the category "white", the analysis conceals the tensions and fractures within settler societies' (2005, p. 274). Silvester argues that heritage and culture played an important role in bolstering the claims of German-speaking Namibians to legitimacy, and also preserving cultural and political opposition within sections of the local white community to the incorporation of Namibia into South Africa as a 'Fifth Province'. He points out that, despite South African efforts to colonise Namibia, the monumental landscape is dominated by tributes to the German colonial period. Nearly all these monuments are held in high esteem and are, therefore, well preserved and protected, while only a few have been neglected and decayed or destroyed by nature. The landscape of Windhoek as the capital city is, in particular, filled with monuments inherited from the German and South African colonial era, with various meaning and significance, such as: the Alte Feste located in Robert Mugabe Avenue, the Curt von François statue on the corner of Independence Avenue, the Hendrick Witbooi memorial in Zoo Park, the Ovambo Campaign memorial in TransNamib Park, and the 'Oudstryders' memorial in Bismarck street.

Erecting the Equestrian Monument

The Equestrian monument is among the oldest statues in Namibia, dating from 1912 in the German colonial era (1884-1915). It is regarded as one of the most prominent landmarks of Windhoek, and is the best known historical war memorial in Namibia. According to Vogt, the Equestrian monument is unique, in that it has a dual significance as art and as a heavily weighted cultural artefact. The statue represents a mounted trooper of the German colonial forces (*Schutztruppe*) in the form of an equestrian sculpture. It came into existence after a 'decision was taken to erect a statue in honour of their German compatriots who were killed in action during the wars with Namibians between 1903-1907 and during the Kalahari expedition in 1908 against Simon Kooper's guerrilla unit based in Botswana. The fallen included 1,525 officers and soldiers, 92 marine officers and soldiers, and 124 civilians' (Vogt, 2004, pp. 104-105).

The site where the Equestrian monument was built was not randomly chosen, but has a history of its own as a concentration camp for the OvaHerero and Nama people. This was regarded as one of the biggest concentration camps during that period. Figure 18.1 shows the Windhoek *Feste* (Fort), with the OvaHerero and Nama prisoners of war camp in the foreground. The statue was the most visible reminder in the capital city of the war of anti-colonial resistance against the Germans and a marker of a concentration camp where many Herero prisoners were held and abused. As the author of a text message to *The Namibian* newspaper argued:

Figure 18.1: Alte Feste and Concentration Camp
(National Archives of Namibia)

The Reiterdenkmal removal is not going to make the history go away! If President Pohamba really wants to stop the mockery of the statue, as he says, replace it with the heroes of that era. Put up a denkmal for that war! People must remember that that war happened![4] It has even been argued that the development of a memorial at the cemetery in Swakopmund should actually be viewed as an 'anti-memorial' that highlights the lack of official recognition given in official state projects to the traumatic memories of communities affected by the 1904-1908 war (Frank, 2012, p. 8).

The monument was designed by the Berlin Sculptor Adolf Kürle following a proposal by the German Commander, Colonel von Estorff, and was erected in 1911 and inaugurated on 27 January 1912, to honour the German Emperor, Kaiser Wilhelm. The ceremony was timed to take place on the Kaiser's birthday and the monument stood at this same site for 97 years. Figure 18.2 shows the inauguration of the monument on the site of the former concentration camp with the Kammergebäude Tower (used to store and repair weapons and ammunition) in the background centre of the photograph.

According to Zeller, the speech delivered by the German Governor, Theodor Seitz, at the unveiling of the statue made it 'clear beyond any doubt that the monument should not be understood simply as a memorial to the dead. Its function was rather to act as a monument to victory, to demonstrate power and mastery' (2003, p. 231). The monument was regarded as one of the most important symbols of the colonial past in Namibia and was officially proclaimed a national monument on 2 January 1969.

---

4   *The Namibian*, sms text message, 12 August 2012.

Figure 18.2: The inauguration of the Reiterdenkmal, 27 January 1912
(Colonial Picture Archive, University Library of Frankfurt/Main)

Up until July 2009, when it was moved, the Equestrian statue monument was situated in Robert Mugabe Avenue, in Windhoek, opposite the Christus Kirche and in front of the Alte Feste.

Commerce and Tourism

The meaning of monuments often changes over time. The Equestrian monument has been used as an icon by commercial manufacturers and tourism promoters. South West Breweries made sure that the statue would become the most visually prominent symbol of Namibia's distinctly colonial German local identity (Silvester, 2005, p. 276). According to Don Stevenson, the Equestrian monument was used as part of the logo of South West Breweries and featured prominently in promotional advertising. However, when the Breweries was renamed Namibia Breweries Limited after independence, the logo was changed because it was viewed as being associated with a colonial symbol (Stevenson, 2009, p. 109). One might argue that the moving of the Equestrian monument in 2009 to give space for the new Independence Memorial Museum resembles what happened with the changing of the logo.

The tourism industry has also given the monument a central role in the marketing of Windhoek and Namibia as a tourist attraction, and there could be various reasons why the tourism industry uses the statue of a German soldier as a way of marketing holidays in Africa. One could be that the tourism industry is built on promoting 'unique' tourist sites to create a 'unique competitive advantage', to construct a particular 'tourist destination'. The fact that Namibia was the only one of Germany's colonies to have a significant settler community has meant that the German cultural flavour has been one of the country's major selling points and that has contributed to the fact that Germany provides the largest number of overseas visitors to Namibia. For example, one-third of all tourists from outside Africa who visited Namibia in 2011 were Germans (Namibia Tourism Board, 2012, p. 42).

The increasing use of new technology to market Namibia does not seem to have dethroned the statue from its iconic place within the branding of Namibia. One tourist company site on the internet describes Windhoek in the following text that reads as follows:

> Windhoek is a wonderful town to while away the day. In downtown Windhoek you can find many examples of German colonial architecture, including the equestrian monument, the Alte Feste fort, Christuskirche (Christ's Church), the well-kept gardens of Tintenpalast (Ink Palace).[5]

This text suggests that one of the primary attractions that enables Windhoek and Namibia to be successfully marketed to the German market is the history of the German period and its cultural legacy.

Commemorations

According to Vogt, for many years, annual meetings of the veteran's federations, with members of different church congregations and language groups, have taken place at the site of the Equestrian monument, while up to this day wreath-laying ceremonies and commemorative services are conducted at the site. The services are performed by Namibians within their traditions and traditional rites and customs and are, thus, a reflection of their constitutionally enshrined cultural rights. According to Article 19 (Culture) of the Namibian Constitution '. . . every person shall be entitled to enjoy, practise, profess, maintain and promote any culture, language, tradition or religion subject to the terms of this Constitution and further subject to the condition that the rights protected by this Article do not impinge upon the rights of others or the national interest'.[6] One can argue whether these customs might have been crucially disturbed by moving the Equestrian monument. However, after the relocation of the monument, wreaths were laid at the new site on Remembrance Day on 11 November 2010, so the statue retains its commemorative role and function as a place of memory. One question that requires further consideration is whether such rituals of remembrance are sufficiently employed as a platform for reconciliation.

---

5 <http://www.ganeandmarshall.com.> {Accessed on 4 December 2009}.
6 < http://www.orusovo.com/namcon>/, The Constitution of the Republic of Namibia. {Accessed on 5 December, 2009}.

Local Interpretation

According to Charles Siyauya 'a German-Namibian will perceive the *Reiterdenkmal* as good heritage, whereas a Nama or Herero will perceive the *Reiterdenkmal* as a heritage that hurts'[7] and as a heritage that 'stands as a visible and prominent reminder of the crimes committed by German forces. By keeping these memories alive, it also supports the demand for reparation from Germany'.[8] Through informal conversations with people from different ethnic groups within Namibia, it emerges that the Equestian monument is meaningful to different people in different ways – the meaning of the statue is not fixed. Some use it simply as a landmark when giving directions, whilst others think it is part of Namibian history, but without being able to explain the specific significance or meaning of the monument. Even though the monument is an inheritance from the colonial period, local people grew acquainted with the monument to the extent that they incorporated it into their urban landscape and inscribed it with new meanings. For instance when the Ovawambo people talk about the City of Windhoek they refer to it as '*koshilando shoka kambe komusamane kalondoloka*' meaning 'the town of a man who never got off his horse'. The Ovaherero and Nama people also have a personal attachment with the Equestrian monument because it was their ancestors who died at the camps, including the one in Windhoek at the site where the monument used to stand. The Ovaherero people refer to the monument as '*ongoro nomundu*' which means 'the man and the horse'. This shows that the statue is not only a 'marker' for German-speaking Namibians and German tourists whose ancestors fought in the war, but also for the Ovaherero and Nama communities, whose ancestors were hanged or died at this site.

Whilst research has recently been conducted on the concentration camps at Swakopmund and Lüderitz, research is still needed on the operation of the camp that was built next to the Alte Feste. Even though various local people interpreted the monument in different ways, there were some who did not appreciate its presence because of the history that the monument represents. The monument has also provided a historical marker for democratic protest, and one claim states that these protests date back decades. In 1959, a few days after the Old Location Uprising in which 11 people were killed, unknown Herero activists covered the rider's head with a linen bag and decorated the rest of the statue with flowers as a 'protest against the atrocities of the white South African minority regime' (Zeller, 2000, pp. 244-245). Another example of the way in which the monument provided a space to visually provoke debate about the past took place in January 2000. Somebody spray-painted the monument with a Nazi swastika and the government had to import products from outside the country to clean the monument.

In 2008, fifty-one white crosses were erected around the Equestrian monument. The crosses were inscribed with names like Handjala, Dauseb, Hamakari, Tsowaseb, Awas, Bushman 35 and Mujoro. One cross carried the words 'Now just another way

---

7 Charles Siyauya, 'An Argument for Keeping Old Names, Monuments', *New Era*, 11 July 2008.
8 Elke Zuern (2012) 'Memorial Politics – Challenging Power and Inequality in Namibia', Draft Paper. <http://www.politicsandprotest.ws.gc.cuny.edu/files/2012/07/Zuern-Memorial-Politics.pdf.> { Accessed on 10 December 2012}.

of slavery'.⁹ The historian and expert on Namibian monuments, Dr Andreas Vogt, said 'The erection of the crosses shows that the *Reiterdenkmal* is an active, lively monument which people still debate and talk about and take a stance on, it is not just a monument which was erected almost 100 years ago and just stands there.' This shows that even though the monument has been accepted as part of the Windhoek's architectural heritage and Namibian history, it continues to be a focal point for debates about our reading of the past.

In 2001, a group called 'The Initiators' approached the Minister of Education with a request for an additional commemorative stone to be mounted next to the Equestrian monument as a way of promoting the 'national policy of reconciliation', and to show their commitment to the policy and to a peaceful future for all in Namibia.¹⁰ The proposed wording on the additional plaque that had been discussed between the initiators and the National Monuments Council read as follows:

> In the spirit of national reconciliation as enshrined in the Constitution of the Republic of Namibia, we, the Namibian heirs and participants of more than a hundred years of modern history, commemorate all victims of war up to the attainment of national sovereignty of Namibia. As citizens of this country we are committed to shape a peaceful future of our motherland Namibia in justice and liberty.

Moved but not Removed

However, in response to the request, Cabinet took the decision to relocate the Equestrian monument to a new site about 50 metres away, infront of the Alte Feste. The context for this was the decision to create a new museum on Namibia's liberation struggle, and the proposal for a plaque that would provide an alternative reading of the monument seems to have been forgotten. The Independence Memorial Museum is described as 'a national monument intended to educate Namibians and tourists about the history of the country's Independence through historical displays.¹¹ It will be honouring those who fought and died for the liberation of Namibia from the very beginning of colonial rule. This includes people who resisted German colonial rule as well as those who resisted South African oppression.

The North Korean company that created both Zimbabw's and Namibia's Heroes Acres was also commissioned to construct the Independence Memorial Museum. Once again the announcement that the museum would be built on an important heritage site led to demands that the opportunity be taken to remember the 1904-1908 war. Hon. Kazenambo Kazenambo MP argued during a Parliamentary debate in June 2008 that 'the horse was a "reference point" to the concentration camp that had been at the site during the war'.¹² The decision to move the monument stirred a local debate in the media and also within the German-speaking Namibian community about both the historical

---

9 Tanja Bause, 'Lone horseman gets company', *The Namibian*, 10 July 2008.
10 Letter from the Initiators to the Chairman, National Monuments Council, Hon. John Pandeni, dated 8 June 2001.
11 C. Maletsky, 'City Icon to Take Last Ride' *The Namibian*, 10 June 2008.
12 Kuvee Kangueehi, 'Reiterdenkmal Debate Divides the House', *New Era*, 23 June 2008.

*Figure 18.3 The Equestrian monument wrapped up
for relocation in 2009
(Harald Koch)*

narrative of the past and the way in which the war of 1903-1908 should be remembered. Vogt alleges that the decision on the construction and location of the museum was made without Parliamentary debate, without the required professional investigation by a team of conservation experts convened by the National Heritage Council of Namibia, and without any organised public debate or consultative workshops to establish the feelings of the public on this important matter.[13] Furthermore, he highlighted the possible negative effects that the relocation of the monument could have on the meaning of the monument and the high risk that the monument would be physical damaged during the move. Figures 18.3 and 18.4 show the Equestrian monument wrapped with protective plastic and being moved to its new site about 50 metres away.

From December 2009 until 10 January 2010, a photographic exhibition called 'History Unbolted' was exhibited at Swakopmund Museum by Tanya Davidow and Nicola Brandt. The same exhibition was displayed at the National Art Gallery of Namibia in Windhoek from 15 January to 15 February 2010 (see Figure 18.5). The text accompanying the photographs read as follow: 'The photographs are intended to

---

13   A. Vogt, 'To move or not to move', *The Namibian,* 18 July, 2008.

Figure 18.4 The removal of the monument in 2009
(Harald Koch)

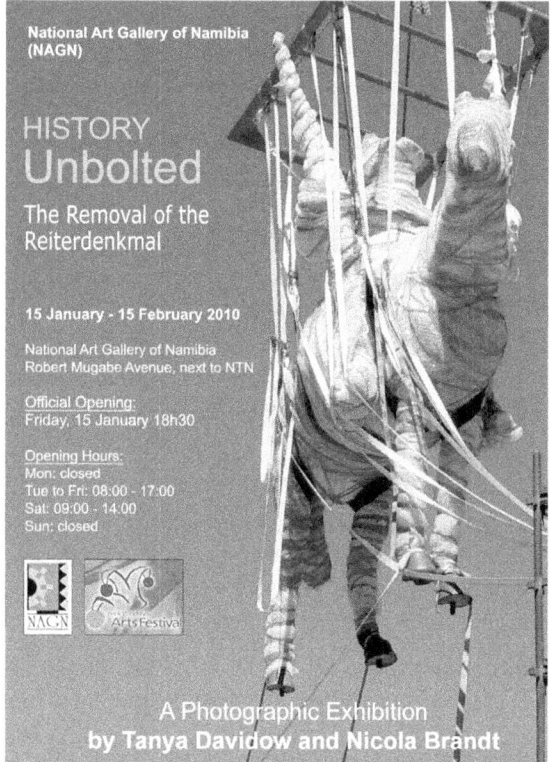

Figure 18.5 Poster advertising the exhibition of
photos of the relocation of the monument
(Nicola Brandt)

Figure 18.6 The completed relocation of the Reiterdenkmal with the Independence Memorial Museum, Alte Feste and Christuskirche in the background
(Lisa Berl)

place the *Reiterdenkmal* at the centre of a narrative that demonstrates how landscapes and structures within landscapes are never natural.'[14] Photos at the exhibition showed various angles of the monument without giving a caption to each photo, thus taking the format of a 'photographic essay'.

Various newspapers in Namibia kept track of the progress of the reconstruction of the foundation of the Equestrian monument at the new location. The completion of the reconstruction targeted the original inaugural date; however, due to the weather (heavy rain), the reconstruction was delayed.

The re-inauguration of the Equestrian monument at the new site took place on 14 November 2010. The translated caption for the photograph of the event in *Die Republikien* read:

> Mostly members of the German community were present at the inauguration ceremony of the new position of the 'Reiterdenkmal' in front of the Alte feste and none of the various governmental institutions invited attended.[15]

The statue was moved to make space for the new Independence Memorial Museum, which is a component of the National Museum of Namibia (see Figure 18.6).

---

14 Nicola Brandt, 'History Unbolted, the removal of the Reiterdenkmal', Exhibition from 15 January to 15 February 2010, National Art Gallery of Namibia, visited on 22 January 2010.
15 'Ruiterstandbeeld ingehuldig', *Die Republikein*, 16 November 2010.

The Namibian government's Medium Term Expenditure Framework (MTEF) states that the Independence Memorial Museum will 'allow all Namibian people and tourists visiting the building to be both educated and inspired by the schematic arrangement of historical displays demonstrating both the history and the rising of the Namibian nation'. The building was constructed by the Mansudae Overseas Projects, a North Korean company 'under the special guidance of Kim Jong Il, the leader' and employing around 4,000 people including 1,000 artists.[16] The company also constructed the Military Museum for the Ministry of Defence in Okahandja, Heroes Acre on the outskirts of Windhoek and the new State House for the President of Namibia. The company was responsible for a number of major monumental projects in other countries in Africa such as the Heroes Acre in Zimbabwe, the Three Dikgosi Monument in Botswana, the African Renaissance Monument in Senegal, a statue of Béhanzin in Benin, a statue of Laurent-Désiré Kabila in the Democratic Republic of Congo and the Dr Agostinho Neto Cultural Centre in Angola.[17]

However, SWANU President Usutuaije Maamberua, reflecting on the symbolic location of the museum, proposed that it should be renamed the 'Genocide Remembrance Centre' because it was built at 'one of the most horrific places, where past genocide activities were committed', which is why it is called '*Orumbo rua Katjombondi*' (meaning 'a place of horror').[18] If the soldier on his horse was a constant reminder of the assumption of German colonial power and its consequences, it has been displaced by a monumental museum that seems to symbolically displace the past with a futuristic design that celebrates and asserts the power of the modern post-colonial state.

Re-moving the Past

As this chapter was being written, the Equestrian monument went through a second relocation and has now been de-proclaimed as a national monument. Significantly it was on 26 August 2013, during a Heroes Day celebration at Omugulugwoombashe, that President Hifikepunye Pohamba announced the final removal of the statue. Omugulugwoombashe was the site of the first battle between Namibian guerrillas and the South African security forces and is now part of Namibia post-independence memorial landscape, as the government has erected a large statue of the Founding Father, Dr Sam Nujoma, at the site. President Pohamba stated: 'The horse rider must be removed. If they want to take it back to Germany it is also fine, we will not have any objections.'[19] The comments stimulated a lively public debate in the media as to whether the horse and its rider reflected German or Namibian history and heritage.

16　The Official Web Site of the Mansudae Art Studio <*http://www.mansudaeartstudio.com/index. php?option=com_content&view=article&id=261&Itemid=50&lang=en*>. {Accessed 22 May 2013}
17　For a more detailed analysis of the North Korean dominance of state heritage projects in Namibia see Meghan Kirkwood, 'Postcolonial Architecture Through North Korean Modes: Namibian Commissions of the Mansudae Overseas Project' (MA, thesis, University of Kansas, 2011).
18　'SWANU wants Independence Museum to be renamed', *The Namibian* 15 June 2011.
19　Elvis Muraranganda, 'Govt presses on with Reiterdenkmal removal', *Namibian Sun*, 24 December 2013.

On 20 December 2013, the National Heritage Council published an advertisement officially proposing the 'de-proclamation of the Equestrian Statue Monument'. The Council argued that: 'This monument is viewed to have lost its real political significance already three years after its erection when Germany lost the territory and was given to the Union of South Africa in 1915.'[20] The Council argued that as the monument has 'lost' its original meaning, it had also lost its relevance to society. However, this argument did not recognise the reality that the meaning of a monument changes over time and that the crucial issue is that of 'interpretation' – the way in which it is packaged and presented and the changing ways in which the public might 'read' the monument.

The public were given 60 days to object to the de-proclamation of the monument. However, five days after the publication of the advertisement by the National Heritage Council, on the night of Christmas Day, the monument was removed and its stand (that had been carefully reconstructed exactly as it had been built at the original site) was demolished. It was reported that people were forbidden to take photographs of the destruction of the monument.[21] No public announcement was made about the future fate of the monument and this gave the impression that the demolition had been impulsive. The statue and its plaque were left standing in the courtyard in the centre of the Alte Feste.

It is commonly argued that the 'heritage significance' of sites changes over time. For example, Ground Zero at Hiroshima in Japan (where the first atomic bomb used in combat exploded) has become a shrine to peace, and the Nanjing Massacre Memorial in China uses a horrific national event to promote international human rights and a specific argument against the abuse of women during conflict. When considering the significance of the 'horse rider', Charles Siyauya argued that the removal of the statue would be 'historical suicide' even though it represented a 'heritage that hurts'. He argued that 'Removing it would remove a significant layer of Namibian History to benefit the subjective view of one group of people and would lead to a distortion of history, destroying evidence of the presence of colonialism and leads to tremendous deficit of factual information.'[22] A contrasting view was expressed by Dr Ngarikutuke Tjiriange, who asked 'Why should we have statues of German colonial killers in Namibia while our own resistance heroes are not recognised and accorded the same respect in Germany?'[23] The polarised debate drew attention to the central question as to whether heritage that reflects or represents the colonial past should be preserved or destroyed, and larger questions about the significance of heritage.

It is argued that when dealing with sites that reflect past conflicts it is important for heritage practitioners 'to deal with stakeholders for whom the particular site remains a site of acute anguish ...Interaction with the community is indispensable.'[24] Some Namibians feel that the statue should be kept on display as a reminder of the German colonial period and its impact on Namibia, so that future generations learn from the

---

20   *Namibian Sun*, 'Govt presses on with Reiterdenkmal removal', 23 December 2013.
21   Ellanie Smit, 'Reiterdenkmal disappears overnight', *Namibian Sun*, 27 December 2013.
22   Charles Siyauya, 'An Argument for Keeping Old Names, Monuments', *New Era*, 11 July 2008.
23   Dr Ngarikutuke Tjiriange, 'Reiterdenkmal removal: A great govt decision', *New Era*, 3 January 2014.
24   William Logan, and Kier Reeves (2009) *Places of Pain and Shame: Dealing with 'Difficult Heritage'*. Abingdon: Routledge, p. 13.

past and it can be used to promote the new values of an independent Namibia, such as freedom and reconciliation.

David Uzzell has argued that when dealing with sites of conflict it is important to make use of 'hot interpretation', which can be used as a tool for 'community development [as] it can bring peoples together rather than be used as an instrument of division'.[25] The argument is that, rather than removing 'heritage that hurts', the modern approach to heritage interpretation is to use such sites as points of engagement to deal with the past. Hot interpretation was reflected in a speech by Mr Koch, at a ceremony on 27 January 2012, to mark the centenary of the statue. Koch stated that 'We are gathered here in memory of all the soldiers and civilians of German descent who died 100 years ago, but we are also here to remember all the other people who lost their lives in that war. This monument should remind us of what happened and it should ensure that something like that does not happen again.' The statue, had (and has) the capacity to serve Namibia as a point of engagement and dialogue about the past, but only if we adopt a more democratic approach to heritage development.

Conclusion

Andreas Vogt argues that 'monuments were set up regarding the commemoration of the most diverse causes, and the most different persons. To respect and to maintain any monument should be a matter of principle'.[26] Our heritage reflects the multiple layers of history in Namibia. The German colonial period was short, but highly significant in shaping Namibia's cultural identity, influencing the architectural forms found in our built environment and determining the economic landscape. Yet whilst heritage sites that reflect the importance of this historical period should be conserved as part of our unique identity as a nation, it is also important that ways are found to ensure that there is a democratic debate and sufficient consultation with stakeholders about the appropriate ways to deal with sites that form 'heritage that hurts'.

It might be argued that the challenge facing the Namibian government is to create alternative heritage sites that will serve as worthy memorials to the painful experience of the different Namibian communities that were most affected by the 1903-1908 war, so that that history is better reflected in our heritage landscape. However, the history of the German colonial period cannot be totally erased without damaging the collective memory of the Namibian population, and there is a compelling argument that such heritage sites should not be destroyed, but that they should be complemented.

Sites such as Shark Island (the notorious prison camp off Lüderitz), *Ozombuzovindimba* (the site where General Lother von Trotha issued his famous extermination order against the Ovaherero) and Ohamakari (the site where the most significant battle of the war took place) should be developed as 'sites of memory' where the stories of those that fought against men like the soldier mounted on his horse can be told. The removal of the Equestrian monument will be meaningless unless the opportunity is also taken

---

25   D. Uzzell and R. Ballantyne (2008) 'Heritage that Hurts: Interpretation in a postmodern world'. In G. Fairclough, R. Harrison, J. H. Jameson Jnr, and John Schofield (eds) *The Heritage Reader*, London & New York: Routledge, p. 512.
26   Andreas Vogt, 'To move or not to move', *The Namibian*, 18 July 2008.

to create an exhibition that discusses the meaning of the monument and adds layers of interpretation to the site to reflect its multiple meanings. Namibians should view heritage sites as an opportunity for debate and dialogue about our shared history, which will reflect our diverse perspectives on the past and form a firm foundation upon which to build our policy of national reconciliation.

Comment: Colonial Monuments – Heritage or Heresy?

André du Pisani

The thorny question of the role and fate of monuments erected to commemorate regimes and their policies that have since been discredited and disgraced, is not solely a Namibian dilemma. This comment will highlight some issues raised by two presentations made at the 2009 *Moments, Memories and Monuments* conference: a paper presented by Ms Helvi Elago (revised for this volume) and a short film produced by Mr Tim Huebschle. The two presentations complement each other as they underscore the validity of approaching monuments and, more usefully, memorial culture, from two distinct, yet complementary perspectives – the written and the visual narrative.

In both presentations, The Equestrian monument (*das Reiterdenkmal* in German), formerly known as the 'Country War Memorial' (*Landeskriegerdenkmal*), provides a useful point of entry into the complexities of the debates around appropriate forms of commemorating the past and envisioning the future in post-colonial Namibia. Paradoxically, the same foundational concerns apply, though admittedly, in a different political and historical context, to Heroes Acre, inaugurated on 26 August 2002.

Helvi Elago's admirable and timely chapter builds on the memorable 1992 South African History Workshop in Johannesburg on '*Myths, Monuments, Museums*' and the earlier work of Phanuel Kaapama, Henning Melber, Jeremy Silvester, Jurgen Zimmerer and others, who wrote reflectively on the Equestrian monument and its place and symbolic meaning(s) in post-colonial Namibia. To her credit, Elago takes the debate further, particularly by locating the discourse around the iconic Equestrian statue and the commodification, material and military culture that the monument has come to represent against the dominant nationalist and nation-building narrative/discourse of the SWAPO-led government, by foregrounding debates about the nature and use (or abuse) of history in the public sphere.

Following Antze and Lambek (1996) and Coombes (2003), the chapter is premised on the understanding that all memory is unavoidably borne out of individual subjective experience and shaped by collective consciousness and shared social and historical processes, so that any understanding of the representation of memory of the past more generally must necessarily take into account both contexts. Public monuments such as the Equestrian monument carry with them temporal repercussions and, when the context within which the monument is viewed is reconfigured, there is the prospect of visitors reading it in new ways.

Annie Coombes, in a ground-breaking book entitled *Visual Culture and Public Memory in a Democratic South Africa*, argues that 'monuments are animated and reanimated only through performance and that performances or rituals focused around a monument are conjunctural. The visibility of a monument is in fact entirely contingent upon the debates concerning the reinterpretation of history that takes place at moments of social and political transition. Their significance is consequently constantly being reinvented but always and necessarily in dialogue with the past' (Coombes, 2003, p. 12).

Helvi Elago locates her reflective chapter in the context when a monument was in the process of being moved and then removed. This in itself marks more than a physical transition, but signifies a moment pregnant with potential for new ways of reading the monument by different publics or constituencies.

Both Helvi Elago's chapter and Tim Huebschler's short film explore the possibilities and impossibilities for rehabilitating a monument with an explicit history as a foundational icon of the former German colonial state. Is it possible to disinvest such an icon of German imperial associations and invest it with new resonances that will enable it to remain a highly public monument despite a new democratic government? Is it possible for the majority of Namibians to simply accept the coexistence of such an oppressive reminder of genocide and imperial imposition? Is it possible to, in the graphic language of Gayatri Chakravorty Spivak, through 'an act of translation', or in the Benjaminian sense of 'supplemental meanings' arrive at a reading against the grain (Benjamin, 1969 and 1986; Spivak 1993). For on a more complex level, 'translation' offers a way of articulating the operations of agency in the construction of historical and public memory. If one proceeds from such an exploration, does the Equestrian monument have significance for many or all Namibians? And if it does, what could this be? In his film, Tim Huebschle concludes the first part by asking: 'History has made us what we are. But why stop there?'

In this context, one is reminded of the celebrated words of the novelist, Samuel Becket: 'History has deformed all of us'.

Award winning filmmaker Tim Huebschle's film has a witty title *Rider without a Horse*, note not 'Horse without a Rider', although the film suggests the inseparability of structure and agency. If the reader will allow me a certain degree of poetic licence, the scene where the rider mounts the horse at the conclusion of the first part of the film reminds one of the moving documentary, *Disgraced Monuments* (1994), by directors Laura Mulvey and Mark Lewis. In this powerful rendition they explore the fate of public monuments under successive regimes in the former Soviet Union, and the apparent endless cycle of monumental sculptures celebrating the favoured leader of the moment, followed inevitably by their iconoclastic dismantling and removal. Just such a sequence was famously captured by the Soviet film-maker Sergei Eisenstein, when he filmed the toppling of the statute of the Czar in *Oktobr* (1927). As the art historian Natalya Davidova comments in *Disgraced Monuments*, in Russia it has always been a case of 'a struggle with the past that was realised through a struggle with monuments', and as a pessimist remarked philosophically in *Disgraced Monuments*, 'Concrete is easier to change than reality'.

Of course, cultural policy and politics in Namibia demand an answer unlike that of the former Eastern Europe, as the second part of *Rider without a Horse* shows. Nonetheless, concrete is easier to change than reality, for reality (more accurately, 'realities'), has/have its/their own ambivalence. In the case of the Equestrian monument, arguably 'Namibia's most well-known historical monument', to paraphrase Andreas Vogt (2004, p. 103) the symbolic schema, the idea and ideal of conquest is achieved through a 'double-life-size statue, reaching a height of 4.5 meters depicting a German *Schutztruppe* cavalryman in full uniform. The soldier faces northwards, i.e. in the direction of Imperial Germany' (Vogt, 2004, p. 104). When first relocated, the soldier faced westwards, gazing out over the undulating hills and blood-red sunsets of the Khomas Highlands. This in itself changed an aspect of the iconography of the monument.

There was however, little apportunity for 'translation', to involve Spivak's term, before the soldier was moved again. The removal men struck on Christmas evening, 25 December 2013, and under the watchful eye of the Namibian police, the Equestrian monument was removed from its pedestal and relocated to the inner court yard of the Alte Feste, the symbol of German colonial past. For now, the Equestrian monument, held upright by poles, seems to have found its last, if somewhat less-dignified, resting place in the inner courtyard. The horse and rider are no longer mounted on a pedestal, and the two-piece bronze memorial plaque that had been an integral part of the monument, lies face-up on the grass next to the monument.

Local news reports had it that some of the granite rocks that formed part of the original pedestal were destroyed with a jack hammer, others seemingly ended up on a dumpsite, while a large remaining rock, ironically, served as part of the foundation for the newly erected monument, designed and built by a North Korean company Mansudae Overseas Projects (MOP) that commemorates the 1903-08 genocide.

Figure 18.7 The Genocide Memorial Statue was unveiled on 20 March 2014 and stands in front of the Alte Feste, a spot previously occupied by the Reiterdenkmal. The statue depicts a man and woman embracing one another breaking the chains of colonialism
(Naitsikile Iizyenda)

The removal of the Equestrian monument and the subsequent construction of the new monument on the very foundations of the former one, raise important ethical and aesthetic questions in the post-colony. So, too, does the relocation of the Equestrian monument to the inner courtyard of the Alte Feste. In both cases, the space of politics and the politics of space, remain contested.

In a letter to the Informanté newspaper, reacting to opinions voiced by some local German commentators that President Pohamba 'has no knowledge of the Namibian law or he does not understand it',[27] the Minister of Information and Broadcasting, Joel Kaapanda, described the Equestrian statue 'as a remnant of Lothar Von Trotha's Extermination Order' of 1905. The Minister added in his letter, [that] the monument 'was erected as a symbol of victory over the Namibian people and colonization of the then South-West Africa by the Imperial Germany'. The minister concluded his letter by stating that 'The Government will make sure that our own history is preserved by getting rid of all colonial vestiges and distortions'.

As the appropriate legal agency, the National Heritage Council published its intent to recommend de-proclamation of the Equestrian monument. The following reasons for this recommendation included, among others:

'This statue was erected in honour of the German soldiers who were killed in action or during the war of colonial resistance with Namibians between 1903-1907 and during the Kalahari expedition in 1908, which were waged in opposition to German colonial rule'.[28]

The Public Notice by the National Heritage Council also quoted from the inaugural speech by the then Governor of German South West Africa, Theodor Seitz, on the 27 January 1912. At that occasion, Seitz, concluded his speech with the following words: 'The venerated colonial soldier that looks out over the land from here announces to the world that we are the masters of this place, now and forever.'

The public was advised that the National Heritage Council would submit its recommendation to the Minister of Youth, National Service, Sport and Culture (MYNSSC) after a period of 60 days from the date the Notice of the proposed recommendation was published. The actual de-proclamation of the Monument took place in January 2014.

The recent events surrounding the Equestrian monument, underlined the importance of such colonial monuments as markers for a struggle with the past. It also brought into sharp relief how divisive such monuments can be in the body politic of newly independent and post-colonial states, such as Namibia. Finally, it emphasised the value of having culture and heritage policies in place that resonate with the needs and aspirations of citizens.

---

27 See *Informanté*, 26 September 2013.
28 National Heritage Council, 'Public Notice - Proposed Recommendation of De-Proclamation of the Equestrian Statue Monument', *Republikein* 20 December 2013.

References

Antze, P. and Lambek, M. (eds) (1996) *Tense Past: Cultural Essays in Trauma and Memory*. London: Routledge.

Benjamin, W. (1969) *Illuminations*. New York: Schocken Books.

Benjamin, W. (1986) *Reflections*. New York: Schocken Books.

Bause, T. 'Lone Horseman gets "company"', *The Namibian*, 10 July 2008.

Bredekamp, H. C. (Jatti) (2007) 'The Cultural Heritage of a Democratic South Africa: An Overview'. In Bothma, T., Underwood, P. and Ngulube, P. (eds) *Libraries for the Future: Progress and Development in South African Libraries*. Pretoria: Library and Information Association of South Africa, pp. 1-12.

Coombes, A. E. (2003) *Visual Culture and Public Memory in a Democratic South Africa: History After Apartheid*. Johannesburg: Wits University Press.

Demissie, F. (ed.) (2012) *Colonial Architecture and Urbanism in Africa: Intertwined and Contested Histories*. Farnham & Burlington: Ashgate Publishing.

Die Republikein, 'Ruiterstandbeeld ingehuldig', 16 November 2010.

[The] Equestrian Monument (Reiterdenkmal), 1912-2014: A chronological documentation of reports, newspaper clippings and photos/illustrations (2014) Windhoek: Kuiseb Publishers.

Frank, C. (2012) 'A Memorial or an Anti-memorial? A Photographic Essay of the Cemetery Memorial Park in Swakopmund', *Postamble*, 8 (1).

Grundlingh, A. (2009) 'A Cultural Conundrum? Old Monuments and New Regimes: The Voortrekker Monument as Symbol of Afrikaner Power in a Postapartheid South Africa'. In Walkowitz, D. J. and Knauer, L. M. (eds) *Contested Histories in Public Space: Memory, Race and Nation*. Durham and London: Duke University Press.

Haufiku, E. 'GDR Tenders Bloat North Korean Riches: Namibian Masses Toil in Bondage', *Informante*, 7 March 2012.

Hell, J. and Steinmetz, G. (2006) 'The Visual Archive of Colonialism: German and Namibia', *Public Culture*, 18 (1).

Informanté, 26 September 2013.

Kirkwood, M. (2011) 'Postcolonial Architecture Through North Korean Modes: Namibian Commissions of the Mansudae Overseas Project'. MA thesis, University of Kansas, Kansas.

Kriger, N. (1995) 'The Politics of Creating National Heroes: The Search for Political Legitimacy and National Identity'. In Bhebe, N. and Ranger, T. (eds) *Soldiers in Zimbabwe's Liberation War*. Oxford: James Currey.

Ladd, B. (2008) *The Ghosts of Berlin: Confronting German History in the Urban Landscape*. Chicago: University of Chicago Press.

Logan, W. and Reeves, K. (2009) *Places of Pain and Shame: Dealing with 'Difficult Heritage'*. Abingdon: Routledge, p. 13.

Marschall, S. (2008) 'The Heritage of Post-Colonial Societies'. In Graham, B. and Howard, P. (eds) *The Ashgate Research Companion to Heritage and Identity*. Farnham & Burlington: Ashgate Publishing.

Maletsky, C. 'City Icon to Take Last Ride', *The Namibian*, 10 June 2008.

Muraranganda, E. 'Govt presses on with Reiterdenkmal removal', *Namibian Sun*, 24 December 2013.

Namibia Tourism Board (2012) *Statistical Report on 2011*. Windhoek: NTB.

Namibian Sun, 'Govt presses on with Reiterdenkmal removal', 23 December 2013.

National Heritage Council, 'Public Notice - Proposed Recommendation of De-Proclamation of the Equestrian Statue Monument', *Republikein* 20 December 2013.

Salvador, C. and Rodrigues, C. U. (2012) 'Colonial Architecture in Angola: Past Functions and Recent Appropriations'. In Demissie, F. (ed.) *Colonial Architecture and Urbanism in Africa: Intertwined and Contested Histories.* Farnham & Burlington: Ashgate Publishing.

Saunders, C. (2007) 'The Transformation of Heritage in the New South Africa'. In Stolten, H. E. (ed.) *History Making and Present Days Politics, the Meaning of Collective Memory in South Africa.* Uppsala: Nordiska Afrikainstitutet.

Silvester, J. (2005) '"Sleep with a Southwester": Monuments and Settler Identity in Namibia'. In Elkins, C. and Pedersen, S. (eds) *Settler Colonialism in the Twentieth Century.* London & New York: Routledge.

Silvester, J. and Elago, H. (2011) *Heritage into Education, Education into Heritage.* Windhoek: Museums Association of Namibia/MDG Achievement Fund.

Siyauya, C. 'An Argument for Keeping Old Names Monuments', *New Era*, 11 July 2008.

Smit, E. 'Reiterdenkmal disappears overnight', *Namibian Sun*, 27 December 2013.

Spivak, G. C. (1993) *Outside the Teaching Machine.* New York: Routledge.

Stevenson, D. (2009) 'The Mysterious Demographics of Beer Drinking'. In Moescher, G., Rizzo, L. and Silvester, J. (eds) *Posters in Action, Visuality in the Making of an African Nation.* Basel: Basler Afrika Bibliographien.

Stolten, H. E. (ed.) (2007) *History Making and Present Days Politics, The Meaning of Collective Memory in South Africa.* Uppsala: Nordiska Afrikainstitutet.

The Namibian, 'SWANU wants Independence Museum to be renamed', 15 June 2011.

The Namibian, sms text message, 12 August 2012.

Tjiriange, N. 'Reiterdenkmal removal: A great govt decision', *New Era*, 3 January 2014.

Tunbridge, J. E. and Ashworth, G. J. (1996) *Dissonant Heritage: The Management of the Past as a Resource in Conflict.* Chichester: Wiley.

Uzzell, D. and Ballantyne, R. (2008) 'Heritage that Hurts: Interpretation in a postmodern world'. In G. Fairclough, R. Harrison, J. H. Jameson Jnr, and John Schofield (eds) *The Heritage Reader*. London & New York: Routledge, p. 512.

Vogt, A. (2004) *National Monuments in Namibia.* Windhoek: Gamsberg Macmillan.

Vogt, A. 'To move or not to move', *The Namibian*, 18 July 2008.

Von Dewitz, C. (2009) *Windhoek Der Klein Stadtfuhrer.* Windhoek: Kuiseb Verlag.

Walkowitz, D. J. and Knauer, L. M. (2009) *Contested Histories in Public Space: Memory, Race and Nation.* Durham & London: Duke University Press.

Werbner, R. (1998) 'Smoke from the Barrel of a Gun: Postwars of the Dead, Memory and Reinscription in Zimbabwe'. In Werbner, R. (ed.) *Memory and the Postcolony: African Anthropology and the Critique of Power.* London: Zed Books.

Zeller, J. (2000) *Kolonialdenkmäler und Geschichtsbewußtsein. Eine Untersuchung der kolonialdeutschen Erinnerungskultur.* Frankfurt am Main: IKO–Verlag für Interkulturelle Kommunikation.

Zeller, J. (2003) 'Symbolic Politics: Some comments on the German Colonial Culture of Remembrance'. In Zimmer, J. and Zeller, J. (eds) *Genocide in German South-West Africa: The colonial war of 1904-1908 and its Aftermath.* Monmouth: Merlin Press.

Zimmer, J. and Zeller, J. (2003) *Genocide in German South-West Africa: The colonial war of 1904-1908 and its Aftermath.* Monmouth: Merlin Press.

Zuern, E. (2012) 'Memorial Politics - Challenging Power and Inequality in Namibia'. Draft Paper.

19 Heritage Education in the School Curriculum: A Critical Reflection

Gilbert Likando

Introduction

This chapter critically highlights the importance of heritage education in the school curriculum in Namibia. It does so in relation to John Patrick's five pitfalls that heritage educators must avoid in the process of designing a heritage education school curriculum or infusing the right content into existing curriculum, namely: *elitism, extreme pluralism, localism, romanticism and anti-intellectualism* (Patrick, 1989). The chapter links this perspective by Patrick of heritage education infusion and integration in the school curriculum to the on-going reform process in education in Namibia. Debates have loomed on how the integration or infusion could be done. While some proponents propose the creation of an entirely new curriculum for heritage education in schools, others argue for the infusion of heritage education content into the current school curriculum by drawing on many disciplines such as history, geography, the natural and social sciences, the arts and literature as the best approach.[1]

Heritage and its Forms of Manifestation

It is imperative at the outset to create an understanding of what the concepts 'heritage', 'history' and 'heritage education' denote. It should be noted as Silvester and Elago (2010, p. 4) have observed, that '…heritage is a word that is commonly used more often than it is understood'.[2] In a broader sense *heritage* can be conceptualised in five major forms as identified by Tunbridge and Ashworth (1996, pp. 1-4). Firstly, it is used as a synonym for any relic's physical survival from the past. Secondly, it refers to objects, buildings, sites and places, and any other non-physical aspect when viewed from the present. In other words, as Sorensen (1990, cited in Tunbridge and Ashworth, 1996, p.1) argued, '…it defines individual heritage in terms of individual memory then collective memory or national memory'. Thirdly, it denotes accumulated cultural and artistic productivity, whether produced in the past or currently. Tunbridge and Ashworth assume that this kind of heritage has been incorporated into a set of activities and

---

[1] Kathleen Hunter's (1992) discussion on heritage education, supports the assertion that heritage education should be treated as an approach to the teaching and learning of people's history and culture that draws on many disciplines.

[2] J. Silvester and H. Elago (2010) *Education into Heritage, Heritage into Education*. Report prepared for the MDGF, commissioned by NPC and UNESCO. Windhoek: Museums Association of Namibia.

preoccupations labelled as 'high culture'. Fourthly, it refers to elements in whole or in part from the natural environment in terms of a 'heritage landscape' including fauna and flora, which are survivals from the past or are seen as, in some sense, original or typical. Finally, it is also conceived as a commercial activity, loosely grouped into what is termed as the 'heritage industry' (1996, p. 2).

It is on the basis of these five distinct meanings that Geraldine O'Brien defines heritage as a '…combination of those things that make us as individuals, the people we are and, on a larger scale, make us the nation we are'.[3] Simply put, it refers to 'those things' which are passed on to future generations. In this context Kwak (2005), advanced the idea of 'inalienability', meaning that heritage is an integral part of one's dignity and identity.

A lucid distinction between heritage and history is depicted in Tunbridge and Ashworth's (1996, p. 6) explanation:

> …both history and heritage make a selective use of the past for current purposes and transform it through interpretation. History is what a historian regards as worth recording and heritage is what contemporary societies choose to inherit and to pass on. The distinction is only that in heritage current and future uses are paramount, the resources are more varied, including much that historians regard as ahistorical, and the interpretation is more obviously and centrally the product that is consumed.

Thus, based on the foregoing explanation, heritage could be understood in two forms, namely: *tangible heritage* and *intangible heritage*.[4] While tangible heritage encompasses not only buildings but also living culture and its numerous forms of expression as reflected in the UNESCO Conventions,[5] intangible heritage includes, '…oral traditions, memories, languages, traditional arts, rituals, knowledge systems, values and know-how that we want to safeguard and pass on to future generations' (Deacon, Dondolo, Mrubata and Prosalendis, 2004, p. 6). Having said that, it is essential not to lose sight of the fact that our ancient knowledge is important, especially the traditional and indigenous knowledge that has been marginalised for so long; but we also need to remember and value more recent heritage such as oral histories of (in the case of Namibia) people who struggled for land, independence and those who lived under apartheid (Pettersson, 2008).[6] It is an undeniable fact that the safeguarding of intangible heritage remained neglected globally for a long time. However, in order to highlight the increasing recognition of the importance of intangible heritage, UNESCO launched two programmes namely the *Living Human Treasures System* (1993) and

---

[3] Geraldine O'Brien focuses on the personal meanings we attach to heritage. See http://www.teachingheritage.nsw.edu.au/1views/1index.html.{ Accessed 24 November 2009}.

[4] Mounir Bouchenaki, UNESCO Assistant Director General for Culture. *Keynote Address, ICOMOS 14th General Assembly and Scientific Symposium*. Victoria Falls, 27-31 October, 2003.

[5] See the Convention Concerning the Protection of the World Cultural and Natural Heritage, UNESCO, 1972. Retrieved from: http://portal.unesco.org/en/ev.phpURL_ID= 17716&URL_DO=DO_TOPIC&URL_SECTION=201.html. {Accessed 28 November 2009}.

[6] Christer Pettersson (2008) *In the Footsteps of Mr Anderson: Milestones in Swedish-Namibia Relations*. The book highlights what could be regarded as intangible heritage in Namibia, among other things.

the *Protection of Masterpieces of Oral and Intangible Heritage of Humanity* (1998). It is worth noting that these programmes bring to light a synchronised relationship that exists between tangible and intangible heritage as Mounir Bouchenaki, UNESCO Assistant Director General of Culture, puts it:

> Symbols, technologies and objects are tangible evidence of underlying norms and values. Thus, they establish a symbiotic relationship between the tangible and the intangible. The intangible heritage should be regarded as the larger framework within which tangible heritage takes on shape and significance.[7]

The implication here is that there is a close interaction between intangible and tangible heritage. Mounir Bouchenaki further argues that intangible heritage should be expressed in tangible manifestations, if it is to be preserved for future generations, in line with the 2003 UNESCO Convention for Safeguarding of the Intangible Cultural Heritage.[8]

The Meaning of Heritage Education

Having looked at the meaning of 'heritage', its different forms of manifestation and its strength as a source of identity, creativity and diversity, it is plausible to argue that education can play an important role in realising heritage's threefold significance:

1) putting tangible heritage in its wider context;
2) translating intangible heritage into 'materiality' - 'freezing' the intangible heritage; and
3) supporting practitioners and the transmission of skills and knowledge (Deacon et al. 2004).

What is heritage education then? It should be noted that it is difficult to provide an all-embracing definition of heritage education. Hence, Hunter (1992, p. 3) claims that 'heritage education means different things to different people and groups, depending on their professional or community orientation'. Within the context of this discourse, Hunter, in her attempt to provide a lucid meaning of the concept 'heritage education', asserts:

> Heritage education is an approach to teaching and learning about history and culture that uses information available from the material culture and the human and built environments as primary instructional resources. The heritage education approach is intended to strengthen students' understanding of concepts and principles about history and culture and to enrich their appreciation for the artistic achievements, technological genius, and social and economic contributions of men and women from diverse groups. Heritage education nourishes a sense of continuity and connectedness

---

[7] Mounir Bouchenaki (2003) *Keynote Address.*
[8] See Article 2 of the *UNESCO Convention for Safeguarding of the Intangible Cultural Heritage,* 2003.

with our historical and cultural experience; encourages citizens to consider their historical and cultural experiences in planning for the future; and fosters stewardship towards the legacies of our local, regional, and national heritage.[9]

It is within this context that it is argued in this chapter that, in Namibia, it is important that we develop a school curriculum covering heritage, or infuse heritage content into the existing school curriculum, drawing on several disciplines such as: history; geography; the natural and social sciences; and the arts and literature.[10] Heritage education, properly conceived, stresses the rich diversity of citizens (people) reflected not only in the built environment as traditionally envisioned, but also through intangible heritage – memories of the past that serve as laboratories of the future (Deacon et al., 2004). Preserving and transmitting this knowledge is vital as 'a unifying and nation-building force' (Ministry of Education and Culture, 1993). The Presidential Commission on Education, Culture and Training affirms the importance to:

> ...safeguard, extend and promote our physical, linguistic and spiritual heritage. It is this rich heritage that promotes us with our unique Namibian and African identity, and which is the foundation for development (Namibia, 1999. p. 213).

This affirmation provides a strong argument for integrating heritage education in the school curriculum in Namibia. Coupled with globalisation, which is feared by some as a cultural bulldozer capable of flattening marginal cultural forms, it is clear that integrating heritage education in the school curriculum should be seen as an urgent priority for the education sector in Namibia rather than just common rhetoric (Deacon et al., 2004).

Heritage Education and the School Curriculum

The French sociologist Pierre Bourdieu conceives school as revolutionary. For him, school and curricula are responsible for the reproduction of society and for legitimating the social hierarchies that dominate society. Furthermore, Abdel Hakim Al Husban maintains that one of the necessary elements for the construction by the citizens of the nation state, is the construction of a cultural and social identity that is in harmony with the particular identity of the state itself.[11] Arguably, cultural heritage plays an important role in this process of state construction. Ultimately, the value of heritage education in the school curriculum should be understood from this angle. It is imperative to address the following questions: How should heritage education be included in the school curriculum? What kind of approach should be followed in this process? The question of how, is also very pertinent in this debate, and can only be answered by examining

---

9   Kathleen Hunter (1988) *Heritage Education in the Social Sciences*.
10   Hunter's discussion on heritage education supports the assertion that heritage education should be treated as an approach to teaching and learning of people's history and culture that draws on many disciplines.
11   Abdel Hakim Al Husban, on *Curriculum and Cultural Heritage: A Case Study from Jordan.* http://tempusheritage.yu.edu.jo/attachments/Act3_Heritage%20education%20in%20Jordan.pdf., {Accessed 26 November 2009}.

the most appropriate and effective ways of placing heritage education within the school curriculum.

There are three basic common approaches (of which two are considered here) advanced by Kelly (2000) in his discourse on the integration of HIV and AIDS education in the school curricula, which could serve as a basis for heritage education to be effectively placed there. First, is the *separate subject approach* – this approach advocates that specific content knowledge (in this case 'heritage education') could be treated as a free-standing subject. The advantage of this approach is that it ensures that the subject is identifiable and manageable and that it receives sufficient emphasis. The approach from Jordan, where a new curriculum called *National Education* was conceived covering the age range of 12 to 18 years, in which a large amount of the content was dedicated to history and cultural heritage, is a classical example.[12] Some proponents of heritage education, such as Patrick, argue that 'there is no need to create a new curriculum in heritage education, but rather there is an imperative to use the existing curriculum in social studies or history more effectively and infuse it with the best content...'[13]. However, the Jordanian approach presents an alternative way of approaching the integration of heritage education in a school curriculum, especially at secondary level where history and geography are stand-alone subjects.

The second approach, the *career subject approach* presents a common scenario where subject content (in this case heritage education) could be part of existing career subjects. In the case of Namibia, it could be part of different subjects such as: geography, history, arts and literature and social studies at primary level. The limitation of adopting this approach, as Kelly (2000) has argued, is that there is a possibility that the new area might lose its identity within the different subjects. Despite this approach's shortcomings, Hunter (1988) supports the infusion of content on heritage education into career subjects through this approach.

In support of the *career subject* approach, Patrick claims that teaching and learning about common themes in geography such as location; place; human environment interactions; the movement of people, ideas, goods; and the formation and change of regions; could be enriched through the use of the built environment.[14] He further argues that the same point can be made about the main themes of historical literacy such as time, chronology, continuity and change, common memory, historical empathy, and the relationship between cause and effect. These ideas can be included in the curriculum more realistically and interestingly through the use of historic places and artifacts.[15]

---

12 See Abdel Hakim Al Husban, in *Curriculum and Cultural Heritage: A Case Study from Jordan.* http://tempusheritage.yu.edu.jo/attachments/Act3_Heritage%20education%20in%20Jordan.pdf.,{Accessed 26 November 2009}.
13 See John Patrick (1989), 'Heritage Education in School Curriculum'. Paper presented at the Planning Forum for the National Centre for Heritage Education, Waterford, Virginia, 16-19 November, 1989.
14 Ibid.
15 Hunter (1988), *Meaning of Heritage Education in the Social Sciences.*

Shortcomings in the Current Namibian School Curriculum

Heritage education should be seen as an induction of young people into an enriched national culture. The current wave of educational reforms in Namibia involves a wide range of critics who have debated the forms of cultural heritage and knowledge that our schools should impart to young people. In the first place, debate on curriculum reform in Namibia seems to have relegated discourse on heritage education in the school curriculum to the periphery. Although most educators agree that the main goals of education in general are to foster intellectual, social, moral, cultural, aesthetic, physical and spiritual development, a critical examination of the school curriculum shows that more emphasis is given to intellectual development at the expense of other values (Republic of Namibia, 1999. p. 209).

A critical reading and analysis of the school curriculum at primary level, where social studies is being offered as a core-subject, and at secondary level, where history and geography and other subjects are being offered as stand-alone subjects, clearly shows that cultural heritage themes are not presented as independent topics or recognised as such in the school curricula. Although a number of topics are being covered in social studies, for example topics on the built environment (particularly those of historical significance that reflect the value and achievements of the preceding generations), much still needs to be done in terms of selecting the right content to be infused into the existing curricula. Even so, Patrick cautions, there are pitfalls to avoid as outlined in my opening paragraph, namely *elitism, extreme pluralism, localism, romanticism, and anti-intellectualism.* Avoidance of these pitfalls (especially for curriculum planners/developers and educators) creates a lever and opportunity to open the way to cultural literacy, and to provide students with the knowledge of key facts and ideas that shape the identity of a community and provide the basis for intelligent and fruitful participation in a community.[16]

According to Patrick, cultural literacy can be enhanced by moving outside the rather sterile pages of the textbooks and worksheets to an examination of the physical landmarks that are the objects of historical preservation. In this way, he argues, abstractions of the past are linked to tangible forms in the present.[17] Simply put, the link between intangible and tangible heritage (which are two sides of the same coin) enhances cultural literacy, a cornerstone of heritage education. However, whilst the importance of heritage education is recognised, educationalists working on curriculum development are cautioned to avoid the five 'pitfalls' that Patrick warns could create obstacles and reduce the benefits of reform of the curricula.

The first pitfall, *elitism,* is conceived as an overemphasis on the dominant political and social figures in the past and a corresponding under-emphasis on the 'underside of history'. Take, for instance, the apartheid system; it successfully used this ideology to inculcate values of superiority (Meighan, 1986). An undertone of racial superiority was reflected in the curriculum prior to independence. However, despite progressive revisions, a critical reading of the school curriculum in Namibia brings to light two important points:

---

16   John Patrick (1989), 'Heritage Education in School Curriculum'.
17   Ibid.

1. The current social studies curriculum (at primary level) does not provide a balance between national, regional, and local heritage. The lack of sufficiently geographically spread material needs to be re-examined, especially when initiatives such as the Heritage Hunt spearheaded by the Museums Association of Namibia (MAN), and UNESCO's proposal on the development of a heritage curriculum for schools and tertiary institutions in Namibia, have provided the materials to start the process[18]. The same sentiments can be expressed about the history and geography school curriculum at secondary level.

2. Developing a heritage curriculum or infusing the right content into the existing curriculum demands us to avoid promoting a false sense of cultural uniformity that denies or ignores the rich, multi-faceted, diversity in our past and present. In support of this idea, Patrick (citing Gary Nash, a prominent social historian) argued, 'the history of the society cannot be properly understood without taking account of the activities of all its constituent parts, which means, people of all classes, regions and conditions'.[19] Thus, heritage education properly conceived takes care of all the cherished variety of history and culture in past and contemporary society.

'Unity in diversity' is a fundamental principle in Namibia, and heritage education has a role to play in fostering this principle (Republic of Namibia, 2001). This brings us to the second pitfall, *extreme pluralism*. It should be stressed that Namibia is a pluralistic society. Therefore, heritage education, in considering the right content to be included in the curriculum, should guard against extreme pluralism, which would foster ethnic group separatism and divisiveness in society, and diminish national unity and identity.[20] Put differently, although as a nation we acknowledge the tension that might exist between the values of unity and diversity in the Namibian society, heritage education, or the content of heritage education, should be able to transcend the boundaries of this tension and honour both.

The third pitfall in Patrick's thesis that needs consideration by educators is *localism*. This refers to an overriding concern with the history and culture of particular places, and corresponding neglect of the larger communities within which these places are situated. The danger of localism in heritage education is that educators or curriculum developers may promote what Patrick terms *parochialism* at the expense of cosmopolitanism.[21] This is not to say local history and culture in the curriculum are not important but, rather, that lessons on local history and culture from local places should not be treated in isolation from the larger picture that demonstrates the complexity and interconnectivity of regional and national history and culture.

---

18   See Outcome 1, in the proposal for '*Sustainable Cultural Tourism in Namibia*', MDG Joint Programme, United Nations and Government of Namibia, 8 November, 2008. http://www.mdgfund.org/sites/default/files/Namibia_Culture%20Joint%20Programme%20Document%20vol.1.pdf
19   John Patrick (1989), 'Heritage Education in School Curriculum'.
20   Ibid.
21   Ibid.

The fourth pitfall to avoid in selecting the right content for heritage education is *romanticism* (understood as an uncritical way of looking at history and culture). Heritage education may simply dwell on 'victories' and the positive, and neglect unpleasant events or ugly elements of the past. It is possible to deliberately omit factual information in order to support a particular ideology. However, it is important to note that failure to consider the danger of romanticism in selecting the right content for heritage education creates what Patrick terms 'collective amnesia' – where unhappy events are not remembered and it is difficult to deal with social tensions and unresolved issues that have historical or cultural roots.[22]

Finally, *anti-intellectualism* is another pitfall to avoid. This might not be a problem in Namibia, as most educators are aware of the obvious benefits of experiential learning. Conversely, it is important to note that, for heritage education to be effective, educators should maintain a balance between experiential learning – leaning through visiting museums, historical sites and monuments to mention a few – and learning via the printed page. Patrick puts it this way:

> Sound heritage education combines cognition and direct sensory experience, academic abstractions and tangible realities, objects in the built environment and documents in the classroom. Certainly visits to historical sites… can enliven education about the past as no classroom can ever do.

Patrick's argument highlights the strength of heritage education in contributing to the common learning and cultural literacy of the students, if a balance between experiential learning and learning through the printed page can be maintained.[23]

Conclusion

The very fact that the school curriculum expresses the experiences, ideas and common values of a given society provides enough reasons to advocate for the introduction of heritage education into the school curriculum in Namibia. Central to the notion of infusing the right content into the existing school curriculum is the avoidance of five acknowledged pitfalls namely: *elitism; extreme pluralism; localism; romanticism; and anti-intellectualism*. Heritage education, therefore, if designed with the right content, has the potential to avoid the pitfalls, and enable young people to learn core values and knowledge that constitute in Patrick's words 'common memory, the unifying elements of our diverse society'.[24]

---

22 Ibid.
23 See Hunter (1988), *Heritage Education in the Social Sciences*.
24 John Patrick (1989), 'Heritage Education in School Curriculum'.

References

Al Husban, A. H. (n.d.) *Curriculum and Cultural Heritage: A Case Study from Jordan.* http://tempusheritage.yu.edu.jo/attachments/Act3_Heritage%20education%20in%20Jordan.pdf. {Accessed 26 November 2009}.

Bouchenaki, M. (2003) UNESCO Assistant Director General for Culture *Keynote Address, ICOMOS 14th General Assembly and Scientific Symposium.* Victoria Falls, 27-31 October 2003.

Pettersson, C. (2008) *In the Footsteps of Mr Anderson: Milestones in Swedish-Namibia Relations.* Johannesburg: David Krut Publishers and Ulwazi.

Deacon, H., Dondolo, L., Mrubata, M., and Prosalendis, S. (2004) *The Subtle Power of Intangible Heritage: Legal and Financial Instruments for Safeguarding Intangible Heritage.* Cape Town: HSRC Press.

Hunter, K. (1988) *Heritage Education in the Social Sciences.* ERIC Clearinghouse for Social Studies/Social Science Education, Indiana University.

Hunter, K. (1992). *Heritage Education: What's Going On Out There?* Washington, DC: American Historical Association.

Kelly, M. J. (2000) 'HIV/AIDS in Relation to Content, Process and Organization Aspects of Education'. In Kelly, M. J. (ed.) *Planning for education in the context of HIV/AIDS.* Paris: UNESCO.

Kwak, S-Y. (2005) 'World Heritage Rights Versus National Cultural Property Rights: The case of the Jikji Human Rights Dialogue'. *Cultural Rights.* Series 2, No. 12. Spring.

Meighan, R. (1986) *A Sociology of Educating.* 2nd Edn. London: Holt, Rinehart and Winston.

Patrick, J. (1989) 'Heritage Education in School Curriculum'. Paper presented at the Planning Forum for the National Centre for Heritage Education, Waterford, Virginia, 16-19 November 1989.

Republic of Namibia (1999) *Presidential Commission on Education, Culture and Training: Report.* Windhoek: Government Printer.

Republic of Namibia (2001) *Unity, Identity and Creativity for Prosperity: Policy on Arts and Culture of the Republic of Namibia.* Windhoek: Ministry of Basic Education, Sport and Culture.

Silvester, J. and Elago, H. (2010) *Education into Heritage, Heritage into Education.* Report prepared for the MDGF, commissioned by NPC and UNESCO. Windhoek: Museums Association of Namibia

Tunbridge, J. E. and Ashworth, G. J. (1996) *Dissonant Heritage: The Management of the Past as a Resource in Conflict.* Chichester: Wiley.

UNESCO (2003) *Convention for Safeguarding of the Intangible Cultural Heritage.* Article 2.

United Nations and Government of Namibia: '*Sustainable Cultural Tourism in Namibia*', MDG Joint Programme, 8 November 2008.

Index

!Gariep 96
!Khara Khoen 45
|Khowesin 39
26th August as Heroes Day in Namibia 23, 289
32 Battalion 4, 194, 211
34 Battalion 234
35 Battalion 234
51 Battalion 210
52 Battalion 210
53 Battalion 210
54 Battalion 210
101 Battalion 234
202 Battalion 234
AAB (Anti-Apartheid Bewegung), 252, 254
AARCLS 2, 6, 22-23, 39, 218, 269
Abrahams, Dr Kenneth 142
Administrator General 179
Afrikaner, Jan Jonker 84
AG9 (1977) 227, 234
AG27 237
Ahtisaari, Martti 267
AKTUR 182, 188
Allgemeine Zeitung 140, 144
Alte Feste 276, 280
Amadhila, Leevi, Naftali 204
Amathila, Ben 6
Amputu, Selma 29
Amwaalwa, Justina 29
ANC 3, 260, 279
Angola 115, 222
Angula, Nahas 222
Apartheid 250, 279
Appolus, Emil 267
archives 2, 4, 22, 92

Arendsnes (Eagle's Nest) Base 225
Auala, Bishop Leonard 129
Ausiku, David 222

Bäetsile 60
Bagani 234
Bantu Affairs Commissioner 156, 166, 172
Bantu Education 153
Basson, Japie 128, 132
Bast, Brother Joseph 107
Basutoland (Lesotho) 117
BaTawana 55, 59
Bathoen, *Kgosi* 60
Bechuanaland (Botswana) 51, 62, 117, 143, 152
Becker, Sarel 132, 183
Berker, Chief Justice Joachim 135, 142
Beukes, Hans 140
Beukes, Hermanus 143
Bierfert, August 108
Blauw, Friedrich 101
Bleek, Wilhelm 91, 98
Blue Book (1918) 39
boers 10, 64, 165
Bosman, Isaac John 62
Bremen 40
Bremen Memorial, 261
Breytenbach, Colonel Jan 216
British South African Company 60
Bruchhausen 40, 45
'Buffalo' Battalion (see 32 Battalion)
Bushmanland 188

Calulo, Battle of 268
CANU 10, 148, 160
Caprivi 148, 211

Carpio, Victorio 135
Cassinga 12, 74, 180, 198, 201, 214, 233, 268
casspir 226
Castro, Fidel 84
Charité 91
Christians, Anna 184
Chunga, *Induna* 155
Collenbrander, A.B. 156
Conradie, Kephas 183
contract labour, see migrant labour 105
Council of Churches in Namibia 259
Cuando Cubango 55
Cuangar (Angola) 109, 112, 222-223
Cuba 84, 223
Cuito Cuanavale 87
Cultural Literacy 303
curfew 212, 224, 229

Dahlmann, Kurt 144
Damaraland 166-167
Darico 58
Davis, Matthias 120
Decree no. 1 (of UN Council for Namibia) 258
Democratic Turnhalle Alliance (DTA) 82, 181-188, 217
diamond mines 116-118, 120
Dickman, René 115
Disho, *Fumu* 112
disinvestment 255
Diyeve, *Fumu* 106
Dos Santos, President Eduardo 84
Du Plessis, Abraham 181-182

Eendobe 210
Eenhana 210-211
Efundula 241

Elifas, *Omukwaniilwa* (King) Fillemon 78, 80, 197
ELCIN 224
ELOC 210
Elundu 211
Endola 28
ENOK 237
Equestrian Monument 276-295
Eriksson, Axel 64
ex-detainees 245, 247, 260

Fagan, Henry 134
Fairfield, Sir Edward 66
Faraday, Robert Arthur 27, 59, 65, 67
Federal Party 129
FELM 269, 271
Filliung, Father Joseph 107
Finaughty, William 151
Finland 266-275
FINNIDA 272
First, Ruth 127, 136-137, 141-142
Fischer, Dr Alfred 168
Fischer, Eugene 90-91
Fisher, Braam 145
FNLA 223
Fouche, Willem 225
Francistown 222
Freedom Park 193
Fritsch, Gustav 91

Garöeb, Moses 35
GDR 253, 260
Geneva Convention 199, 200
Genscher, Hans Dietrich 259
Gerber, Dr 113
Germany 278
Gciriku 116
Gibbons, Hill 58

Gibeon, 39-40
Gochas 45
Goldblatt, Advocate Israel 9-10, 127, 164
Goliath, Andreas 97, 100
Goliath, Petrus 95, 61, 101
Goodenough, William 67
Goold-Adams, Major Hamilton 62, 64
Green Party 258
Grootfontein 107, 114, 116, 162
Groth, Pastor Siegfried 254, 260
Guchab 112
GwaShitumwa, Mumbandja, 30

Hahn, 'Cocky' 75
Haiyaka, Jerobiam 212
Haiyaka, Lovisa Taukuheke 212
Hall, Judge Cyril 130
Hambukushu 112
Hammar, August 58
Hamukwaya, Jonas 225, 230
Haneb 97
Hangala, Leake 268
Harris, Rutherford 60
Hartikainen, Aarne 267
Haupindi, Lorenz 175
Hausiku, Rev. Heikki 237
Heinnen, Erkki 210
Hermann, Father B. 107
Hermandungu, Father Ludwig 107
Herero Chiefs' Council 129, 130, 136, 181
Hereroland 78, 108
heritage education 298-305
Heroes Acre 39, 51, 193, 276, 285, 292
Holy Family Mission (Katima Mulilo) 153-154, 156 161
Hompa 55
Hornkranz 55
Hoornkrans 39, 45

Hornbostel, Erich von 89

iconoclasm 18, 278
Ihamäki, Rev. Mikko 267
Impalila 152
Information Centre on Southern Africa (ISSA) 254
Informationsstelle Südliches Afrika 252
International Court of Justice 135, 178, 211
International Red Cross 199
Ithana, Pendukeni 202
Ithete, *Hompa* Himarwa 107
Itula, Aili Andreas 31
Iyambo, Lahja 30
Iyambo, Mandume 'Kayala' 224
Iyambo, Nicky 267
Iyambo, Patrick 30
Iyambo, Uushona 30

jackal stories 98-99
Jamba 235
Jasson, Voitto 222
Joubert, Mathys Andries 62
Juva, Archbishop Mikko 267

Kaakunga, Maria 268
Kabajani, Richard Kapelwa 157
Kai|Khauan 45, 47
Kahimemua 48
Kaishungu, Loth 201
Kakoto, Moses 209
Kakuchi 235
Kalomoh, Ndeulitufa 224, 232
Kalunduka, Tomas 210
Kambombo, Kayele 268
Kameeta, Bishop Zephania 262
Kampungu, Dr Romanus 133, 173, 176
Kandjimi, *Hompa* Hawanga 109, 111, 115

Kandjimi, Moses 227
Kandjimi Murangi Secondary School 228, 235
Kandjimi, Pius 227,
'Kandove' 79
Kangayi, Jaako 230
Kankondi, Raimo 268
Kanyetu, *Hompaghona* 59-61
Kapulwa, Aili 213
Kapulwa, Paulus 210
Kapuuo, Clemens 127, 132, 135-137, 142, 166, 178, 217
Karasburg 165
Karuaera, Rev. Bartholomew 130, 132, 135-136, 138, 142
Kasamane (see Dickman, René) 115
Kasheshe 153
KaSheshere, Katiku 60
Kassinga massacre (see Cassinga)
Katanga, Kaduma 225
Katima Mulilo 151, 162, 234
Katjipuka, Hanganee Kavezeri 224
Katjire (see Schoenfelder, E.) 118
Katutura 195
Kaunda, President Kenneth 84, 156
Kavango 9, 55, 66, 105, 108, 119, 171, 204, 221
Kavango Education Act 171
Kavango Legislative Council 11, 170-177, 232
Kavikunua, Nikodemus 43
Kaxumba kaNdola (see Tuhadelini, Eliaser) 73
Keetmanshoop 165
Kekkonen, Urho 267
Kenya 270, 276
Kerina, Mburumba 131
Khan 112
Khorixas, 161, 166

Kizito College 153
Koevoet 194, 204, 208, 212, 225, 229
Kooper, Rev. Markus 8, 140
Kozonguizi, Jariretundu 131, 144
Kruger, C.E. 152, 156
Kuhangua, Jacob 148
Kunene 166
Kürle, Adolf 281
Kutako, Hosea 8, 84, 136, 140
Kwanza Sul 268, 272
Lambert, Andries 66

Landeshauptmann 66
landmines 195, 204, 208, 216, 218, 227
Lång, Birgitta 268
Legislative Assembly 178
    Caprivi 168
    Kavango 232
    Ovamboland 79, 81, 200
Lempp, Ferdinand 128, 132, 135, 137
Leutwein, Maj. Theodor 45, 66, 158
liberation struggle 148, 150, 157, 170, 197, 207
    archival material 3-4, 7, 16, 25
    heroine of 36
    songs in the 71-78
Lichtenecker, Hans 8 89
life-casts, 90-91
Liljeblad, Emil 267
Linyanti 155
Livingstone 152
Lloyd, Sgt. Edwin 60
Lozi Kingdom 149
Lubango 245, 259
Lubowski, Anton 198
Lüderitz, 112, 116, 258, 291
Lunganda (see Iyambo, Patrick) 30
Lukonga, Alfred Siloiso 155

Lukongo, Jackson Mazasi 155
Lusaka 161

Maamberua, Usutuaije- 289
Mafulo 155
Maherero, Samuel 38, 51, 84, 99
Mahangu 34
MAKSA 254
Malawi 85, 114
Majavero, *Hompa* Alfons 173,
Mansudae Overseas Projects 289, 294
Marriage Act (No 81 of 1963) 243
Mashabbi, Headman 62
Mashare 234
mass graves 13, 194, 201-203, 209
Masubiya 164
Maswahu, Vernet 160, 162, 168
Matongo Greenwell 157
Mauni 234
Maxuilili, Gotlieb Nathaniel 35, 73
Mazanza 172
Mbamba, Dr Alpo Mauno 222
Mbambo, Klemens 107
Mbeki, Thabo 203
Mbumba, Nangolo 222
Mbunza 116
Mbwalala, Ruben 200-201
McKiernan, Gerald 58, 65
Memory of the World 7, 39
migrant labour 9, 171
Minnaar, Dan 132, 135, 137
missionaries 41, 43, 58, 122, 150, 153, 210, 241-242,
   Catholic 106-109, 122
   Finnish 210, 266-268, 271
Mize, Bishop Robert 129, 137, 140
Moffat, John 62-63
Mogodi, Khukhwi 62

Mollison, Theodor 90
Mossamedes 64
Mpasi, *Hompa* Daniel Sitentu 229, 232-233
MPLA
Mpungu 234, 236
Mudge, Dirk 171, 181, 188
Müller, Franz 59, 62
Mundia, Nalumino 156
Mupekaka 79
Muremi, Nimrod 231
Musese 233-235
Museums Association of Namibia 194, 218, 303
Muunda, Timoteus 217
Muyongo, Mishake 168, 160
Muzogumwe 222
Myllymäki, Väinö 268

Nakatana, Joe 268
Nalishuwa, Alfred Tongo 154, 160, 162
Nama 39
Nampadi, *Hompa* 107
Namibia Peace Plan 435, 258
Namibia Project (Bremen) 257, 268
Namibian newspaper 144, 195, 217
Nankudhu, John, Otto 22
National Archives of Namibia 2, 5-7, 22-23, 39-40
National Heritage Council 286, 290, 295
National Museum of Namibia 288
Native Administration Proclamation (1928) 243
Native Commissioner 75, 115-116, 119-120
National Reconciliation 201
Naulila 109
Nchindo, Robert 151
Ndadi, Aune 30

Ndjoba, Rev. Cornelius 79, 209, 217
Ndopu, Zacharia 154, 160
Nduuvu, Nangolo Trade Union Centre 268
Nehale lyaMpingana 83,
Nehova, Ndaiponofi 249
Nelengani, Louis 140
Nepara 227, 230, 234
Nestor, Gideon 237
Nestor, Mufenda 222, 231, 237
Nestor, Silas 231
Ngamiland 66
Nganjone, Levy 127, 136
Ngavirue, 'Zed' 127, 135, 145
Ngombala, *Litunga* 149
Ngondo, Rudolf 232
Niehaus, Advocate 128
Nkurenkuru 112, 115, 221-222, 234
Nikodemus, Drothea 28
NNF 11, 183
Northern Labour Organisation 9, 105, 118, 120
Northern Rhodesia 118-119, 150, 152,
Northern Rhodesia Cold Storage Commission 152
NUDO 181
Nujoma, President Sam 83, 85, 130, 148, 156
Nyangana, *Hompa* 55, 58-59, 61, 64, 107, 111, 115

Odendaal Commission 151, 171, 178, 223
Odendaal Plan 211
Ohamakari 49, 291
Ohangwena 211, 207
Ohangwena region 13, 207, 211
Ohopoho 163-164
Okahandja 38, 43, 47-48, 51, 289
Okahao 30

Okankolo 211
Okongo 207
Old Location 198
   shooting 130
O'Linn, Advocate Brian 129, 143
Omakakunya (see Koevoet)
Omauni 212
Omongwa 210
Omufimba 212
Omugulugwoombashe, Battle of 22, 29, 197, 211, 222
Omukwetu 197, 204
Omundaungilo 210
Omupembe 213
Onamatadiva 210
Ondangwa 116, 212, 216
Ondjolo 244
Operation Barnacle 204
oral history 5, 24-26
orature 93, 99, 101
Oshakati 212-213, 216, 234
Oshakati State Hospital 212-213,
Oshalumbu 217
Oshana 209-210
Osire 231, 237
Otavi 112
Ottawa Convention (199) 205
Oukwanyama 84, 210
Oudstryders Memorial 280
Ovahimba 263
Ovambo Campaign Memorial 280
Ovamboland 105, 170, 200, 210-212, 221, 234, 266
   Administration 111, 125
   Bantustan Authority 185
   election (1973) 185
   Homeguard 194
   Legislative Assembly 79, 81, 200

Peoples Congress 72
traditional authority 185
Owamboland (see Ovamboland)
Ozohoze 136
Ozombuzovindimba 291

Palapye 62
Passarge, Siegfried 57, 58
Paton, Alan 135, 142
petitions to UN, 140, 145
phonograph 89, 94
Pienaar, Louis 179
PLAN 5, 71, 157, 179, 193, 203, 208, 216
Pöch, Rudolph 91
polygamy 241-242
Pretoria 167
Pretorius, J.W.F. 189
propaganda 14, 77, 223

rape 243, 246
Reagan, President Ronald 84
Rehoboth Basters 44, 47
Reinhard, Brother Anselm 107
Reinhardt, Georg 59, 62
Reiter Denkmal (see Equestrian Statue)
Rietmond 40
Resolution 435, 180, 186
Rhenish Mission 25, 254
Rhodes, Cecil 60, 62, 277
Riarua, Asser 43
Robben Island 29, 73
Ruacana 192, 210
Rundu 162, 222

Saarinen, Merja 268
SADF 77, 179, 208, 212, 236
Sadwere, Hermine 228

Sakaria, Lazarus, 'Chinaman' 222
San 210
Scheepers, Frederick 59, 62
Scherz, Ernst Rudolf 132
Shikwambi, Aira 249
Schimming, Ottilie 142
Schoenfelder, E. 118
Schuckmannsburg 149
Schulz, Aurel 58
Scott, Rev. Michael 129, 131, 139,
Sector 10, 234
Sector 20, 234
Sector 70, 234
security police 137-139, 141-143, 212, 228
Sekgoma, *Kgosi* 55, 59, 62-66
Sesheke 157, 161
Shaanika, Kaapanda 268
Shakadya, Gerhard 175
Shangheta, Hafeni 213
Shantjefu 7, 55, 68
Shark Island 51, 291
Shambyu 116
Shifidi, Immanuel 28-29
Shikongo, Hanyango 210
Shikongo, Sakeus 210
Shipanga, Andreas 143, 267
Shiyagaya, Toivo 179
Shityuwete, Helao 222
Shongola (see Hahn, 'Cocky') 74
Sibitwane, Litunga 149
Sillery, A 57
Simanya 234
Simbwaye, Brendan 10, 137, 149, 160, 198
Simubali, Adrian Waluka 154
Sirongo, Rev. Nathaniel 233
Siteketa, Severinus 230, 237
Siyave, Romigius 231

skulls 262
slave trade 113
Smith, Hannes, 'Smithie' 137
solidarity movement 252-261
South Africa 117
Southern Labour Organisation 105, 118, 120
Southern Rhodesia (see Zimbabwe)
South West News 135, 145
statues 277, 280
street names 261, 278
Struggle Children 203
Swakopmund 112
Swanepoel, Lt. Piet 139-140
SWABC 74, 77
SWANLA (South West Africa Labour Association) 72, 105, 121
SWANU (South West Africa National Union) 82, 130, 144
SWAPO (South West Africa People's Organisation) 4, 7, 10-11, 14, 16, 148, 178-179, 260
    Elders' Council, 246
    Family Act (1977) 247
    Womens' Council 249
    Youth League 244, 246
SWAPOL 226
SWATF (South West Africa Territorial Force) 4, 77, 79, 208, 234
SWP (South West Party) 128-129, 132

Taapopi, *Omukwaniilwa* Josea 188
Tambo, Oliver 130
Tanzania 222
Taskinen, Liisa 268
Terrorism Trial 73, 169,
Thomas, Charles 57, 60, 65
Tjamuaha, Maharero 42
Tjiueza, Wilfried 93, 97, 99

trade unions 267-268,
trauma 13, 26, 31, 33
Truth and Reconciliation Commission (SA) 201-202
Tsumeb 9, 74, 114, 116,, 118, 193
Tswanaland 182
Tuhadeleni, Eliaser 27
Tuhadeleni, Priskila 27, 33
Turnhalle Conference 179

uKangwali 116, 221
UN (United Nations)
    Resolution 435 (1978) 12
    Security Council 178
    Trusteeship 133-134, 152
UNIN (United Nations Institute for Namibia) 178, 257
Union of South Africa 132-133, 183, 290
UNIP 150, 156-157, 161
UNITA 2, 222
UNSWP 128
uranium 258

Vaalgras 38, 51, 97
Vaatz, Marga 128, 132
Vagciriku 7, 55
Vakwangali 107
Vashambyu 59, 107
Vedder, Heinrich 41
Vesikko, Markku 268
Veterans' Affairs, Ministry of 5, 203
Viana Camp 268, 272
Vigne, Randolph 127, 132, 140
Vimbari 113
Voice of Namibia 75, 87
Volkmann, *Oberleutnant* 107
von Hornbostel, Erich 89

von François, Major Curt 39, 45, 58, 66, 106
von Luschan, Felix 91
von Trotha, Gen. Lothar 258
Voortrekker Monument 279
Voster, John 86

Walvis Bay 35, 184, 198
Warmbad 161, 164
wax cylinders 89-90
Weise, Phillip (see Wiesel, Phillip)
Welwitschia (see Khorixas)
West Germany 252
West German Banks 255
Weyulu, Stefanus 217
Wiesel, Phillip 57, 59, 65-66
Windhoek 59, 74, 107, 259
Windhoek Advertiser 140, 195, 217
Windhoek Observer 145, 186, 195, 214, 217
Witbooi, *Kaptein* Hendrik 38-51, 98-99
Witbooi, Hendrik, Diary of 39
Witbooi, *Kaptein* Izaak 97
Witbooi, *Kaptein* Moses 38
Witbooi, *Kaptein* Samuel 137, 140
Witboois (see |Khowesin)
WNLA 120, 151, 168
Wulff, August 40

yaKadha, Iita 74-75
yaLuwayo, Ndatoolomba 74-75
ya Toivo, Toivo 140

Zambia 75, 84, 118, 150, 156, 167, 222
ZANU 84
Zimbabwe 71, 75, 120, 127, 260, 277, 289

About the cover photograph

Man on a Drum © John Liebenberg 1985

On 26 August 1985, the gathering on Freedom Square in Katutura to commemorate Namibia Day was prohibited, and the South African Special Police Task Force was determined to implement the ban. A makeshift stage was built with 44-gallon drums. Halfway through the commemoration the Task Force came, kicked it down and attempted to disperse the crowd with several rounds of teargas. The commotion brought more people from their homes into the street. During the mêlée a man rolled some drums together and clambered on top of them. He waved a SWAPO flag amidst clouds of teargas. He lasted a few minutes before round after round of rubber bullets forced him to flee. The Task Force then kicked the drums into a riverbed and spent the rest of the afternoon chasing people from one street to the next.

This single act of defiance illustrates the resilient nature of Namibia's resistance to oppression.

www.ingramcontent.com/pod-product-compliance
Lightning Source LLC
Chambersburg PA
CBHW081539300426
44116CB00015B/2681